The public has long been painfully aware of the economy's current instability. The contemporary recession has brought to the foreground problems which have been germinating for decades. Falling real wages, inconsistent productivity growth, and the loss of international competitiveness in major industries are all outgrowths of long-term developments that predate the current crisis. As the United States moves from a position of global economic leadership to one of economic interdependence, we need new approaches to explain the dramatic changes in the U.S. economy.

It is the underlying premise of this volume that the inadequate and uneven performance of the American economy that has persisted for over two decades can only be understood within a historical context that spans at least a half century. Moreover, the contributors to this book are united in their conviction that economic instability and unemployment in the contemporary United States are ultimately not cyclical but structural, resting on an outmoded institutional organization of the economy. To recapture economic growth, structural reform of the U.S. economy is urgently needed.

This collection of essays, written by leading scholars, presents a systematic analysis of the nation's economic woes. The authors furnish more than hard-hitting criticisms of the U.S. economy. They also attempt to offer solutions to America's most pressing economic problems.

Understanding American economic decline

Understanding American economic decline

Edited by

MICHAEL A. BERNSTEIN and DAVID E. ADLER

Published by the Press Syndicate of the University of Cambridge
The Pitt Building, Trumpington Street, Cambridge CB2 1RP
40 West 20th Street, New York, NY 10011-4211, USA
10 Stamford Road, Oakleigh, Melbourne 3166, Australia

First published 1994

Printed in the United States of America

Library of Congress Cataloging-in-Publication Data
Understanding American economic decline
/ edited by Michael A. Bernstein, David E. Adler.
p. cm.
Includes index.
ISBN 0-521-45063-2. – ISBN 0-521-45679-7 (pbk.)
1. United States – Economic conditions – 1945– 2. United States – Economic policy. I. Bernstein, Michael A. (Michael Alan), 1954 – II. Adler, David E.
HC106.5.U42 1994
330.973 – dc20 93-48755
CIP

A catalog record for this book is available from the British Library.

ISBN 0-521-45063-2 hardback
ISBN 0-521-45679-7 paperback

For Teresa Odendahl and Vanessa Drucker

Contents

Foreword: Writing about the economic future

ROBERT L. HEILBRONER

It has always been the ambition of economics to anticipate the future. I do not mean that the discipline has ever pretended to an ability to make hard-and-fast predictions – along with the rest of social inquiry, economics had a hard enough time explaining the past. I am speaking of another kind of ambition that differs from true prediction in that its arguments rarely concern specific events, much less explicit timetables. This aspect of economics can be described as *historical vision,* with the odd twist that the word "historical" refers to the future rather than the past. That is why I have used the deliberately imprecise term "anticipate" to describe the unique ambition of economics, whose increasing unreliability constitutes an important underlying premise of this book.

Writing about the ideas of the great economists many years ago, I called their future-oriented visions "scenarios." The word was intended to emphasize the drama-laden character of their exercises in social analysis, in which a few simple assumptions about human and physical nature formed the basis for complicated narratives involving the rise and fall of social classes and the viability of entire social orders. Marx is, of course, the textbook case in point, but the description applies as well to Adam Smith and John Stuart Mill, John Maynard Keynes and Joseph Schumpeter. By way of contrast, no such single large-scale historical vision is present in these essays. As the book's title announces, the theme of decline is central to its multifaceted analysis, but the theme does not have the focused dialectical inevitability that characterized Marx's apocalyptic drama or the ironic character of Schumpeter's tragicomedy. This is, therefore, a volume of essays that reflects a different appraisal of our historical situation from that of the past. Decline is seen as a blend of economic malfunction and political lack of will – neither of them "inevitable" in the classical sense, both of them perhaps remediable, at least to some extent, by appropriate policy measures.

Economic malfunction differs from past prognoses because it does not suggest that somehow capitalism has lost *its historic élan vital* – the drive to accumulate capital. Stagnation has appeared in every capitalist nation over the last two decades, but the cause is not seen as a climacteric of the system's trajectory, reflected in a collapse of confidence that brought on the Great Depression. Rather, stagnation appears to be one of those periods of relative saturation that regularly follow transformational booms – the lackluster sequel to the railroad age and the automobile age and, in our case, the age of the jetliner, creator of the largest new industry of the postwar world, tourism.

Thus the malfunction of the last decades appears to be rooted as much or more in the quality as in the quantity of investment. Production processes have been automated, largely to the disadvantage of the middle levels of skill. Business organizations have been radically slimmed down under the impetus of new communication and information networks, to the detriment of employment as a whole and middle management in particular. And although it plays only a small part in the essays to follow, it ought to be noted that the continued expansion of output, even at its laggard pace, has begun to manifest an ominous effect on the environment – the first hints of an environmental overreach of truly frightening proportions.

As a result, economic failure appears at two levels. At the macro level, post-transformational doldrums have once again slowed down the pace of advance below that needed to assure full employment. Meanwhile, at the micro level the new technologies of the system are exerting powerful effects on social and economic life – quickening the pace of production, economizing on storage, eliminating redundancy, enhancing the use of high-science technology – alas, without providing the propulsive capabilities of the older "transformational" technological leaps. Hence investment brings social problems without the accompanying economic vitality that would make those problems easier to address.

We do not know whether a new transformational rejuvenation awaits us. Meanwhile, however, decline has been intensified and prolonged by a second element, also different from the scenarios of the recent past. This is the lack of the political will needed to offset, or even to take the place of, spontaneous growth. Curiously enough, although we cannot explain the misbehavior of investment, there is no lack of explanations for the political aspect of decline. In part it reflects the then unforeseen inflationary consequences of the great boom of the 1960s. Today the fear of inflation serves as a reason – and more significantly, a rationale – for a general wariness concerning government expenditures. In part, the lack of will can be seen as a "normal" swing of the political pendulum from the New Deal Left to the Reagan–Bush Right, but it probably reflects as well the growing political conservatism of the more successful unionized working class during the earlier boom years.

No doubt there are other specific explanations as well. But what is important to all the diagnoses and remedies of these essays is the recognition that a political negativism has seriously compounded the difficulties of the economic sector. Much of the stagnation and social disarray of what is now almost twenty-five years of decline could have been alleviated had government itself been utilized as a source of transformational change, but this was far beyond the political possibility curve. Here we should note that in a volume of this title written thirty, twenty, even ten years ago, the word "socialism" would surely have appeared as an imaginable alternative social formation. That possibility is not in any of these essays. For better and for worse – it is important to stress the conjunctive – it is a limitation placed on our political and economic futures by the fate of the Russian aberration.

In such a setting of antipathetic political attitudes, one can see why "prediction" becomes impossible, and even "anticipation" hazardous. Nevertheless, anticipation is what we all hunger for, and it is what this book is about. Can the American decline be corrected? Is the vision of a high employment, high social responsibility capitalism a possibility – not as a scenario of inevitable change, but as a political and economic framework toward which perceptible progress can be made? In one way or another, the essays that follow are all concerned with this central question.

As I have said, the essays take the measure of what must be done, without pretending to a degree of foresight that is not possible in today's world. Our authors observe the economy from many vantage points, comparing its behavior with that of other capitalisms, analyzing the political and economic failures of crucial sectors, such as finance and corporate organization, seeking perspectives on its historic position in the larger global setting. No single unified "scenario" underlies these essays because none exists in an age in which economic behavior has become less dependable and politics more strategic. Instead, we find many appraisals as to what can be done, within the limits of our historical situation.

Taking the measure of our current situation is, however, only half the task of this ambitious effort. Anticipation – no matter how tentative – requires prior diagnosis, and diagnosis in economics, as in medicine, ordinarily takes place in a language that the patient does not understand. To repair that serious breach of communication is a second important purpose of this undertaking. In no way does that make this a book of economic "popularization." Its authors are interested in describing overlooked or misperceived aspects of the current economic scene, not in setting forth readable versions of conventional views. But their purpose lies not only in presenting new perceptions about our economic prospects, but in communicating the meaning of these perceptions in ways that will engage, not bewilder, their readers.

Perhaps that is only to say again that *Understanding American Economic Decline* begins from the premise that a better-working American economy will not emerge spontaneously from the dynamics of the system. It will require new political mechanisms, and these mechanisms in turn require a new degree of political will. The essays that follow cannot provide the political and institutional changes required to halt and reverse the trend of American social and economic life. What they can and do provide is the informed understanding from which to construct a more prosperous and equitable American economy.

Preface

Consider a nation in which family income is growing at a brisk rate, and has done so, with only brief interruptions, for nearly twenty years. The number of individuals classified as poor falls steadily, from roughly 40 million to just under 25 million in less than a decade. Unemployment is low. Just one working parent, as is common in this economy, can easily support an average family. It is a fundamental belief of this society, and a not unrealistic one given continually improving economic and social conditions, that children will surpass their parents' standard of living. This nation's economic competitiveness on world markets is unchallenged. Its currency is an international standard of value. The nation is globally hegemonic; its domestic economy is little affected, let alone dominated, by outside competitors.

And this nation's government attracts "the best and the brightest." Though many question the government's foreign policy aims, few doubt its effectiveness and efficiency, as exemplified by a wide variety of public works programs. The government is seen, on the whole, as beneficial, providing unemployment insurance, social security, medical coverage for the elderly, and ultimately, economic stability and growth.

This nation, of course, was the United States of only thirty years ago, during a time of prosperity which all Americans born before 1960 can remember. Rapid material growth rates were matched by equally optimistic attitudes on the part of policy makers. One of the most widely read and influential economics texts of its time could state, "The reason for virtual disappearance of great depressions is the new attitude of the electorate . . . Economic science *knows how* to use monetary and fiscal policy to keep any recessions that break out from snowballing into *lasting* chronic slumps."[1]

And now consider an economy in its worst depression since the 1930s. Close to one in three college graduates takes a job which does not require a college degree, and the downward economic slide for non–college graduates is even more severe. Real wages have been flat or falling for decades, predating the current slump. Two-income families are a necessary though not always adequate strategy for keeping household income from falling.

Internationally, productivity growth in this economy has been lagging behind that of other industrial nations for almost two decades. Industry after industry has experienced a loss in international competitiveness. Trade deficits soar. This nation no longer clearly dominates the world economy. And the government is seen as ineffectual and inefficient. Indeed, government itself is seen as the source of many of the nation's economic troubles.

For most of the American public, this hypothetical contrast is all too real. They have experienced what they perceive to be a steady economic decline for the past several decades. Diminished expectations generated by inadequate economic performance have expressed themselves both in rising middle-class resentment and powerful discontent among the poor.

Many policy makers also share the public's bewilderment and anxiety. The self-assurance of the economics doctrines of the 1960s, which claimed to know how to achieve simultaneously acceptable rates of growth, unemployment, and inflation, has been shattered.

In their place, new policy prescriptions to combat the recession are eerily reminiscent of economic doctrines widespread in the early days of the Great Depression of over a half century ago. Much of current economic thought holds that fiscal policy cannot lower unemployment and that balanced budgets are the only successful approach to maintaining growth. Yet received wisdom has not allowed policy makers to formulate effective responses to the recession or to the long-term decline. The economy has failed to prosper in the wake of three administrations committed to supply-side economics. This failure indicates the sterility of existing mainstream economic theory.

This volume of original essays argues that recent U.S. economic deterioration has deep structural, historical, and institutional roots rarely ad-

1 Paul A. Samuelson, *Economics, 8th Edition* (New York: McGraw-Hill, 1970), 250.

dressed by mainstream economic theory and policy. The origins of the current crisis go beyond mere policy errors or cyclical fluctuations to involve profound issues of institutional organization including the U.S. financial system, government–business relations, labor–business relations, and inter- and intrafirm cooperation. We attribute U.S. economic problems and slow growth rates to an economy structured and organized in ways better suited to the 1950s than the 1990s.

The essays in this volume all share this institutional and historical perspective. This approach is largely outside the focus of mainstream economic theory – theory which has yet to offer a convincing explanation of contemporary economic decline in the U.S. Although our methodological approach is not easy to model or quantify, qualitative phenomena such as institutional arrangements do have quantitative impacts as seen in fluctuations in national growth rates. One goal of this volume, therefore, is to inspire a new approach to economic analysis, one where formal models have meaningful applications. Some of the essays investigate the theoretical limitations of the mainstream perspective. Others demonstrate that mainstream policy, in particular supply-side economics, has not only failed to strengthen the economy but weakened it.

The anthology analyzes the underlying causes of America's persistent economic difficulties, the ineffectiveness of current policy responses, the social impact of the difficulties, and finally what must be done to get the economy back on track.

Our contributors have conceived their essays on these topics as broadly as possible. The first part includes two essays providing a historical overview of the growth and development of the American economy since 1945. The essays in the second part, concerned with structural change in more recent decades, focus on such issues as corporate behavior and strategies, the transformation of labor productivity in major manufacturing and service industries, and the macroeconomic consequences of the Cold War period. Policy concerns are explicitly addressed in the third part with essays on current economic stagnation and the contradictions of recent policy making, the failure of Bush/Reaganomics, and a comparison of national strategies for the enhancement of global competitiveness. The distributional and social impacts of contemporary American economic performance and policy form the fourth part and frame the essays, which discuss the changed position of organized labor, the effect of structural change on the gender and racial distribution of employment opportunities, the social impact of income inequality on minority populations, and intergenerational downward mobility in recent years. A concluding part offers observations on the economic policy puzzles and persistent growth difficulties that face the nation.

Our approach has profound policy implications, a major concern of the authors. Current economic policy debates are largely limited to arguments over short-term policies such as income tax cuts or revision of capital gains assessments or federal budget deficits. This book suggests that these preoccupations of political leaders and pundits do not address the underlying causes of American economic decline. They therefore offer inadequate solutions to long-term slow growth. The policy initiatives proposed in this book call for more substantive reforms that are institutional in nature – focusing on such matters as technology, labor training, income distribution, and financial and managerial practice.

Most discussion of U.S. economic decline has been intellectually unsatisfying. One common argument is simply to deny that the U.S. has suffered from a loss in international competitiveness. Another response is to acknowledge a decline, but to give it no credence, saying in effect: so what if times are tough? This nihilistic argument does not attempt to explore the origins of contemporary economic stagnation. Theories or journalistic accounts that do acknowledge there are problems with the U.S. economy and attempt to investigate how these problems arose are hampered by limitations in mainstream economic theory itself. Mainstream models are not well suited to discussing actual experiences of growth which are situated in a nation's history as well as its institutional, political, and social structure. Though these factors can be forced to fit into conventional economic analysis, the resulting equation is too reductive to yield meaningful insight into why and how nations grow. More to the point, mainstream theory, with its formal preoccupations, is in general not really concerned with why the United States has experienced a relative decline or why other industrialized countries are on a more rapid growth trajectory. What went wrong in the United States, why its economy has declined, is not just a question left unanswered by mainstream economics; it is a question rarely asked by mainstream economics. The essays in this volume confront U.S. economic decline head on, investigating its roots in U.S. historical and economic and political structures. And a meaningful and accurate diagnosis of what is really wrong with the U.S. economy is a necessary step towards national economic renewal.

David E. Adler

Acknowledgments

As with all publications, this volume is the product of the joint labor of several people. Some of them are identified in the table of contents, but there are others who are not. Mention should be made of six of them here. Michael Edelstein, Chair of the Department of Economics of Queens College in the City University of New York, lent decisive support and encouragement at a very early stage in our work. Mary Klemme and Lorel Wirkus, of the Department of History at the University of California, San Diego, provided exemplary word-processing and clerical assistance. Janis Bolster and Robert Racine, our production editor and copy editor, respectively, also deserve special mention.

In particular, we would like to take this opportunity to express our sincere thanks to Frank Smith, Executive Editor at Cambridge University Press, who played a crucial role – both editorial and intellectual – in bringing this project to completion. Frank's commitment to this endeavor was essential to its realization. For that, and for the rather adroit ways in which he often combined sympathetic encouragement with a bracing impatience, we are most grateful.

Michael A. Bernstein
David E. Adler

Understanding American economic decline

Historical perspectives

Often lacking in mainstream analysis of the contemporary problems of the American economy is a historical context within which to situate current events. While quantitative change is clearly a most important focus for economic investigation, qualitative transformations in the nation's economic life also figure prominently in aggregate performance. For this reason, it is necessary to situate within analytic studies of recent economic difficulties in the United States a sharply focused awareness of long-term historical forces that have molded both the causes of and the reaction to contemporary economic decline.

The two essays in this part seek to provide this historical sensibility. Michael A. Bernstein provides a broad outline of American economic history in the late twentieth century. David M. Gordon offers a systematic look at the declining fortunes of the American economy in the postwar era.

1

Understanding American economic decline: the contours of the late-twentieth-century experience

MICHAEL A. BERNSTEIN

> [W]e have been witnessing not merely a depression and a bad recovery . . . but the symptoms of a permanent loss of vitality which must be expected to go on and to supply the dominating theme for the remaining movements of the capitalist symphony . . .
>
> –Joseph A. Schumpeter, *Capitalism, Socialism and Democracy* (New York: Harper & Row, 1962), 111

I. INTRODUCTION

Will a "permanent loss of vitality" be the defining characteristic of the economic history of late-twentieth-century America? Not very long ago, during the Great Depression of the 1930s, many economic experts had wondered if capitalism would survive at all. Today many of them fear that the American economy is weak and failing, destined to be a second-echelon participant in a new twenty-first-century world economic order. That sense of foreboding is shared by the public. Most Americans, at least of the lower and middle classes, believe that their children will not sustain a standard of living equal to their own.

After World War II, the views of those who had argued that the Great Depression was symptomatic of a profound weakness in the mechanisms of capitalism appeared hysterical and exaggerated. As the industrialized nations sustained dramatic rates of growth during the 1950s, the economics profession itself became increasingly preoccupied with the development of Keynesian theory and the management of the mixed economy. The presumption was that the Great Depression could never be repeated owing to the increasing sophistication of economic analysis and policy formulation. Indeed, the belief became commonplace that the business cycle was "tamed" and "obsolete."

The erratic performance of the American economy in the past three decades has eroded this notion. Serious questions have been raised concerning political obstacles to the management of cyclical instability and our ability to diagnose and correct economic maladies. The confidence of the Keynesian Revolution has been shaken.

Even so, our current anxieties are not paralleled by a firm conviction as to what intellectual strategies would be most fruitful in the formulation of effective public policy. Mainstream economic theory remains wedded to an analytical framework that eschews close attention to historical and institutional parameters. This persistent aversion to long-term and institutional theories of economic instability and crisis stems in large part from the methodological predilections of contemporary economists. Secular and institutional mechanisms are exceedingly difficult to model and therefore to subject to modern hypothesis testing. They are also not directly studied by means of partial or general equilibrium argument. The ever-increasing role of economists in government and in the private sector has turned attention away from the study of historical events and processes toward the investigation of contemporary policy formulation and execution. In the context of economic history, this development has substituted arguments concerning what should have been done by the appropriate authorities for analysis of what actually happened and why. In the literature on economic instability itself, earlier questions regarding the causes of fluctuations have been discarded in order to examine what should be done once cycles begin.

Regardless of the prejudices or tendencies of contemporary economic analysis, the inadequate performance of the American economy since the early 1970s has brought the question of long-term and institutional change back to the fore. Debates concerning so-called reindustrialization and industrial policy have become more common and intense. The disruptive impacts of industrial life cycles and the emergence of revitalized foreign competition in several major industries have garnered increasing attention from American economists and political scientists. In this context, it is imperative that we reassess our analytical understanding of business cycles and macroeconomic instability, as well as our grasp of the twentieth-century evolution of the American economy as a whole. By doing so, we may not only win a better appreciation of the challenges we face in our efforts to rectify the shortcomings of the American economy; we should also become more aware of the distinctive and altogether novel ways in which American prosperity had been achieved in the immediate post–World War II era.

II. THEORIES OF ECONOMIC INSTABILITY

A. Basic theory

Any conception of economic instability or of cycles in economic performance must explain how, over time, markets fail to provide for balanced growth. Persistent or intermittent unemployment of labor or capital are symptomatic of some difficulty in reaching what economists call equilibrium. In a capitalist economy characterized by a fair degree of competition in major markets, unemployment (or inflationary overemployment) of any resource should generate price changes that will serve to eliminate the distortion and "clear" the market in question. This equilibrating mechanism of modern markets may generate periodic swings in economic performance known as business or trade cycles. Obstacles to such equilibration may lead to sustained periods of instability or depressions.

If one were to imagine a simple economy in which one sector made consumption goods and another capital goods, given a particular endowment of resources and technology with a fixed population of given demographic characteristics, balanced performance would involve a virtual steady state in which the output of both sectors would be totally utilized in each production period. There would be no unemployment, of either human or produced inputs, and a simple reproduction of economic life from period to period would ensue. But the assumptions embedded in this exercise – two-sector production, fixed technological and resource endowments, fixed population, and so on – belie the argument. Economies, at least capitalist ones, do not exhibit such constancy. It is this variability in the conditions affecting economic life that is the source of instability.

As population growth changes, as technological know-how is altered, as the composition and interaction of economic sectors is transformed, the ingredients of the growth process similarly change. Moreover, given the decentralized nature of decision making among households and firms in a capitalist economy, fluctuations in economic activity may emerge simply out of recurrent inconsistencies in coordination among various and numerous activities. In all these regards, cyclical volatility as well as long-term swings in economic growth are inherent in the workings of capitalist economies.

Some economic theorists as well as economic historians have tried to discern three general patterns in the cyclical performance of modern economies. Periodic waves of fifty years or more were examined by the Russian statistician N. D. Kondratieff in the 1930s. He argued that these "long waves" were associated with the introduction and dispersion of major inventions and dramatic alterations in resource endowments owing to such things as mineral discoveries, transportation and communication breakthroughs, and war. The Juglar cycle, a wave of approximately ten years' duration, appeared to be linked with population movements. A swing of about forty months' length, dubbed the Kitchin wave, was understood to have the appearance of a typical inventory cycle.

Simon Kuznets, Moses Abramovitz, and Richard Easterlin were successful in documenting the existence of waves of some fifteen to twenty years in length in the U.S. case. Such swings, according to these investigators, demonstrated that in the United States and other industrialized countries, economic growth throughout the nineteenth and twentieth centuries proceeded on the basis of intermittent accelerations in output growth and resource utilization. Perhaps most striking, such periods of acceleration were usually followed by serious downturns in economic activity. It seemed clear that these oscillations involved changes in resource endowments (including the size and age composition of the population) and alterations in the intensity of resource use.

Whether of the secular or short-run sort, business cycles embody one of the central puzzles of modern economic life. Sustained (that is to say, uninterrupted) economic growth requires continuing increases in investment expenditures that are large enough to make additions to productive capacity, create jobs, and expand output. Yet, in the absence of technical change, the rate of net investment will fall to zero as soon as the rate of increase in consumption (and hence in sales revenue) levels off. For consumption expenditures to rise consistently, there must be net investment to create jobs and maintain consumer income levels, or injections of spending from elsewhere in the economy such as the government, foreign trade, and from major resource discoveries or territorial expansion. This is an essential paradox of capitalist growth and the reason why growth often takes the form of accelerations and pauses (or "booms" and "busts"). Indeed, the foundation of the mathematical theory of business cycles is found in what is known as the "accelerator model" of investment behavior.

The acceleration principle, as it is sometimes known, is premised on the idea that an economy's capital stock (inventory, machinery, tools, and the like) will grow when the level of output is growing. As sales for a firm increase, and thus as inventories run down and capacity is utilized at higher rates, there will be an incentive to invest in more plant and equipment, and to hire more labor to increase production and meet greater demand for a firm's product. But when sales cease to grow, or start growing at a slower rate, net investment will fall to zero as firms seek to adjust to new economic circumstances. A reduction in the rate at which new capacity is purchased, and at which new jobs are thus created, will lead to a falling off in economic activity, or a recession. A recovery, at least in theory, will occur when the ratio between sales and capital stock rises (owing to the reduction in capital occasioned by disinvestment in the downturn) to a point where firms think it appropriate to resume net investment. Two essential concepts emerge from this fundamental characterization of the trade cycle. It is assumed that businesspeople will seek to maintain some target ratio between the level of sales and the size of their capital stock. Furthermore, and as a consequence of this plausible behavioral assumption, sales must rise at a sufficient rate simply to keep investment level, let alone to stimulate net investment. In other words, fluctuations in consumption in capitalist economies generate undulations in investment behavior that lie behind the trade cycle. But investment itself largely determines the level of and rate of growth in consumption due to its impact on job creation and employment. Cyclical instability is, therefore, an essential and unavoidable characteristic of capitalist enterprise.

B. Circulation crises and financial panics

Counterposed to the intermittent volatility of the real economy are perturbations in the monetary and financial system. These too can cause wide gyrations in output and employment and can even, at times, lead to general interruptions of economic activity often called, in the course of American history, "panics." What distinguishes circulation crises and financial panics from so-called real business cycles is that they have often emerged independent of movements in inventory, population growth, technical change, and the like. Their propagation appears linked, in many cases, with institutional and regulatory constraints on the financial and banking sectors of the economy.

A financial crisis, in its simplest form, can emerge if there is an inadequate supply of currency in the system. If a national money supply is tied to the availability of a particular precious metal such as gold or silver, fluctuations in the supply of that medium will cause changes in national output. A rapidly growing money supply will, all other things remaining the same, initiate an inflationary boom as greater amounts of dollars "chase" a given output of goods and services. Conversely, should the money supply shrink, a deflationary spiral will ensue with concomitant impacts upon output, employment, and investment. Obviously, changes in the growth rate of the money supply can occur even in a paper money system in which a central monetary authority or political events alter that growth rate over time.

In a decentralized banking system, with a hard money (i.e., precious metal) base, the potential for financial disruption is great. There exist no unambiguous lines of authority in the event that a particular region or urban area suddenly requires an increase in circulating medium. Similarly, should some banks fail, owing to a deterioration in general economic conditions, poor management, or sheer bad luck, a decentralized institutional system of finance offers no mechanism by which liquidity can be restored. As banks close their doors, firms must cease operations and lay off workers; households will need to cut back consumption expenditures or substitute nonmonetary forms of exchange in their daily activities. An economic convulsion is the result.

Interestingly enough, circulation problems arising out of decentralized or hard money systems may have their genesis simply in the seasonal fluctuation of economic activity. In an agricultural economy at harvest time, for example, farmers will accumulate large cash reserves as they sell their crops. At the same time, merchants, shippers, and packers will require loans in order to process and move farm crops to market. Often such agents are located in cities or metropolitan areas distinct from the farm belts they serve. If there is no clear channel by which farmers' cash reserves can be recycled to those banks financing the wholesale trade, an interruption in commerce will result.

Financial panics may also occur when and if depositors lose confidence in the security of their bank-held assets. Fractional-reserve banking, and its unique profitability and ability to stimulate economic growth, is premised on the notion that every demand deposit will not be drawn upon at once. Yet if depositors sense some difficulty in the robustness of the banking system, a "run" can develop in which all deposits are in fact drawn down at the same time. In the face of such an onslaught, individual banks have little choice but to lock out their customers. Of course, as one bank pursues this strategy, the ingredients of wholesale panic are further supplied. Such inherent fragility in the private banking system can only be compensated for by governmental institutions that establish lenders of last resort, in the form of a central or national bank, or insurance systems by which the value of all deposits is secured to some minimum. Once again, even with respect to the monetary circulation and financial mechanisms of modern economy, the possibility of crisis and volatility is ever present.

C. Effective demand failures

Shortfalls in national output may also occur due to reductions in the level of demand. As consumption falls and firm sales are reduced, a cumulative downturn may develop whereby reductions in demand cause a decrease in investment and employment which itself furthers the decline in consumption as workers lose income. It is even possible that an economy may gravitate toward an "equilibrium" position, that is, a state of affairs from which there seems no tendency to depart, in which significant amounts of capital and labor are unemployed. This deviation of actual from potential output may be the result of distortions in the price mechanism, by which adjustments in wages and prices that might bring about full employment of resources are obstructed, or due to misperceptions on the part of wealth holders and workers as to the economic alternatives available to them. Capital might be hoarded, rather than productively invested, owing to a lack of confidence; labor might be withdrawn from the market in the (mistaken) impression that wages will rise in the near future. Virtual economic stagnation can be the ultimate result.

Tendencies toward underconsumption (or its mirror image, overproduction) may be derived from short-term changes in the distribution of income or long-run transformations in the structures of capital accumulation. Downward inflexibility of prices, caused by the concentrated structure of industry or the impact of labor unions, may intensify the effective demand problem and prevent the price system from reaching a new equilibrium at full employment. On the one side, "sticky prices" limit the already constrained purchasing power of consumers. On the other, to the extent that noncompetitive pricing predominates in the capital goods sector, producers are less willing to buy new plant and equipment. High real wages, held up by union pressure or government policy, may further contribute to persistent disequilibrium in labor markets. Yet lowering wages in an economy with highly concentrated and thereby imperfect markets can result in a reduction in real wages as prices remain high. The effective demand crisis is thereby exacerbated. Only if price adjustments are general, economy-wide, and followed rapidly by increased investment can a deflationary recovery process succeed.

Price inflexibility that is an outgrowth of capital concentration and imperfections in markets has especially negative implications for economic performance in the intermediate to long run. In highly concentrated industries, a downturn in the business cycle may result in perverse reactions that make the slump worse. The net revenue of firms with a great deal of market power may be so attenuated in a slump that strategies of price reduction may be viewed as unfeasible. There may even be incentives to raise prices in order to compensate for the reduction in the volume of sales.

If price reductions do not occur when the economy-wide rate of growth declines, the necessary adjustment of sectoral rates of expansion to the aggregate rate requires reductions in individual firms' rates of capacity utilization. If industrial structure were more competitive, however, excess capacity would not result from a decline in the rate of growth; rather, prices would fall. Reductions in capacity utilization imply not only lower national income but also higher unemployment. In the presence of underutilized capacity, firms will be disinclined to undertake net investment. A cumulative process will thereby be established wherein a decline in the rate of growth, by generating reductions in the rate of capacity utilization, lead to a further decline in the rate of expansion as net investment is reduced. Individual firms, believing that decreases in investment might alleviate their own burden of excess capacity, merely intensify the problem economy-wide. It is this "fallacy of composition," assuming that what is good for the individual is good for the whole, that is the basis of most macroeconomic difficulties in capitalist systems.

Effective demand failures may also be generated by declines in the rate of population growth or reductions in the rate at which innovations and new technologies are introduced into the economic system. As population growth falls off (assuming some minimum level of affluence of the population as a whole), the growth of major markets such as housing, transportation, and food production also slackens. Economic growth is thereby jeopardized and may only be resumed by the introduction of new technologies and products that can absorb larger investment outlays to expand production and employment once again. If these are not forthcoming, the only solution may be some form of exogenous spending (such as governmental deficit spending) to augment consumer purchasing power.

It is also possible that in more affluent societies, an ever-increasing volume of savings is generated. Such savings may eventually find no outlets except at unrealistically low rates of interest – rates at which investors may prefer to hold their wealth in cash rather than securities, bonds, or other titles to real capital. This would constitute a monetary parallel to the real problem of a potentially vanishing set of investment and technological opportunities. In other words, at very low rates of interest, the demand for money becomes so high as to create a "liquidity trap." As money accumulates in cash hoards, the decline in productive spending makes the downturn worse. As one distinguished macroeconomic theorist, Michal Kalecki, once put it: "Capitalists get what they spend; workers spend what they get." If either workers' consumption spending or capitalists' investment outlays decline, recession or depression is the result.

D. Compositional and structural distortions

Persistent unemployment, lagging capacity utilization in major industries, and inadequate rates of net investment in a national economy may also be the outgrowth of transformations in the composition of national product. Simple accelerator models of the business cycle fail to capture this complexity of modern economies because functional relationships between sales and investment obscure the influence of secular changes in the mix of industries constituting the national aggregate. Long-range prospects for expansion underlie the decision making associated with large investment obligations. The size and rate of growth of the relevant market are of primary concern. To the extent that firms in an industry during the trough phase of a business cycle have pessimistic expectations regarding their markets, a revival becomes dependent on either the creation of wholly new, promising markets (i.e., products) or the stimulus of new expenditures arising outside the industry. Highly concentrated sectors bolster the potential for economic stagnation. The reluctance to compete and expel excess capacity in these markets intensifies the gloom of the environment in which enterprise plans are formulated, besides contributing to the state of depressed sales and net revenues that makes investment upturns more and more difficult.

Product innovation requires large net revenues or adequate access to external sources of funds – both of which are less available in a slump. External stimuli must be sufficiently large to have an adequate effect. Secular changes in the growth performance and potential of various industries must offset declines in certain groups with rises in others. The chance that such changes in sectoral performance will proceed smoothly is small.

Secular transitions in development involve the decline of old and the rise of new industries. These alterations in the composition of national output tend to be discontinuous and disruptive not because of imperfections in markets but rather because of forces inherent in the accumulation of capital over time. First, the ongoing expansion of the capitalist economy is coterminous with the advance of scientific and technical knowledge that transforms production technique, cost structures, and the availability of raw materials and that creates entirely new inputs and outputs. Consider, for example, the emergence of fossil fuels, the replacement of natural fibers with synthetics, and the rise of internal combustion as a means of locomotion. Entire industries are made obsolete or virtually so, while new ones are created. Second, the structural milieu in which product and technical changes take place is itself a product of economic growth.

The concentration and increasing specificity of capital may interfere with the movements of inputs required for smooth transitions in sectoral activity. The decline in competitive pressure in highly concentrated industries not only makes entry difficult, because of pricing strategies, but also exit. Large amounts of capital are fixed in plant and equipment, their liquidation neither encouraged by a competitive environment nor practical if the industry is in long-run decline. The hesitancy of large firms to liquidate in depressed times may also be due to a reluctance to relinquish goodwill and the technical specialization of labor and organization, and to uncertainty as to the growth potential of new markets.

Concentration of capital may lead to unequal access to investment funds, which obstructs further the possibility of easy transitions in industrial activity. Because of their past record of profitability, large enterprises have higher credit ratings and easier access to credit facilities, and they are able to put up larger collateral for a loan. Equity issues by such firms are more readily financed and sold, and such firms can avoid takeovers more easily than small firms. Large firms, too, may have commonalities of interest with financial institutions through interlocking directorates. All these factors may impede the flow of capital out of old and into new sectors, thereby making worse shortfalls in aggregate economic performance.

Compositional and structural change in economies may also precipitate serious unemployment problems that interfere with the achievement of full employment output. New industries may have differing capital intensities and skill requirements, relative to older sectors, that complicate (or possibly prevent) the absorption of unemployed workers. The problem may be twofold: newer industries may not grow fast enough to provide employment opportunities for those laid off in older sectors; but even if higher growth rates are achieved, the newer industries may require different amounts and altogether different kinds of labor for their production. Structural unemployment may be the troubling and persistent consequence.

Finally, changes in the relationship of a national economy to the world economic system may also be responsible for wide fluctuations in macroeconomic behavior. A resurgence of competition from other national systems previously excluded from or inadequately prepared for international commerce may affect the fortunes of domestic industries grown used to protected or exclusive markets. Transformations in international currency systems, whereby a nation's monetary unit that had previously served as *numeraire* and means of international transaction is rapidly integrated into a general floating currency system, will also profoundly change the performance characteristics of that economy. Inflationary pressures at home may translate into an export boom as a currency is devalued; while deflationary patterns may yield an upswing in imports to the detriment of domestic producers. Policy flexibility and independence may also be constrained as a nation's economy becomes more integrated with economies elsewhere. Domestic changes in fiscal and monetary policy will have international trade consequences as well. Modulations of interest rates, for example, will affect the flow of capital across national borders as investors compare rates of return in various nations.

National economic performance may also, in a mature setting, require increasing involvement of the state. Maintaining outlets for net investment expenditure might involve deficit spending to bolster demand, direct government purchases of goods and services (particularly of public goods such as infrastructure and defense), and government oversight of the penetration of foreign markets. These efforts might be paralleled by rising outlays by private firms on sales efforts, distribution mechanisms, and means to enhance consumer credit. While for some economic theorists, fiscal and monetary mechanisms stand as instruments of periodic countercyclical policy, for others governmental involvement in mature economies may be a permanent (and ever-increasing) feature of modern industrial systems.

In many respects, economic instability in modern states would appear to be the outgrowth of coordination problems whereby the plans of private firms do not meld appropriately to maintain balanced growth over time. Business cycle theorists have long understood that if investment decision making could somehow be coordinated by some central authority, with aggregate demand augmented accordingly, there would not necessarily arise interruptions in the growth process. The expansion plans of one firm would be met by those of its suppliers and its consumers, and so on. Such organization of national economic activity has in fact most often been achieved, in capitalist settings, during wartime. The difficulty of course is that systemization of private planning by sovereign authority is inconsistent with the operation of economic systems premised upon the rights of private property and wealth accumulation.

To protect against unemployment and economic instability, the freedom to accumulate may be curtailed within the context of national planning. Yet to endorse unfettered accumulation of wealth may be to leave society open to divisive and potentially catastrophic political turmoil when a dramatic flagging of business activity occurs. Planned systems can often eradicate income volatility and unemployment, but they apparently cannot ensure adequate rates of growth in material welfare and income. Capitalist systems, by contrast, have unprecedented records when it comes to the massing of wealth and raising of living standards, but unemployment and income fluctuations cannot be eliminated except under extraordinary conditions.

III. THE CONTEMPORARY AMERICAN RECORD

World War II achieved in the United States what the New Deal could not – economic recovery from the Great Depression of the 1930s. Unemployment fell to only 7% by the time of the Japanese offensive at Pearl

Harbor. American entry into the war brought almost instantaneous resolution of the persistent economic difficulties of the interwar years. Rationing, federal planning, and price controls provided for the efficient and rapid diversion of resources from civilian to military production. Unemployment fell to 1.2% by 1944. And, while hardly inspired by specific economic concerns, President Roosevelt's "arsenal of democracy" nevertheless contained vivid policy lessons for economists, politicians, government officials, and the public at large.

Yet as World War II came to a close many economists and businesspeople worried about the possibility of a drop in the level of prosperity and employment to one far below that of the war. But these apprehensions proved to be unwarranted. By 1946, aggregate spending did not fall and unemployment did not even reach 4%. Although recessions occurred between 1945 and the mid-1970s, most of them lasted only about a year or less, and none of them remotely approached the severity of the Great Depression of the thirties. During these three decades American manufacturing output steadily increased with only minor setbacks. According to the Federal Reserve Board's index, manufacturing production doubled between 1945 and 1965 and tripled between 1945 and 1976.

Such robust economic performance is hardly surprising in wartime – especially when conflict is global and, with few exceptions, kept outside of a nation's own boundaries. What is most striking about the American economic experience linked with World War II was the enduring growth and prosperity of the *postwar* years. Consumption and investment behavior played a major part in this great prosperity of the late forties and fifties. On the domestic side, reconversion was itself an investment stimulus. Modernization and deferred replacement projects required renewed and large deployments of funds. Profound scarcities of consumer goods, the production of which had been long postponed by wartime mobilization needs, necessitated major retooling and expansion efforts. Even fear of potentially high inflation, emerging in the wake of the dismantling of the price and wage controls of the war years, prompted many firms to move forward the date of ambitious and long-term investment projects. On the foreign side, both individuals and governments were eager to find a refuge for capital that had been in virtual hiding during the war itself. Along with a jump in domestic investment, therefore, a large capital inflow began in late 1945 and early 1946.

Domestic consumption was the second major component of postwar growth. Bridled demand and high household savings due to wartime shortages, rationing, and controls, coupled with the generous wage rates of the high-capacity war economy all contributed to a dramatic growth in consumer spending at war's end. The jump in disposable income was bolstered by the rapid reduction in wartime surtaxes and excises. And the baby boom of the wartime generation expressed itself economically in high levels of demand for significant items like appliances, automobiles, and housing. G. I. Bill benefits additionally served to increase the demand for housing and such things as educational services with associated impacts on construction and other industrial sectors.

Foreign demand for American exports grew rapidly in the immediate postwar years. In part the needs of devastated areas could only be met by the one industrial base that had been nearly untouched by war-related destruction. Explicit policy commitments to the rebuilding of allied and occupied territories, such as the Marshall Plan in Europe, also served to increase the foreign market for the output of American industry. Even so, one of the most powerful influences on the impressive postwar growth of the American economy was the unique and special set of arrangements developed for international trade at the Monetary and Financial Conference of the United Nations in 1944.

When the allied nations' financial ministers gathered at Bretton Woods in New Hampshire, just before the war's end, they were concerned to reconfigure world trade and financial flows such that the disputes so characteristic of the interwar years 1919–39 could be avoided and stability maintained. Along with the creation of the International Bank for Reconstruction and Development (known today as the World Bank) and the International Monetary Fund, the conference decided to establish fixed exchange rates between the U.S. dollar and all other internationally traded currencies. The value of the dollar itself was set in terms of gold at $35 per ounce. This installed a benchmark against which the value of all other currencies was measured. As the American economy was, by far, the most powerful at the time, it seemed prudent and indeed necessary that its currency play such a central international role. Moreover, the other industrialized nations of the day were powerless to stop the United States from assuming this central position in world finance.

American postwar prosperity and the benefits of world economic leadership continued throughout most of the 1950s. The added fiscal stimulus of the Korean War also played a role in maintaining the high levels of growth and employment characteristic of the decade. Republican President Dwight Eisenhower, carrying on in the tradition of his Democratic predecessor Harry Truman, repeatedly committed his administration to the practice of compensatory demand management. But the prosperity of the fifties, while robust and impressive, nevertheless weakened by 1957. This set the stage for the arrival of a new brand of economics in Washington, imbued with the doctrines of Keynesianism. From the "New Frontier" policies of John Kennedy, to the "Great Society" agenda of his successor Lyndon Johnson, through the declaration of a "New Federalism" by Richard Nixon, there ensued an era of sustained central government intervention in the nation's economic life. The self-assurance of many, but not all of the "new" economists of the early 1960s, that the goal of achieving simultaneously acceptable levels of unemployment and inflation could be realized, has more recently been shattered. But throughout the sixties and much of the seventies, and for some even during the eighties, the perceived obligation of government to secure overall economic stability was not seriously questioned and remained one of the more important changes of twentieth-century American economic history.

By the 1970s, a quarter century of American prosperity was in jeopardy. The growth rate of the G.N.P. fell after several years of sturdy expansion. Unemployment rates reached disquieting levels, and the attendant downturns were persistent rather than transitory. After the dramatic rise in oil prices in 1973, the economy deteriorated. Measured in constant prices, the annual average compound growth rate of the G.N.P. fell from 4% (for the period 1960–73) to 1.8% (for the period 1973–82). Annual unemployment rose from 4.8% of the labor force in 1973 to 8.3% two years later. But in 1975 a sustained recovery began as the rise in food and fuel prices slowed. As a result the inflation rate fell in the next few years from over 12% to between 5 and 7%. Nevertheless, a 1979 revolution in Iran led to great oil price increases and an inflation rate of 16% during the first half of 1980. Although there was a modest upswing in late 1980, the United States by 1981–2 experienced the worst recession since the Great Depression. The unemployment rate alone rose to 10%. Overall, the decennial average rate of unemployment was, for the 1980s, approximately 6.9%.

The poor macroeconomic performance of the 1970s was in fact initiated by an exogenous shock. In the wake of the Yom Kippur War of 1973, the Organization of Petroleum Exporting Countries (O.P.E.C.) instituted a series of price increases for crude oil that had disastrous consequences for the United States and other industrialized economies. The price of crude rose 12% in June of 1973 and then took off with the October war in the Middle East. Oil prices rose 66% in October and doubled in January of 1974. From 1952 to 1965 the average inflation rate for the American economy (based on the consumer price index) stood at 1.3%. In the following seven years it rose to 4.1%, and for the decade of the seventies to 8.8%. For 1972–82, it is estimated that the total change in the American cost of living was some 133%. Poor crop yields in 1971 and 1972 because of a drought in the nation's agricultural regions contributed to the inflationary spiral.

The O.P.E.C. shock, while different in form, had many of the same consequences as the 1929 stock debacle. Real incomes fell dramatically. Many bank portfolios and the economic position of investors were imperiled. The confidence of consumers and investors was dealt a serious blow. Investment declined as firms became more and more hesitant and as households postponed major expenditures. Profit margins shrank as the costs of production rose. Capacity utilization and employment consequently shrunk. The cumulative oil price increases of the 1970s also had a devastating impact on the American balance of payments – a $40 billion deficit in fuel imports alone by decade's end. As the G.N.P. growth rates noted above show, the American economy fell, rose, and fell again during the rest of the seventies. This combination of seeming economic stagnation and high inflation gave rise to a new economic label – "stagflation."

There were numerous factors forestalling recovery in the seventies. The fiscal crisis of the Vietnam era and its related international financial development – the demise of the Bretton Woods system – fundamentally altered the relationship of the American economy to world markets. Where trading partners in the past had been content to hold their dollar reserves – essentially financing the American trade deficit – the deterioration in the value of the dollar pursuant to the war inflation and increasing political resistance abroad changed that behavior.

With the collapse of the Bretton Woods system in 1970–71, the United States was freed from the burden of maintaining a fixed exchange rate; the resultant devaluation of the dollar improved America's export position, at least potentially. But the other consequence of the policy change was inflation. Thus on the very eve of the O.P.E.C. price explosion, the United States had already been placed in an extremely vulnerable economic condition. In addition to the monetary changes, technological factors made themselves felt in the early seventies that suggested that an industrial "retardation" was under way. This loss of international competitiveness further weakened the American economy.

As early as the 1960s the nations devastated by World War II (most significantly Japan and the then Federal Republic of Germany) had reestablished their economic presence in world markets. They possessed an advanced technological base owing to the recent rebuilding of their major industries and their relative insulation, under international treaties and agreements (exemplified by the erection of a "nuclear umbrella" by the United States), from the burdens of defense spending. Consequently, their major industries – automobiles, electronics, and steel – became powerful competitors with their American counterparts. This was the real corollary to the financial crisis precipitated by O.P.E.C. and agricultural price increases. And it was a dramatic expression of the loss of America's leadership in the world economy as a whole.

Many scholars have focused on what they see as a managerial failure of American enterprise in the sixties and seventies in meeting foreign competition. A focus on short-term profitability and sales, rather than long-term investment and revitalization has been blamed as a major cause of management's failure to keep America first among industrial equals. Certainly the case of the automobile industry suggests that American producers were locked in a kind of technological rigidity that left them exposed to the full impact of superior Japanese technology – especially when the O.P.E.C. price rise qualitatively altered the demand for cars toward lighter, more fuel-efficient vehicles. The peculiar incentives established by American tax codes, and what is often called the present-mindedness of the American corporate elite, may have been factors in this managerial failure.

But there appear to have been other factors involved in the technological deceleration of some major sectors of American industry. The stimulus afforded by World War II and the Korean conflict brought all of American industry out of the crisis of the thirties. Indeed, it has been suggested that wartime production and the military procurement of the cold war years have been responsible for much of the prosperity of the American economy in the entire postwar era. It would appear, however, that the fiscal stimulus of an enduring defense establishment, while providing a short-run fillip to national income, may in the long run have weakened major sectors of the economy and curtailed their ability to develop and compete on a world scale.

Table 1.1. *U.S. trade in manufactured goods, 1965–80 (Annual averages; billions of dollars)*

Years	Exports	Imports	Trade ratio[a]
1965–69	20.3	16.6	0.1
1970–73	35.1	34.8	0.004
1974–76	71.7	57	0.11
1977–80	101.4	103.6	−0.01

[a]Trade ratio = (exports − imports)/(exports + imports).
Source: U.S. Department of Commerce, *International Economic Indicators* (September, 1974, and September, 1984).

Nowhere was the deterioration in overall American economic performance during the seventies more vividly stated than in the international trade statistics. U.S. trade in manufactured goods was transformed during the seventies. By 1977–80 the ratio of net exports to total manufacturing trade turned negative for the first time since 1940 (see Tables 1.1 and 1.2). America's market share of exports of manufactures steadily eroded. And almost all of the major manufacturing sectors saw their trade performance worsen. Exceptions included fields in which the United States held a virtually unassailable technical lead (such as aerospace and aviation) or where public policy had taken an active role in obstructing the worsening trend (such as leather and lumber products). Accompanying the alteration in the competitiveness of American industry in the world economy was the restructuring of the nation's labor market and changes in the productivity of labor in core manufacturing industries.

As the international competitiveness of domestic industry weakened, both rates of employment and levels of labor earnings suffered in what had previously been major industrial venues. A transition to a service economy yielded relatively fewer well-paying and secure jobs than at any time since the 1930s. In 1979, 43% of the nonfarm labor force worked in service and retail trade. In fact, during the 1970s, these two sectors had accounted for 70% of all the new private sector jobs created in the economy at large. Within the service sector, the growth in employment was concentrated in such activities as restaurants, hospitals, nursing homes, medical and dental offices, and business services (that ranged from personnel services and data processing to custodial operations).

Table 1.2. *Trade ratios for selected industries, 1967 and 1977*

Industry	1967	1977	Change 1966 to 1977
Textile mill products	−0.36	0.03	0.39
Turbine generators	0.41	0.78	0.37
Leather and leather products	−0.24	−0.02	0.22
Telephone and telegraphic equipment	0.19	0.33	0.14
Wood pulp	−0.22	−0.12	0.10
Paper and paperboard	−0.37	−0.30	0.07
Aerospace	0.80	0.82	0.02
Steel	−0.16	−0.68	−0.52
Rubber tires and tubes	−0.11	−0.51	−0.40
Apparel	−0.54	−0.86	−0.32
Machine tools	0.13	−0.12	−0.25
Photographic equipment	0.38	0.17	−0.21
Automobiles	−0.01	−0.21	−0.20
Chemicals	0.49	0.30	−0.19
House appliances	0.01	−0.14	−0.15
General industrial machinery	0.72	0.57	−0.15
Construction machinery	0.91	0.76	−0.15
Computers	0.78	0.65	−0.13
Farm machinery	0.17	0.15	−0.02

Source: U.S. Department of Commerce, *Survey of Current Business: 1980, U.S. Industrial Outlook for 200 Industries with Projections for 1984.*

Employment growth in such activities as these far outpaced that in the industrial arena throughout the 1970s; this trend continued through the 1980s.

The jobs created in these new growth areas of the contemporary American economy were quite different from those in which earlier generations had made their livings. Service workers tended to work shorter hours and earned lower hourly wages than their peers in manufacturing. A large percentage of these positions, as well, were "dead end" ones insofar as the prospects for further training and ultimate promotion to supervisory responsibility were quite meager. A vast proportion of these new jobs developed in nonunion settings with lower wage levels and drastically reduced benefits compared to jobs in manufacturing. Not surprisingly, therefore, women and minorities (and generally younger workers) accounted for substantial shares of the employment in these newer service industries. In short, the changing structure of the national economy, linked in part with the effects of America's increasing economic interdependence with the rest of the world, led to the generation of new jobs that paid less, had less security, and offered fewer opportunities for advancement than the industrial posts that for generations had underwritten the life-cycle incomes of whole families. Of course, nostalgia about the loss of semi- and high-skilled jobs in basic industries like automobiles and steel had to be tempered with the recognition that international competition often lowered the prices for some of these major products within the United States.

The changing manner in which the U.S. economy did business with the rest of the world was perhaps the single most striking characteristic of the period after 1980. By 1988, for example, the major export from the West Coast of the United States was waste paper. The major imports to that coast were automobile parts, furniture, and textiles. Various American manufacturing sectors steadily shrank in size since the early seventies when foreign competition made its presence felt in no uncertain terms. But as this process of global restructuring of commerce proceeded, many (but not all) American manufacturing firms themselves became part of what was called the "hollowing out" of the nation's industrial base. As imports jumped 51% during the early eighties, and as exports declined by about 2%, American firms embarked on investment strategies (in many cases stimulated by public policy) that, while individually profitable, tended to accelerate the deindustrialization trend. In 1989, for example, the General Electric Company used reserve funds to purchase $10 billion of its own stock rather than to make new acquisitions or invest in new technology with which to meet the growing competition from abroad. General Motors in 1990 operated seventeen assembly plants in Mexico that employed a total of approximately 24,000 workers. The company discussed plans to invest in an additional twelve factories in Mexico. For the year 1990, it was estimated that some 300,000 automobiles were imported from Mexico as a result of direct American corporate initiatives.

Throughout the 1980s one major sector of American industry did not suffer from atrophy – the defense industries. The presidential administration of Ronald Reagan embarked on a decade-long process of expansion in the armed services, resulting in the largest peacetime increase of American forces and weapons systems in history. By the end of the eighties, the United States economy annually allocated close to $300 billion in resources to the military. Strikingly enough, the profit rate on defense contracts far outstripped that in consumer durables industries. From 1970 to 1980 the average rate of profit earned on Department of Defense contracts was about 19.4%, as compared with 14.4% in durable goods manufacturing. For the first half of the 1980s, defense industry profit rates averaged 23.3%, while durable goods producers managed only 10.6%.

The Reagan military buildup brought new and difficult pressures to bear on the American economy. Compared with most other major industrial nations, the United States committed a far greater percentage of its G.N.P. to defense spending, approximately 6.1% annually by the end of the 1980s. France, for example, allocated 3.5%, the former Federal Republic of Germany 3.1%, and Japan a bit less than 1%. This development prompted some investigators to worry that the diversion of national resources to defense projects impeded the ability of American industry to increase productivity, innovate, and generally confront the overseas competition that had made such profound inroads in the world economy since the early seventies. From the mid-1970s to the mid-1980s, American manufacturing productivity grew roughly by 2% as compared to 7.3% for Japan, 3.3% for West Germany, and 2.3% for Great Britain. While it had once seemed that defense research and production could "spin-off" new techniques and products to benefit the private sector, concern grew that military production weakened domestic manufacturing. To what extent these anxieties were valid constituted a new and exciting area of research for economists, economic historians, and technologists. Of course, it is important to remember that the whole idea of a peacetime military expansion after World War II had been sold in part to Congress and local public officials on the basis of all the resources and funding that would flow their way. Military bases brought jobs to local communities and profits to local businesses. Defense spending in general also created better paying jobs that provided higher purchasing power for the other products of domestic industry.

Rising by almost 120% through the course of the 1980s, from $134 to $294.9 billion, military spending in the United States also had a profound economic impact by virtue of its contribution to a federal budget deficit and, thereby, the public debt. The cumulative federal deficit for the

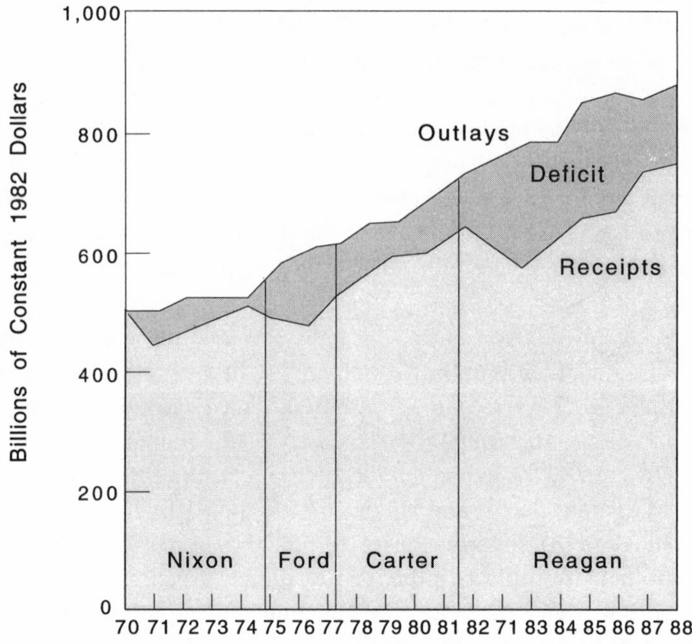

Figure 1.1. Federal budget deficits, 1970–88. *Source:* U.S. Department of Commerce, as reported in Gary M. Walton and Hugh Rockoff, *History of the American Economy* (San Diego: Harcourt Brace Jovanovich, 1990), p. 561.

eighties came to approximately $2 trillion. As the budget deficit grew from 2.7% to 5.2% of G.N.P. during the first Reagan term (1981–84), it became clear that a substantial portion of the increase was due to increased military spending. Paralleled by a burgeoning trade deficit (that reached almost $200 billion by the end of the decade), the imbalance between federal revenues and expenditures emerged as one of the most serious challenges facing the American economy in the nineties. (The burgeoning federal deficits of recent decades are portrayed in Figure 1.1.)

IV. CONCLUSIONS AND HYPOTHESES

A. Countercyclical policy formulation

From the 1890s to the Great Depression of the interwar period, countercyclical economic policy was virtually unknown. Economists were in fact limited by deep-seated intellectual prejudices in the formulation of compensatory measures. The lack of a comprehensive theory of macroeconomic behavior (prior to the advent of the Keynesian Revolution) was paralleled by the absence of reliable and systematic data on the fiscal and monetary mechanisms of government. The notion of government spending itself was suspect. Budget deficits were equated with national economic ruin, and the plausible yet inaccurate analogy drawn between a family's finances and those of the state reigned supreme in economists' minds. The fallacy of composition was not yet part of economists' lexicon.

Business cycle theory was in a similarly inchoate and uninformed state. Most economists viewed the cycle as a therapeutic cure for intermittent yet never well-explained overflows of the economic mechanism. Cycles could not be tamed, much less made obsolete. The notion of potential output and an appreciation of the losses incurred when actual national output fell below that capacity (or full-employment) ceiling were yet unexplained. As a result, there was a thoroughly inadequate understanding of the process of inflation. There certainly was no conception that a slack economy would not suffer accelerating inflation under a regime of restitutive fiscal spending. Ignorance contributed to (though it does not fully explain) the virtual impotence and in some cases the unintended perversity of economic policy during the thirties.

With the 1940s experience of economic intervention and planning by the federal government, and the emergence of a bipartisan commitment to aggregate demand management under the Eisenhower administration, there quickly arose a consensus regarding the benefits of fiscal activism. During the "New Frontier" years of John Kennedy's presidency, and throughout the terms of Lyndon Johnson, the use of the federal government's authority over taxation and monetary policy, as an instrument of countercyclical control for the national economy, was common and widely accepted. During the 1970s, however, the fiscal burdens of both the Vietnam War and the redistributive efforts of Johnson's "Great Society" programs inspired an increasing resistance to the practice of Keynesian demand management. The faltering economic performance of the late seventies, epitomized by the very high levels of the "misery index" (the sum of the rates of inflation and unemployment), laid the foundations for a major transformation in American economic policy in the 1980s.

The emergence of so-called supply-side economics (or "Reaganomics") as a new blueprint for federal economic policy was inspired by a widespread belief that the period of American economic leadership in world affairs, the anticipated "American Century" of the preceding seventy-five years, might be coming to an end. Henceforth, the economic prosperity of Americans would be increasingly dependent upon developments elsewhere in a vast global marketplace. Two developments during 1978, in fact, each rooted in what were perceived to be past failures of governmental economic policies, appeared to signal the beginning of a return to policy approaches that predated the New Deal.

One was a popular movement, termed a "taxpayers' revolt," to limit government spending and tax revenues. Prompted by some successes of this movement in state and local referendums (in particular, the passage of Proposition 13 in California in 1978 that limited property tax assessments), some national political leaders jumped on the bandwagon of economy in government in order to push proposals to limit federal employment and spending.

The second development resulted from the battering of the dollar in foreign exchange markets as holders of dollars sold them in large amounts because they feared that American economic policies would continue to cause stagflation, weak capital formation, and limited real economic growth. In response the Federal Reserve Board moved to support the dollar through monetary stringency, and President Jimmy Carter promulgated a wide-ranging program that included voluntary guidelines for wage and price increases, further measures to support the dollar's international value, and a renewed pledge to hold down government employment and spending in order to reduce the large federal deficits of the previous decade. These developments reflected a growing belief among some national leaders and many middle-class Americans that government policies requiring ever-larger spending programs, deficit financing, and money creation (to ease the interest rate pressures that deficits would otherwise generate) were more a cause of stagflation than a solution.

Ronald Reagan's stunning landslide victory over Jimmy Carter in the 1980 presidential election signaled a transition from Keynesian-style demand management to the allegedly new strategies of supply-side economic theory. Believing that the fundamental source of the problems facing the contemporary American economy had to do with supply problems rather than with demand fluctuations, the supply-side theorists focused their policy proposals on the means by which macroeconomic supply conditions might be improved. Increasing supply, it was presumed, would overcome the twin problems of stagnation and inflation that had troubled the economy since the early seventies.

Supply-side theory focused on what were believed to be the distortions created by large government spending, high taxation of income, and inordinate governmental regulation of economic affairs. Excessive income taxation, it was argued, stifled productive effort, for example, by discouraging overtime work. It robbed individuals of the fruits of enterprise and risk bearing. Finally, it distorted economic decision making so as to slow economic growth and create the very fiscal pressures that contributed to the problems of stagflation in the first instance. The solution would involve a radical reduction in taxes, a systematic shrinking of government programs and, thus, federal agency budgets, and the elimination of costly regulatory measures.

In February of 1981, the newly elected Reagan administration presented its "Program for Economic Recovery" to the Congress. Inspired by the arguments of supply-side economists, the proposal called for the control of federal spending, the reduction or elimination of a wide variety of social entitlement and redistributive schemes dating back to the days of the New Frontier and the Great Society, and the aggressive reduction of tax rates on incomes. In particular, it called for 10% annual reductions in marginal income tax rates for three years beginning in the summer of 1981. Along with this economic platform, the President's program also provided for the implementation of investment incentives for private business (by means of accelerated depreciation), and streamlining or elimination of a host of regulatory codes, and monetary stringency. The hope, along with the expectation that such measures would stimulate growth through investment, jobs creation, and greater labor productivity, was that the federal budget might be balanced by 1984 with concomitant savings on interest payments and a lessening of the loanable funds shortages caused by a massive government presence in capital markets.

By August of 1981, the Economic Recovery Tax Act was made law – thereby implementing, in the form of income tax reduction, a major component of the Reagan supply-side program. Over the next three years, major cuts were made in such programs as unemployment insurance, food stamps, aid to families with dependent children, Medicaid, student loans, retirement benefits, grants for mass transportation, and benefits to import-impacted industries. Paralleling such transformations in fiscal policy, a strict anti-inflationary money policy was also pursued. The results were mixed. On the one side, inflation was strikingly reduced. From 9% in 1981, the annual rate of increase in the price level fell to 3.5% by the end of Reagan's first term. Unemployment, after rising to 9.7% in 1982, fell to about 7.5% in 1984–85, and to 5% by the end of 1988. But, consistent with the Reagan administration's belief that an "inflation threshold" existed, job idleness was not pressed below the 5% achieved by the end of 1988. In this, the Reagan White House sharply distinguished itself from the Keynesian-style full employment commitments of both Democratic and Republican predecessors. Moreover, owing to the fiscal crisis dramatized by the extent of the federal debt, the presidential administration of Bill Clinton, as well as its immediate successors, faces the difficulty of implementing fiscal demand management even if it wishes to do so. In this ironic sense, although the Reagan administration practiced Keynesianism in its dramatic expansion of military spending while at the same time reducing federal taxes, Reaganomics did unambiguously achieve one particular policy objective: it has made the future use of Keynesian-style spending policies distinctly problematic if not impossible.

B. Economic interdependence and the end of the "American Century"

Far from being the dominant economic power of the day in the early 1990s, the United States became one member of a new set of major industrial powers. The increased interdependence created by the latest economic restructuring of the world posed both vast opportunities and difficult challenges for the American economy. U.S. policy making had to take into greater account the demands and actions of other nations. Trade performance, access to technology, productivity, and the general level of economic welfare within the United States were more affected by those of other nations. Making the transition from world economic leadership to world economic cooperation and interdependence was clearly the major task that stood before the American economy in the 1990s. Not surprisingly, this challenge left much of the American public fearful and apprehensive regarding the future.

Other challenges also emerged for the American economy as it approached the turn of the century. The need for job training and broader educational initiatives, in order to improve the nation's international competitiveness, became apparent. Day care provision, increasingly important in a society where many families had two household heads earning income, also emerged on the national political agenda – although, interestingly enough, in the 1992 presidential campaign it was almost never mentioned. Medical insurance, exceedingly costly and in 1990 unavailable to as many as 30 million Americans, potentially came to constitute, under some reform proposals, a major claim on the federal budget. All these policy conundrums portended dramatic and difficult choices for the Congress, the executive branch, and the taxpaying public.

In addition to the general challenges afforded by foreign competition, political and economic developments around the world also had tremendous significance for the current and future performance of the American economy. The political devolution and liberalization of the former communist-bloc nations created a set of potential opportunities for American business without parallel in earlier decades. Some American firms began operations in the former Soviet and other Eastern European economies in the early 1990s. Meanwhile, the Commonwealth of Independent States and several of the East European nations approached the United States for massive foreign aid to assist in the transition to more privatized economic practices. The extent to which such opportunities for American overseas investment and such further demands upon the federal budget could be realized was unclear.

The changing structure of the world economy continued to pose additional challenges to the United States. Free trade pacts with Canada and Mexico had the capacity to restructure the way business was done in the Western Hemisphere. How a large American trading zone would affect industries within (and outside) the United States was hard to predict, but it was clearly possible that low-cost Mexican labor would provide a powerful competition for manufacturing and assembly activities in the United States. The continuing unification of Europe, epitomized by the reunification of Germany and the expansion of a European free trade zone, while potentially jeopardized by internecine warfare in the Balkans and trans-border disputes regarding monetary and exchange-rate policy, nonetheless created the single largest economic entity in the world. Along with enduring discussions as to the possibility of establishing a single European currency unit, it seemed clear that continued diplomatic efforts by the European nations could succeed in counterposing to the United States, and other large economic systems, the impressive economic powers of the entire European continent. How the U.S. economy might confront such new challenges from a rapidly changing political-economic world system constitutes one of the central questions for public discussion as the turn of the century approaches.

That for over two centuries prior to World War I, Americans had always had to secure their livelihoods with constant reference to the world market suggests that the American economic experience in the twentieth century has been altogether unique. Special historical and institutional circumstances, some the result of conscious design and others fortuitous, combined to create a remarkable prosperity and a virtually global economic hegemony after the war decade of the 1940s. The nation's economic fortunes have more recently weakened – as these circumstances have themselves changed. In turn, the confidence that future growth will be adequate to redeem the economic expectations and hopes of all Americans, the overwhelming proportion of whom had grown accustomed to the novel affluence of the late twentieth century, is now greatly suspect.

Reclaiming the economic stability and expansion that characterized the postwar era in the United States will pose dramatic challenges both to policy makers and to political representatives. The seeming paralysis that has surrounded four successive presidential administrations and nine congresses, in efforts to formulate effective economic policy, bodes ill for the immediate future. Similarly, the vast majority of economic analysts focus a disproportionate amount of their energy either on political nostrums (such as "supply-side theory") or abstract and academic debates. Meanwhile, a full resolution of the economic difficulties facing the nation remains elusive.

Whether American economic decline will be reversed or, instead, in the words of Joseph Schumpeter with which this essay began, "supply the dominating theme for the remaining movements of the capitalist symphony," will depend in large measure on the ability of Americans – politicians, policy makers, businesspeople, working people, and consumers – to stake out new political and economic initiatives with which to secure the welfare of present and future generations. Success in that task will clearly require the courage to criticize and refashion a wide variety of political and economic practices and arrangements that have been, and in many respects still are, taken for granted. Indeed, historical changes on a world scale, that have currently jeopardized American economic growth, have already made this task essential and urgent. Toward the end of encouraging such critical evaluation of present economic conduct and policy, and with a view to demonstrating the promise of new and alternative approaches to understanding contemporary economic history and events, the essays in this volume have been prepared.

REFERENCES

Trade cycle theory

Moses Abramovitz, "The Nature and Significance of Kuznets Cycles," *Economic Development and Cultural Change* 9 (April, 1961), 225–48.

American Economic Association, *Readings in Business Cycle Theory* (Homewood, Ill.: Richard D. Irwin, 1951).

Michael R. Darby, "Three-and-a-half Million Employees Have Been Mislaid: Or, an Explanation of Unemployment, 1934–1941," *Journal of Political Economy* 84 (February, 1976), 1–16.

James S. Duesenberry, *Business Cycles and Economic Growth* (New York: McGraw-Hill, 1958).

Irving Fisher, *Booms and Depressions: Some First Principles* (New York: Adelphi Company, 1932).

Milton Friedman and Anna J. Schwartz, *A Monetary History of the United States, 1867–1960* (Princeton, N.J.: Princeton University Press, 1963).

Robert A. Gordon, *Business Fluctuations* (New York: Harper & Row, 1955).

Alvin H. Hansen, *Full Recovery or Stagnation?* (New York: Norton, 1941).

Michal Kalecki, *Selected Essays on the Dynamics of the Capitalist Economy, 1933–1970* (Cambridge University Press, 1971).

John Maynard Keynes, *The General Theory of Employment, Interest, and Money* (London: Macmillan, 1936).

Charles P. Kindleberger, *Manias, Panics, and Crashes* (New York: Basic Books, 1989).

N. D. Kondratieff, "The Long Waves in Economic Life" (W. F. Stolper, trans.), *Review of Economic Statistics* 17 (November, 1935), 105–15.

Simon Kuznets, *Modern Economic Growth: Rate, Structure, and Spread* (New Haven, Conn.: Yale University Press, 1966).

"Long Swings in the Growth of Population and in Related Economic Variables." *Proceedings of the American Philosophical Society* 102 (February, 1958), 25–52.

Robert E. Lucas, "An Equilibrium Model of the Business Cycle," *Journal of Political Economy* 83 (December, 1975), 1113–44.

Wesley C. Mitchell, *Business Cycles: The Problem and Its Setting* (New York: National Bureau of Economic Research, 1927).

A. W. Phillips, "The Relation Between Unemployment and the Rate of Change of Money Wage Rates in the United Kingdom, 1861–1957," *Economica* (n.s.) 25 (November, 1958), 283–99.

Paul A. Samuelson, "Interactions Between the Multiplier Analysis and the Principle of Acceleration," *Review of Economics and Statistics* 21 (May, 1939), 75–78.

Joseph A. Schumpeter, *Business Cycles: A Theoretical, Historical, and Statistical Analysis of the Capitalist Process* (New York: McGraw-Hill, 1939).

The American record

Robert E. Baldwin, *Trade Policy in a Changing World Economy* (Chicago: University of Chicago Press, 1989).

Paul A. Baran and Paul M. Sweezy, *Monopoly Capital: An Essay on the American Economic and Social Order* (New York: Monthly Review Press, 1966).

William J. Baumol and Kenneth McLennan, *Productivity Growth and U.S. Competitiveness* (New York: Oxford University Press, 1985).

Michael A. Bernstein, *The Great Depression: Delayed Recovery and Economic Change in America, 1929–1939* (Cambridge University Press, 1989).

Alan S. Blinder, *Economic Policy and the Great Stagflation* (New York: Academic Press, 1979).

Barry Bluestone and Bennett Harrison, *The Deindustrialization of America: Plant Closings, Community Abandonment, and the Dismantling of Basic Industries* (New York: Basic Books, 1982).

Robert M. Collins, *The Business Response to Keynes: 1929–1964* (New York: Columbia University Press, 1981).

Robert W. Degrasse, Jr., *Military Expansion, Economic Decline: The Impact of Military Spending on U.S. Economic Performance* (New York: Council on Economic Priorities, 1983).

Richard A. Easterlin, *Population, Labor Force, and Long Swings in Economic Growth: The American Experience* (New York: National Bureau of Economic Research, 1968).

Ralph E. Freeman (ed.), *Postwar Economic Trends in the United States* (New York: Harper & Row, 1960).

John Kenneth Galbraith, *The Great Crash: 1929* (Boston: Houghton Mifflin, 1972).

Robert A. Gordon, *Economic Instability and Growth – The American Record* (New York: Norton, 1977).

Charles P. Kindleberger, *The World in Depression: 1929–1939* (Berkeley: University of California Press, 1973).

Paul Krugman, *The Age of Diminished Expectations: U.S. Economic Policy in the 1990s* (Cambridge, Mass.: MIT Press, 1990).

Naomi R. Lamoreaux, *The Great Merger Movement in American Business, 1895–1904* (Cambridge University Press, 1985).

William E. Leuchtenberg, *Franklin D. Roosevelt and the New Deal, 1932–1940* (New York: Harper & Row, 1963).

R. D. Norton, "Industrial Policy and American Renewal," *Journal of Economic Literature* 24 (March, 1986), 1–40.

Recent Economic Changes in the United States (Report of the Committee on Recent Economic Changes of the President's Conference on Unemployment; Herbert Hoover-Chairman) (New York: McGraw-Hill, 1929).

Robert B. Reich, *The Next American Frontier* (New York: Penguin Books, 1983).

Nathan Rosenberg, *Technology and the Pursuit of Economic Growth* (Cambridge University Press, 1991).

George Soule, *Prosperity Decade: From War to Depression, 1917–1929* (New York: Holt, Rinehart, & Winston, 1947).

Herbert Stein, *The Fiscal Revolution in America* (Chicago: University of Chicago Press, 1969).

David A. Stockman, *The Triumph of Politics: How the Reagan Revolution Failed* (New York: Harper & Row, 1986).

James Tobin, *The New Economics One Decade Older* (Princeton, N.J.: Princeton University Press, 1974).

Harold G. Vatter, *The U.S. Economy in World War II* (New York: Columbia University Press, 1985).

2

Chickens home to roost: from prosperity to stagnation in the postwar U.S. economy

DAVID M. GORDON

There can be little doubt that the twentieth century had become, by the 1950s, the American Century. In 1948 the United States economy accounted for roughly 45 percent of total global industrial production while real U.S. gross domestic product was nearly twice as large as the sum of real GDP in the U.K., Germany, France, and Japan combined.[1] Building on the Bretton Woods system, the power of U.S. corporations and the structure of postwar global finance assured that the dollar – backed by gold – was the pivotal international currency. U.S. military and nuclear power not only waged the Cold War against the Soviet bloc but was also deployed to keep the world safe for democracy and capitalism, mostly capitalism.

It seemed, indeed, that the sun might never set on the American Empire. "World opinion? I don't believe in world opinion," financial and presidential adviser John J. McCloy remarked scornfully in 1963. "The only thing that matters is power."[2]

This essay relies heavily on joint work with Samuel Bowles and Thomas E. Weisskopf, although they bear no responsibility for its presentation or conclusions. Significant passages in this essay have been reproduced, by permission, from *After the Waste Land,* by Samuel Bowles, David M. Gordon, and Thomas E. Weisskopf (Armonk, N.Y.: M. E. Sharpe, 1990).

1 Global industrial production data summarized in David M. Gordon, "The Global Economy: New Edifice or Crumbling Foundations," *New Left Review,* No. 168, March/April 1988, Table I. Comparison of real GNP based on data presented in Angus Maddison, *Phases of Capitalist Development* (Oxford: Oxford University Press, 1982), Tables A1, A6–A8.

2 Quoted in Alan Wolfe, *The Limits of Legitimacy: Political Contradictions of Contemporary Capitalism* (New York: The Free Press, 1977), p. 176.

Sic transit gloria imperiae. By the early 1980s the U.S. economy was no longer hegemonic, barely still dominant. The dollar had fallen from its pinnacle and U.S. trade deficits were beginning to soar nearly out of control. U.S. productivity growth lagged far behind its pace in other leading competing economies such as Japan and West Germany. The dreams and aspirations of U.S. workers and households were becoming clouded with hardship and uncertainty. Economic problems seemed pervasive. "It would be necessary to go back to the 1930s and the Great Depression," pollster Daniel Yankelovich concluded in 1979, "to find a peacetime issue that has had the country so concerned and so distraught."[3]

As background and foundation for many of the subsequent chapters in this book, this essay provides a brief overview of the rise and demise of postwar U.S. economic power. The essay begins with a summary of key indicators of U.S. economic performance in the postwar period, emphasizing the shifting tides from boom to stagnation. The second principal section then outlines the institutional foundations of the postwar U.S. economic system, sketching both the structural buttresses of prosperity and the sources of erosion of that institutional system. I conclude with an analysis of the burdens and inflexibilities imposed on the U.S. economy by the hierarchical structures upon which the U.S. corporate system was built. In the end, I argue, the U.S. economy was dragged into stagnation and crisis in large part by the costs of the very structures of power which had initially established its place in the sun. By the 1970s, it appears, the chickens had come home to roost.

THE TRAJECTORY OF THE POSTWAR U.S. ECONOMY

> Things are going much better in the economy than most people realize. It's our attitude that is doing poorly.
>
> – G. William Miller, Chair, Federal Reserve Board, 1978[4]

This section examines the performance of the U.S. economy in the postwar period, concentrating on its shift from boom to stagnation. I focus here on the years through the end of the 1970s. In our joint essay elsewhere in this volume, Samuel Bowles, Thomas E. Weisskopf, and I complete the story by examining the effects of right-wing economics on eco-

3 Quoted in William Bowen, "The Decade Ahead: Not So Bad If We Do Things Right," *Fortune,* October 8, 1979, p. 88.

4 Quoted in *Business Week,* January 15, 1978, p. 64.

nomic performance during the 1980s, extending most of the indicators introduced here through 1989.

One of the problems in tracing the performance of any capitalist economy is separating trend from cycle. The economy continuously moves up and down its short-term roller coaster. In tracking its performance over the longer term, as a result, observations and measurements are crucially sensitive to the particular points in the cycle from which one begins calculations. Any economy can appear buoyant, for example, as it recovers from the pits of a deep recession or depression. Many of those enjoying momentary respite from economic hardship may feel, to borrow the title of a mid-1960s novel by Richard Farina, "been down so long it looks like up to me"[5] – even though, over the longer run, economic performance might not have improved at all.

In this essay, following relatively standard procedure, I control for the short-term effects of the business cycle by tracking the economy from one business-cycle peak to the next. And following the method deployed in joint work with Bowles and Weisskopf, I identify business-cycle peak years by looking at the ratio of actual gross national product (GNP) to "potential" GNP. The ratio of actual to potential GNP reaches a cyclical peak at the stage of an expansion when the economy's productive potential is most *fully* utilized.[6]

By this measure, there were seven business-cycle peaks in the period from the late 1940s through the late 1970s: 1948, 1951, 1955, 1959, 1966, 1973, and 1979. One can best study the economy's performance during the years of stable prosperity by examining data for the *entire* boom period from 1948 to 1966, ignoring the several short-term cycles in between. Then, in order to sharpen our focus on the contours of subsequent decline, I compare the boom period with two periods of economic

5 *Been Down So Long It Looks Like Up To Me* (New York: Random House, 1966).

6 The procedure for estimating potential output follows a method developed by the Council of Economic Advisors during the 1970s. For presentation and discussion of that method, see Peter K. Clark, "Potential GNP in the United States, 1948–80," *Review of Income and Wealth,* June 1979. For detail on our method of extending the CEA estimates of potential output, see Samuel Bowles, Thomas E. Weisskopf, and David M. Gordon, "Business Ascendancy and Economic Impasse: A Structural Retrospective on Conservative Economics, 1979–87," *Journal of Economic Perspectives,* Winter 1989, Data Appendix.

stagnation: the first phase from the cyclical peak of 1966 to that of 1973, and the second phase from the cyclical peak of 1973 to that of 1979.

Macroperformance

We can look first at some relatively standard measure of aggregate economic performance. Table 2.1 presents a set of data useful for this preliminary evaluation.

One common indicator focuses on output growth, normally measured as the rate of growth of real GNP. Beginning with this simple measure (row 1), we can see clearly the symptoms of stagnating economic performance after the mid-1960s. Real GNP growth averaged a healthy 3.8 percent a year from 1948 through 1966, then dropped to 3.1 percent in 1966–73 and subsequently dipped further to 2.5 percent in 1973–79.

Table 2.1. *From boom to stagnation: the deteriorating performance of the U.S. postwar macroeconomy*

	Phase Averages		
	1948-66	**1966-73**	**1973-79**
[1] Real GNP growth rate (%)	3.8	3.1	2.5
[2] Real productivity growth rate (%)	2.6	1.8	0.6
[3] Rate of inflation (%)	2.2	5.0	7.7
[4] Index of monetary pressure (%)	-1.4	0.7	-0.8
[5] Rate of unemployment (%)	4.9	4.6	6.8

Sources: Growth rates are annual rates, calculated as logarithmic growth rates. Levels are calculated as average annual levels. *ERP* refers to *Economic Report of the President*, 1991.

[1] Rate of growth of real GNP ($1982): *ERP*, Table B-2.

[2] Rate of growth of output per hour of all persons, nonfarm business sector (1977 = 100): *ERP*, Table B-46.

[3] Rate of change of GNP price deflator: *ERP*, Table B-3.

[4] Rate of change of real money supply (M2) minus rate of change of real GNP: Real M2 from *Business Conditions Digest*, Series No. 106, adjusted for difference between rate of change of consumer prices, *ERP*, Table B-58, and rate of change of GNP deflator, *ERP*, Table B-3. Rate of change of real GNP same as in row [1].

[5] Rate of unemployment in civilian labor force: *ERP*, Table B-32.

But is a decline in real GNP growth from 3.8 percent to 2.5 percent really so significant? How does one evaluate the impact of such a slowdown in economic growth?

The answer depends in part, of course, on how much benefit people derive from that economic growth. Do they have to work harder and harder to sustain it? Do its benefits flee the country or get plowed back into maintaining the existing capital stock?

Taking some of these complications into account, many economists prefer to focus on real GNP *per capita,* controlling for the size of the population which aggregate economic output is supposed to support. Bowles, Weisskopf, and I prefer an alternative measure of aggregate economic performance which we label "hourly income" – real net national income per hour of work. Hourly income differs from per capita GNP in three respects: (1) it deducts from gross national product the "capital consumption allowance" – that part of output needed simply to maintain the existing aggregate stock of structures and equipment; (2) it adjusts for inflation with a price index reflecting changes in the prices of *purchased* rather than produced commodities; and (3) it substitutes total *hours of work* for total population as the standard against which real income should be measured.[7]

None of these modifications is particularly controversial, but the third one – dividing by hours of work rather than population – is quite important. By focusing on hourly income, we can pay close attention to the standard of living we attain *in return for the amount of work we must perform in order to achieve that standard of living.* Increases in per capita GNP may not be desirable if we must work too many additional hours to achieve them.

Figure 2.1 presents data on average annual rates of growth of *hourly income.* These data underscore impressions of the turn from prosperity to stagnation. Hourly income grew rapidly from 1948 to 1966, slowed noticeably from 1966 to 1973, and declined even more dramatically from 1973 to 1979. By the evidence of this figure, the collapse of prosperity after the mid-1960s appears dramatic indeed.

There is one obvious source of these dramatic declines in hourly in-

7 For a detailed discussion of the concept of hourly income and its advantages over per capita GNP as a measure of the average level of well-being in a society, see Samuel Bowles, Thomas E. Weisskopf, and David M. Gordon, *Beyond the Waste Land: A Democratic Alternative to Economic Decline* (Garden City, N.Y.: Anchor Press/Doubleday, 1983), Appendix A.

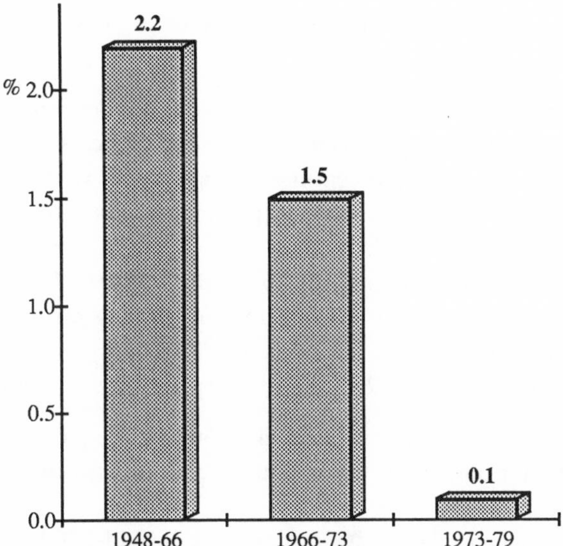

Figure 2.1. Growth of hourly income: average annual percent change in real net national income per hour.

come: the slowdown in the rate of growth of hourly output, or labor productivity. Hourly *income* did not grow as fast after the mid-1960s largely because hourly *output* did not rise as rapidly as during the postwar boom. Using the same benchmark years, we find (Table 2.2 row [2]) that the average annual rate of growth of U.S. hourly output – defined as real nonfarm business output per total employee hour – slowed from 2.6 percent in 1948–66 to 1.8 percent in 1966–73 and then again to 0.6 percent in 1973–79.[8]

8 Aggregate hourly income, defined as real net national income per hour of work, is conceptually very closely related to aggregate hourly output (productivity), defined as real net domestic output per hour of work. The only differences involve three technical distinctions: (1) real net national *income* is the nominal value of net national income/product divided by a *purchased*-output price index, while real *output* is the same nominal value of net national income/product divided by a *produced*-output price index; (2) *national income* includes income received by U.S. nationals from their activities abroad (e.g., foreign investment) and excludes income received by foreigners from their activities within the United States, while *domestic output* includes output produced by foreigners in the United States but excludes output produced by U.S. nationals abroad; and (3) the denominator in hourly income is hours of work by U.S. nationals anywhere, while the denominator in productivity is hours of work by all people within the United States.

Judged by historical precedents in the United States earlier in the century, further, this decline in productivity growth rates seems relatively pronounced:[9]

- The economy's performance during the postwar boom compares favorably, for example, with the relatively prosperous years in the United States from the turn of the century through 1929, with productivity growth roughly 30 percent more rapid in the 1948–66 phase than during the 1901–29 period.
- By contrast, productivity growth during the stagnant 1966–79 cycle appears even more languid than during the Depression of the 1930s. Average annual productivity growth in the 1966–79 years was almost a fifth slower than from 1929 to the late-Depression peak of 1938.

These comparisons provide further indication that the erosion of macroperformance after the mid-1960s is notable and, by historical standards, relatively severe.

One additional correlate of stagnation after the mid-1960s was mounting inflationary pressure, giving birth to a new term – "stagflation" – for a new macroeconomic phenomenon – the unexpected combination of stagnating demand and accelerating price growth. Data for the rate of inflation are presented in row [3] of Table 2.1. They show a moderate and tolerable average annual rate of change of output prices of 2.2 percent a year in the 1948–66 boom. They then show an accelerating pace of inflation, rising to 5.0 percent in 1966–73 and 7.7 percent in 1973–79.

A traditional homily in economics suggests that inflation results when "too much money chases too few goods." We can assess the relative contribution of "too much money" and "too few goods" to accelerating inflation with a couple of simple calculations. "Too much money" would contribute to rising inflation if and when the rate of growth of the real

9 Data for 1947–79 from sources for row [2] in Table 2.1. Data for 1900–46 for nonfarm business sector real output from *Historical Statistics of the United States* (Washington, D.C.: U.S. Government Printing Office, 1976), Vol. I, Series D-684. (Business cycle peaks for pre-WWII cycles defined by peaks in series for capacity utilization, measured as the ratio of real GNP, from Nathan S. Balke and Robert J. Gordon, "The Estimation of Prewar Gross National Product: Methodology and New Evidence," *Journal of Political Economy* 97:1, February 1989, Table 10, to real potential GNP, from "natural real GNP" in Robert J. Gordon, *Macroeconomics* (Boston: Little, Brown, 1990), 5th ed., Table A-1.)

money stock exceeded the rate of growth of real output. Row [4] of Table 2.1 provides such an "index of monetary pressure," defined as the difference between the rates of change of the real money supply (M2) and of real GNP. If this measure is negative, it means that monetary factors were restrictive, with the money supply "leaning against" output pressure. If it is positive, it means that monetary influences were accommodating, amplifying inflationary pressure resulting from output growth. By this standard, as we can see from the table, "too much money" contributed to the acceleration of inflation in 1966–73, when the money supply grew relatively rapidly, but not at all in 1973–79, when money growth was restrictive.

A reasonable measure of "too few goods" is provided by the data for productivity growth. If productivity growth is buoyant, this means that the supply of goods is expanding rapidly relative to the resources available to produce them and inflationary pressure is unlikely to build. If productivity growth is tepid, by contrast, the supply of goods is expanding slowly relative to available resources, other things equal, and inflationary spurts may be likely because demand pressure bumps up against relatively limited supply. Looking back at row [2] in Table 2.1, we can see that "too few goods" made a marginal contribution to accelerating inflation in 1966–73, when the productivity slowdown was just beginning, but that it apparently made a major contribution in 1973–79, when productivity growth dropped abruptly. By the middle to late 1970s, it thus appears that the productivity slowdown – rather than demand-side pressure – played a crucial role in shaping the trajectory of deepening stagflation.

A final standard index of macroperformance focuses on unemployment. Conventional expectations through the late 1960s had anticipated a fairly sharp trade-off between inflation and unemployment. If the former went down in recessionary times, the latter would be expected to go up – and *vice versa*.

Beginning in the early 1970s, however, these expectations were confounded. Row [5] of Table 2.1 provides data on the rate of unemployment in the civilian labor force. Unemployment had remained above 5 percent during much of the 1950s but had begun to drop significantly by the mid-1960s. Thanks in part to the additional demand pressure generated by the Vietnam War, the unemployment rate fell below 4 percent in 1966–69, contributing to a somewhat lower average in 1966–73 than for the entire boom from 1948 to 1966. After the early 1970s, however, unemployment rose dramatically at the same time as the pace of inflation accelerated. Stagflation had taken firm roots. Many U.S. households were bound to be caught in a squeeze between slack labor markets and spiraling prices.

Further, the magnitude of the U.S. economic crisis was reflected in the international as well as the domestic arena. U.S. corporations lost much of the competitive advantage they had enjoyed in the early postwar period. In 1951, for example, the U.S. economy accounted for 30 percent of the world trade of the sixteen leading industrial nations; by 1971, the U.S. share had fallen to 18 percent.[10]

Even more dramatically, the U.S. economy took a running nose dive in the international rankings by per capita GDP. The United States ranked number one in 1950, in 1960, and again in 1970 – still more than 20 percent ahead of its nearest competitor. By 1980, however, the U.S. had dropped to number eleven (not counting the oil-rich Middle Eastern states), trailing Switzerland, Sweden, Norway, Germany, Denmark, Luxembourg, Iceland, Finland, the Netherlands, and Belgium in that order.

Despite these relative advances, however, other nations were suffering economically as well. All of the advanced capitalist economies experienced significant declines in the growth of output and productivity during the 1970s. Even in Japan, buoyantly successful in the postwar period, the rate of growth of GNP was less than half as rapid in the 1970s as it was in the 1960s.[11]

The worldwide character of the economic crisis thus emphasizes the extent to which the turn toward stagnation in the United States involved broader developments in the global economy, witnessing a generalized slowdown in the advanced economies, as well as specific tendencies within the domestic economy, underlying the slippage in the relative standing of the U.S. economy among the advanced countries.

Deteriorating well-being

However portentous the turn toward stagflation, stagnation in aggregate macroindicators does not by itself guarantee deteriorating working and

10 OECD, *National Accounts, 1950–1980,* Vol. I (Paris: OECD, 1982). Data for subsequent comparison of per capita GNP from ibid., p. 88 (with comparisons in current prices at current international exchange rates).

11 *Economic Report of the President,* 1991 (Washington, D.C.: U.S. Government Printing Office, 1991), Table B-110.

Table 2.2. *Impact of stagnation on people's well-being*

	Phase Averages		
	1948-66	1966-73	1973-79
[1] Rate change, real spend. hourly earnings (%)	2.1	1.1	-0.8
[2] Average hours worked per capita	659	691	707
[3] Rate change, real median family income (%)	3.1	2.2	-0.1

Sources: Growth rates are annual rates, calculated as logarithmic growth rates. Levels are calculated as average annual levels.

[1] Real after-tax hourly earnings of production workers ($1989): Thomas E. Weisskopf, "Use of hourly earnings proposed to revive spendable earnings series," *Monthly Labor Review*, November 1984, pp. 38–42, and annual updates by the present author.

[2] Hours worked divided by population: *National Income and Product Accounts*, Table 6.11:1; *Current Population Reports*, Series P-25.

[3] Real median family income ($1989): *Current Population Reports*, Series P-60, No. 160, Table 11.

living standards for the vast majority of households. It is plausible, though not particularly likely, that stagnation of aggregate output could squeeze net new investment or replacement investment or government services – but that wages, hours, and income might continue to improve substantially for most households.

Unfortunately for millions of Americans, however, the turn from prosperity to stagnation took its toll directly and fairly immediately. Table 2.2 reviews some of the most important indicators of this deteriorating well-being.

Roughly 90 percent of U.S. households depend on wage and salary income for their survival.[12] For this vast majority, two principal trends determine the level of income available to their households: take-home pay per hour of work and the total hours worked to support household members. Table 2.2 presents some basic data on both earnings and hours of the postwar period.

12 See Institute for Labor Education and Research, *What's Wrong with the U.S. Economy?* (Boston: South End Press, 1982), p. xi and notes, for analysis of the income sources of the bottom 90 percent of U.S. households in 1980. Underlying data are from Internal Revenue Service, *Statistics of Income, Individual Income Tax Returns.*

Row [1] presents data on the rate of change of the average production worker's take-home pay – or *real spendable hourly earnings.*[13] Production workers comprised 81.3 percent of total employment in 1979[14] and represent that group in the labor force which is most clearly dependent on wage and salary income. Spendable hourly earnings measure the average worker's hourly wage and/or salary income plus other compensation – for example, medical benefits – minus personal income taxes and Social Security taxes. These earnings are expressed in constant dollars in order to adjust for the effects of inflation on the cost of living.

The data show a clear pattern. The average worker's real after-tax pay grew rapidly through the mid-1960s; its growth slowed in the first phase of stagnation, until the early 1970s, and then declined fairly sharply through the rest of the 1970s. By 1979, workers' take-home pay had fallen 6 percent *below* its postwar peak in 1972.

Row [2] presents data on average annual *hours worked per capita* by the U.S. population. This measure reflects the total amount of labor which U.S. households committed to the economy in order to support themselves and their dependents. The data on hours approximately mirror the data on real spendable hourly earnings. Not shown directly in the table, average hours per capita declined fairly steadily from the late 1940s until the early 1960s – as workers and households were able to take advantage of rising wage and salary income; hours fell from a peak during the Korean War of 704 hours per year to a postwar low of 627 hours in 1961. As row [2] indicates, this resulted in what turned out to be a relatively low average workload during the full 1948–66 period.

Average hours then rose in the mid-1960s when real earnings growth

13 For many years the Bureau of Labor Statistics provided a standard statistical series on "real spendable *weekly* earnings." This series was discontinued in December 1981 because it was judged that the average workweek had changed substantially over time (with shifts among part-time and full-time workers) and that the calculations made in the series for taxes were unrealistic. Although there is some validity to these claims, we believe that it is essential to be able to provide a continuous statistical series on the purchasing power of the take-home pay of production workers. We therefore developed an alternative series on real spendable hourly earnings, which is free of the two problems in the weekly earnings series. See Thomas E. Weisskopf, "Use of Hourly Earnings Proposed to Revive Spendable Earnings Series," *Monthly Labor Review,* November 1984.

14 Based on *Employment and Training Report* (Washington, D.C.: U.S. Government Printing Office, 1981), Table C-3.

began to slow. They continued to rise during the 1973–79 phase as households tried to stave off the squeeze of declining real hourly earnings (row [1]).

This increase in average annual hours per capita reflected an increase in the number of household members working outside the home, and not an increase in average hours per week. Faced with stagnating and then declining real spendable earnings, additional family members, particularly married women, sought work. The percentage of the adult population working or looking for work outside the home – a figure which had been roughly constant over the postwar period – began to rise in the mid-1960s, climbing from 59 percent in 1966 to 64 percent in 1979.[15] This extra labor helped sustain total household earnings, making possible continued increases in household consumption levels.[16] As the 1970s progressed, *Business Week* noted in 1980, it became more and more important to take into account "the sweat that goes into producing [household] income."[17]

This squeeze shows up quite clearly in data on real median family income (row [3]), a measure of the standard of living which the typical U.S. family could afford as the postwar period progressed. Families could sustain rapidly improving living standards during the decades of prosperity, with real median family income rising at an average annual rate of 3.1 percent in 1948–66. After the mid-1960s, however, the slowdown in hourly earnings began to take hold, with the rate of growth of real median family income in 1966–73 falling 30 percent below its pace during the boom years. After the early 1970s, finally, stagnation became fully manifest, with real median incomes actually declining slightly from 1973 to 1979. Despite the substantial increases in average hours worked (row [2]) in the second phase of stagnation, the decline in hourly take-home pay (row [1]) was so severe that family incomes could not keep pace with inflation.

By the second phase of stagnation, in short, the typical U.S. family was racing simply to stay in place. Prosperity had clearly given way to eroding well-being. The bloom was off the economic rose in the United States.

15 *Economic Report,* 1991, Table B-32, column for civilian labor force participation rate.

16 For a recent analysis of the increase in working hours since the 1960s, see Juliet B. Schor, *The Overworked American: The Unexpected Decline of Leisure* (New York: Basic Books, 1991).

17 *Business Week,* January 28, 1980, p. 73.

INSTITUTIONAL FOUNDATIONS OF THE POSTWAR ECONOMY: CONSTRUCTION AND DECAY

> America has embarked on a career of imperialism, both in world affairs and in every other aspect of her life. . . . The path of empire takes its way, and in modern times . . . the scepter passes to the United States.
>
> – Management consultant, 1941[18]

> Between the fall of Vietnam and the fall of the Shah of Iran, the U.S. has been buffeted by an unnerving series of shocks that signal an accelerating erosion of power and influence. Although the shocks themselves have occurred primarily in the military and foreign policy arenas, they have deep-seated economic and monetary roots.
>
> – "The Decline of U.S. Power," *Business Week*, 1979[19]

Stagflationary pressures did not pass unheeded during the 1970s. Analyses of stagflation became a major growth industry in economics. Two standard kinds of explanations for the erosion of prosperity emerged within mainstream economics.

Those of relatively more conservative persuasion tended to regard the U.S. government as the principal culprit, ascribing deteriorating macroperformance to ill-advised and increasingly pervasive government interventions in the private economy.[20] In an introduction to a major collection of papers, *The American Economy in Transition*, published in 1980, for example, Martin Feldstein, Harvard economist soon to become chair of the Council of Economic Advisers under Ronald Reagan, concluded ominously:[21]

> The expanded role of government has undoubtedly been the most important change in the structure of the American economy in the postwar period. The extent to which this major change in structure has been the cause of the major decline in performance cannot be easily assessed. . . . Nevertheless, there can be no doubt that government policies do deserve substantial blame for the adverse experience of the past decade.

18 Quoted in William Appleman Williams, *Americans in a Changing World* (New York: Harper & Row, 1978), p. 314.

19 *Business Week*, March 12, 1979, p. 36.

20 For two rhetorical examples of this late-1970s conservative view, see Jude Wanniski, *The Way the World Works* (New York: Simon & Schuster, 1978); and William E. Simon, *A Time for Truth* (New York: McGraw-Hill, 1978).

21 "The American Economy in Transition: Introduction," in Feldstein, ed., *The American Economy in Transition* (Chicago: University of Chicago Press, 1980), p. 3.

By contrast, those of relatively more liberal inclination were inclined to blame the economy's deterioration on a variety of unanticipated "shocks" or "surprises" which distorted and disrupted an otherwise healthy economy.[22] For example, Robert J. Gordon, a leading liberal macroeconomist from Northwestern University, concluded at the end of the 1970s that "in the postwar period external events were the most important single destabilizing force, most obviously in the direct impact of Korean and Vietnam defense expenditures on real GNP and in the effect of the formation of the OPEC oil cartel in the 1970s on inflation and unemployment."[23] If only these shocks had been properly anticipated, according to this view, then stagflation might not have occurred.

Both of these orientations take the institutional structure of the private economy as given. Conservatives assume that the private sector in the postwar period was functioning according to the principles of perfect competition and that it would have continued to function effectively if the government had only minded its own business. Liberals assume that the prevailing mix of private and public sectors would have continued to enjoy smooth sailing if only turbulent weather hadn't intervened. In neither case is much attention paid to the actual structure and functions of private-sector institutions themselves. Nor do these mainstream economists imagine that the internal structure and contradictions of those institutions themselves might conceivably account for the turn from boom to bust.

Many economists outside the mainstream take the institutions of the private sector much more seriously. For some of us, indeed, these institutions hold the key to understanding the trajectories of capitalist economies in general and the fate of the postwar U.S. economy in particular. In our view, socioeconomic institutions shape relations among capitalists, workers, and other classes or groups of economic actors; they define the role of the state in the economy; and they determine the external relations of the capitalist sector with foreign capitalists and with other co-existing modes of production.

Following one line of approach, this perspective has been formalized in

22 Two useful examples of this inclination from the late 1970s are Otto Eckstein, *The Great Recession – With a Postscript on Stagflation* (Amsterdam: North-Holland Publishing, 1978); and Alan S. Blinder, *Economic Policy and the Great Stagflation* (New York: Academic Press, 1979).

23 "Postwar Macroeconomics: The Evolution of Events and Ideas," in Feldstein, ed., *The American Economy in Transition*, p. 156.

recent years through analyses of prevailing "social structures of accumulation" (SSAs) – the constellations of institutions which condition growth and accumulation in a given capitalist economy.[24] If the constituent institutions of an SSA are operating smoothly and in a manner favorable to capital, capitalists will find their productive activities profitable and they will feel confident about the potential returns from investing in the expansion of productive capacity. But if the SSA begins to become shaky – for example, because some of its constituent institutions begin to lose their effectiveness and legitimacy, and/or because heightened class conflict or international rivalry begin to pose challenges to capitalist control – then capitalists will find production less profitable and will begin to cut back on domestic capital formation and instead devote their wealth to their own consumption, to financial investment, or to investment abroad. A slowdown of economic growth and a rise in unemployment will be likely to result. Under these circumstances costly social and economic conflicts often intensify, further eroding overall economic performance and reducing people's living standards.[25]

Viewed through the lenses of the SSA perspective, the postwar U.S. economy was based upon a new social structure of accumulation arising out of the ashes of the 1930s and the conflicts of World War II. In the account of the postwar U.S. SSA developed in my joint work with Bowles and Weisskopf, four main institutional dimensions provided the principal buttresses of U.S. corporate power in the postwar period and, building upon that power, the dynamics of rapid growth and accumulation.[26] We

24 The concept of a social structure of accumulation was introduced in David M. Gordon, "Up and Down the Long Roller Coaster," in Union for Radical Political Economics (ed.), *U.S. Capitalism in Crisis* (New York: Union for Radical Political Economics, 1978), and further developed and applied in David M. Gordon, Richard Edwards, and Michael Reich, *Segmented Work, Divided Workers: The Historical Transformation of Labor in the United States* (New York: Cambridge University Press, 1982). See also David M. Gordon, Thomas E. Weisskopf, and Samuel Bowles, "Power, Accumulation and Crisis: The Rise and Demise of the Postwar Social Structure of Accumulation," in R. Cherry et al., eds., *Macroeconomics from a Left Perspective,* Vol. I of *The Imperiled Economy* (New York: URPE, 1988).

25 A recent exploration of the foundations and implications of the SSA approach is available in David Kotz, Terence McDonough, and Michael Reich, eds., *Social Structures of Accumulation: The Political Economy of Growth and Crisis* (Cambridge: Cambridge University Press, 1994).

26 See Samuel Bowles, David M. Gordon, and Thomas E. Weisskopf, *After the Waste Land: A Democratic Economics for the Year 2000* (Armonk, N.Y.: M. E. Sharpe, 1990), Ch. 5.

refer to these four institutional dimensions as *Pax Americana,* the limited capital–labor accord, the capitalist–citizen accord, and the containment of intercapitalist rivalry. The subsequent turn of stagnation, we argue, was conditioned by the emergence of conflicts and contradictions along each of these four institutional axes.

In order to understand the deteriorating performance of the U.S. economy, by virtue of this argument, it becomes necessary to trace the construction, consolidation, and decay of each of these four institutional foundations. I provide here a brief review of each of those four dynamics of institutional development and crisis in turn.

Pax Americana

The United States emerged from World War II as the world's dominant economic and military power. In subsequent years, U.S. economic dominance assured a stable climate within which capitalist trade, investment, and output could grow rapidly throughout much of the world. Insistent U.S. leadership helped to lower tariffs and other barriers to trade. Marshall Plan aid to devastated European economies facilitated their economic recovery. U.S. direct private investment abroad contributed as well to the reconstruction and development of capitalist enterprise in many parts of the world.

For a time, at least, the system worked in the interests of both the U.S. and other active participants in the global economy. The dollars pumped into the world system by U.S. investment and foreign aid quickly returned through growing demand for U.S. exports. Booming foreign markets and stable world market conditions raised both corporate profits and private business expectations; this stimulated high rates of U.S. capital investment at home as well as abroad. Domestically, U.S. corporate leverage in international markets helped promote high rates of growth and capacity utilization.

None of these benefits emerged through private initiatives alone. The U.S. government adopted an increasingly interventionist international stance. U.S. corporations enjoyed huge productivity advantages at the beginning of the postwar period, to be sure, but aggressive political support of foreign investment and imposing military power joined to bolster this private-sector leverage. Drawing from a varied tool kit, the U.S. government built the military, economic, and political machinery to police much of the world.

Table 2.3 reviews some of the key indicators of the foundation which

Table 2.3. *Institutional axis I: construction and erosion of* Pax Americana

	Phase Averages		
	1948-66	1966-73	1973-79
[1] Rate change, real value of dollar (%)	0.0[a]	-2.8	-2.9
[2] Rate change, real U.S. foreign dir. invest. (%)	7.2[a]	4.0	1.4
[3] Defense outlays as percent of GNP (%)	9.0	7.7	5.0
[4] Rate change, rel. crude materials prices (%)	-2.0	1.1	-0.1
[5] Rate change, real cost of imports (%)	-0.6	1.6	3.8

[a] Figure is for 1951–66. See also text note #27.

Sources: Growth rates are annual rates, calculated as logarithmic growth rates. Levels are calculated as average annual levels. *ERP* refers to *Economic Report of the President*, 1991.

[1] Rate of change, (real) multilateral trade-weighted value of the U.S. dollar: 1967–79, *ERP*, Table B-109, column for real series adjusted by changes in consumer prices; 1951–66, individual country exchange rates from U.S. Bureau of Labor Statistics, "Output Per Hour, Hourly Compensation, and Unit Labor Costs in Manufacturing, Twelve Countries, 1950–1982," unpublished tables, January 1984.

[2] Rate of change, real value of U.S. private direct investment abroad ($1982): U.S. Department of Commerce, *Selected Data on U.S. Direct Investment Abroad, 1950–76* (Washington, D.C.: U.S. Government Printing Office, 1982), and *Survey of Current Business*, updates various years. Deflated by price deflator for private nonresidential capital stock (1982 = 100), based on real and nominal series from U.S. Department of Commerce, *Fixed Reproducible Tangible Wealth in the United States, 1925–85* (Washington, D.C.: U.S. Government Printing Office, 1987).

[3] National defense outlays as percent of GNP: Defense outlays, 1948–61, *Historical Statistics of the United States* (Washington, D.C.: U.S. Government Printing Office, 1976), Series Y-473; 1962–79, *Statistical Abstract, 1989*, Table 526; GNP, *ERP*, Table B-1.

[4] Rate of change, ratio of nonagricultural crude materials price index to GDP price deflator: Crude materials prices from U.S. BLS disaggregated price data available from *Citibank Database*; GDP price deflator from *National Income and Product Accounts*, Table 7.4.

[5] Rate of change, ratio, imports price deflator to exports price deflator: *ERP*, Table B-3.

Pax Americana provided for U.S. economic prosperity – as well as its subsequent erosion:

- The Bretton Woods system featured fixed exchange rates, with each individual national currency pegged to the value of the dollar. This exchange-rate stability fostered international trade and economic growth. Row [1] witnesses this fixed-exchange-rate regime, with the real value of the dollar remaining approximately constant throughout the boom period.[27]

- Reflecting the stability of the global economy and the favorable international access provided to U.S. corporations, U.S. foreign direct investment (row [2]) soared during the boom years. In the 1948–66 period, the real value of U.S. foreign investment increased by 7.2 percent – nearly twice the rate of growth of U.S. GDP.
- Driven by the political and military support which the U.S. government provided for *Pax Americana,* military expenditures also remained at very high levels after World War II and the Korean War. National defense outlays as a percent of GNP (row [3]) averaged 9.0 throughout the whole 1948–66 period, down somewhat from their post-WWII peak of 13 percent during the Korean War.
- U.S. capital gained access to foreign raw material and energy supplies on increasingly favorable terms. The relative price of nonfarm crude materials (row [4]), almost all of them imported, declined by an average 2.0 percent a year during the boom years, reflecting in particular the favorable access to imported oil which U.S. corporations and the government had been able to engineer during and after World War II.
- U.S. sellers sold in a seller's market and U.S. buyers bought in a buyer's market. One essential indicator of foreign market access is the real cost of imports, or the ratio of U.S. imports prices to U.S. exports prices. The lower the real cost of imports, the greater the quantity of goods and services that can be purchased abroad by a unit of real output produced in the U.S. economy. Between 1948 and 1966, the real cost of imports (row [5]) declined at an average annual rate of 0.6 percent a year, indicating that U.S. firms were able to purchase their input supplies on increasingly favorable terms. For U.S. corporations, the benefits of *Pax*

27 Official published data for the multilateral trade-weighted value of the dollar extend back only to 1967. From 1950 through 1966, the dollar values of almost all individual currencies remained approximately constant, with a few notable exceptions such as France's sharp devaluation in 1956–58. For the purposes of discussion, I have ignored these exceptions and treated the multilateral value of the dollar *as if* it remained exactly constant through 1966. For data on the dollar values of twelve leading individual currencies, see U.S. Bureau of Labor Statistics, "Output Per Hour, Hourly Compensation, and Unit Labor Costs in Manufacturing, Twelve Countries, 1950–1982," unpublished tables, January 1984.

Americana showed up on the bottom line: as the imports grew relatively less expensive, everything else equal, domestic profitability could improve as well.[28]

None of these benefits occurred by accident. President Kennedy affirmed the principles of private–public partnership at the beginning of his administration, addressing a group of executives: "Our [national] success is dependent upon your profits and success. Far from being natural enemies, government and business are necessary allies. . . . We are anxious to do everything we can to make your way easier."[29]

Beginning in the early to middle 1960s, however, U.S. corporations faced growing challenges in both the First and the Third worlds. These challenges substantially weakened the international position of U.S. capital. By the mid-1960s, the structure of *Pax Americana* was tottering.[30]

The first challenge came from the recovery and increasing competitive vigor of corporations in Europe and Japan. By the mid-1960s, Japanese and European firms were enhancing their market shares at the expense of U.S. corporations not only overseas but also at home in the United States.[31]

This mounting international competition had many sources, but one of the sources of declining competitive advantage was undoubtedly the burden of U.S. military expenditures. The military role of the United States was indispensable in helping to police the postwar international system, but it also constituted an enormous drain on the productive capacity of the United States.[32]

28 For an analysis of the importance of the real cost of imports (the terms of trade) to domestic profitability, see Samuel Bowles, David M. Gordon, and Thomas E. Weisskopf, "Power and Profits: The Social Structure of Accumulation and the Profitability of the Postwar U.S. Economy," *Review of Radical Political Economics,* Spring–Summer 1986, 132–67.

29 Quoted in Wolfe, *The Limits of Legitimacy,* p. 214.

30 For detailed analyses of the demise of *Pax Americana* and the consequent changes in the structure of the global economy, see Joyce Kolko, *Restructuring the World Economy* (New York: Pantheon Books, 1988); and Mario Pianta, *New Technologies Across the Atlantic: U.S. Leadership or European Autonomy* (Brighton: Wheatsheaf Books, 1988).

31 Data on this mounting import competition is provided in the section below on intercapitalist rivalry. For a useful analysis of mounting competition among the advanced countries, see Philip Armstrong, Andrew Glyn, and John Harrison, *Capitalism Since 1945* (Oxford: Basil Blackwell, 1991), especially Ch. 10, "The Eclipse of U.S. Domination."

32 For an insightful analysis of the effect of the U.S. military on the U.S. econ-

Could this drain have been avoided? In retrospect we can see that the postwar international financial system required *both* a strong U.S. economy *and* a strong U.S. military – the former to reinforce the dollar's role as key currency, and the latter to stabilize the political relationships necessary to enforce U.S. access to foreign markets and secure the uninterrupted flow of dollars around the globe. But these requirements turned out to be as much competing as complementary, with military spending eventually sapping the economy's strength. When this contradiction became acute, by the mid-1960s, monetary stability began to unravel. There had been a growing glut of U.S. dollars on world money markets, partly as a result of defense expenditures abroad. Foreign countries became increasingly reluctant to hold dollars, sensing that the dollar's official exchange rate was overvalued, and demanded gold from Fort Knox instead. Eventually, by the early 1970s, the U.S. severed the relationship between gold and the dollar, effectively renouncing the dollar-based system of fixed exchange rates. With that declaration, the inevitable became actual and the foundations of international monetary stability were shattered.

Challenges from the Third World also began to undermine U.S. international domination in the 1960s. Foreign liberation movements came increasingly to focus their ire on the United States. The U.S. government initially rebuffed these challenges without much difficulty – as in Guatemala and Iran in 1954. But the failure of the Kennedy administration to overthrow Castro in the 1961 Bay of Pigs Invasion, and especially the long and humiliating failure to stem the revolutionary tide in South Vietnam marked a significant and escalating erosion of the U.S. government's capacity to "keep the world safe" for private enterprise.

A final challenge in the world economy came from exporters of raw materials, primarily in Third World nations. With U.S. political economic power teetering after the mid-1960s, the economic bargaining power of some of the Third World raw-material-exporting nations increased substantially. The OPEC cartel was the most visible and important example. In conjunction with multinational petroleum companies, it succeeded in shifting the terms of the oil trade sharply against the oil-importing nations, first in 1973 and then again in 1979.

The final two columns of Table 2.3 help us trace some of the consequences of this erosion in U.S. international political economic power:

omy, see Tom Riddell, "Military Power, Military Spending and the Profit Rate," *American Economic Review,* May 1988, 60–65.

- Although the Bretton Woods system was not officially and finally dissolved until 1971–73, exchange rates began to fluctuate as early as 1967–68 when the drain on Fort Knox gold began in earnest. As a result, the real value of the dollar began to decline during the first phase of stagnation, falling at an accelerating rate from 1970 to 1973 and resulting in an average annual rate of change (row [1]) of −2.8 percent in 1966–73. When Bretton Woods was formally buried in 1973, the dollar was still apparently overvalued, resulting in a continuing decline of 2.9 percent per year in 1973–79. No longer officially the world's key currency, the dollar's sharp decline underscored how artificially inflated its value had become by the end of the boom years. The international hegemon had begun to seem more and more like a paper tiger.
- With mounting Third World hostility toward the U.S. as well as increasing global economic instability in the new flexible-exchange-rate regime after 1973, U.S. corporations became more and more reluctant to take the risks of direct investment abroad: the rate of growth of real U.S. foreign direct investment (row [2]) slowed considerably during the 1966–73 and 1973–79 phases, respectively, virtually ceasing its growth altogether in the middle to late 1970s.
- After increasingly successful challenges to U.S. political and military power, and with mounting demands on economic resources at home, the U.S. military machine became increasingly difficult to sustain. National defense outlays as a percent of GNP (row [3]) fell slightly during the 1966–73 phase, even with the Vietnam War effort at its peak. Then, with strong public reaction against the Vietnam War debacle, relative defense expenditures fell further in 1973–79 – to less than 60 percent their boom-phase levels.
- The rebellion of foreign raw materials exporters blew the cost of U.S. imported raw materials through the ceiling. Largely as a result of the OPEC oil price hike in 1973, the rate of change of relative nonfarm crude materials prices (row [4]) in 1966–73 reversed its earlier decline, now growing at a pace of 1.1 percent a year. And then, thanks in part to another oil price hike in 1979, relative crude materials prices maintained those higher levels during the 1973–79 phase, with an effectively zero rate of change from the previous cycle.
- As we saw above, the real cost of imports (row [5]) had improved during the boom period. After the mid-1960s, however, it began to rise, first increasing by 1.6 percent a year in 1966–73 and then even more substantially by 3.8 percent a year in 1973–79. This cost increase hit

U.S. corporations where they felt it most acutely, below the bottom line.

The limited capital–labor accord

The battle for postwar prosperity was also won on the home front. The limited truce between corporations and labor was a second essential element of the postwar SSA.

The limited capital–labor accord involved a restructuring of labor–management relations after the 1940s.[33] For those millions of U.S. workers to whom the accord was limited, it provided the carrot of real wage growth, improved job security, and better working conditions in return for acquiescence to complete corporate control of the production process and allocation of the profits from production. For those millions excluded from the accord, by contrast, corporations continued to wield a heavy stick of intensive supervision and the threat of job dismissal – with wages, job security, and working conditions continually falling behind those in the more advantaged sectors.

In many industries covered by the informal accord, corporations explicitly retained absolute control over the essential decisions governing enterprise operations – decisions involving production, technology, plant location, investment, and marketing. This set of corporate prerogatives was codified in the "management rights" clauses of most collective bargaining agreements. In return, unions were accepted as legitimate representatives of workers' interests. They were expected to bargain on behalf of labor's immediate economic interests, but not to challenge employer control of enterprises. Unions would help maintain an orderly and disciplined labor force while corporations would reward workers with a share of the income gains made possible by rising productivity, with greater employment security, and with improved working conditions.

There *were* productivity gains, as shown in Table 2.1, and there were real wage gains as well, as shown in Table 2.2. Job security also improved; the aggregate unemployment rate dropped to 3.8 percent by 1966, roughly one-quarter of its average level during the 1930s. But there was more to the limited capital–labor accord than simply its correlates in productivity growth, wage gains, and job security. Table 2.4 provides some of the key data for analyzing the contours of postwar capital–labor relations.

33 See Gordon, Edwards, and Reich, *Segmented Work, Divided Workers,* Ch. 5.

Table 2.4. *Institutional axis II: construction and erosion of limited capital–labor accord*

	Phase Averages		
	1948-66	**1966-73**	**1973-79**
[1] Intensity of supervision (ratio)	0.18	0.21	0.22
[2] Union representation rate (%)	31.6	27.1	24.2
[3] Index of earnings inequality (ratio)	1.36	1.45	1.37
[4] Frequency of industrial accidents (rate)	3.5	4.1	5.1
[5] Cost of job loss (ratio)	0.31	0.21	0.22

Sources: Growth rates are annual rates, calculated as logarithmic growth rates. Levels are calculated as average annual levels.

[1] Ratio of nonproduction/supervisory employees to production/nonsupervisory employees: *Handbook of Labor Statistics* (Washington, D.C.: U.S. Government Printing Office, 1981), Table C-3.

[2] Union members as percentage of nonfarm employment. Union members: 1947–57, *Historical Statistics of the United States*, Series D591; 1958–77, U.S. Bureau of Labor Statistics, "Directory of National Unions and Employee Associations," Bulletin 2079, September 1980, Table 6; 1978–79, U.S. Bureau of Labor Statistics, "Corrected Data on Labor Organization Membership," USDL, 81-446, September 1981. Nonfarm employment: *Economic Report of the President*, 1991, Table B-43.

[3] Weighted ratio of white male earnings to female and to black male earnings, for persons with income during year: Median income data from *Current Population Reports*, Series P-60, No. 162.

[4] Lost workday cases due to injury and illness, manufacturing, per hundred full-time employees: 1971–79, *Statistical Abstract*, various years; 1948–70, Peter Arno, "The Political Economy of Industrial Injuries," unpublished Ph.D. dissertation, New School for Social Research, 1984, Table 6.

[5] Portion of year's pay expected to be lost if dismissed from job: Samuel Bowles, David M. Gordon, and Thomas E. Weisskopf, "Business Ascendancy and Economic Impasse: A Structural Retrospective on Conservative Economics, 1979–87," *Journal of Economic Perspectives*, Winter 1989, Data Appendix.

In order to take full advantage of their renewed control, corporations dramatically expanded their supervisory apparatus. Overall, the resources devoted to managerial and supervisory personnel climbed significantly. Between 1948 and 1966, for example, the ratio of supervisory to nonsupervisory employees in the private business sector increased by nearly 75 percent – from roughly thirteen supervisory employees per hundred nonsupervisory employees to more than twenty-two. For the period as a whole, this ratio, labeled in Table 2.4 as the "intensity of supervision" (row [1]), averaged 0.18.[34]

While the accord benefited some workers, it excluded others. The percent of nonfarm workers who were union members reached its peak at the time of the AFL–CIO merger in 1954 and then began to decline gradually through the mid-1960s as the limits on the accord held firm; the union representation rate (row [2]) averaged only about one-third for the full 1948–66 period. Meanwhile, unorganized workers, women, and minorities lost ground. The wages of workers in the "core" sector of industry outstripped those of workers on its periphery, increasing from 1.3 times noncore workers' earnings in 1948 to 1.5 times in 1966.[35] Income inequality by race and gender also increased through the 1960s. Row [3] presents a composite index of the degree of income advantages for white male over female and black male workers. This index of earnings inequality rose substantially from a ratio of 1.20 in 1948 to 1.45 in 1966, averaging 1.36 for the period as a whole.

Beginning in the early 1960s, two problems eventually emerged to shatter the limited capital–labor accord. The first involved those who had been excluded from its benefits, while the second involved the internal contradictions of the accord itself.

Corporations showed little interest in expanding the breadth of the accord, first of all, and unions grew comfortable with their privileges as

34 Not all the employees designated by official data as "nonproduction" or "supervisory" personnel are exclusively managers or supervisors, but by far the largest portion are. In 1980, for example, there were 13.9 million "supervisory" workers on private nonfarm payrolls. In the same year, according to detailed occupational data, there were approximately 11.5 million managers, clerical supervisors, and blue-collar worker-supervisors in the private sector. (This is an approximate estimate because detailed data on government supervisory personnel were not available from the census; the number reported here reflects an approximate deduction from the total number of managers and supervisors for those in government, assuming that equal proportions worked in those categories in both the public and private sectors.) All the rest of the 13.9 million certainly have supervisory responsibilities, since it appears that at least 8 million or so employees who are not managers or supervisors *also* supervise other employees. For data see *Employment and Training Report,* 1981, pp. 152–53; and Institute for Labor Education and Research, *What's Wrong with the U.S. Economy?* p. 220.

35 See Gordon, Edwards, and Reich, *Segmented Work, Divided Workers,* Figure 5.1A.

"insiders." As a result, the ranks of unions continued to drop as a percentage of nonfarm employment, with the union representation rate (row [2]) dropping to 27.1 percent in 1966–73 and further to 24.2 percent in 1973–79. The net effect for the labor movement was a significant narrowing of its reach.

As the ranks of those excluded from the benefits of the accord continued to swell, protest against the racism, sexism, and distributive injustice of the accord emerged through four different but effective movements: the civil rights movement, the welfare rights movement, the organization of the elderly, and the women's movement. These movements all led to government efforts at accommodation, including efforts at ensuring equal opportunity and affirmative action. Many of these programs cost money, and their growing costs reflected the mounting and increasingly expensive requirements of containing resistance to an unequal distribution of power and privilege. These movements helped eventually to provide real economic gains; as we can see in row [3], for example, earnings inequality by race and gender peaked in the 1966–73 phase and then began actually to decline as the government programs of the 1960s eventually took effect.

The accord began to encounter increasingly serious resistance from *inside* as well. Several factors contributed to this challenge. The first involves an apparent shift in attitudes and working conditions.

Rising real wages, heightened job security, and improved working conditions were increasingly taken for granted – as memories of the Depression receded and young workers replaced those who had struggled through the 1930s. This decline in *material* insecurity apparently led to greater concern about occupational health-and-safety issues, influence over workplace decisions, and opportunities for meaningful and creatively challenging work.[36] These spreading concerns could conceivably have been accommodated, but they tended to run up against the vast apparatus of bureaucratic control. The increasing intensity of supervision worked well for those workers who understood and still believed in the terms of the initial bargain, but it was less and less likely to remain effective when it confronted a labor force which – by age, education, and temperament – was increasingly resistant to arbitrary authority.

36 As the authors of the Report of a Special Task Force to the secretary of Health, Education, and Welfare, *Work in America* (Cambridge, Mass.: M.I.T. Press, 1972), concluded, "It may be argued that the very success of industry and organized labor in meeting the basic needs of workers has unintentionally spurred demands for esteemable and fulfilling jobs" (p. 12).

Compounding and partly precipitating these shifts in focus was a serious reversal of the improvement of working conditions during the postwar boom. Part of this reversal is captured by data on industrial accidents, presented in row [4] of Table 4. During the boom years, the industrial accident rate had declined fairly continuously, dropping by roughly 30 percent from 1948 to the early 1960s and resulting in a relatively low average rate of 3.5 in 1948–66. But mounting competition and declining profitability led to an intensification of the pace of production, with the accident rate climbing steadily through the two principal phases of stagnation. By 1979, the accident rate had reached a level roughly 80 percent higher than its levels of the early 1960s.

Rather than responding to frustration and friction in production by cutting back on the supervisory apparatus, however, corporations responded with further increases in the scale and scope of their institutions of production control. The intensity of supervision (row [1]) increased further to 0.21 in 1966–73 and then again to 0.22 in 1973–79. Nor were these continuing increases inevitable features of advanced technological societies. In deepening its top-heavy, hierarchical systems of management, U.S. corporations departed more and more noticeably from the more cooperative systems of labor relations practiced in leading competitors such as West Germany and Japan. By the late 1970s, for example, the ratio of administrative and managerial personnel to total nonfarm employment was almost three times as high in the United States as in West Germany and Japan.[37] Relying on top-down supervision was an expensive and apparently addictive habit. The bureaucratic burden was not easy to lift.

These contradictions of hierarchical organization were complemented by another and clearly critical problem for capital: the declining effectiveness of the traditional source of capitalist leverage over the workforce, the threat of unemployment. This threat is based on two simple facts of life in a capitalist economy: workers depend on getting jobs in order to live, and a significant number of workers at any time are stuck without a job.

Two developments in the postwar period reduced the effectiveness of this threat. First, the unemployment rate fell to unusually low levels in the mid-1960s. Second, the social programs won by social struggle in the

37 Based on commensurable tabulations of national occupational statistics, these comparative data are summarized and documented in David M. Gordon, "Who Bosses Whom? The Intensity of Supervision and the Discipline of Labor," *American Economic Review,* May 1990, 28–32.

1930s – social insurance, unemployment compensation, and others – were greatly expanded and augmented by new 1960s programs such as Medicaid, Medicare, food stamps, and Aid to Families with Dependent Children (AFDC). The combined effect of all these programs was to provide some cushion for those laid off from work.

To document this phenomenon and assess its relative impact, several of us have combined the two effects – lower unemployment and the cushion provided by social programs – into a single measure of the "cost of job loss."[38] This measure represents the portion of a year's expected overall income which is lost by a worker who is laid off. It varies with both the likelihood of remaining without a job for a long time – as when unemployment rises – and with the relative income lost when a worker is unemployed. The higher this measure, the greater the cost to the worker of job termination and the greater the potential corporate leverage over their workers through the threat of dismissal.

Row [5] of Table 2.4 traces the "cost of job loss." The cost of job loss was highest during the boom and significantly lower during the first phase of the crisis – boding poorly for the effectiveness of corporate threats of dismissal. It did rise marginally in the second phase, but remained on average well below its boom level. Moreover, the modest recovery from 1973 to 1979 was accomplished largely by rising relative unemployment (see row [5] of Table 2.1), not by further extensions of transfers and welfare benefits – underscoring the apparently enduring dependence of corporations on high unemployment for enhanced employee control.

Measured by the cost to workers of losing their job, employers' leverage over workers declined by roughly a third from the boom period to the first phase of crisis. This was bound to loosen their hold over labor and undermine their ability to maintain the profitability of production. There are several indications that workers began to take advantage of this reduced corporate leverage.[39]

38 The detailed sources and methods of estimating the cost of job loss are originally presented in Juliet B. Schor and Samuel Bowles, "Employment Rents and the Incidence of Strikes," *Review of Economics and Statistics,* November 1987. The data series is maintained and updated by the present author.

39 See Gordon, Edwards, and Reich, *Segmented Work, Divided Workers,* Ch. 5; and Bowles, Gordon, and Weisskopf, *After the Waste Land,* Chs. 5–6, for detailed discussion of these reactions.

I focus here on only one indicator, the frequency of strike activity. Because of the relatively cooperative contours of the postwar accord, strikes declined during the postwar boom itself; the number of workers involved in strikes as a percentage of all trade union members – the group of workers most likely to engage in strike activity – dropped substantially through the early 1960s.[40] But then, as workplace friction mounted after the mid-1960s and employer leverage eroded, strikes spread in the 1966–73 phase, increasing by 40 percent over their relatively low levels in the previous business cycle from 1959 through 1966. Only when unemployment rates climbed and corporations began to mount a sustained counteroffensive against labor did strike frequency subside again, declining by nearly 40 percent from 1966–73 to 1973–79.

It appears, on the basis of these several indicators, that the effectiveness of corporate control over labor was beginning to decline after the mid-1960s – as a result of both friction within the bureaucratic shell and the increasingly muted effect of the unemployment threat. This erosion of the limited capital–labor accord appears to have resulted in significantly reduced labor effort in production in the 1966–73 cycle, contributing to the first phase of slowdown in productivity growth.[41] With that productivity slowdown, profit margins also suffered mounting pressure, contributing to a decline in profitability after the mid-1960s (see data below). As the truce between capital and labor began to dissolve, so did one of the central foundations of U.S. corporate power and aggregate economic prosperity.[42]

40 Full documentation of this strike frequency variable is provided in Bowles, Gordon, and Weisskopf, "Business Ascendancy and Economic Impasse," Data Appendix.

41 See Thomas E. Weisskopf, Samuel Bowles, and David M. Gordon, "Hearts and Minds: A Social Model of U.S. Productivity Growth," *Brookings Papers on Economic Activity,* 2:1983, 381–441; and Bowles, Gordon, and Weisskopf, *After the Waste Land,* Ch. 7.

42 For reasons of space constraints, I concentrate here on developments during the 1966–73 phase. In 1973–79, corporations began to fight back, armed with the ammunition of rising unemployment, and a kind of political standoff or stalemate between workers and corporations emerged – with the level of conflict much higher and the effectiveness of the accord substantially diminished compared to the boom years. For more on this part of the story, see Bowles, Gordon, and Weisskopf, *After the Waste Land,* Ch. 6.

The capitalist–citizen accord

The Depression generated more than labor struggles. Millions also battled for tenants' rights and public housing, for social security and public assistance, for protection against the vagaries of life in capitalist economies. After World War II, these demands were at least partially accommodated. The state began trying to smooth the rough edges of the market economy without compromising the reign of profits as a guide to social priorities.

Three aspects of the expanded state role during the postwar boom years were crucial.

First, the government sought to reduce macroeconomic instability, hoping to avoid the kind of economic downturn which had threatened the survival of all the leading capitalist economies in the 1930s. Macropolicy sought quite modestly to moderate and guide the cycle, not to eliminate it, in the interests of political stability and profitability.

From the late 1940s to the mid-1960s, this effort succeeded. The results were felicitous: the first five postwar business-cycle recessions were more than two-thirds less severe – measured by the magnitude of their average-output slowdown – than business cycles during the comparable period of expansion after the turn of the century.[43]

Second, direct public support of business increased substantially at all levels of government – federal, state and local. This support became evident on both the tax and the expenditure sides of the ledger:

- On the expenditure side, government contracts provided guaranteed markets for many major corporations, especially in military production, while government subsidies favored many private businesses, particularly in nuclear power and agriculture. Even more important, government expenditures on transportation, communications, and other infrastructural facilities, as well as on education and research, lowered the costs of business for almost all private firms. Some of the resulting economic benefits were passed on to consumers through lower prices, but firms also profited from this public largesse.
- On the tax side, the government moved quickly and insistently to lower the tax burden on capital. This effect can be measured by an index constructed in joint work with Bowles and Weisskopf which we call

43 Based on data in Jeffrey Sachs, "The Changing Cyclical Behavior of Wages and Prices," *American Economic Review,* March 1980, Table 2.

Table 2.5. *Institutional axis III: construction and erosion of capital–citizen accord*

	Phase Averages		
	1948-66	**1966-73**	**1973-79**
[1] Capital's share of tax burden (%)	37.5	28.5	26.4
[2] Personal transfer, share potential output (%)	5.9	8.6	10.7
[3] Rate change, index govt. bus. regulation (%)	3.8	16.1	10.3

Sources: Growth rates are annual rates, calculated as logarithmic growth rates. Levels are calculated as average annual levels.

[1] Share of total taxes falling on income from capital: Samuel Bowles, David M. Gordon, and Thomas E. Weisskopf, "Business Ascendancy and Economic Impasse: A Structural Retrospective on Conservative Economics, 1979–87," *Journal of Economic Perspectives*, Winter 1989, Data Appendix.

[2] Real personal transfer payments divided by potential output: Personal transfer payments, *National Income and Product Accounts*, Table 1.9:15, deflated by GNP price deflator, *Economic Report of the President*, 1991, Table B-3; potential output, from same source as in row [1].

[3] Rate of change, index of government expenditures on regulation of business: Same source as in row [1].

"capital's tax burden." It represents an estimate of the share of taxes at all levels of government which are borne by income from capital. Capital's tax burden had been heavy during World War II and continued to weigh mightily through the Korean War, reaching its post-WWII peak in 1951 of 45 percent of total taxes falling on capital income. It then fell continuously through the mid-1960s as government repeatedly sought to honor President Kennedy's prescription that "we are anxious to do everything we can to make your way easier" – dropping to only 33 percent in 1966. The average level during the boom years (row [1] of Table 2.5) was 37.5 percent.

Finally, the state committed itself to at least a margin of economic security for all Americans, whether aged, unemployed, or simply poor. Over most of the postwar period, up to 1966, unemployment insurance coverage grew, the size of the unemployment check relative to workers' take-home pay increased slightly, and the sum of social insurance, education, health, and general assistance programs inched upward as a fraction of GNP. These programs provided real benefits to many people but were nonetheless contained within the larger framework of capitalist priorities. For example, the distress of unemployment was reduced only by limited cash transfers to those who lost their jobs, not by structural changes guaranteeing everyone a job on a continuous basis.

The expanded state role thus provided benefits both to capital and to many citizens. Throughout the boom period, however, the central priority of profitability remained unchallenged. Charles Wilson, president of General Motors and President Eisenhower's designated secretary of defense, told his confirmation hearing in 1952 that "what was good for our country was good for General Motors, and vice versa."[44] Eric Goldman later reflected on the uproar which Wilson's comment provoked: "After all, was he not speaking precisely the feeling of generations of Americans who had labored . . . in the firm belief that what was good for their businesses was good for America, the land of business?"[45] As long as millions could benefit alongside business, the logic of profitability could continue to prevail.

But the bottom line was not to continue unchallenged for long.

As we saw in the previous section, several movements began during the 1960s to demand state cushions from the bumpy road of capitalist growth. As a result, fueled by expanding expenditures for Medicare, social security, and public assistance, transfer payments began to rise significantly in the mid-1960s. Row [2] in Table 2.5 charts this mounting burden of state expenditures, tracking the percentage of potential output committed to personal transfer payments at all levels of government. Averaging a modest and sustainable 5.9 percent during the boom years, the transfer share rose to 8.6 percent in 1966–73 and further to 10.7 percent in 1973–79 – nearly double its level in 1948–66. More and more citizens were insisting that their "entitlements" deserved at least as high a priority as government support for business.

A second challenge to the logic of profitability followed close behind. Beginning with occupational health-and-safety campaigns in the Oil, Chemical, and Atomic Workers Union and in the United Mine Workers, and equally with Ralph Nader's effective public mobilization around issues of consumer safety and product design, fueled by the notorious

44 Quoted in Eric F. Goldman, *The Crucial Decade and After: America, 1945–1960* (New York: Vintage, 1960), p. 239.

45 Ibid., p. 240.

Pinto exploding-gas-tank scandal, sustained by Love Canal and the periodic burning of the Cuyahoga River, a wide variety of movements emerged to challenge the hallowed identity of private greed and public virtue. The oldest of these movements – conservation – enjoyed a veritable rebirth and transformation in the late 1960s and early 1970s, sparking a series of popular and often militant campaigns demanding environmental protection, alternative energy sources, and a halt to nuclear power.

Although these movements were largely disconnected and focused on single issues, they had the combined effect of raising doubts about the primacy of private profitability in determining resource allocation and economic decision making. By the early 1970s, these several insurgencies had won a series of major legislative and legal victories, creating a sequence of agencies with major responsibility for corporate regulation – the National Highway Safety Commission (1970), the Occupational Safety and Health Administration (1970), the Environmental Protection Administration (1970), the Consumer Safety Administration (1972), the Mine Enforcement and Safety Administration (1973), and several others.

The increasing importance of such regulatory agencies is illustrated in row [3] of Table 2.5, which depicts the growth of an index of U.S. government regulatory expenses over the postwar period. After growing no more rapidly than real output during the boom years, government regulation took off in 1966–73 and continued its rapid growth in 1973–79.

The drive for government regulation pinched and business yelped. The government tried to ease the pain by continuing to lighten capital's tax burden; the share of taxes borne out of capital income (row [1]) fell further in 1966–73 and 1973–79. But this relief was not enough to salve the business community's discomfort. With mounting intensity beginning in the mid-1970s, corporations sought to roll back regulation and overcome citizen opposition. "We should cease to be patsies," one corporate executive urged at a series of management conferences in 1974–75, "and start to raise hell."[46]

The containment of intercapitalist rivalry

Large corporations in the United States emerged from World War II more powerful than ever. As the postwar period progressed, their power in-

46 Quoted in Leonard Silk and David Vogel, *Ethics and Profits: The Crisis of Confidence in American Business* (New York: Simon & Schuster, 1976), p. 67.

Table 2.6. *Institutional axis IV: containment and intensification of intercapitalist rivalry*

	Phase Averages		
	1948-66	**1966-73**	**1973-79**
[1] 200 largest firms' share industrial assets (%)	52.8	59.8	58.0
[2] Index of import competition (%)	5.6	8.6	10.3

Sources: Growth rates are annual rates, calculated as logarithmic growth rates. Levels are calculated as average annual levels.

[1] Ratio of real imports to real GNP: *Economic Report of the President*, 1991, Table B-3.

[2] Share of industrial assets owned by largest 200 firms: *Statistical Abstract*, 1985, Table 886, 1977, Table 923, and unpublished U.S. Bureau of the Census data.

creased – and their vulnerability to intercapitalist competition diminished. This protection against competition occurred both domestically and internationally.

On the domestic front, large firms could use their monopoly or oligopoly positions to raise prices higher than would have prevailed in competitive markets. They could gain access to more favorable investment opportunities and use their funds to buy up more vulnerable competitors.

The indicator in row [1] of Table 2.6 illustrates one aspect of this process. The largest 200 firms in the United States were able dramatically to increase their ownership share of total industrial assets through the late 1960s, benefiting from both their general power and leverage throughout the postwar years and an intense merger wave in the late 1960s: their asset share increased from 47 percent in 1948 to 61 percent in 1971, with the 1948–66 average of 52.8 percent increasing to 59.8 in 1966–73. The largest corporations came more and more to dominate the economic landscape, forming the core of what Harvard economist John Kenneth Galbraith called the "new industrial state."[47]

For a time, at least, U.S. corporations were also able to enjoy considerable advantages over their foreign competitors. U.S. corporate size and power enabled them to achieve economies of scale and to afford new technology and product design while many foreign corporations lagged

47 *The New Industrial State* (Boston: Houghton-Mifflin, 1971), 2nd ed.

behind. The key role of the dollar and the flood of dollars circulating through the global economy provided ready markets for products made in the United States. And foreign competitors simply had difficulty penetrating U.S. domestic markets because of the scale and scope, as Harvard business historian Alfred D. Chandler, Jr., calls it, of U.S. corporations.[48] Through the boom period, as a result, imports averaged only 5.6 percent of GNP (row [2] of Table 2.6).

In the first decade and a half of the postwar period, in short, the great majority of large U.S. corporations did not have to worry much about price competition from rival suppliers of their product markets, and they could generally maintain a substantial margin of price over production cost. The containment of intercapitalist competition contributed to healthy balance sheets and high profits. By the early 1960s, however, new threats to the cozy position of the U.S. industrial giants began to loom on the horizon.

A first challenge came from the increasingly intense and effective competition waged by rival corporations in Europe and Japan. Having recovered from the devastation of World War II, and having built up their plant and equipment with the best of modern technology, these corporations were increasingly successful in competing with U.S. corporations – first in overseas markets and then also at home in the United States.

Imports had remained a low and constant or declining share of GDP over most of the postwar era. Around the mid-1960s, import penetration suddenly escalated. Between 1960 and 1970, imports rose from 4 to 17 percent of the U.S. market in autos, from 4 to 31 percent in consumer electronics, from 5 to 36 percent in calculating and adding machines, and from less than 1 to 5 percent in electrical components.[49] This import penetration showed up quickly in the aggregate data. As row [2] of Table 2.6 shows, the import share rose from 5.6 percent in 1948–66 to 8.6 percent in 1966–73 and then again to 10.3 percent in 1973–79.

But foreign competition was by no means the only challenge to the cozy oligopoly positions that had been enjoyed for so long by so many major U.S. corporations. A second challenge emerged from within the United States, in the form of growing domestic competition in many

48 *Scale and Scope: The Dynamics of Industrial Capitalism* (Cambridge, Mass.: Harvard University Press, 1990).

49 The industry data are from *Business Week,* June 30, 1980, p. 60, based on Commerce Department data.

industries. In part this growing competition could be attributed to the economic boom itself, which opened up new opportunities for "outsider" firms to break into markets previously controlled tightly by "insiders." And in part it was the result of increasingly effective antitrust activity on the part of a federal Justice Department pushed into action by a public growing more and more distrustful of big business.

In a major study of long-term trends in competition in the U.S. economy, economist William G. Shepherd concluded:

> The U.S. economy experienced a large and widely spread rise in competition during [the period from] 1958 [to] 1980. . . . Tight oligopoly still covers nearly one-fifth of the economy, but that share is down by half from 1958. Pure monopoly and dominant firms have shrunk to only about 5% of the economy, while the effectively competitive markets now account for over three-fourths of national income. Most of the shift appears to reflect three main causes: rising import competition, antitrust actions, and deregulation. Each has been important, but antitrust actions have had the largest influence.[50]

Row [1] of Table 2.6 shows the impact of this increased competition on the largest 200 firms' asset share: After a steady rise in their share of industrial assets through the early 1970s, the largest 200 firms' share actually declined some in the 1973–79 phase as new and rising giants began to challenge for market control.

U.S. corporations were thus pressured after the mid-1960s by increasingly intense product market competition and intercapitalist rivalry. Their ability to raise prices over costs to protect their profit margins, and their ability to close their own ranks against challenges from below, diminished apace.

The rise and decline of the SSA: profitability and accumulation

In a capitalist economy, two of the central barometers of the economy's vitality are provided by the level of profitability and the pace of accumulation. If the postwar economy had turned from prosperity to stagnation, this shifting dynamic should surely be evident in data on the rate of profit and the pace of accumulation.

50 William G. Shepherd, "Causes of Increased Competition in the U.S. Economy, 1939–80," *Review of Economics and Statistics*, November 1982, p. 624.

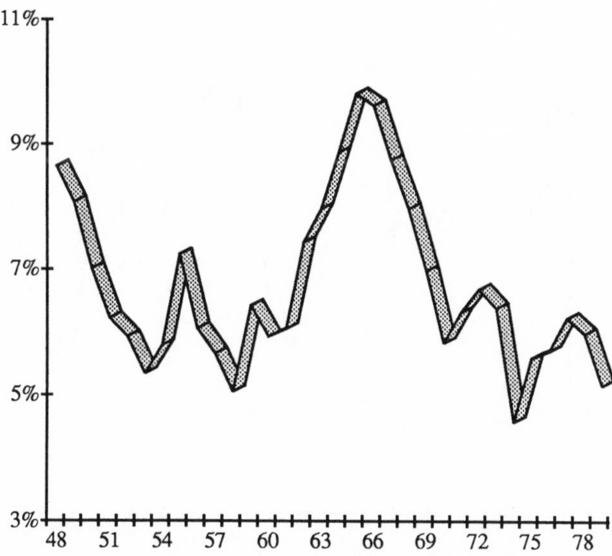

Figure 2.2. Declining profitability after the mid-1960s: net after-tax rate of profit, nonfinancial corporate business sector (NFCB).

The behavior of the (net) after-tax profit rate for U.S. corporate business is graphed in Figure 2.2. When the postwar U.S. social structure of accumulation was working well, profitability recovered from short-term recessions and achieved levels more or less comparable to its pre-recession peaks. Despite the depths of the 1957–58 and 1960–61 recessions, for example, the after-tax rate of corporate profits was far higher in 1965 than it had been in 1955, before these two recessions. After 1966, however, corporate profitability did not recover from the stresses of economic downturn. Following the recession of 1969–70, the after-tax profit-rate peak in 1972 was one-third lower than it had been in 1965. After the recession of 1974–75, once again, the after-tax profit-rate peak in 1977 had fallen below its 1972 peak. Operating through its normal cyclical mechanisms, *the U.S. economy was unable to reverse this process of decline by itself.*

The behavior of the (net) rate of capital accumulation by U.S. corporate business from 1951 to 1979 is graphed in Figure 2.3. This index measures the rate at which corporations are expanding their productive capital stock – one important determinant of the future productive potential of the U.S. economy. Like the rate of profit, the rate of capital

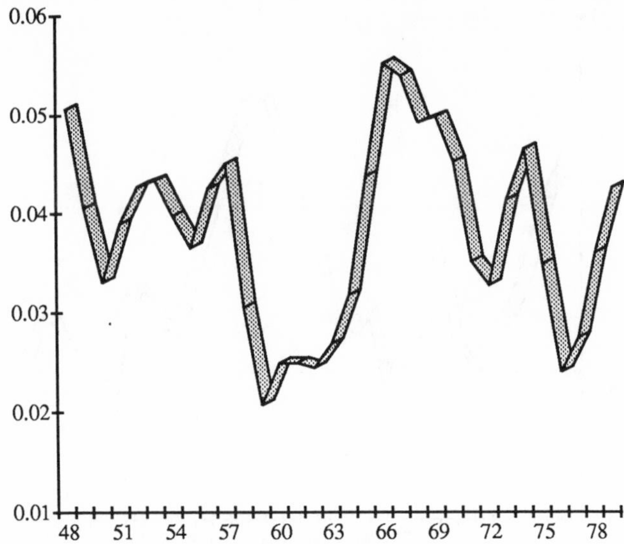

Figure 2.3. Stagnating accumulation after the mid-1960s: rate of growth of NFCB real net fixed nonresidential capital stock.

accumulation displays a pattern of significant cyclical fluctuations. The long-term trend in accumulation is not so clearly differentiated between the boom and the crisis periods as in the case of profitability. There is, however, an unmistakable downward trend in the accumulation rate after the mid-1960s; each cyclical peak and each cyclical trough after 1965 is lower than the previous one, just as in the case of profitability. As the pace of accumulation slowed, so did the productive potential of the economy.

Is there a link between the processes of institutional consolidation and decay outlined in the previous sections and the trends in profitability and accumulation sketched here? Bowles, Weisskopf, and I have been able to develop quantitative analyses which provide strong support for that connection.[51] The postwar SSA worked for U.S. capital as long as the several

51 Our most recent econometric analysis of U.S. corporate profitability is reported in Bowles, Gordon, and Weisskopf, "Business Ascendancy and Economic Impasse," Table 3. This model includes as explanatory variables seven quantitative indexes of capitalist power, which together reflect all four principal structures of the postwar SSA in the United States. Our regression (shown in row [3-1] of "Business Ascendancy") of the annual net after-tax rate of profit on variables accounts for 91 percent of the variance of U.S. profitability from 1955 to 1986. In a separate (unpublished) regression estimated for the period from 1955 to 1979, this same model accounts for 95

institutional foundations of its domination were effectively unchallenged. Once people began to challenge those power relations both at home and abroad, corporations could no longer enjoy the booming profits to which they had grown accustomed; stagnating investment was one of the perilous consequences.

THE COSTS OF KEEPING PEOPLE DOWN

> Even in the best state which society has yet reached, it is lamentable to think how great a proportion of all the efforts and talents in the world are employed in merely neutralizing one another. It is the proper end of government to reduce this wretched waste to the smallest possible amount, by taking such measures as shall cause the energies now spent by mankind in injuring one another or in protecting themselves against injury, to be turned to the legitimate employment of human faculties, that of compelling the powers of nature to be more and more subservient to physical and moral good.
>
> – John Stuart Mill[52]

percent of the variance of U.S. corporate profitability. Movements in the seven SSA variables account for 70 percent of the drop in the net after-tax rate of profit from the 1959–66 business cycle, when the profit rate reached its peak, to the 1973–79 cycle. (To determine the proportion of the decline in the net after-tax profit rate from 1959–66 to 1973–79 explained by different sets of independent variables, we used the same method described in our article "Hearts and Minds," Table 4.)

We have developed a parallel quantitative analysis of the slowdown in the pace of accumulation after the early 1970s in David M. Gordon, Thomas E. Weisskopf, and Samuel Bowles, "Power, Profits, and Investment: The Postwar Social Structure of Accumulation and the Stagnation of U.S. Net Investment since the Mid-1960s," New School for Social Research, Working Paper in Political Economy, No. 12, January 1993. Since profitability is a central determinant of investment, and since our SSA analysis helps illuminate the postwar trajectory of the rate of profit, we ought to be able to trace the influence of institutional consolidation and decline on investment *through* the mediating role of profitability. We find that an analysis of the investment slowdown which takes into account the erosion of the underlying institutional environment does a much better job of explaining annual movements in investment than one which ignores that environment. Through that analysis, for example, we find that the continuing erosion of capitalist power in the 1973–79 cycle accounts for fully three-fifths of the slowdown in investment from 1966–73 to 1973–79.

52 John Stuart Mill, *Principles of Political Economy* [1848] (London: Longmans, Green & Co., 1920), p. 979. I am grateful to Maurizio Franzini and Samuel Bowles for bringing this quote to my attention.

If the stagnation of the U.S. economy after the mid-1960s had been purely the result of surprises or shocks, it might have been possible to adjust to the dislocations, fairly quickly steering the ship back on course within a relatively short period. But the institutional foundations of the SSA were enduring and relatively inflexible, making it difficult to shift course in midstream. Worse still, the postwar SSA built upon hierarchical relations of domination and subordination which could not so easily be abandoned.

Conflict and domination is generally more costly than cooperation and reciprocity. And once challenges to power begin to emerge, it is more likely than not that the powerful will respond – not by relinquishing it – but rather by extending and deepening their systems of control. If and when this course is chosen, it promotes tendencies toward the garrison state. An ever-increasing fraction of the nation's productive potential must be devoted simply to keeping the have-nots at bay.

These costs of keeping people down may be illustrated by a series of calculations of the scope and trends in what Bowles, Weisskopf, and I call "guard labor" and "threat labor."

In any society a significant number of people do not produce goods and services directly but rather enforce the rules – formal and informal, domestic and international – that govern economic life. The presence of some guard labor in an economy is hardly an indictment of an economic system: it is a fact of life that rules are necessary and that they do not enforce themselves. But some rules are harder to enforce than others, and some economic structures must rely more heavily on guard labor than others. In the workplace, for example, it takes large expenditures on surveillance and security personnel to enforce rules which workers often perceive as invasive, unfair, unnecessary, and oppressive.

It should come as no surprise, given the analysis of the preceding sections of this essay, that the amount of guard labor in the postwar U.S. economy was mammoth. We include the following enforcement activities in our estimates of guard labor – workplace supervisors, police, judicial, and corrections employees, private security personnel, the armed forces and civilian defense employees, and producers of military and domestic security equipment. By our estimates, for example, guard labor constituted fully 20 percent of nonfarm employment plus the armed forces in 1966.[53]

53 The full estimate of guard labor includes those in "supervisory occupations"; police, judicial, and corrections employees; private security guards; and military personnel on active duty, civilian employees of the Defense

Added to this burden is another category of unproductive labor in an inegalitarian society – the wasted activities of what we call "threat labor." As noted earlier, employers in conflictual workplaces rely on the threat of job dismissal to help intimidate their workers and extract greater labor intensity from them. The more hierarchical and conflictual the workplace, the more important the presence of this threat becomes. And the greater the reliance on this threat, the more important it becomes that unemployed workers clamor outside the workplace for jobs, making the threat of dismissal credible. We include three groups in our estimate of threat labor in the United States – the unemployed, "discouraged workers," and prisoners. Threat labor comprised another 6 percent of nonfarm employment plus the armed forces in 1966.[54]

We can use these estimates of guard and threat labor to characterize the trajectories of institutional development in the postwar U.S. economy. To trace the evolution of the garrison state, I express these hierarchical

Department and those in defense-related employment. The data for those in supervisory occupations are based on the percentage of employees defined (in U.S. Department of Labor, *Dictionary of Occupational Titles* [Washington, D.C.: U.S. Government Printing Office, 1977], 4th ed.) as having "supervisory" or related "relations with people." Police, judicial, and corrections employees are drawn from U.S. Department of Justice, *Criminal Justice Statistics* (Washington, D.C.: U.S. Government Printing Office, various years); and *Historical Statistics,* numerous series. Data for private security guards are taken from *Statistical Abstract,* various years; and *Historical Statistics,* series D589, D591. Military personnel on active duty, civilian employees of the Defense Department, and those in defense-related employment are drawn from *Statistical Abstract,* 1989, p. 335. More detailed definitions, sources, and methods of our calculations, encompassing business cycle peaks from the late 1940s through the late 1980s, are available in a supplementary memorandum upon request from the present author.

54 The category of threat labor includes the unemployed; "discouraged workers" who would be unemployed if they had not dropped out of the labor force because they could not find work; and prisoners. The total number of unemployed are taken from *Economic Report,* 1990, Table C-33. The definition for the number of discouraged workers is drawn from *Statistical Abstract,* 1989, p. 395; data are based on U.S. Bureau of Labor Statistics, *Labor Force Statistics Derived from the Current Population Survey,* 1948–87, BLS Bulletin No. 2307, August 1988, Tables A-22, A-25. The number of prisoners is taken from U.S. Department of Justice, *Sourcebook of Criminal Justice Statistics, 1988* (Washington, D.C.: U.S. Government Printing Office, 1989), Table 6.31. As with the calculations on guard labor, more detailed definitions, sources, and methods for the estimates of threat labor are available in a supplementary memorandum upon request from the author.

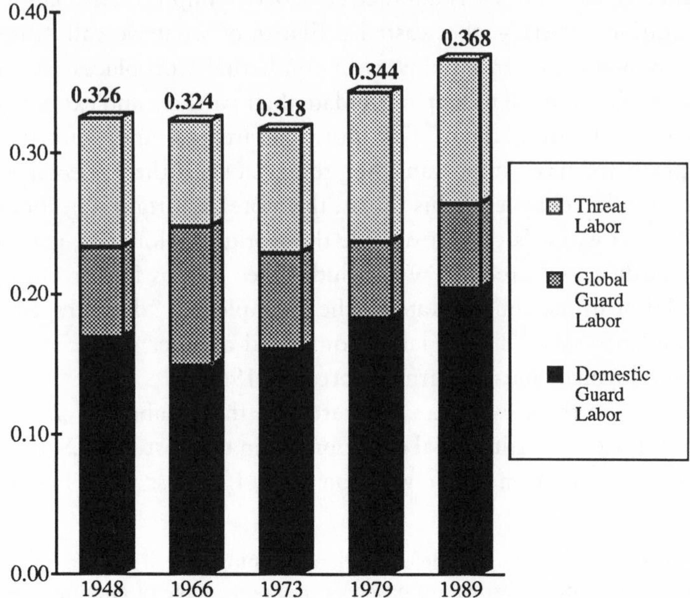

Figure 2.4. The costs of keeping people down: ratios of guard and threat labor to productive employment, 1948–89.

burdens as the ratio of guard and threat labor to all "productive" labor in the nonfarm economy – that is, all employment not devoted to guard activities. And I organize the data into three main categories: (1) "domestic guard labor," the sum of all "supervising" occupations as well as police, courts, corrections, and private guard employees; (2) "global guard labor," the sum of active-duty military personnel, civilian Pentagon employees, and defense-related employment; and (3) "threat labor," the sum of the unemployed, discouraged workers, and all federal and state prisoners.

Figure 2.4 plots these respective ratios for the postwar period at business-cycle peaks, extending the series through the end of the 1980s to anticipate a bit of the story outlined in the later essay by Bowles, Weisskopf, and myself. The graph traces the evolution of what could be fairly called a garrison state in the U.S. economy.

In 1948, for example, there were a total of nearly 33 people filling guard or threat roles for every 100 employed in "productive" slots – including 17 as domestic guard labor, 6.5 as global guard labor, and 9 as threat labor.

In the boom years from 1948 to 1966, the total burden of guard labor remained roughly constant, reflecting the consolidation of the postwar SSA. But some interesting changes in the composition of the garrison state took place. Because of the burdens and responsibilities of policing the world, on the one hand, the global guard labor ratio rose by 50 percent from 0.064 in 1948 to 0.10 in 1966. Because the carrot of the limited capital–labor accord rewarded some workers and allowed production relations to function effectively in some (limited) sectors without relying so heavily on either supervision or the threat of dismissal, on the other hand, the domestic guard labor ratio and threat labor ratio both diminished slightly, with the domestic guard labor ratio declining from 0.17 in 1948 to 0.15 in 1966 and the threat labor ratio falling from 0.09 to 0.08.

After the onset of stagnation in the mid-1960s, the total relative size of the garrison state again remained roughly constant – reflecting in part the inertial character of such hierarchical institutions. Again, however, some important changes in its internal composition occurred. Responding to friction at the workplace and the initial erosion of the limited capital–labor accord, corporations intensified their supervision of workers, with the domestic guard labor ratio increasing back to 0.16 in 1973. Corporations also became somewhat more dependent on the threat of dismissal, with the threat labor ratio increasing from 0.08 in 1966 to 0.09 in 1973.

Then, in the period of what we call mounting "political stalemate," the system came to rely more and more heavily on guard labor to try to beat back challenges to corporate power. The global guard burden continued to decline somewhat, in the period of the wind down from the Vietnam conflict, but domestic guard and threat activities more than compensated for that contraction. The domestic guard labor ratio increased once again, rising from 0.16 in 1973 to 0.18 in 1979. And the threat labor ratio grew as well, climbing from 0.09 in 1973 to 0.11 in 1979.

During the 1980s, as Bowles, Weisskopf, and I argue in our subsequent essay, right-wing economics relied even more heavily on direct assertion of hierarchical power in an effort to restore capitalist control. In the 1979–89 cycle, as a result, the garrison state increased its relative size even more. Remilitarization resulted in the global guard labor ratio rising back to 0.06. Increasing reliance on the stick in production generated a further increase in the domestic guard labor ratio from 0.18 in 1979 to 0.20 in 1989. And although the unemployment rate fell slightly (see row [5] of Table 2.1), the threat labor ratio remained roughly constant as the relative ranks of both discouraged workers and prisoners swelled.

By 1989, after more than two decades of stagnation and crisis, the garrison state had swelled to gargantuan proportions. We estimate that roughly 34 million Americans were engaged in guard and threat labor in 1989 – over a third more people, for example, than all those employed in manufacturing industries at all occupational levels.

This is not an easy kind of economy to transform. Those who are used to exercising power over subordinates do not easily or willingly relinquish it. Or at least these are some of the lessons we might draw from the preceding analysis.

The American Century depended on the open and aggressive assertion of hierarchical power. The American Century began to ebb when workers, citizens, and foreign buyers and sellers began to challenge that power. U.S. corporations tried for a time to roll back those challenges. As we show in our later essay on the 1980s, however, the right-wing and business offensive ultimately failed either to restore underlying capitalist power or to revive the stagnant economy.

As the American Century continues to sputter to its ignominious conclusion, it is surely time for us to begin to organize our economy on more democratic foundations. Our joint analysis of the waste embedded in the postwar U.S. economy – the waste of misdirected and underutilized resources as well as of garrison employment – persuades us that a successful and effective program for economic recovery can advance rather than suppress the values of democracy, community, and fairness.[55] The American Century is not an experience which many of us should pine nostalgically to repeat.

55 See Bowles, Gordon, and Weisskopf, *After the Waste Land,* Chs. 11–14.

Institutional and structural perspectives

The overwhelming majority of economists tend to focus their investigations of macroeconomic performance on discrete, quantitative variables – measured and understood within the contours of a theory of competitive markets. Yet, much as historical forces have an array of qualitative impacts on specific economic conditions, so too do institutions and the particular structures of given markets. This is all to say that changes in institutional behavior, the links between domestic and international markets, and the interaction between private economic behavior and governmental policy all play a crucial role in determining particular aggregate outcomes.

The four essays in this part provide some insight regarding these institutional and structural parameters and their relationship to contemporary American economic decline. William Lazonick investigates the consequences of changes in the ways corporate management behaves for macroeconomic performance. The evolution of financial institutions is also significant in this regard, and this matter is addressed by Jane Knodell. Global economic interdependence has clearly transformed the structure of the contemporary American economy – although the exact mechanisms by which that international context has affected domestic industries has been poorly understood. James K. Galbraith and Paulo Du Pin Calmon have significant new research findings to report on this complicated issue. Finally, Jeffrey A. Hart offers a much needed comparative perspective on the ways in which various nations have tried to formulate effective corporate structures and governmental policies to further economic growth. The relative success or failure of these efforts has much to do with the institutional and structural characteristics of individual national economies themselves.

3

Creating and extracting value: corporate investment behavior and American economic performance

WILLIAM LAZONICK

TIME HORIZONS, VALUE CREATION, AND INNOVATION

During the 1980s and early 1990s, a common criticism of America's industrial leaders was that they had "short time horizons" (see Jacobs 1991; Porter 1992). Managers who value present over future returns to their companies tend to avoid investment strategies that require considerable developmental periods before a flow of earnings can be realized. Yet these developmental – or innovative – investments are what enterprises need to sustain their competitive positions on global markets and what a national economy needs to maintain and enhance the standards of living of its people.

Pressured by the financial community, it is alleged that industrial managers favor investment strategies that make use of productive resources that have already been developed and hence can generate earnings immediately without incurring large capital outlays. Meanwhile, America's competitors, and particularly the Japanese, are investing in innovation. By adopting short time horizons, according to this line of argument, American industry has been managing its way to economic decline (Hayes and Abernathy 1980).

Is this charge of short-termism against American industry warranted? If it is true that those who control America's major business corporations have short time horizons and hence avoid innovative investment strate-

This essay draws heavily on a number of the author's recent works, most of them published. Rather than encumber the text with detailed bibliographic sources, where appropriate I refer the reader to these works.

gies, then how did the United States become such a powerful industrial nation in the past? Have the time horizons of America's top managers always been short, or is their truncated vision a relatively new phenomenon? Has the financial community – Wall Street – always exerted equivalent pressure to generate short-term earnings, or has that pressure increased over time? And, is Wall Street really to blame, or does its proclivity for the short term reflect more fundamental problems in the organization of the American economy? If those who control American industry do indeed have short time horizons, what can policy makers in business and government do to elongate them? Specifically, what can be done to give strategic decision makers in the major American corporations the incentives and abilities to invest in innovation?

To answer these questions, we cannot just focus on the incentives and abilities of those who wield decision-making power in America's industrial corporations. They are actors in a larger social drama that over the past few decades has been reshaping the ability of Americans to produce at home and compete abroad. To begin to address the problem of short time horizons, we require an understanding of the social forces in American society that are encouraging, and often compelling, those people who control our economic resources to think about generating returns today rather than higher productivity tomorrow. We also have to ask for whom the returns are being generated, and what effects the distribution of returns are having on the incentives and abilities of Americans, as individuals and as members of organizations, to engage in innovation.

Basic to comprehending the problem of short time horizons is an understanding of the conditions under which industrial corporations pursue innovative investment strategies as well as the conditions under which investments in innovation are successful. The distinction between long and short time horizons is really a distinction between *innovative* investment strategies that entail a developmental period before they generate returns and *adaptive* investment strategies that reap the returns on past investments (see Lazonick 1991:ch. 3; 1993a). To understand corporate investment behavior and economic performance, we must explain what takes place during the innovation process that ultimately yields the returns that make investments in innovation worthwhile. We must also explain why enterprises that engaged in innovative investment strategies in the past turn to adaptive strategies that merely live off their prior successes.

The innovation process expands the ability of an enterprise, industry, or economy to produce high-quality, low-cost goods and services. That is, it augments our ability to *create value* – to produce goods and services that we need at prices that we can afford. The adaptation process, in contrast, makes no attempt to augment the quality and lower the cost of goods and services but, at best, merely seeks to reproduce the value-creating capability of the enterprise, industry, or economy. In a world of innovation, those who simply try to do what worked before will soon find themselves left behind. In its extreme form, the adaptation process can entail disinvestment that, by extracting value today without putting any new value-creating capabilities in its place, reduces our ability to create value tomorrow.

Whether innovative or adaptive, value creation is a social process in which numerous participants contribute to the generation of goods and services with expectations of sharing in the returns. In doing so, these participants are generally both value creators and value extractors. They contribute to the generation of goods and services that society values, but they also extract a portion of this value as a reward for their contributions.

Of critical importance to whether investment strategies are innovative or adaptive is the balance between value creation and value extraction. Innovation enables an enterprise, industry, or economy to create more value than it extracts, whereas adaptive investments may entail the extraction of more value than is created. What matters for economic prosperity is the balance between the forces that determine value creation and value extraction.

Because value creation occurs over time, it is not always evident at any point in time which activities are net value creators and which are net value extractors. For example, an innovative entrepreneur who eats beans while working eighty-hour weeks to create a new product *may* be on balance a value creator. Whether or not he or she is a net value creator depends on the success of his or her innovative strategy. If, in the end, he or she creates nothing of value, even the consumption of beans may represent a net value extraction. The activities of a portfolio investor who commands the highest possible rate of interest for the use or his or her financial resources *may* be on balance value extracting. Whether, from a social point of view, the rate of interest received represents net value extraction depends on what the borrower does with the financial resources.

Nevertheless, there is a difference between the goals and activities of the innovative entrepreneur and the portfolio investor that have important implications for the balance between value creation and value extraction in the economy. The innovative entrepreneur is actively engaged in the attempt to create value while the portfolio investor is actively engaged in the attempt to extract value. There is no guarantee that those who engage in value creation will be successful, but without their attempts to create more than they extract, an increase in a society's value-creating abilities cannot, and will not, take place. It is also clear that the success of those whose prime purpose is to extract value makes the possibilities for the success of innovative strategies all the more difficult. If sustained economic prosperity is what we are after, it is of critical importance that we understand the relation between the value-creating forces and the value-extracting forces at work in our society, and how this relation has evolved over time.

In this essay, I outline the evolution of the forces for value creation and value extraction in the American economy during the twentieth century. I shall argue that during the first half of the century, the value-creating forces were ascendant, and indeed made the United States the most powerful industrial economy in the world. For this reason, and with obvious oversimplification, I call the first half of the century the "era of value creation." During the second half of the century, the value-extracting forces have become increasingly powerful in the American economy, and I call this half of the century the "era of value extraction." If, as appears to be the case, the "American century" is at an end, it is because for decades we have been living too much off the past rather than investing for the future.

The problem that American society faces is not just that, as we extract more value than we create, we are harvesting the fruits of an era when we created more than we extracted. Our problem is also that other nations, especially in Asia, are enjoying their own eras of value creation based on continuous investments in innovation that are destroying even the value of our own innovative investments of the past. If Americans do not take steps to regenerate the forces for value creation, sooner or later the United States will not have much value to extract.

Indeed, for some people "sooner" has already come. The ability to extract value in the American economy is highly unequal. There are already large segments of American society that are overrepresented by blacks, Hispanics, and women who possess neither the power to create value or extract value. A reinvigoration of the forces for value creation in the American economy is essential to respond to the challenge of not only foreign competition but also domestic social decay.

THE FORCES FOR VALUE CREATION

To create value, an enterprise, industry, or economy requires six "Ms": money, management, manpower, machines, materials, and markets (the following is adapted from Lazonick and Mass 1993). An explanation of how each of the six Ms contributes to the value-creation process provides an analytical framework in which to consider the evolution of the forces for value creation in the United States over the course of this century.

Money, or finance, plays a critical role in the value-creation process because those who control money get to choose what type of strategy an enterprise, industry, or economy will pursue. An innovative strategy inherently entails fixed costs because expenditures have to be made on "machinery" (i.e., plant, equipment, and motive power) and certain types of manpower (including those who inhabit the managerial structure) with a time lag before the receipt of returns. These fixed costs are high because of not only the scale of investments but also the developmental period that (by definition) must occur before the investments that entail fixed costs can generate returns.

Those who control money may or may not make strategic decisions that entail innovation – they may or may not act as entrepreneurs. Strategic decision makers can, and often do, decide not to be innovative but produce on the basis of resources that already exist within the company or that can be readily purchased on factor markets. They choose an adaptive strategy (see Lazonick 1991:ch. 3). When they do choose to innovate, strategic decision makers must keep financial resources committed to the innovation process until productive capabilities are sufficiently developed and utilized to generate returns. A failure to generate returns at any point in time may be a manifestation not of a failed strategy, but of the need to commit even more financial resources to an ongoing learning process (Lazonick 1993a). To keep money committed to the innovative investment strategy, those who control money must have intimate knowledge of the problems and possibilities of the investment strategy, or entrust their money to strategic managers who have such knowledge.

Management is required to plan and coordinate all of the specialized activities – the specialized division of labor – that must be integrated for an innovation to emerge. The innovative efforts that count for economic development invariably involve continuous, cumulative, and collective learning (Lazonick 1993a). Continuous learning results in the improvement of skills. Without continuous learning, acquired capabilities atrophy. Cumulative learning permits the use of acquired technological capabilities as the foundations for acquiring new capabilities. Without cumulative learning, more complex capabilities cannot build on fundamental capabilities already acquired. Collective learning enables a highly specialized division of labor to develop complex technology and generate productivity. Without collective learning, the planned coordination of the specialized division of labor is an economic burden rather than an economic benefit. By planning and coordinating the specialized division of labor, management's role is to ensure the continuity, cumulativity, and collectivity of the learning process.

Manpower – or labor power to be gender neutral at the sacrifice of alliteration – is the input into the innovation process that can potentially learn. But, because of the continuous, cumulative, and collective character of the learning process, individuals cannot just learn as they please. Central to the innovative strategy is investment in the capabilities of those people who comprise the specialized division of labor that management must plan and coordinate. Strategic decision makers ("money") do not invest in all of the people whom they employ, but only in those people whom they expect to participate in the collective learning process. Strategic decision makers do not want to invest in people who will exit the enterprise with their human assets. Nor do they want to invest in people who will use their voice within the enterprise to subvert rather than support the process of innovation.

Machines combine with manpower to transform materials into products. Innovation in machinery is both skill-displacing and skill-augmenting. It is skill-displacing because certain productive capabilities that once resided in manpower can not be more effectively performed by machines. It is skill-augmenting because innovation in machinery requires the application of new knowledge to develop machinery and utilize it effectively in the production process. Machines can affect the productivity levels attained in manufacturing a given product and the quality of what is produced. There is generally an intricate relation between innovation in materials and innovation in machines (see, e.g., the cases in Lazonick and Mass 1993). Innovation in machines and materials both in turn depend on the complementary skills of manpower.

Materials are the substances that people as labor power transform into products. As such materials become embodied in work in process – components, parts, and intermediate goods. An understanding of the character of these materials in their raw and semi-processed states is critical for the innovation process to take place. A key innovation may entail the creation of new materials through chemistry or the blend of materials that enter the production process. The quality of materials and semi-processed inventories will affect the ways in which machines and manpower are developed and utilized. As in the case of machinery, materials innovation can affect both the productivity of a given product and the quality of the product produced.

Markets provide the opportunity to generate returns on the investment in innovation. Privileged access to markets is often a critical condition for innovation to take place. As a general rule, the more innovative the strategy, the higher its fixed costs (see Lazonick 1991:ch. 3; Lazonick 1993a). Even with lower wages and interest rates, enterprises and industries that engage in an innovative strategy may be at a competitive disadvantage during the period of time that they are developing their productive resources and increasing the utilization of these resources by expanding their market share.

As has long been recognized by the "infant industry" argument for tariff protection, privileged access to home markets may be required for a period of time to develop and utilize productive resources sufficiently to generate a higher quality product at a lower unit cost than foreign competitors. The protection of markets, that is, creates opportunities for indigenous innovation that otherwise would not be taken up. An import-substitution strategy that entails indigenous innovation eventually creates the possibility for export expansion if the products of indigenous innovation have access to markets abroad. Integral to the analysis of indigenous innovation is how a nation protects its home markets and gains access to foreign markets.

Given this framework, how can we characterize the forces for value creation that enabled the United States to become world dominant by the middle of the twentieth century? In a process of dynamic expansion, all of the six Ms of enterprise are individually identifiable but inextricably interlinked. Our discussion of the forces for value creation will begin with money and end with markets with the management of manpower, machines, and materials completing what, in current business jargon, is quite appropriately called the "value chain" (see Porter 1985).

Innovation requires financial commitment so that high fixed-cost investments in physical and human resources (machines and manpower) can be transformed into high-quality, low-cost products that markets will absorb (the following arguments draw on Lazonick 1992). For a new venture, this financial commitment comes from the entrepreneurs themselves, from relatives or former business associates who trust the capabilities and integrity of the entrepreneurs, or from venture capitalists who make it their business to acquire an intimate knowledge of the entrepreneurs and the industry in which their capital is being invested. For those who have money to allocate, it is only a profound knowledge of the entrepreneurs and their business plans that can reduce the uncertainty inherent in a new venture. For this reason, new ventures are virtually never financed by impersonal capital markets.

It is only when, through a continuous process of reinvestment and organizational learning, new ventures have been transformed into going concerns that shares in the enterprise are issued to the public. Even in this case, however, the purpose in going public is (contrary to the folklore that emanates from Wall Street) generally not to finance the expansion of the enterprise but to monetize the cumulated investments of the original owner-entrepreneurs and their private partners. The function of the stock market is to permit the transfer of ownership from the original entrepreneurs and their backers to the shareholding public. The vast majority of the new shareholders have played no role in building up the company. Nor, as portfolio investors, do they want to play such a role now that they have acquired ownership rights. But for the ease of disposing of their shares on a highly liquid market, the new shareholders would not have been willing to take ownership stakes in the companies concerned.

It was only when the Great Merger Movement of the turn of the century gave Wall Street the opportunity to create a highly liquid market in industrial securities that this transfer of ownership of successful industrial enterprises from the original entrepreneurs to portfolio investors could occur. Until the late 1890s, a market in industrial (as distinct from railroad and government) securities did not exist. With J. P. Morgan taking the lead, Wall Street financed the mergers by selling to the wealth-holding public the ownership stakes of capital-intensive, high-technology companies that had transformed themselves from new ventures into going concerns during the rapid expansion of the U.S. economy in the decades after the Civil War. The concentration of market shares that resulted from the mergers made the new combinations attractive to the wealth-holding public, as did the stringent listing requirements of the New York Stock Exchange, the scrutiny of bond-rating agencies (chiefly Moody's and Standard and Poor's), and government regulation of trading subsequent to the Armstrong investigation of 1905. As a result, stock holding became widespread and fragmented.

Left in control of investment decision making in companies such as International Harvester, General Electric, and American Telegraph and Telephone were career managers. The new chief executives were by no means new recruits to these organizations. In industries in which the specialized divisions of labor that had to be planned and coordinated were complex, the owner-entrepreneurs of the late nineteenth century had recruited managerial personnel to build their new ventures into sustainable going concerns. Sustained competitive advantage went to those enterprises that built managerial organizations that could plan and coordinate the innovation process.

When a national market for industrial securities was created at the turn of the century, the existence of these managerial structures permitted dynamic enterprises to continue to flourish when ownership was separated from control. With the original entrepreneurs retiring from the scene, the most able, energetic, and visionary career managers could now rise to strategic decision-making positions. With ownership fragmented among tens or hundreds of thousands, and in some cases millions, of shareholders, the new strategic decision makers were left free to allocate corporate revenues to innovative investments that built on the organizational and technological capabilities that their enterprises already possessed.

In the wake of the Great Merger Movement, critics of the new combinations, many economists among them, viewed the merged companies' enhanced control over product prices as monopolistic practices that, in effect, permitted big business to extract value at the expense of the dependent consumer. In fact, for most companies, control over the level and volatility of prices enhanced their abilities to pursue innovative investment strategies. When successful, the innovative strategies enabled these companies to lower prices to consumers while increasing the wages and salaries of their workers and the dividends of their shareholders.

The critical issue for the development of the American economy was not product-market concentration and administered prices per se, but what the strategic decision makers in industry did with their enhanced control over market forces. Retained earnings, leveraged with money raised through long-term bond issues, financed not only the building of state-of-the-art plant and equipment for manufacturing but also the world's most up-to-date research laboratories and far-flung marketing facilities. To generate new knowledge and make as full use as possible of existing resources, the major industrial corporations also invested heavily in people. As we shall see, these investments were confined largely to those line and staff personnel who were deemed to be part of the management structure. The managerial enterprises that dominated the American economy invested very little in the skills of workers on the shop floor.

Investments in managerial organization did not just occur in the private sector. In the case of U.S. agriculture, similar investments that constituted a veritable managerial revolution were made by the federal and state governments to generate new knowledge of relevance to America's millions of farmers and to diffuse it to them on their farms (Ferleger and Lazonick 1993). The managerial revolution that, as Alfred Chandler (1977) has shown, began on the railroads during the second half of the nineteenth century, pervaded the American economy during the first half of the twentieth century.

These investments in managerial organization were supported by complementary private and public investments in the nation's educational system. Entrepreneurial fortunes of the late nineteenth century – and especially those of Carnegie and Rockefeller – endowed philanthropic foundations that reshaped the system of education from the primary through the university levels to fit the needs of a modern industrial society. At the same time, the nation's public institutions of higher education – the land-grant college system – developed to service the research and personnel needs of agriculture and industry. By the 1920s these massive investments in education formed solid underpinnings for the innovative strategies of the nation's industrial enterprises.

Within the industrial corporations, the building of managerial structures continued during the first half of the twentieth century to ensure the transformation of innovative investments in manpower and machines into high-quality, low-cost products. The management structure consisted of staff personnel who supplied the enterprise with knowledge and line personnel who ensured that their subordinates put that knowledge into action.

To plan and coordinate these line and staff activities to achieve the corporation's goals, it was not enough to train the relevant manpower to do particular tasks. The training of thousands of individuals had to be planned and coordinated so the particular tasks added up to a coherent whole. The problem was not a purely technocratic exercise. These thousands of individuals had to be motivated to utilize their skills to achieve common goals. Central to the managerial revolution in American business was the creation of incentive systems and accounting systems that sought to transform individualistic Americans into "organization men."

The inhabitants of the managerial structure were in fact (until the 1960s) almost exclusively men. More than that, they tended to be white, Anglo-Saxon, Protestant men who, within the corporate structure, were "members of the club." Their salaried status signified their long-term attachment to the enterprise; they were, in effect, what the Japanese have called "permanent employees." With their education, training, and cultural cohesion, these managerial personnel constituted a formidable collective productive force.

Left out of the "club" were women, who were often required to give up their employment upon marriage, and shop-floor workers, who increasingly came from a variety of non-"Wasp" backgrounds. These were the "hourly" workers who, in theory at least, could be hired and fired at will. In practice, those blue-collar workers who tended expensive machinery that had to be operated continuously and at high speeds to generate returns had to be motivated to maintain the pace of work. Despite a general lack of skill on the shop floor, managers still relied heavily on the complementary labor of operatives to achieve high throughput and low unit costs (see Lazonick 1990:ch. 7).

To elicit the desired responses from blue-collar workers, management used various methods such as piece-rate incentives, close supervision, extreme specialization of labor, and employee welfare plans. What worked best, however, was the ability of the company to offer workers long-term employment security as well as wages and work conditions that were above the prevailing norms for manual labor. The companies that were best able to offer such employment were those that, through investments in management, machines, and manpower, had gained distinct and sustained competitive advantages in their particular industries. By gaining the cooperation of labor on the shop floor, these companies were able to build their organizational capabilities, increase the value created by their investments, and extend their competitive advantages.

Once management had generated competitive advantage in one product market in one geographic area, it could try to use its organizational capabilities to capture market shares in new industries and in new locales. In the United States, dominant enterprises implemented what has become known as the multidivisional structure (Chandler 1962) to accomplish this task. With their highly integrated organizations already in place, dominant enterprises could engage in continuous innovation by building on their existing knowledge and facilities. Such enterprises were able to expand nationally and then internationally, while also channeling their financial resources into new product development that built on the unique capabilities that these companies already possessed.

From the outset of American industrialization in the early nineteenth century, entrepreneurs had had a problem recruiting and attracting skilled labor (the following arguments draw on Lazonick 1990: chs. 7–9). The existence of abundant land and an expanding economy meant that skilled labor had ample alternative opportunities, and could therefore command high wages without necessarily contributing high productivity. It was to avoid being dependent on the skills of a highly mobile, highly paid workforce that American strategic decision makers sought to embody the strength and skill requirements of work in machines and materials rather than in manpower. To pursue this strategy, which in its time was innovative, those with money had to employ staff personnel who could develop the machines and materials and line personnel who could ensure high rates of utilization of the machines and materials. The business enterprise also had to recruit large numbers of unskilled workers to tend the machinery and transfer the materials from one machine to another on the shop floor.

Toward the end of the nineteenth century, the rapid expansion of the American industrial economy attracted massive numbers of unskilled labor from eastern and southern Europe who became the primary source of blue-collar labor in the mass-production industries. The very real threat that these workers posed to existing craft labor (mostly of northern and western European origins) in the United States led to the growth of craft unionism under the umbrella of the American Federation of Labor. The attempt by these craft workers to maintain the traditional boundaries and prerogatives of their trade increased the resolve of management to run non-union shops and to take the need for the exercise of skill off the shop floor by embodying it in machines and materials. In cases where new machine technologies did not yet exist, the short-run response of management to craft labor was to make key skilled workers members of the managerial structure.

Increasingly, however, the technical specialists and professionals who became salaried managers were recruited from the nation's colleges and universities – institutions that during the first two decades of the century went through a massive transformation to provide pre-employment foundations for careers within the burgeoning managerial organizations. Within the managerial structure, management development programs provided these employees with extensive training that moved them around and up the managerial hierarchy, in the process gradually transforming them from specialists to generalists. This career-long process of development and promotion entailed a long-term commitment of the enterprise to the managerial employee and elicited a profound identification of the employee with the goals of the enterprise.

Such skill development systems did not prevail on the shop floor because a prime role of the managerial organization as it evolved in most American enterprises was to develop and utilize machines and materials in ways that would make it unnecessary for blue-collar workers to be in the possession of substantial skills. Increasingly, blue-collar workers were recruited from the vocational tracks of high schools in which the restricted conceptual and analytical content of their education conformed to the limited skill requirements of the jobs in which they would eventually find employment. These jobs did, however, require workers who would cooperate in supplying continuous effort to high-speed production processes for sustained periods of time. The structure and content of the routinized schooling that they received for some thirteen years before entering the workplace provided value-creating socialization for the subsequent routinized jobs.

During the 1920s, as American manufacturing boomed, the most successful corporations began to share the gains of innovation with shop-floor workers in the forms of somewhat higher wages and considerably more employment security than had previously been available in industry or were currently available elsewhere in the economy. These employment conditions reinforced the willingness of shop-floor workers to cooperate in the value-creation process and to forego union organization. Even after restrictions were put on immigration in the 1920s, the offers of remunerative and stable employment for unskilled workers drew hundreds of thousands of men off the American farms and into the factories.

This dynamic of growth collapsed in the 1930s. It collapsed, not because American industry did not have enough value-creating capability but because it had too much. As I shall discuss later, even with workers in the mass-production industries earning somewhat higher wages, there was too much value creation and not enough value extraction to sustain demand. In part this imbalance between supply and demand was because of a saturation of existing markets for consumer durables. In part it was because millions of families in farming, mining, and less capital-intensive manufacturing industries (textiles foremost among them) found themselves squeezed between cutthroat competition in their product markets and highly mobile labor in their labor markets, and hence extracted little from the boom of the 1920s.

As the depression deepened in the early 1930s, corporations that had dominant shares began to lay off their blue-collar workers, thus driving the depression deeper. These same corporations did not in general lay off their managerial employees. Strong balance sheets, the legacy of the 1920s, enabled these companies not only to keep their managerial organizations intact but actually to expand them. During the 1930s, for example, there was a significant increase in the number of research personnel employed by the major industrial corporations.

These industrial corporations were, therefore, well prepared to cooperate with the government in stepping up production for the war effort of the early 1940s. Before World War II, the government's main involvement in the generation and utilization of technology was in the agricultural sector. Now the government became deeply involved in chemical and electronic research for military purposes. After World War II, the Cold War sustained this government involvement. In addition, as a legacy of the New Deal and building on biotechnology advances in state-supported agricultural research, the federal government took responsibility for showing the way in medical research. Research laboratories in major corporations, universities, and the federal government gave the United States the most formidable capability for developing new knowledge in the world.

Also present in the American economy were formidable organizational capabilities for embodying this knowledge in new products and processes that took the American system of mass production to new productivity heights. As had been the case earlier in the century, American industry excelled at producing special-purpose, mass-production technologies that obviated the need for the exercise of skill on the shop floor. Further aiding the achievement of high-throughput production with deskilled production workers was the easy access of American mass-production enterprises to abundant supplies of high-quality natural resources. These resources were secured partly from within the boundaries of the United

States and partly from the worldwide exploitation of resources by U.S. multinational corporations.

As always in the twentieth century, the main job of shop-floor workers in American corporations was to feed materials into machines. What distinguished the 1940s and 1950s from the 1920s and 1930s was that now these workers had industrial unions to bargain with the corporations. The industrial unions did not, however, challenge the right of management to control the development of technology, including the right to continue to neglect investment in the blue-collar labor force. What the unions did win was the protection of seniority in layoffs and rehiring, thus giving workers a high degree of employment security as long as the companies did not undergo massive downsizings. In practice, seniority was also the basis for movements up the blue-collar wage structure.

By securing the employment and earnings of blue-collar workers, this industrial relations system elicited cooperation on the shop floor, even as it made no attempt to upgrade the skills of workers or harness their creativity. Given the extraordinary organizational capabilities embodied in the managerial structures of the major industrial corporations, however, cooperation on the shop floor was all that was needed in the 1940s and 1950s to make American industry the most powerful collective force for value creation in the world.

THE FORCES FOR VALUE EXTRACTION

Adam Smith made famous the notion that the sole end of production should be consumption. He had a point. Even those of us who get intrinsic enjoyment out of our work still seek to extract the economic value that we create.

Building on Adam Smith's metaphor of the invisible hand of market forces, economists have elaborated a theory of the market economy in which each participant gets to extract just that value that his or her factors of production create. In the real world, however, for any particular participant in the economy, the relation between value creation and value extraction is not so clear cut. Contrary to the orthodox economist's conception of an individualistic market economy, value creation in the real world is a collective process in which it is impossible to isolate the value created by each individual participant. It is also a process in which differences in collective power enable some groups of people to extract more than they create and other groups of people to create more than they extract.

Indeed, if taken too far, attempts to align individual rewards with individual contributions may very well interfere with the teamwork that is central to the value-creation process, and reduce the amount of value created by the team as a whole. In addition, where innovation is involved, the value that will be available for extraction is inherently uncertain at the time that the innovative production contributions are being made. It is the relation of people to the organizations through which they create value, not impersonal market forces, that determines how today's productive contribution will be rewarded if and when in the future returns to the innovative investments have been generated.

Value is extracted in the form of wages, salaries, interest, dividends, and taxes. As such, the ability of different groups – labor, management, creditors, owners, and the government – to extract value determines the distribution of income. As I have already emphasized, in and of itself value extraction performs an indispensable economic function; it creates the demand for goods and services that justifies the supply of these goods and services. Without such demand, producers would stop creating value.

In a world of innovation, however, one never expects demand to be in equilibrium with supply. By creating more value than previously existed, the innovation process assures that any tendency toward equilibrium of supply and demand will be disrupted. What matters for long-term economic growth is whether those who extract value use that value in ways that can augment the creation of value in the future.

Specifically, to what extent do they use a portion of the value they extract to finance the next round of innovative investments? Or to what extent do they spend the value they extract in ways that actually erode the organizational capabilities that are critical for innovative investment strategies to succeed? Value created and value extracted are not independent of one another. An increase in the amount of value created opens up new possibilities for extracting value, while an increase in the amount of value extracted can erode the capabilities for creating value. In the previous discussion of the forces for value creation in the United States, I explained how, in the "era of value creation," American companies secured the committed finance to permit them to develop and utilize new technologies. Now I shall explain how, in the "era of value extraction," the forces for value extraction have been undermining the value-creating capabilities of enterprises and industry in the American economy.

To illuminate the critical role of the relation between value creation and value extraction in the economy, and to elaborate the historical background to the era of value creation, let me begin by explaining why the trauma of the Great Depression of the 1930s could occur in the midst of what I have called the "era of value creation." The 1920s was a period of unprecedented economic expansion, with productivity growth in manufacturing averaging 5.6 percent per year over the decade. For manufacturing workers as a whole wages fell by almost 6 percent between 1920 and 1929, while managerial salaries rose by 22 percent and surpluses in the capital account rose by 63 percent. In the most dynamic industries, however, the distribution of income was markedly different from the average. In automobile manufacture, for example, wages rose by 24 percent between 1920 and 1929, while salaries rose by 15 percent. Over the same period capital surpluses in the automobile industry rose by 193 percent (see Lazonick 1990:ch. 7).

During the 1920s, the major manufacturing corporations paid out over 60 percent of their net income to shareholders as dividends. Yet the retained earnings of these companies were so great that they were able to fund all new investment in plant and equipment internally. They also took advantage of the booming stock market to sell shares, which they then used either to bolster their cash reserves or to pay off previously acquired debt (a financial strategy remarkably similar to that employed by Japanese corporations in the late 1980s). A large amount of this excess cash was lent to stock-market speculators on the New York call market as brokers' loans, thus fueling the stock market boom (see Lazonick 1992).

In this way the phenomenal value-creating capabilities of the major industrial corporations set the stage for the Great Crash of 1929. The product markets for consumer durables and houses had shown signs of saturation as early as 1928, but the financial disruption that occurred in the aftermath of the Great Crash took much needed credit out of the hands of farmers and other small businesspeople (in, among other sectors, mining and textiles) who, throughout the 1920s, had been mired in "cutthroat competition." The resultant bankruptcies further diminished the demand for the mass produced goods of the dynamic manufacturing sector. Unburdened by debt, the major companies could cut back production rather than engage in cutthroat competition. By 1931 major companies such as General Motors and General Electric were laying off blue-collar workers in droves, thus depressing consumer demand, and the economy as a whole, even further.

The Great Depression was not caused by a lack of productive capabilities but rather by the inability of formidable productive capabilities to find sufficient access to markets. Even in fragmented sectors such as textiles, mining, and agriculture, that were described as "sick" in the 1920s, the United States led the world in technology and hence value-creating potential. A major goal of the New Deal was to rectify this situation by permitting farmers and workers, whose purchasing power was essential for the existence of mass markets, to extract more of the value created by mass production. In agriculture, price supports and commodity credits made it possible for the farmer to invest in new technologies. In manufacturing, labor legislation made it possible for blue-collar workers to organize unions and engage in collective bargaining to raise wages and stabilize employment. In addition, the New Deal put in place social welfare programs that entailed a transfer of money from the wealthier segments of society who had more money than they could spend to the poorer segments of society who needed more money to spend.

Despite these changes, the redistribution of income that occurred in the late 1930s was not sufficient to generate sustained recovery. It took the entry of the United States into World War II and the consequent mandate to mobilize resources for military purposes to unleash the productive potential of the American economy. Once unleashed, the economy kept booming even after the war ended, in part because of pent-up consumer demand that households could finance from their wartime savings, in part because of a much expanded role of the government in building American infrastructure and military capability in the context of the Cold War, and in part because of the enhanced power of unions in the growing economy to extract value that was then used to buy American goods and services. In the quarter century or so after World War II, the United States was also able to extract value through its access to cheap materials around the world, the low revenues in the rest of the world in effect increasing the amount of value created that could be extracted by workers, managers, financiers, and governments in the United States.

Up to the 1950s, the forces for value extraction tended to support rather than undermine the forces for value creation. The higher wages of workers not only expanded mass markets. Combined with the renewed promises of employment stability, the higher wages of workers in the mass production industries gave them incentives to cooperate in the value-creation process. Within managerial organizations, a structure of hierarchical salary differentials evolved that provided managers with incremental rewards over the course of their careers as they progressed from lower-level to middle-level to upper-level positions. Government taxes were used to build social infrastructure such as schools, hospitals, and highways that directly and indirectly supported the value-creation process. From World War II, the government also began to spend heavily on basic scientific research in medicine and weapons, in addition to its existing commitments to agriculture. Even government funding of military-related research generated new knowledge that found uses in commercial applications.

Beginning in the 1950s and continuing over the ensuing decades, however, forces for value extraction gained strength. These forces adversely affected the dynamic interaction of the six Ms, and thereby undermined the value-creating capabilities of business enterprises. The opposition of the forces of value extraction to the forces of value creation took decades to unfold. In historical retrospect, however, we can see the process whereby the ability to extract value by various groups in the American economy became separated form the ability to create value. Leading the forces for value extraction was the financial sector (the following arguments draw on Lazonick 1992).

Up until the late 1970s – when the American financial system was deregulated, American industrial corporations had access to inexpensive finance. Wealth-holding households placed their money in life insurance policies, bank accounts, and, if they were willing to face the risks, common stocks. The institutional investors of the era of value creation – insurance companies, commercial banks, and mutual savings banks – channeled household savings into industrial investments by holding corporate debt. In a regulated financial environment, holders of bank deposits and insurance policies got low but stable returns on their savings while the dominant industrial corporations, with their investment-grade ratings from Wall Street, had, again by virtue of their dominance, access to relatively low-cost funds for industrial expansion. During the 1940s the yield in Moody's Aaa-rated corporate bonds averaged 2.71 percent, varying between a low of 2.53 percent in 1946 and a high of 2.83 percent in 1942.

As for the shares of the industrial corporations, they were held primarily by households that bought them on the secondary market with the expectation of receiving dividends and capital gains. With share holding widespread and fragmented, these households had little ability to influence the payout ratios – the proportion of current earnings that were paid out as dividends – of the companies that they ostensibly owned. Shareholders who did not like the dividends that they were getting from holding the stocks of a particular company could simply call their stockbrokers and sell their shares.

From the 1950s, however, a new type of share holder arose – the institutional investor. Before the 1950s, the only significant institutional investors that held corporate securities were the insurance companies, and, as prudent institutions, their portfolios consisted of massive amounts of corporate bonds but very small amounts of corporate stocks. The growth of mutual funds and pension funds in the American economy manifested the collectivization of the savings of millions of American wage and salary earners. The specific purpose of a mutual fund is to generate high yields for its members by collectively giving them access to professional money managers who can buy and sell large blocks of stock. Because individual wealth holders can buy and sell shares in mutual funds as easily as they can buy and sell shares of individual stocks, there is vigorous competition among mutual funds to attract investors. In the attempt to generate the higher yields that can attract investors, the mutual funds are constantly buying and selling large blocks of stocks.

During the 1950s, when the mutual funds became significant financial institutions, common stocks accounted for 85 percent of their assets compared with 30 percent of the assets of pension funds and only 3 or 4 percent of the assets of life insurance companies. During the 1960s the mutual funds played an important role in the conglomeration movement by buying up blocks of stock of target companies that were rumored to be in play, and selling them to the conglomerate raiders at higher prices.

The specific purpose of a pension fund is to provide for its members in retirement – a goal that, under conditions of sustained economic growth, might best be achieved by holding stable portfolios of securities for the long term rather than by buying and selling in an attempt to boost short-term yields. Hence the tendency of pension funds at mid-century to put the majority of their assets into long-term bonds. Over the past few decades, however, with American industrial corporations subject to intense pressures from foreign competitors and domestic value extractors, long-term investments have become increasingly uncertain investments. At the same time, pension-fund managers have been under pressure from their beneficiaries to match the yields of the mutual funds. They sought to do so by increasing the proportion of their holdings in stocks from 30 percent in the 1950s to 50 percent in the 1980s. More importantly, as pension funds grew by leaps and bounds, the proportion of all equities

Table 3.1. *Average annual yields on corporate bonds and common stocks, 1950–92*

	Real interest on bonds* (percent)	Dividend/price ratio on stocks** (percent)
1950–54	0.39	5.85
1955–59	2.12	3.94
1960–64	3.29	3.20
1965–69	2.21	3.18
1970–74	1.63	3.47
1975–79	0.67	4.69
1980–84	5.43	5.06
1985–89	6.45	3.58
1990–92	4.51	3.28

* Moody's Aaa.
** For all common stocks listed on the New York Stock Exchange.
Source: Economic Report of the President, 1993, Government Printing Office, 1993, 416, 428, 453.

outstanding in the United States that they owned increased from 2 percent in 1955 to 22 percent in 1985.

The Employee Retirement Income Security Act (ERISA) of 1974, as interpreted by the Department of Labor in 1978, provided government sanction to the pension funds to search for higher yields by getting involved in riskier investments. Accordingly, during the 1980s, the pension funds became the major source of the burgeoning size and number of "venture capital" pools in the United States, an occurrence that might have boded well for value creation had these pools really been providing the financial commitment required to transform new ventures into going concerns. In fact, these "venture capital" pools became major players in the search for higher yields, with the timing and amounts of value extracted from these new ventures often ensuring that they would not become self-sustaining going concerns.

The trends in the yields on stocks and bonds from the 1950s to the early 1990s reveal the success of the institutional investors' search for higher yields. As Table 3.1 shows, the yield on stocks, as measured by the dividend–price ratio, was already high in the 1950s. What is important for the relation between value extraction and value creation, however, is not the yield on stocks per se but whether the dividends paid out to generate this yield constrain the investment strategies of the industrial corporations. In the 1950s yields on stocks were high because, in an era of rapid growth and high profitability, stocks were undervalued (an overhang from the Great Depression) and companies could afford to take on debt. They could, therefore, pay out reasonable amounts of dividends while still retaining enough earnings to finance expansion. In the late 1970s and up to 1987, however, stocks were overvalued and companies were approaching or surpassing the debt-to-equity ratios that were consistent with financial stability. Yet, in response both to pressures from the institutional investors for higher yields and the availability of new forms, and norms, of corporate debt, companies paid out excessive amounts of dividends to maintain high yields and took on too much debt to keep themselves in cash.

American industry has always relied on retained earnings as the foundation for long-term corporate investment. By the 1980s and early 1990s, as the value-creating capabilities of foreign competitors were becoming more formidable, earnings began to flow out of American companies at an unprecedented rate. The proportion of after-tax profits distributed as dividends was already high at 44 percent in the 1960s and 45 percent in the 1970s. Yet it rose to 60 percent in the 1980s and climbed to 85 percent in the early 1990s. As for external finance, in the decades prior to the 1980s real interest rates on Moody's Aaa corporate bonds averaged as low as 0.39 percent in 1950–54 and as high as 3.29 percent in 1960–64. Yet in 1980–84, this yield averaged 5.43 percent, and in 1985–89, 6.15 percent. In the early 1990s, amidst prolonged recession, these real interest rates abated somewhat from the levels of the 1980s, but remained high by historical standards.

The successful search for higher yields – the enhanced ability of wealth holders to extract value from the economy – has made money more expensive and less committed to the value-creation process. More than that, however, the forces for value extraction have served to erode the organizational capabilities of those productive enterprises that are central to the value-creating economy. The erosion has been most evident at the top of the industrial corporation where top managers, who constitute the critical link between investment strategy and organizational structure, have increasingly turned from value creation to value extraction. From the 1950s, even before the advent of financial pressures from Wall Street and the institutional investors, top managers of major American corporations were developing both the incentives and abilities to extract more value for themselves rather than, as had been the case in the era of value creation, use their control over money to invest in the future of their productive organizations.

In the 1950s stock options became a standard form of top management compensation in major corporations. In the late 1940s, the top executives of a sample of fifty Fortune 500 manufacturing companies derived less than 3 percent of their total after-tax compensation from stock-based rewards. But 1950 tax legislation that favored corporate compensation in the form of capital gains combined with increases in common stock prices on the New York Stock Exchange at a rate of 24 percent per year between 1949 and 1956 created new opportunities for value extraction by top managers. By 1953 after-tax compensation from stock-based rewards had risen to 14 percent, and by 1955 it had jumped to 20 percent, thus permitting a 58 percent increase in total after-tax compensation for these executives from 1950 to 1955.

Stock options need not necessarily bias top managers against innovative investment strategies. The stock options received by strategic decision makers in the American industrial corporations could typically be exercised over a period of ten years. Short time horizons were not therefore built into these compensation schemes. In a rising stock market, however, options exercised earlier added to income earlier, and the exercise of existing options could form the basis for the granting of new options. And the fact is that from the late 1940s to the late 1960s, the stock market in the United States was generally on the rise.

As stock-based rewards came to represent a substantial proportion of executive compensation, the tendency was for beneficiaries to consider them as basic earnings rather than as a reward for superior performance. For example, when stock prices declined substantially in 1969 and 1970 – the first large decline since 1947 – stock-based compensation of the Fortune 500 executive sample fell to only 12 percent of total compensation but was replaced by other forms of income. The lesson for top managers was to be concerned with short-run stock market performance so that they could exercise their options early, establish a higher level of base pay, and get more options.

The ability of top managers to buy stocks at a discount transformed career employees into substantial owners. The exercise of stock options meant a stream of dividends if the managers held onto the stocks or, in a rising market, capital gains if the managers (usually after a restricted period) sold the stocks. During the 1950s ownership income began to dwarf compensation income for top managers. With capital gains income over twenty times dividend income in the early 1960s, top managers gained a palpable interest in preventing even short-run declines in the value of their companies' stocks. Along with the ever more powerful managers of institutional financial portfolios, the strategic decision makers who ran America's major industrial corporations increasingly developed an interest in focusing on the "bottom line" of their companies' quarterly corporate reports.

In the process, these top managers began to view their own interests as distinct from the interests of other managers (never mind blue-collar workers) lower down the corporate hierarchy. Manifesting this divergence of interest was the increasing tendency for the pay of top managers of industrial corporations to be determined by "market" forces external to their organizations – for example, the pay of other top managers or of Wall Street financiers – rather than by a structure of incentives and rewards internal to their particular organizations. While the real average after-tax earnings of American wage and salary earners fell by 13 percent during the 1970s and 1980s, the real average after-tax compensation of CEOs of major American corporations increased by 400 percent. In 1981 the average compensation of the twenty-five highest paid executives of U.S. non-financial enterprises was $2.46 million; by 1988 this figure was almost five times higher at $12.22 million (see Lazonick 1992, 1993b).

The value-extracting capabilities of American top executives became particularly evident when their compensation was compared with that of their counterparts abroad. In 1990 the salary and bonus compensation of CEOs of the thirty largest U.S. corporations was on average $3.1 million. For British CEOs (who had also increased their power to extract value from earlier decades), the comparable figure was $1.1 million; for French and German CEOs, $0.8 million; and for Japanese CEOs $.05 million (*New York Times,* January 20, 1992). The availability of stock options to American top managers, but not to Japanese top managers, made the international gap in CEO compensation all the more striking – especially when, as was increasingly the case, the enterprises that Japanese managers directed were outcompeting the enterprises over which the American managers presided.

This enhanced value-extracting power of America's top industrial managers has weakened their incentives to engage in innovative investment strategies. Their ability to command high salaries depends on their cooperation with the financial community in pursuing adaptive investment strategies that generate the "free cash flow" that can be extracted from these corporations rather than dedicate these revenues to investment for the future.

Indeed, quite in keeping with this perspective of an erosion of the organizational capabilities of American industrial corporations, as those at the top of the American industrial corporations have fared extremely well, the employment security and pay of those further down the corporate hierarchy have deteriorated. As a result, the best and the brightest of young Americans have much less incentive to pursue careers as technical specialists in the industrial corporations. At the same time, fueled in large part by the flow of earnings out of these corporations, alternative employment for these people as value extractors in the financial sector have grown more attractive. In 1989 the average compensation (salary and bonus) for the more highly paid stratum of corporate finance and merger and acquisitions specialists at the top ten securities firms was $450,000 if they entered the firm in 1983, $300,000 if they entered in 1986, just over $200,000 if they entered in 1987, and about $140,000 if they entered in 1988. The average compensation of the lower-paid specialists ranged from just under $300,000 if they entered in 1983 to "only" $100,000 if they entered in 1988 (*Wall Street Journal,* Dec. 8, 1989:C1 and C5). In 1993, after several years of recession the *average* annual pay of employees at Wall Street was over $130,000 (*New York Times,* Sept. 30, 1993:B5). As the forces for value extraction have become ascendant, it is not only with the Japanese that American industry must compete (see Bok 1993).

Meanwhile, American industry was simply not making the types of investments that were required to remain competitive on global markets (the following discussion draws on Lazonick forthcoming). The recession of the late 1980s and early 1990s greatly accelerated the tendency that had been building since the early 1980s to terminate the employment of salaried personnel. To some (as yet undetermined) extent, this downsizing represents a necessary rationalization of overstaffed corporate bureaucracies. There is a danger, however, that forced downsizings might be diminishing the abilities of U.S. industrial enterprises to pursue innovative investment strategies. The inability of the enterprise to offer long-term employment security and income growth even to its salaried employees may reduce the organizational commitment of those salaried employees whom the company retains. As shown by the recent experience of many dominant U.S. companies (including IBM), the most able and experienced employees may look outside the company for employment. If and when they do in fact leave the company, they take with them skills acquired through in-house training and experience. The company not only loses its investments in human resources but often finds that these resources are subsequently at the service of direct competitors. The loss of human resources as well as competitive advantage makes the company reluctant henceforth to invest in the skills of its key personnel.

The long-term result of such responses is an erosion of organizational capabilities within the enterprise without any guarantee that the reduction of investment in human capabilities and the reconstitution of comparable organizational capabilities will occur elsewhere in the economy.

The number of scientists and engineers per 10,000 labor force participants in the United States was sixty-five in 1970 and sixty-six in 1986. The Japanese, who had only half the number of scientists and engineers per 10,000 labor force participants as the United States in 1970, had caught up with the United States by the mid-1980s. During the last half of the 1980s, R&D expenditures as a percent of GNP were about equivalent in these two nations – about 2.8 percent. But the much greater role of the military in U.S. R&D expenditures (about 30 percent of the total for the United States and virtually nothing for Japan) reduces the impact of U.S. R&D investment because of a lack of spillover from military to civilian applications. One reason for the lack of spillover in particular and of the decline in U.S. leadership in technological development more generally may be a neglect of long-term generic (or "pre-competitive") research at the corporate level of major industrial enterprises, with the R&D focus devoted overwhelmingly to product and process development at the divisional level.

Evidence from Japan is that its major high-technology corporations that in the past emphasized applications of technology as part of the process of catching up are now using some of the returns from catching up to finance central research laboratories in which to generate knowledge about the technologies of the future. As for the present, analyses of patent citations show that by the beginning of the 1990s, Japan was forging ahead in virtually every high-technology field.

If a reversal in long-term technological capability between U.S. and Japanese industrial corporations is taking place, it may also be affecting the different ways in which U.S. and Japanese industrial enterprises are making use of the unparalleled public-sector research capabilities of major American universities. Unlike the United States, where over a century ago, the U.S. federal government, through the Department of Agriculture, began funding basic research, the Japanese never developed universities for this purpose. Instead, as part of the process of catching up, Japanese companies applied scientific knowledge generated abroad to Japanese industrial requirements. But now that they have caught up, Japanese high-technology companies have been establishing close links between U.S. universities and their central research laboratories. U.S. industrial corporations, in contrast, appear to be increasingly interested in making use of university research capabilities for applied rather than basic research. If so, it may be that in the future Japanese companies will use the basic-research capabilities of U.S. universities to help them forge ahead in high-technology industries such as aerospace, medical equipment, chemicals, and biotechnology, while, by failing to make use of these basic-research capabilities, U.S. companies will forgo a powerful means of catching up.

As for an industry such as automobiles in which the U.S. clearly fell behind in the 1980s, what the Japanese have shown in recent years is their ability to gain competitive advantage even when manufacturing in the United States by transplanting the modes of shop-floor work organization that have already worked so well in generating exports from Japan. A key component to Japanese success in the United States has been the willingness of Japanese transplants to invest in the capabilities of shop-floor workers. Yet these are precisely the investments that dominant U.S. mass producers have been reluctant to make in the United States.

In competition with the Japanese over the past quarter century, the organization of work on the shop floor has been the Achilles heel of U.S. manufacturing. With its managerial structures in place, American industry may have entered the second half of the twentieth century in the forefront in the development of productive resources. But its weakness lay in the utilization of productive resources manufacturing processes in which large numbers of shop-floor workers had to interact with costly plant and equipment.

Into the 1960s, U.S. enterprises dominated in the mass production of automobiles and consumer electronics by making investments in special-purpose machinery that then required the cooperative efforts of masses of relatively unskilled labor to generate high levels of productivity. Aided by a centralized union movement, these enterprises secured a degree of shop-floor cooperation from production workers by offering them more employment security and better pay than could be found elsewhere in the U.S. economy. But the major industrial enterprises did not provide these blue-collar workers with substantive training. Nor did they ever make explicit, and hence more secure, the long-term attachment of the "hourly" employee to the enterprise. Without this commitment of the organization to the individual, one could not expect the commitment of the individual to the organization that might have enabled U.S. mass producers to respond quickly and effectively to the Japanese challenge.

Production workers in the United States receive much less training and tend to be much less skilled than their counterparts in Japan or Germany. Historically, the deskilling of shop-floor work in the United States arose out of successful managerial strategies to introduce mass-production technologies that could take the control of work organization out of the hands of craft workers and make use instead of inexperienced and untrained immigrant labor. The development and utilization of these mass-production technologies required investment in skills. But those who received extensive training were better educated technical specialists who were integrated into the managerial structure as salaried employees with the potential for rising up the managerial hierarchy. It was on this organizational and technological foundation that U.S. industrial enterprises achieved their positions of global industrial leadership.

The problem for the United States is that it has been in those mass-production industries in which the United States was once pre-eminent that the Japanese have changed the organizational and technological foundations of industrial leadership by developing and utilizing the skills of production workers as well as technical specialists. They have done so, moreover, on the basis of a mass-education system that since the late nineteenth century has provided the pre-employment cognitive foundations for the subsequent skill development of production workers as well as technical specialists in the workplace.

In the United States, the unskilled shop-floor worker is the product of an inferior primary and secondary education that sufficed as long as the U.S. model of skilled technical specialists and unskilled production workers yielded global competitive advantage. But the educational requirements of industrial leadership have changed. Numerous comparisons of educational achievement among the OECD nations have shown that the United States ranks at or near the bottom.

One might expect that a nation such as the United States, with its historic commitment to equal opportunity through mass education, would quickly respond to the changed educational requirements of global competition by upgrading the cognitive capabilities of its future workforce. In the past, the captains of industry have recognized the need to improve the education of the masses. Much of the funding of mass schooling after the turn of the century came from the philanthropic foundations established by major industrialists. That was, however, in the "era of value creation" when the U.S. economy was rising to its position as global industrial leader. Despite a general consensus in the United States that investments in mass education are the top priority for industrial regeneration, the wealthiest Americans have shown little interest in making the funding available, either through philanthropic means or through tax-financed government expenditures.

The failure to provide high-quality mass education in turn constrains attempts by industrial employers to develop the skills of production workers to complement advanced process technologies. U.S. industry underinvests in the training of its shop-floor workers, both relative to its own investments in managerial personnel and the investments of its international competitors. Given this lack of in-house training and the difficulty in utilizing advanced process technologies (e.g., robotics) on the shop floor, U.S. industrial enterprises tend to search for alternative, less technologically complex, investment strategies.

If present-day U.S. industrialists are unwilling or unable to take the lead in effecting the necessary educational and training transformations, one might expect that the workers themselves, through their unions, would apply pressure on business and government to make such investments in human capabilities. In many western European nations and to some extent in Japan, unions play precisely this role, be it through direct participation in investment decisions at the enterprise level or through political representation in local and national governments. In the United States, however, the 1970s and 1980s witnessed a dramatic weakening of the labor movement at precisely the time when unions needed to be brought into the investment decision-making process in both the private and public sectors. To do so the adversarial business unions of the 1950s and 1960s needed to be transformed into partners of industry. Instead, through plant closings and legal rulings, the union movement was weakened. The sharp decline of union membership from over 20 percent of wage and salary workers in the early 1980s to less than 15 percent in the early 1990s reflects a longer run trend that manifests the erosion of organizational capabilities in the United States.

The weakening of the U.S. labor movement is also reflected in the decline in the real wages of U.S. manufacturing workers over the past two decades. Real hourly wages have been declining in manufacturing since the late 1970s, and from 1978 to 1990 real weekly wages declined by well over 10 percent. This decline in the real wages of manufacturing workers manifests the growing inequality in income distribution that characterized the 1980s and persists in the 1990s. More than that, however, it also manifests an erosion of organizational capabilities. Within a major manufacturing enterprise (which was the type most apt to be unionized), well-established arrangements for sharing productivity gains with workers provide the social basis for generating the gains to be shared (see Lazonick 1990:chs. 8–10 and Appendix). The willingness of workers to supply high levels of effort increases productivity, while the cooperation of workers in the utilization of productivity-enhancing process technologies creates incentives for employers to invest in these technologies. A loss of control over the supply of effort on the shop floor, therefore, makes employers reluctant to invest in advanced machine technologies as well as the skills of shop-floor workers needed to complement these machines. The long-run decline in real manufacturing wages manifests these perverse impacts of prevailing labor–management relations on shop-floor technological change and productivity growth. The inability of masses of Americans to extract value from the economy is integrally bound up as both cause and effect of their inability to create value.

CONFRONTING THE IDEOLOGY OF OWNERSHIP

From the perspective of value creation and value extraction, therefore, the problem of short time horizons does not simply reside in the heads of strategic decision makers. The structure of the American economy combined with the rise of formidable foreign competition have generated incentives for strategic decision makers in American industry to pursue adaptive investment strategies. As I have argued, the forces for value extraction have been gathering power in the United States since the 1950s. But it was the movement for financial deregulation and other "free-market" ideologies that were put into practice during the years of the Reagan administration that permitted the forces for value extraction to overwhelm the forces for value creation.

What the American economy now needs is massive value-creating investments in many dimensions. We need to invest in schools from kindergarten through grade 12 so that in the world of work masses of people will have the value-creating capabilities to make their enterprises and industries competitive. We need to invest in higher education so that it turns out people who are adept at products that are good for our physical and mental health rather than turning out people who are adept at manipulating financial markets for their own personal gain. Within enterprises, we need investments in research and development specifically and in human capabilities more generally – not only in the management structure where such investments have traditionally been made but also on the shop floor where deskilled work has traditionally prevailed. To truly create value for people, these investments at the levels of the society and the economy must be sensitive to environmental and social concerns. Indeed, as a society, we need new measures of "value" that go deeper than money to gauge our ability to generate goods and services that elevate human existence.

As a step toward achieving these goals in the United States, power over investment decision making in both business and government must shift from the value extractors to the value creators. As a pre-requisite, such a shift will require an ideological revolution in the way in which Americans think about what the forces for value creation actually are. Unfortunately, it is not only conservatives who espouse the belief in the efficacy of the free-market economy. In the late 1970s, financial deregulation was a Democratic initiative, and for decades before that many liberal economists had preached what I have called the "myth of the market economy" (Lazonick 1991).

Such an ideological revolution will be a hard sell. Many if not most critics of "short-termism" in American industry are unwilling to contemplate the shift in control over strategic decision making that an eradication of the problem would entail. Obsessed with an ideology of ownership, they look to financial markets to direct the American economy toward the long term. For example, in a book entitled *Short-Term America: The Causes and Cures of Our Business Myopia* (1991), Michael T. Jacobs, a former director of corporate finance in the United States Treasury Department under Reagan, bemoans the impact of the financial revolution of the 1980s on investment in America's industrial future. Yet he still retains a misguided faith in the role of financial markets to determine the nation's industrial development. "In spite of the many shortcomings of our present equity markets," Jacobs (1991:74) argues,

> the collective wisdom of our markets is still the best judge of economic value. Poor information, rather than poor judgment, is the root of inappropriate evaluations. If we allow companies to ignore their stock price,

> there will be no mechanism to force them to deploy resources more efficiently. Consequently, pursuit of other goals at the expense of maximizing the value of the corporation would not only violate the directors' fiduciary responsibility to the shareholders, it would also undermine the capitalistic system which we have always relied on to satisfy the long-run interests of employees, communities, and customers.

This statement misconceives the forces for value creation that made the American economy the world's most powerful in the past. It was precisely when stock prices were low and shareholders had little power to extract higher yields that the top managers had both the incentives and abilities to invest for the long term. The stock market does not exist, and never has existed, to finance industrial development. Rather, as I outlined in this essay, from the perspective of value creation, it has existed to permit collective business organizations to invest for the long term unconstrained by the abilities of individual property owners and by their desires for value extraction. Underlying the financial revolution that has played a major role in shortening the time horizons of American managers has been the rise of the collective power of property ownership in America's major industrial corporations. In the successful search for higher yields, the collective power of stock ownership has become a force for value extraction that has overwhelmed, surpassed, and ultimately undermined the forces for value creation.

In a recent study, *Capital Choices: Changing the Way America Invests in Industry* (1992:3), Michael E. Porter of the Harvard Business School has recognized that "the U.S. system of allocating investment capital is threatening the competitiveness of American firms and the long-term growth of the national economy." Porter (1992:3) argues that many American corporations have been investing "too little in those assets and capabilities most required for competitiveness (such as employee training), while wasting capital on investments with limited financial or social rewards (such as unrelated acquisitions)." He views short time horizons, ineffective corporate governance, and the high cost of capital as symptoms of "a much broader problem, involving the entire system of allocating investment capital within and across companies."

Competitiveness, Porter (1992:4) argues,

> requires sustained investments in a wide variety of forms, including not only physical assets but also intangible assets such as R&D, employee training, and skills development, information systems, organizational development, and close supplier relationships. These "softer" investments are

of growing importance to competition and are also the most difficult to measure and evaluate using traditional approaches to evaluating investment alternatives.

Yet, in the American economy, such investments have been made on a massive scale in the past (and continue to be made on an apparently lesser scale today), albeit more within the managerial structure and less on the shop floor. What needs to be confronted, and what Porter avoids, is why the interests of, and pressures bearing on, those doing investment decision making at the levels of both business and government have changed.

Porter's very use of the adjective "intangibles" to refer to human assets is a clue to the bias that now pervades the American business community. Investments in human assets are quite tangible to the people who possess them. These assets are acquired through educational institutions, government-sponsored and business-sponsored training programs, and particular employment opportunities. When these human assets are in demand, the asset bearers get jobs, employment security, and decent pay. When combined with the productive capabilities of others and appropriate physical assets, these human assets generate returns not only for the people who possess them but also for the organizations of which they are an integral part.

When top managers as strategic decision makers invest for the sake of these organizations – that is, when they act as value creators – they count the allocation of capital to human assets as critical investments and the higher standards of living that result as basic returns. When they invest for the sake of themselves and the financial community, they see both the allocations of capital to, and the returns from, human assets as expenses that reduce the amount of value that they can extract. When top managers view their mission as "creating value for shareholders" – which during the 1980s became a typical refrain – they tend to neglect investments in human assets precisely because assets that reside in humans are assets that shareholders cannot own.

Why have America's foreign competitors not fallen victim to the value extractors? Porter (1992:9) repeats a common misconception when he states that in Germany and Japan "the dominant owners are principals rather than agents and hold significant ownership stakes." In terms of investment decision making, the principals in Germany and Japan are managers and workers. For reasons having to do with an ideology of collectivism and the organization of labor, in both Germany and Japan ownership has been subordinated to membership. Porter (1992:10–11) implicitly recognizes the subordination of ownership in investment decision making when he argues that "in both Japanese and German companies, the dominant goal is to ensure the perpetuation of the enterprise. . . . Financial controls and capital budgeting are practiced in Japan and Germany, but investments are heavily driven by technical considerations and the desire to ensure the firm's long-term position in the business."

To get the American system of capital allocation back on track, Porter's (1992:14) prime recommendation is to "expand true ownership throughout the system . . . to include directors, managers, employees, and even customers and suppliers." To do so is to endow membership with the rights of ownership – control over the disposition of the assets and the allocation of the revenues of the corporation. The irony is that control by the "membership" over the capital allocation process in American industry is nothing new. Such control characterized the "era of value creation."

Back then, however, the membership was a club of white Anglo-Saxon Protestant men – the "organization men." When organizations make investment in people they in effect define these people as members with the rights and responsibilities that membership entails. Today, the investments required to be competitive on a global scale demand a much more inclusive definition of membership than prevailed in the past – one that cuts across gender, ethnic, race, and class lines. For those who recognize the importance of these investments in organizational capabilities, the first step is to confront the ideology of ownership that dominates American thinking on corporate governance. It is an ideology that, in the name of "creating value for shareholders," is denying the rights of corporate membership to millions of Americans who could be creating value while legitimizing the destructive activities of those who wield wealth and power by extracting value.

REFERENCES

Bok, Derek, *The Cost of Talent: How Executives and Professionals are Paid and How It Affects America,* Free Press, 1993.

Chandler, Alfred D., *Strategy and Structure: Chapters in the History of American Industrial Enterprise,* MIT Press, 1962.

The Visible Hand: The Managerial Revolution in American Business, Harvard University Press, 1977.

Ferleger, Louis, and William Lazonick, "The Managerial Revolution and the Developmental State: The Case of U.S. Agriculture," *Business and Economic History,* 22, 2, 1993:68–102.

Hayes, Robert, and William Abernathy, "Managing Our Way to Economic Decline," *Harvard Business Review, 58,* 1980:66–77.

Jacobs, Michael T., *Short Term America: The Causes and Cures of our Business Myopia,* Harvard Business School Press, 1991.

Lazonick, William, *Competitive Advantage on the Shop Floor,* Harvard University Press, 1990.

Business Organization and the Myth of the Market Economy, Cambridge University Press, 1991.

"Controlling the Market for Corporate Control: The Historical Significance of Managerial Capitalism," *Industrial and Corporate Change,* 1, 1992:445–88.

"Learning and the Dynamics of International Competitive Advantage," in Ross Thomson, ed., *Learning and Technological Change,* St. Martin's Press, 1993a.

"Industry Clusters and Global Webs: Organizational Capabilities in the American Economy," *Industrial and Corporate Change,* 2, 1993b:1–24.

"Social Organization and Technological Leadership," in William J. Baumol, Richard R. Nelson, and Edward N. Wolff, eds., *Convergence of Productivity: Cross-National Studies and Historical Evidence,* Oxford University Press, forthcoming.

Lazonick, William, and William Mass, "Indigenous Innovation and Economic Development: Is Japan a Special Case?" paper presented to the annual meeting of the Economic History Association, Tucson, Arizona, October 2, 1993.

Porter, Michael E., *Competitive Advantage,* Free Press, 1985.

Capital Choices: Changing the Way America Invests in Industry, Council on Competitiveness, 1992.

4

Financial institutions and contemporary economic performance

JANE KNODELL

1. INTRODUCTION

In the decade between 1935 and 1945, the U.S. financial system was transformed from a system in structural collapse to one which provided a stable and effective underpinning to economic expansion, both domestically and abroad. At the outset of the 1990s, the U.S. finds itself with a financial system that once again exhibits growing instability, that is developing without direction, and that is increasingly out of sync with the nation's most pressing capital needs.

The postwar financial system was shaped by New Deal legislation which reorganized finance after its collapse in the Great Depression and by the Bretton Woods international monetary system, which established new monetary ground rules after World War II. It is generally thought to have worked well in meeting the needs of U.S. economic growth up to the late 1960s, when inflationary pressures caused internal contradictions within the financial system to emerge. Since then, the financial system has undergone a market-driven restructuring process which has significantly changed the financial landscape. The financial system in place in the early 1990s reflects on the one hand the tremendous ability of private finance to adapt to changing macroeconomic conditions, and its questionable ability to lead the U.S. economy out of decline on the other.

This chapter will explain how New Deal legislation created a new financial infrastructure for postwar growth, how the macroeconomic environment of finance was transformed over the course of the postwar period, and how financial institutions responded to changing macroeconomic conditions. In concluding, the chapter will draw out the implications of finance's adaptive responses for U.S. economic performance.

2. THE NEW DEAL AND THE REORGANIZATION OF FINANCE

New Deal legislation adopted in the 1930s included a set of laws designed to jump-start the paralyzed financing process in the short run and create a more stable and accessible financial system in the long run. The goal of stability was pursued by the creation of a sector of "core" financial intermediaries operating with public safety nets. The goal of broadening access to credit was pursued by the creation of new public financial intermediaries and agencies which introduced and diffused new financing instruments and shared the risk associated with the development of new credit markets with private finance. A new division of labor between the public sector and the private sector and between "core" financial intermediaries and capital-market-based intermediaries took shape as these two goals were simultaneously pursued.

Creating a stable financial core

The core consisted of commercial banks and thrift institutions and their public-safety-net institutions, the Federal Deposit Insurance Corporation, the Federal Reserve Banks, the Federal Savings and Loan Insurance Corporation, and the Federal Home Loan Banks. The public safety net operated on both the asset and liability sides of banks' and thrifts' balance sheets. Core intermediaries could secure funds by borrowing on the collateral of their assets at Reserve Bank or Home Loan Bank discount windows, and deposit insurance enhanced institutions' ability to attract funds from the general public by sustaining public confidence in deposit instruments.

The quid pro quo for the public safety net was more extensive regulation. The logic of New Deal regulation of core intermediaries was to ensure their profitability, hence their stability, by insulating them from the open capital markets and by limiting competition between and within segments of intermediaries.

The core was insulated from the potentially destabilizing effects of the equity market by the Glass–Steagall Act, which prohibited a financial firm from engaging in both commercial and investment banking, and by the Securities Exchange Act of 1934, which gave the Federal Reserve the power to define the maximum loan-to-value ratio on loans collateralized by securities. In addition, commercial banks were prohibited from owning corporate securities other than the debt instruments of highly credit-rated corporations. Still, by providing short-term finance to brokers for carrying inventories of corporate securities, and to mortgage companies for carrying inventories of mortgages, commercial banks continued to be a pivotal link between the core and the capital markets.

Outside of the core, the financial system crafted by New Deal legislation consisted of capital-market-based financial institutions, investment banks, and insurance companies. Whereas "core" intermediaries gathered deposits and held assets, many of them nommarketable, customized portfolio loans, capital-market-based financial institutions underwrote, distributed, and held financing instruments with secondary markets. Because core intermediaries were prohibited from performing financial intermediation across state lines, interregional finance was performed largely by capital-market-based institutions.

The investment banking industry specialized in underwriting and distributing new issues of corporate equity and debt, most of the former to households (which owned over 90% of all corporate equity in 1950) and most of the latter to insurance companies (which faced regulatory limits on ownership of corporate equity). New Deal legislation did not envelope capital-market-based institutions in safety nets, but it did increase the level of regulatory oversight over the security markets by creating the Securities and Exchange Commission, which was charged with maintaining orderly securities markets and overseeing compliance with expanded disclosure and registration requirements and standards for public offerings of securities.

Corporate fixed investment has been financed primarily with retained earnings and depreciation allowances during the postwar period. Corporate bonds, purchased predominantly by life insurance companies, have been the primary source of external funds, followed by bank credit (used primarily for working capital) and mortgages. The stock market has played a relatively small role in financing the corporate sector, contributing only 8% of all external finance and 3% of total finance over 1945–70; instead the stock market's role has been to "facilitate the rearrangement of the asset and stock portfolios of individual investors and investor groups."[1]

1 See Lintner, "The Financing of Corporations," and Goldsmith, *Capital Mar-*

The central mechanism used to limit competition among core intermediaries was the Federal Reserve Board's Regulation Q, which prohibited the payment of interest on demand deposits and placed interest rate ceilings on savings and time deposits issued by banks. In addition, asset restrictions carved out distinct debt underwriting niches for various core intermediaries (commercial lending for commercial banks, housing finance for savings and loans and mutual savings bank, consumer lending for credit unions).

Broadening access to housing finance

In addition to providing a public safety net for designated "core" financial intermediaries, New Deal legislation expanded the role of the public sector in other directions as well. It created new public financial intermediaries and agencies which infused capital and liquidity into distressed financial institutions in the 1930s and expanded markets for private finance once the crisis passed. The discussion here will focus on the housing and nonfarm business sectors of the economy although similar programs were developed for agriculture as well.

In the housing sector, the Home Owners' Loan Corporation (HOLC), established in 1933, was authorized to sell government-guaranteed bonds and to use the proceeds to purchase defaulted home mortgages from financial institutions; these mortgages were then converted into performing loans by refinancing them as fully amortized twenty-year loans (instead of the short-term loans and five- to ten-year partially amortized loans with balloon payments underwritten previously). The HOLC (along with the Treasury) also subscribed to the capital of newly forming federal savings and loan associations.[2]

The Federal Housing Administration, established by the 1934 National Housing Act, provided insurance on loans to rehabilitate, construct, and acquire residential housing. Unlike conventional mortgages, FHA-insured mortgages were fully amortized loans with maturities of twenty-

ket Analysis and the Financial Accounts of the Nation. For a good discussion of institutional changes in the postwar U.S. equity market which focuses on the replacement of individual equity investors with institutional equity investors, see Kregel, "Institutional Investors and Financial Markets in Britain, the U.S.A. and Germany."

2 See Saulnier, Halcrow, and Jacoby, *Federal Lending and Loan Insurance*, ch. 8.

five or thirty years; they also had higher maximum loan-to-value ratios than conventional loans. In 1944, the Veterans Administration (VA) loan guarantee program was established, which had even more liberal underwriting criteria than the FHA program. These credit instruments broadened access to home ownership by reducing monthly mortgage payments and reducing the size of the down payment requirement, and were used disproportionately by middle-class home buyers.

FHA mortgage insurance changed housing finance underwriting criteria in two ways. First, FHA underwriting criteria were directly applied to a growing proportion of the stock of mortgage debt as financial institutions acquired FHA-insured mortgages. By 1953 FHA- and VA-insured mortgages comprised over half of the mortgage holdings of insured commercial banks, insured mutual savings banks, and life insurance companies.[3] Second, FHA and VA loans exerted a demonstration effect on conventional mortgages, which over time took on many of the characteristics of FHA and VA loans.[4]

The creation of the Federal National Mortgage Association (FNMA) in 1938 complemented the FHA's mortgage insurance programs. FNMA issued federally backed securities and purchased FHA- and VA-insured mortgages; as a "buyer of last resort," it reduced the liquidity risk associated with thirty-year mortgages. FNMA also "seasoned" mortgages as a direct lender in new FHA mortgage insurance programs with as-yet marginal market acceptance.

The FHA and VA mortgage insurance programs laid the basis for the eventual development of a national secondary market for insured mortgages. They created the basis for a secondary market by standardizing the mortgage instrument and appraisal techniques, which made the packaging of mortgages possible.[5] They were also a major factor in the transformation of mortgage banking companies into intermediaries between borrowers (builders and home buyers) and institutional investors, primarily insurance companies but also commercial banks, usually located in different geographic regions. Local correspondents of mortgage companies were particularly active in areas where the demand for housing finance

3 Ibid., p. 305.

4 Hayes, *Bank Lending Policy,* 1st ed., p. 152.

5 Jackson, in *Crabgrass Frontier,* shows that the FHA's appraisal techniques undervalued urban property and produced a suburban bias to FHA's programs, and therefore to metropolitan development.

exceeded the supply capacity of local core intermediaries, such as the Pacific, East North Central, and West South Central regions.[6]

The housing finance system which grew out of New Deal legislation, then, involved not only thrift institutions, but also commercial banks (which provided construction loans, "warehouse" loans for insured mortgages in the pipeline to institutional investors, and conventional mortgages), mortgage companies (which underwrote and packaged insured mortgages), and insurance companies (which held blocks of insured mortgages in portfolio). While direct participation by commercial banks in federally insured mortgages was limited, the credit quality of their residential construction and "warehouse" loans was predicated on the availability of permanent finance to the home buyer, which came to be predicated on FHA insurance.

In the housing finance system reorganized by New Deal legislation, then, the public sector absorbed credit risk and liquidity risk for private finance. Federal mortgage insurance was a credit-risk-pooling mechanism whose social cost took the form of the Treasury guarantee on the liabilities of the insuring entity. The federal government reduced liquidity risk for core intermediaries with deposit insurance, which stabilized the flow of funds into core intermediaries, and with lender of last resort lending for holders of federally insured mortgages. Again, to the extent that the liabilities of deposit insurance corporations were ultimately backed by the Treasury, the federal government absorbed some of the liquidity risk while reducing the level borne by private finance.

Broadening access to business finance

The federal role in nonfarm business finance took on similar forms to that in housing, but differed in the greater emphasis on direct lending. The latter was performed by the Reconstruction Finance Corporation (RFC), created by the RFC Act of 1932. The RFC was initially empowered to lend to distressed financial institutions and railroads, but its authority was expanded repeatedly, as circumstances demanded, to infuse capital into banks (1933) and to lend to private business (1934). Federal Reserve banks also received authority to lend directly to business in 1934.[7]

6 See Klaman, *The Postwar Rise of Mortgage Companies.*
7 See Saulnier et al., *Federal Lending,* ch. 7.

The RFC's direct loans filled a variety of capital market gaps. First, by having an intermediate term to maturity, the amortized "term" loans (five- to nine-year maturities) supplied by the RFC filled the gap between the short-term lending performed by commercial banks and the long-term finance provided by the capital market. Second, they served borrowers with marginal creditworthines due to the age of the firm, the age of the firm's industry, the size of the firm, and/or the degree of leverage of the firm's financial structure. Finally, they filled the gap between capital-surplus and capital-deficit regions, being placed disproportionately in the West South Central, Pacific, and East North Central regions.

The interest rate on RFC loans, in contrast to private sector loans, was invariant over the cycle and across borrowers. As a result of this policy, larger loans subsidized smaller loans. The RFC's interest rate was lower than those of commercial banks on smaller loans, especially smaller term loans, but higher on larger loans.

Much of the direct lending performed by the RFC and by Federal Reserve banks took the form of a deferred participation arrangement with commercial banks, under which a loan was underwritten by either the RFC or the bank, with the bank initially funding the loan, paying a participation fee to the RFC for its promise to purchase a specified percentage of the loan upon demand from the bank. Participation loans were larger on average than direct loans and involved primarily medium-sized and larger commercial banks seeking to meet loan requests that exceeded their legal loan limits.

Almost half of the participation loans originated between 1934 and 1947 were national defense loans made under wartime powers; the volume of participation loans and the average loan size rose sharply during WWII and the Korean War. The Federal Reserve Board responded to the financing requirements of defense mobilization with Regulation V, under which the federal government guaranteed loans to war contractors by any lending agency (including Federal Reserve Banks and the RFC).[8] Between 1934 and 1947, 60% of the participation loans went to manufacturing and mining firms, one-third of these going to metals and metal products firms.

After the RFC came under increasing criticism for competing with commercial banks in the business loan market, it was dissolved and replaced with the Small Business Administration (SBA) in 1953. Many of

8 Ibid., p. 485.

the RFC's defense mobilization functions were taken over by the Defense Department budget. The SBA developed the loan participation model into a loan guarantee program under which commercial banks performed credit evaluations and the SBA guaranteed up to 90% of the principal and interest on loans written for longer maturities than would otherwise be provided by the commercial banking system. While the SBA retained the RFC's emphasis on longer-term lending and on providing debt finance to smaller firms, it lost the industrial-targeting aspect of the RFC's lending program and increasingly supported lending to service sector firms in local economies.

The RFC made much of its impact on commercial bank lending policies through term loan participations with commercial banks, which demonstrated that "the risks of lending [to new, small enterprise] may be kept within tolerable limits by taking appropriate collateral security. Undoubtedly, many bankers who gained familiarity with lending operations . . . through participation in a defense loan guaranteed by a federal agency have been led to continue them without federal cooperation."[9]

This section has demonstrated how federal credit programs put in place following the Great Depression provided the underpinning to the expansion of two key sectors of the postwar economy, housing and defense. At the same time, they "undoubtedly exerted a net expansive influence on the markets for private financing institutions" by "relieving them of assets believed to be illiquid or undesirable" and by raising the demand for private credit both directly (as "marginal" business borrowers were seasoned into bank-worthy borrowers) and indirectly (e.g., as federal support for housing finance created new demands in the housing construction sector).[10]

In both business and housing finance, federal credit programs promoted long-term institutional intermediation, long-term debt finance provided within the context of a lender–borrower relationship. The amortized loan expanded the universe of qualifying borrowers and loosened the connection between past income and creditworthiness, which was particularly important for recently unemployed households and new firms. However, as the amortized loan found a permanent and growing place in the portfolios of thrift institutions, commercial banks, and insurance companies, the profitability of major intermediaries became to vary-

9 Ibid., p. 281.
10 Ibid., P. 282.

ing degrees reliant on an interest rate structure which would be transformed by growing inflationary pressures in the late 1960s.

3. THE TRANSFORMATION OF THE MACROECONOMIC ENVIRONMENT OF FINANCE

The macroeconomic environment of finance was transformed over the course of the postwar period from an environment that was consistent with New Deal–crafted financial institutions to one that was not. The dividing point between the two phases was the late 1960s–early 1970s, the period spanning the Vietnam War boom and the collapse of the Bretton Woods international monetary system.

Institutional factors shaping U.S. inflation policy played a central role in the transformation of the macroeconomic environment of finance. One important factor was the degree of independence of the Federal Reserve from the federal government. After the 1951 Accord between the Federal Reserve and the Treasury, the link between monetary policy and the management of the federal debt was weakened while the link between monetary policy and price inflation was strengthened. In addition, the Accord expressed the central bank's institutional preference for using the level of interest rates to control inflation, not more interventionist policies such as credit controls or binding income policies.[11]

Labor market institutions narrowed the range of choice of anti-inflation policy instruments as well. Adversarial industrial relations and decentralized decision making within the trade union movement made "the co-ordination of wage and price settings in individual markets with a national goal of overall wage and price stability [e.g., income policies] impossible."[12] Finally, an ideological belief in the social optimality of market outcomes placed a serious political limit on any inflation policy which exerted a significant degree of social control over either the allocation of credit or the distribution of income.

Adherence to the interest rate approach to inflation policy during the

11 Epstein and Schor, "The Federal Reserve–Treasury Accord and the Construction of the Postwar Monetary Regime," show that Truman's Treasury Department supported the Accord in order to block the Council of Economic Advisers' proposal to use credit controls instead.

12 See Cornwall, "Inflation as a Cause of Economic Stagnation." I have applied his general argument about the effect of labor market institutions on the feasibility of income policies to the specific case of the postwar U.S.

Vietnam War mobilization, instead of incomes policies, fiscal policy, or the demand-side credit controls which had been used during World War II and the Korean War, created a monetary regime which facilitated credit and price inflation in the 1970s, and would thereby have a long-lasting impact on core intermediaries and the supply of finance.[13]

1950–1966

This period was generally characterized by stability in interest rates, inflation rates, and exchange rates. On the real side of the economy, GNP growth was high by historical standards during this period, and recessions were increasingly mild. During the 1949–54 and 1954–58 business cycles, output declined 2.8% and 3.1%, respectively, from peak to trough; during the 1958–61 and 1961–70 cycles, output declined only 0.3% and 0.4%, respectively, from peak to trough.[14] Real output grew at an average annual rate of 3.8%.

The rate of inflation during this period was low and stable, averaging 2.2% and ranging between −1% and 3% in 1952–65. The gap between potential and actual GDP (the GDP gap) was positive for the last half of the 1948–66 period at the same time that actual GDP growth was strong by postwar standards, averaging 3.8% per year. The positive GDP gap of the late 1950s and early 1960s was not due to weak actual GDP growth on average, but rather to strong potential GDP growth which lifted the inflation ceiling on real economic growth and moderated inflationary pressures.

The design of monetary institutions together with the conduct of monetary policy also contributed to price stability. During this period, the Federal Reserve "leaned against the wind," allowing the Treasury bill rate to rise and free reserves (unborrowed reserves net of required reserves) to

13 "Demand-side" credit controls, which work by limiting the demand for credit as opposed to the supply, were used successfully during the Korean War mobilization. Regulation W increased the down payment requirement on consumer durables and set an upper limit to the repayment period; similarly, Regulation X increased the down payment requirement on higher-priced housing. Note that the effectiveness of such credit controls was enhanced by the widespread use of credit by households (one of the by-products of New Deal reforms). See Campagna, *U.S. National Economic Policy 1917–1985*, pp. 219–20.

14 See Howard Sherman, *The Business Cycle*, p. 16.

fall as real economic activity approached cyclical peaks.[15] As Treasury bill rates rose, the yield spread between Treasury bills and saving deposits at thrift institutions rose, as did the yield spread between long-term bonds (corporate and government) and mortgages, particularly guaranteed mortgages (the interest rates on which were subject to ceilings). The result was a flow of funds out of thrift institutions and a shift away from mortgages, especially guaranteed mortgages, by nonthrift housing lenders (commercial banks and insurance companies). Hence, a monetary ceiling was imposed on residential construction spending as the pace of economic activity accelerated, relieving aggregate demand pressure on prices during booms.[16]

Figure 4.1, showing the level of short-term and long-term interest rates over 1954–91, and Figure 4.2, showing the spread between long-term and short-term credit instruments over the same period, illustrate the distinctive structure of interest rates during the period before 1970, albeit one that began to disintegrate after 1966.

This structure is characterized by a general "stickiness," or invariance, of the long-term nominal interest rate vis-à-vis movements in the short-term nominal rate and the inflation rate: the long-term interest rate reflected the market's belief that long-term rates would continue to drift moderately upward, as they had in the recent past. These expectations were conditioned by the experienced stability of the long-term rate over the immediate postwar period, when the Federal Reserve "pegged" the long-term rate.[17] The generally low level of interest rates was the residual effect of the large stock of liquidity in the form of short-term Treasury bills (issued to finance the World War II defense mobilization) in the portfolios of corporations and banks.

As a result, during the expansions of 1954–57, 1958–60, and 1961–69, the long-term rate trended upward and exhibited mild cyclicality within a moderate range of interest rates while the short-term rate showed stronger cyclical fluctuations within a much wider band. Move-

15 The following discussion draws heavily on Cornwall, *Growth and Stability in a Mature Economy,* ch. 9.

16 In addition, Cornwall shows that with the onset of recessions and easy money, the flow of funds back into thrift institutions and the renewed availability of guaranteed mortgages stimulated residential construction, which led the economy out of recession.

17 Corporate bond rates, which were "pegged" to the government bond rate, were also stable over the cycle, as was the volume of corporate bond issues.

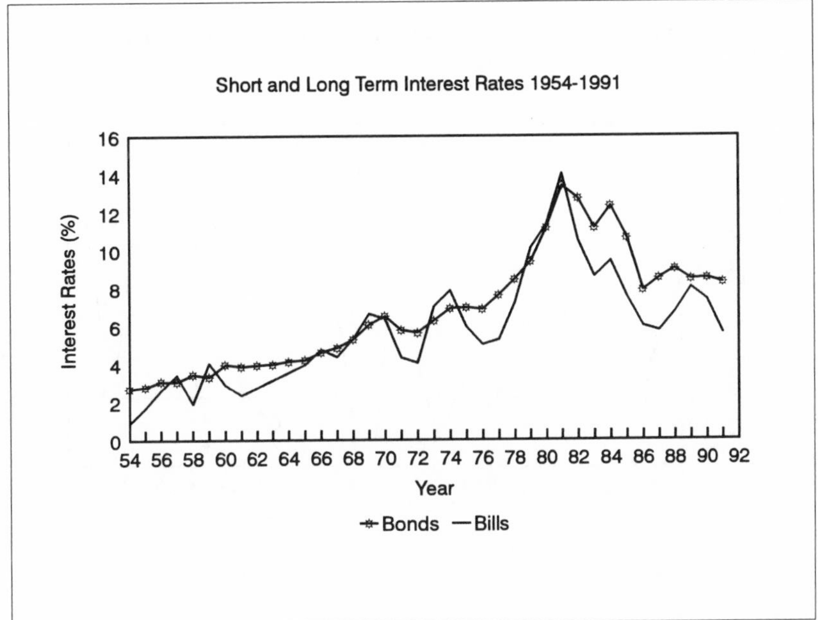

Figure 4.1. Yields on three-month Treasury bills and thirty-year Treasury bonds.

ments in short-term rates did not drive comparable movements in long-term rates. Neither did changes in the rate of inflation feed into long-term rates, as in 1954–56, when the inflation rate rose, or in 1957–60, when the inflation rate fell.

This interest rate environment, combined with stability in core intermediaries' deposit bases, encouraged longer-term financial intermediation and was one factor that induced liberalization in commercial lending policy during this period.[18] Term loans by large commercial banks were booked at progressively longer maturities during this period and reached a new population of firms, namely, growing, sub-prime firms. These firms lacked direct access to the capital market and needed flexible lending

18 According to one study of commercial bank lending policy in the postwar period, the policy of providing fixed-rate lending was based on "a view of the world which presumed that interest rates would fluctuate around a reasonably level trend and that setting a fixed rate in relationship to a historical average would be reasonable." See Hayes, *Bank Lending Policies,* 2d ed., p. 148.

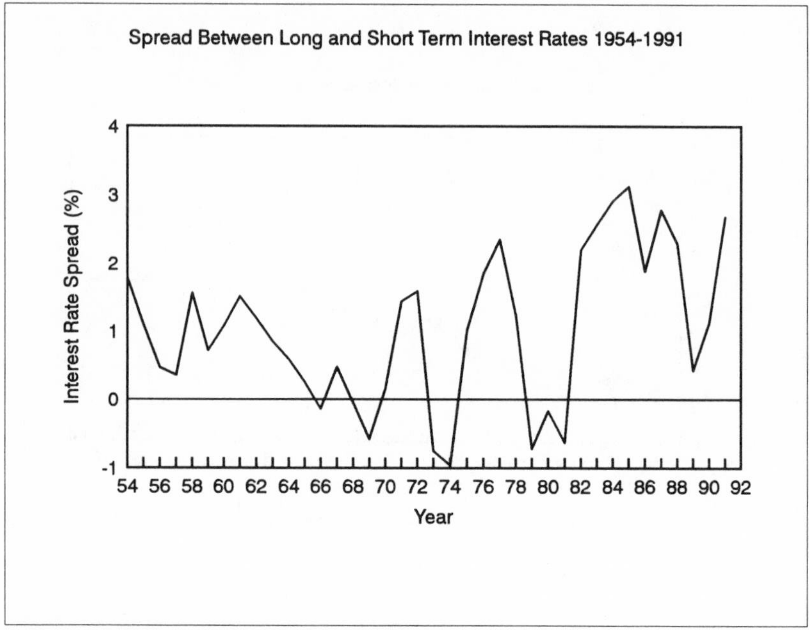

Figure 4.2. Yield on thirty-year Treasury bonds minus yield on three-month Treasury bills.

arrangements to accommodate the changing capital requirements characteristic of rapid growth. By the early 1960s, maturities on term loans had been extended from two to three years to five years.[19] By the early 1970s, many major commercial banks were booking ten- to twelve-year term loans for large prime borrowers.[20]

The spread, which is also an indicator of the shape of the yield curve, was positive at all phases of the cycle until 1966, when the pattern started to change. The yield curve flattened during expansions, as the Federal Reserve allowed short-term rates to rise, and then got steeper during recessions as short-term rates fell. As long as yield curves sloped upward, operating conditions were profitable at the margin for core intermediaries, which borrowed short and lent long.

19 Prior to the 1960s, banks were hesitant to lend at longer maturities for fear of a recurrence of the 1930s shrinkage of their deposit base. See Hayes, *Bank Lending Policies,* 1st ed., p. 101.

20 However, because they wanted to protect their ability to meet prime borrowers' needs during tight money periods, banks remained reluctant to lend to sub-prime borrowers at maturities longer than five years.

Throughout most of this period, commercial banks were protected from competition with the open money markets because market interest rates were below the regulated ceiling on their time deposits. However, the first episode of disintermediation, the flow of funds out of money center banks and into the open markets, took place during this period, in 1959. When Treasury bill rates rose above the ceiling on time deposits, corporations withdrew time deposits with large New York banks and purchased Treasury bills.

This instability in deposit bases undermined large banks' asset growth and potentially their ability to fulfill loan commitments. In order to attract corporate deposits back, New York banks introduced the large ($1 million and over) negotiable (resellable) certificates of deposit (CD) in 1961, when Treasury bill rates had dipped below the ceiling.[21] As Treasury bill rates rose above the 3% ceiling on six-month CDs between 1962 and 1965, regulators repeatedly prevented an outflow of funds to the money market by raising the ceiling on CDs.

The Bretton Woods system, which defined the parameters of the postwar international monetary regime, remained intact throughout this period. Under the Bretton Woods system, the dollar played the role of the key currency, meaning that its value was fixed in terms of gold, and other nations' exchange rates were then pegged to the dollar. The Bretton Woods system successfully created a stable international monetary framework for national economic growth up to the 1960s, when the "dollar shortage" gave way to the "dollar glut."[22]

The U.S. lost gold to its major trading partners every year between

21 The interest rate on negotiable CDs was still subject to a ceiling (3% in 1961). However, the ability to resell a 3% six-month time deposit before it matured elevated the effective yield on the time deposit above the lower (2.5% and 1%) ceilings placed on shorter-term time deposits offered by thrifts and smaller banks.

22 However, Volcker, citing Robert Triffin's *Gold and the Dollar Crisis,* noted that the founders of the Bretton Woods system had created "a world monetary system dependent upon American deficits [to build up stocks of the reserve currency and to finance economic growth], the very same deficits that everyone came to decry in the 1960s as destabilizing [insofar as they undermined confidence in the reserve currency]." Volcker and Gyohten, *Changing Fortunes,* p. 39. Keynes argued that another inherent flaw in the Bretton Woods system was its deflationary bias resulting from the fact that it contained adjustment mechanisms forcing deficit countries to adjust (deflate), but no adjustment mechanisms forcing surplus countries to adjust (inflate).

1958 and 1968; this both indicated declining confidence in the dollar and undermined the convertibility of the dollar into gold at the fixed price of $35.00. Starting in 1961, the U.S. took policy measures designed to stem the gold outflow, such as Roosa bonds, swap arrangements with foreign central banks, Operation Twist, and voluntary restraints on capital outflows. The accelerating inflation of the late 1960s caused growing price level disparities between the U.S. and Europe and Japan, further weakening foreign asset demand for the dollar.

In summary, between 1950 and 1966, the macroeconomic environment was conducive to the long-term financial intermediation at the core of the New Deal financing system. Short- and long-term interest rates were relatively stable around a gradually rising trend, and there were no international shocks to the domestic financial system. But by the mid-1960s, contradictions between a financing system centered around long-term financial intermediation and the modality of inflation policy were beginning to appear. Rising market interest rates were threatening the stability of money center banks' deposit bases and eroding their profitability. In addition, structural shifts in the international distribution of economic power were undermining the Bretton Woods system.

1966–1973

During the interim between the golden years of the 1960s and the turbulent years of the 1970s, tensions in the domestic and international monetary systems came to a head. Domestically, the will and ability of U.S. monetary and fiscal authorities to effectively address the Vietnam War inflation were tested and failed. The lack of social control over the price level destabilized domestic credit markets and caused international confidence in the dollar to erode to the crisis point.

Evidence of aggregate demand pressure on prices became evident in 1966, when the rate of inflation rose from 1.9% to 3.5% amid other signs that GNP was rapidly approaching full-employment output. There was some restraint in the federal budget, but not on the scale needed to adequately slow the growth of private sector demand: acknowledging the thinness of public support for the Vietnam War, President Johnson refused to propose a tax increase in the 1966 budget.[23] In addition, the

23 Paul Volcker, who worked for the Treasury Department during the Kennedy and part of the Johnson administrations, believes that the failure to exercise

wage and price guidepost policy, which had worked reasonably well in 1962–65, broke down as the rising inflation rate eroded political support for the guideposts.[24]

Given the inadequacy of the fiscal policy response, the burden of inflation policy fell on the Federal Reserve. The monetary experience of 1966–70 deserves detailed attention here. A pattern of interaction between the monetary authorities and the private sector developed during this period which became characteristic of episodes of credit market instability in the 1970s and which led to the deregulation of interest rates.

In the summer of 1966, the Board of Governors tried to slow the rate of growth of bank loans with supply-side credit controls.[25] It raised the reserve requirement on CDs and kept the ceiling on CDs below the Treasury bill rate. Money center banks lost corporate deposits to the open market; "Lending to all but the most established and necessitous [business] customers was halted abruptly."[26] In response, corporations turned to the commercial paper market as both suppliers and demanders of funds, and major banks liquidated municipal securities and turned to the Eurodollar market as a substitute source of funds. In 1966, the Board of Governors responded to this circumvention of its policy by the large banks by announcing its intent to place a reserve requirement on Eurodollar CDs in order to control the growth of bank credit funded through the Eurodollar market. However, the board took no action in 1966, and an inflow of funds through the Eurodollar market offset the outflow of funds from CDs.

The rate of growth of overall bank credit did fall in 1966, but growth in business loans remained rapid as banks rationed nonprime loan customers. The Federal Reserve eased credit after residential construction plummeted and crisis threatened the municipal security market.[27] The Federal Reserve promptly supplied liquidity through the discount win-

fiscal restraint during the Vietnam War buildup "would undermine the credibility of the Keynesian doctrine that was the foundation for the . . . New Economics . . .," and was the initiating event of the subsequent inflation of the 1970s. *Changing Fortunes,* p. 38.

24 See Campagna, *National Economic Policy,* pp. 318–21.

25 "Supply-side" credit controls seek to slow the growth of bank credit by restricting banks' ability to lend.

26 See Wojnilower, "The Central Role of Credit Crunches in Recent Financial History," p. 287.

27 See Wolfson, *Financial Crises,* pp. 49–50.

dow and brought open market interest rates below the ceiling on CDs in early 1967.

By the summer of 1967 the growth recession was over, the threat to place reserve requirements on Eurodollars had been withdrawn, and Federal Reserve Chair William McChesney Martin was referring to the Eurodollar market as a "safety valve." It was a safety valve in two senses. First, it prevented large banks from pulling deposits away from thrifts and smaller banks when open market rates rose above the ceiling on CDs again later in 1967.[28] Second, by financing the U.S. balance of payments deficit and thereby lifting the monetary ceiling (albeit only until 1969), the Eurodollar market became the "ad hoc means of war finance": the U.S. used the Eurodollar market to monetize the balance of payments deficit driven by the military buildup.[29]

After 1967, the expansion and the defense buildup resumed with vigor. Nominal aggregate demand expanded 9.2% in 1968 and 7.9% in 1969; the rate of inflation rose to 4.7% in 1968 and 6.2% in 1969. Short-term rates also rose and broke through the 5%, 6%, and 7% barriers for the first time in the postwar period, in 1967, 1968, and 1969, respectively; the yield curve was inverted for two years (1968–70), the longest period in postwar experience.[30] However, the rise in rates did little to slow the growth in credit; annual business short-term credit growth rose from 8% in 1968 to 20% in 1969.

The Eurodollar market performed its "safety valve" function throughout the expansion, until 1969, when the Bundesbank enforced the balance of payments constraint on domestic expansion. In order to force the U.S. to finance the war out of domestic resources, the Bundesbank signalled that it was considering revaluing the mark, which convinced the Federal Reserve to place reserve requirements on Eurodollar deposits. A credit crunch ensued, followed by recession in 1970.[31] When Penn Central's default on its commercial paper in June 1970 threatened borrowers in that market with an unexpected cutoff of funds, the Federal Reserve

28 In 1966, when the ceiling on bank CDs was held below open market interest rates, large banks attracted funds away from thrift institutions and smaller banks by issuing $100,000 CDs, whose yields exceeded those of thrifts' and banks' time deposits. See note 22 and Wolfson, *Financial Crises,* p. 48.

29 See Dickens, "The Great Inflation and U.S. Monetary Policy in the Late 1960s."

30 The short-term rate referred to is that on three-month Treasury bills.

31 See Dickens, "Great Inflation," pp. 12–14.

responded by opening the discount window wide and suspending the ceiling on short-term CDs, allowing the money center banks to act as lenders of last resort.

In the international arena, U.S. inflation and balance of payments deficits over 1966–70 hastened the demise of the Bretton Woods monetary system. In late 1967, the U.S. balance of payments deteriorated badly under the pressure of heavy public and private capital exports, stimulating a speculative movement into gold and out of the dollar. The speculation was stemmed by mandatory restraints on capital exports in 1968, but the relief was temporary. In anticipation of another serious speculative attack on the dollar, President Nixon suspended the convertibility of the dollar into gold in 1971. Between 1971 and 1973, a modified version of Bretton Woods allowing for exchange rate movements within a band around "central values" was put in place, but gave way in 1973 to floating exchange rates after renewed speculation against the dollar.

The monetary events of 1966–70 were formative in reshaping the domestic and international monetary regimes. In the domestic arena, the experience demonstrated the limits and consequences of anti-inflation policy working through higher market interest rates.[32] It showed that this kind of policy is only as effective as the demand for credit is responsive to increases in the rate of interest; during 1966–70, the rise in interest rates did little to slow the demand for credit in the context of vigorous growth in nominal aggregate demand.[33] It also showed that monetary restraint would give way to monetary ease whenever financial crisis threatened – supporting earlier credit expansion. Finally, it became clear during this period that the willingness of foreign portfolio managers, private and

32 This discussion draws heavily on Wojnilower, "Central Role of Credit Crunches."

33 Pollin, "Stability and Instability in the Debt–Income Relationship," p. 349, argues that around 1966, there was a structural shift in business demand for credit which had the character of "necessitous borrowing" in light of declining profits. Similarly, Goldsmith, *Capital Market Analysis*, p. 35, notes the "spectacular" increase in corporate bond issues in 1965–70, which was "the result of a considerable increase in corporations' fixed capital expenditures and the difficulty of expanding bank and mortgage credit . . . it seems hardly an exaggeration to say that on the demand side the sharp acceleration in the supply of corporate bonds was the most important single factor tightening the capital market in the late 1960s and driving up the level of long-term interest rates."

public, to hold dollars had become a binding constraint on U.S. monetary policy and a fatally weak link in the Bretton Woods system.

The monetary experience of the late 1960s brought about changes in the conduct of domestic monetary policy. As Wojnilower has argued, the 1966 credit crunch gave an "impetus . . . to the search for alternatives to flash points such as rate ceilings that cornered the Federal Reserve in stark yes-or-no situations. The circumstances were ripened for a shift of policy focus to the monetary aggregates."[34]

1973–1980

The 1970s, in contrast to the golden era of 1950–66, was a period of tremendous volatility in interest rates, inflation rates, and exchange rates in the context of a rise in interest rates and the inflation rate and a depreciation of the dollar over the course of the decade. These developments led ultimately to a dramatic shift in the Federal Reserve's operating techniques in 1979.

In addition, GNP growth slowed in the 1970s, and the deepest recession of the postwar period was experienced. The average rate of real output growth fell to 2.5%, and real output fell 4.6% during the recession of 1974–75.

As Figure 4.3 shows, the level and volatility of the rate of inflation rose considerably during the 1970s. The rise in the average decadal rate of inflation was propelled by two dramatic upward spurts in the rate of inflation, in 1973–74 and in 1977–80. Numerous factors were at work, including the slowdown in potential GNP growth and productivity growth after 1973, inflation in primary commodity prices (notably oil), the downward stickiness of prices and money wages during recessions, the building of expected inflation into wage and price increases, and the depreciation of the dollar after the initiation of floating exchange rates in 1973.[35]

34 See Wojnilower, "Central Role of Credit Crunches," p. 288. In fact, Federal Reserve Chair Burns introduced monetary aggregates as an operating target for the first time in 1970.

35 On downward wage stickiness, see Julie Schor, "Wage Flexibility, Social Welfare Expenditures, and Monetary Restrictiveness." By the 1970s, labor and commodity markets had taken on the quality of "fix-price" markets in which, as Cornwall describes in "Inflation as a Cause of Economic Stagnation," p. 106, wages and prices "do not respond directly to downward shifting demand curves unless such shifts are large and prolonged."

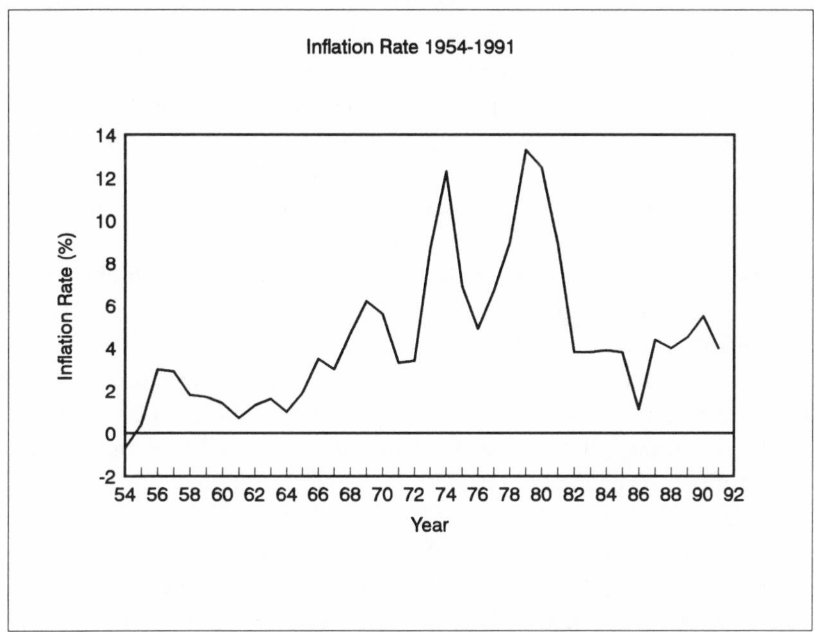

Figure 4.3. Annual rates of increase in consumer prices.

Furthermore, the monetary mechanism which had slowed residential construction spending and price level inflation during earlier booms was no longer in place. With the relaxation of interest rate ceilings on thrift deposits and the growth of the secondary mortgage market in the 1970s (see below), rising nominal interest rates during the boom did not lead to an outflow of funds from the housing sector, as they had in earlier postwar booms.[36] In addition, real estate was in strong demand as an inflation hedge because nominal mortgage rates, while high by historical standards, were low in relation to expected rates of increase in house prices. In the absence of an effective monetary ceiling, nominal aggregate demand grew rapidly, reaching annual rates of 16% in the third quarter of 1978.

Inflationary pressure fed directly into the short-term credit market.

36 Wojnilower emphasizes this point in "Central Role of Credit Crunches," concluding that "The institutional changes of [the 1970s] to free financial markets from kinks that caused crunches have also greatly intensified the propensity of the economy to excessive credit expansion and inflation" (pp. 278–79).

Rising rates of inflation in 1973–74 and 1977–79 stimulated growth in the demand for short-term credit by widening the gap between nominal internal funds (linked to the past prices) and nominal working capital spending (linked to current prices). The resulting rise in short-term interest rates, reinforced by contractionary monetary policy, did little to inhibit either business credit demand or the supply of credit; growth in business short-term credit demand proceeded at a rapid pace (reaching annual rates of 30% at the interest rate peaks of 1974 and 1980).[37]

The long-term end of the credit market was slower to respond to rising rates of inflation compared with the short-term end of the market. Figure 4.4 shows the real long-term interest rate, the difference between the nominal long-term interest rate and the current rate of inflation. A fall in the real long-term rate denotes a failure of the nominal rate to keep up with a rise in the inflation rate. Real long-term rates fell from the outset of both inflationary spurts and were negative throughout the periods of accelerating rates of inflation, 1972–74 and 1978–80.

Long-term interest rates were also slow to respond to rising short-term interest rates. While long-term rates showed more cyclicality during 1970–77 than they had before, they were still substantially more stable than short-term rates around an upward trend not substantially steeper than that of the 1960s. As a result, as shown in Figure 4.2, there were large shifts in the yield curve during 1970–77, and the yield curve was inverted for prolonged periods of time during the "tight money" phases of business cycles (1973–74 and 19[illegible]-81).

These prolonged periods of negative real interest rates and inverted yield curves broke the pattern of stability in long-term nominal rates; bondholders and bond speculators had been burned, and ceased to believe that future long-term rates would follow a moderate upward trend.

37 In fact, the rise in rates during booms may have stimulated "credit hoarding" – borrowing to avoid higher rates in the future or future constraints on the availability of funds. See Moore, "Wages, Bank Lending, and the Endogeneity of Credit Money," on the interest-insensitivity of the business demand for short-term credit.

At this time, the Federal Reserve was targeting the Federal Funds rate believed to be consistent with a permissible range of money supply growth. As Earley and Evans point out in "The Problem Is Bank Liability Management," the Federal Reserve's use of the money supply as a control variable hid the "credit explosion" of the 1970s, when the narrowly defined money supply grew on average at an annual rate of 5% while bank credit and total credit grew twice as fast, and at roughly the same rate as nominal GNP.

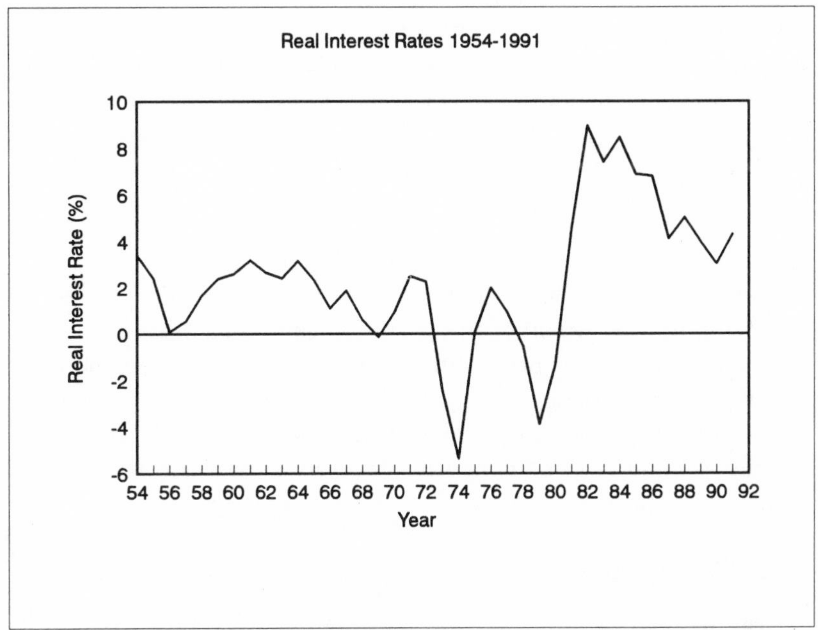

Figure 4.4. Inflation-adjusted yield on thirty-year government bonds.

After 1977, the "stickiness" of the nominal long-term interest rate vis-à-vis increases in the inflation rate broke down, and the nominal rate rose from 7% to 11% in 1980, with much of this increase concentrated in 1979. Long-term rates showed more sensitivity to changes in current short-term rates after 1979, when long-term rates climbed an unprecedented 200 basis points in the course of a year.

In the late 1970s, the rapid inflation in both the long and short ends of the credit market was intensified by an unstable dynamic linking the two. On the one hand, increases in short-term interest rates started to weigh more heavily in the formation of bond speculators' interest rate expectations. On the other hand, the rise in long-term nominal rates accelerated the rise in short-term rates as borrowers sought to borrow short-term in order to avoid locking into high long-term rates.

The dollar lost much of its exchange value against foreign currencies during the 1970s, with major losses in value taking place during the inflationary surges of 1973–74 and 1977–80. Real U.S. interest rates were below those of its major trading partners from late 1978 until 1981, weakening foreign demand for the dollar. Another exchange crisis threatened in late 1978, requiring a large-scale "rescue" of the dollar by foreign central banks and the IMF, augmented by a full percentage-point increase in the discount rate. After strengthening in the beginning of 1979, the dollar weakened again in the summer; President Carter appointed Paul Volcker Chair of the Federal Reserve soon thereafter.[38]

1980–1993

In accepting his appointment, Volcker announced that the Federal Reserve's top priority would be to squeeze the embedded inflation expectations out of wage and price setters in the economy through monetary restraint. To achieve this, the Federal Reserve abandoned interest rate targeting (increases in which had, in Volcker's view, been too cautious to be effective) and targeted nonborrowed reserves, purportedly to control money supply growth, instead.

After a large decline in real output in the second quarter of 1980, the Federal Reserve eased its target, and interest rates fell sharply while the rate of inflation continued to rise. The Federal Reserve returned to a policy of restrained growth in nonborrowed reserves in late 1980 and stuck with it well into the deep recession of 1981–82. Interest rates reached their postwar peak after the onset of recession as necessitous borrowing against declines in current income drove short-term credit demand. In 1981, the rate on three-month Treasury bills approached 15% while the Federal Funds rate reached 19%, and the prime rate reached 20%.

This was a high-interest-rate inflation policy with a vengeance; in contrast to past episodes of policy-induced higher interest rates, this time rates were allowed to reach whatever level was necessary to slow the growth in nominal spending. The unemployment rate rose from 7.6% in 1981 to 10.8% at the end of 1982; the capacity utilization rate in manufacturing fell from 78.5% in 1981 to 67% at the end of 1982; real output fell 3.3% from peak to trough; and the GDP gap reached the postwar high of 6% of actual GDP in late 1982. The sharp and prolonged decline in aggregate demand produced enough slack in labor and product markets to weaken labor's bargaining power and reduce the rate of inflation, which started to fall in 1981–82.

38 Georgian banker and Carter advisor Bert Lance sent Carter the message that "if he [Carter] appoints Volcker, he will be mortgaging his re-election to the Federal Reserve." See Greider, *Secrets of the Temple,* p. 47.

During the expansion of 1982–90, the inflation rate remained in the 3–4% range for the most part, dipping as low as 1.1% in 1986. While nominal interest rates fell as well, they did not fall as much as the rate of inflation; this was particularly true of long-term interest rates. After-inflation long-term rates remained "stuck" at historically high levels throughout the expansion and hovered in the 6–8% range during 1983–86, dipped down to 4% in 1987, then stayed in the 4–6% range during the 1990–91 recession and into the subsequent recovery. Real U.S. interest rates exceeded those of its foreign trading partners from 1981–86, fuelling the appreciation of the dollar and putting downward pressure on import prices.

Similarly, the spread between long-term and short-term interest rates was stuck at historically high levels throughout much of the 1982–90 expansion (falling only with the rise in short-term rates at the end of the expansion). The long-term rate was particularly sticky downwards during the 1990–91 recession, when the spread reached the postwar high of 400 basis points.

The steep yield curves characteristic of much of the period after 1982 and the high level of real interest rates reflected the persistence of inflation fears in the bond market.[39] The falling inflation rates of the 1980s were contingent on the maintenance of high rates of unemployment which weakened labor; the 1980s did not establish that the U.S. had found a way to control inflation when labor markets are close to full employment. Thus, the possibility of a repeat of high interest rates in the future remains latent in labor market and central banking institutions. So long as this is true, low long-term real interest rates depend on restrictive aggregate demand policy and slow economic growth.

4. THE INSTITUTIONAL RESPONSE OF FINANCES

The transformations in the macroeconomic environment associated with stagflation (slow growth with inflation) led to a restructuring of the financial system, as its major components – core intermediaries, financial markets, and regulatory agencies – responded to the rising levels of interest rate risk and credit risk.

After 1966, stagflation exposed financial institutions, particularly core

39 My colleague Tracy Mott has noted that the bond market acts not on the basis of its own inflation expectations, but on the basis of its perception of the Federal Reserve's inflation expectations, because when the Federal Reserve starts to worry about inflation, interest rates rise.

intermediaries, to higher levels of both interest rate risk (as interest rates rose and fluctuated widely) and credit risk (as GDP growth slowed). In response, commercial banks and thrifts took a variety of steps to insulate themselves against or compensate for rising interest rate risk and credit risk. The less regulated open market segment of the financial system seized on the opportunities presented by the weakness and problems of core intermediaries, and has grown in relative importance. Finally, regulators of core intermediaries reacted to the problems of "their" industry by easing regulations in the early 1980s, then tightening them in the early 1990s.

Operating problems of core intermediaries

The rise in interest rates in the 1970s, and particularly the rapid rise in rates in the late 1970s, posed two problems for long-term institutional intermediation: fund shifting and profit squeezing. Fund shifting is the movement of funds among intermediaries or from intermediaries to the open markets in response to changing relative yields among saving vehicles. Profit squeezing occurred when core intermediaries' return on funds did not keep up with the rising cost of funds because of the older long-term fixed-rate loans in their portfolios. Both problems were experienced to varying degrees by thrift institutions, commercial banks, and insurance companies.

Thrift institutions (savings and loans and mutual savings banks) suffered fund shifting to commercial banks and the open market during tight money periods throughout the earlier part of the postwar period. As noted earlier, such thrift disintermediation helped prevent excessive aggregate demand pressure on the price level and ended with the onset of recession and lower prices.

However, in the early 1960s, thrift disintermediation of a noncyclical and potentially permanent character took place as commercial banks in major urban markets, having exhausted the ability to fund asset growth by selling government securities, started to attract large-denomination consumer deposits away from thrifts. The result was interest rate competition between thrifts and banks and the erosion of thrifts' profitability. In 1966, this competitive escalation in interest rates was brought to a halt by the extension of interest rate ceilings to thrifts, set at twenty-five basis points above the ceiling on bank deposits, and by the Federal Reserve's decision not to allow the ceilings to rise as open market rates rose.

After 1966, thrifts' small deposits were protected from commercial bank raiding, and regulation Q ceilings, constant through the 1970s, preserved profit margins. However, the problem of fund shifting to the open money market remained, intensifying in the mid-1970s as the widening gap between money market rates and the rate on savings deposits induced entry by money market mutual funds. Money market mutual funds offered the opportunity to earn money market yields to small savers who could not buy money market instruments (with denominations of at least $100,000) directly.[40]

In the late 1970s, thrifts were given the authority to issue money market certificates, which enabled them to arrest fund shifting to mutual funds.[41] However, this only substituted the profit squeezing problem for the fund shifting problem. While the yield curve was inverted in 1978–82, thrifts were paying higher interest rates on money market certificates than they were charging on new mortgages; insured savings and loans had operating losses throughout 1979–82 as a result.

Major commercial banks, as noted in the previous section, first experienced fund shifting to the open market in the late 1950s; they responded by developing a new deposit instrument that evaded interest ceilings on short-term deposits (six-month negotiable CDs). The new instrument was effective in preventing fund shifting out of money center banks until 1966, when the ceiling was held below open market rates; however, other instruments for preventing fund shifting were developed (including Eurodollar deposits and commercial paper issued by bank holding companies), and by 1973 the ceilings on large-denomination negotiable CDs were suspended, never to be reinstated.

After 1970, major commercial banks did not lose deposits during tight money phases of the cycle, but they did face a profit squeeze since their interest-sensitive liabilities exceeded their interest-sensitive assets.[42] Large banks' term loans, which had become a significant proportion of their commercial loan portfolio, kept banks' interest earnings from keeping up with increases in short-term interest rates. However, at the end of the

40 Money market mutual funds buy large pools of money market instruments and sell small-denomination ownership shares in the pool to investors.

41 The money market certificate required a $10,000 minimum deposit (the minimum denomination of Treasury bills) and its interest rate was tied to the six-month Treasury bill.

42 Therefore, when short-term interest rates rose, the cost of funds rose more rapidly than the return on funds, which was a blend of higher interest rates on new loans and lower interest rates on old loans.

1970s, when interest rates were at their most volatile, the return on bank equity rose for both large banks and small banks: large banks had adjusted to the volatile interest rate environment (see below), and small banks had fewer interest-sensitive liabilities than assets (so that when interest rates rose, their return on funds rose faster than their cost of funds).[43] Bank earnings, unlike thrift earnings, were relatively immune to the spike in interest rates at the end of the 1970s.

Life insurance companies also experienced disintermediation during the 1970s. As the yield on conventional life insurance policies fell relative to open market investment opportunities, voluntary terminations of life insurance policies rose. In addition, as open market rates rose above the regulated interest rate ceilings on policy loans (5–8%), policyholders took advantage of the opportunity to borrow at rates lower than prevailing market rates.[44] As a result, life insurance companies were forced to substitute low-interest-earning policy loans for higher-yielding market securities.[45]

While thrifts and life insurance companies were more exposed to rising interest rate risk than commercial banks, credit risk disproportionately affected commercial banks. Mortgage insurance protected thrifts and life insurance companies against rising default risk (mortgage delinquencies rose steadily between 1978 and 1986) on the insured segment of their mortgage portfolios (mortgages with a 20% down payment or less); the large percentage of owner equity was a cushion against default risk on the non-insured segments of mortgage portfolios. In contrast, commercial banks were not insured against the credit risk which emerged after the deep recession of 1981–82 and the disinflation of 1982–86.

Disinflation was most dramatic in the food, energy, and housing sectors: the rate of inflation in food prices fell from 11% in 1979 to 2.1% in 1983, in energy prices from 30.9% in 1980 to 0.7% in 1983, and in upper Midwest housing prices from 10.7% in 1977–80 to 1.9% in

43 See Flannery, "How Do Changes in Market Interest Rates Affect Bank Profits?"

44 This was a contractual obligation written into traditional life insurance policies.

45 See Curry and Warshawsky, "Life Insurance Companies in a Changing Environment," p. 237, who note that in 1980, life insurance companies were earning 8.06% on their assets, far below the 11.94% yield on corporate bonds.

1980–83.[46] The quality of commercial and industrial loans in these sectors deteriorated as nominal income and asset growth fell far below that expected when the loans were contracted; the result was higher rates of loan losses and bank failures between 1982 and 1985, particularly in states with important agriculture and energy sectors. Falling commodity prices, amplified by the rising value of the dollar, adversely affected the performance of loans extended by money center banks to developing countries as well.

Rise of market-based intermediaries

Table 4.1 shows that the relative share of core intermediaries in total assets owned by financial intermediaries has fallen from 88% in 1950 to 56% in 1990, while that of pension funds has risen from 8% to 26% and that of market-based intermediaries from 4% to 18%. Market-based intermediaries either raise funds primarily from the open money and capital markets or acquire assets primarily from the open money and capital markets. The open market has also gained at the expense of financial intermediaries, particularly banks; the commercial paper market's share of short-term business finance rose from 3% in 1966 to 15% in the early 1990s.

Finance companies, money market mutual funds, and the commercial paper market, which D'Arista and Schlesinger have described as the "parallel banking system," accounted for much of the growth in market-based intermediation. Money market mutual funds issue shares and invest in money market instruments, notably commercial paper; finance companies borrow from banks and the open markets, notably the commercial paper market, and lend to businesses and households.[47] The unregulated parallel banking system has had distinct cost advantages over core intermediaries.

Money market mutual funds pay higher yields on shares than commercial banks can pay on comparable bank products because of their lower costs of intermediation. Money market mutual funds are not required to

46 The rate of disinflation in energy prices is distorted by the 1979 oil price shock. Rates of disinflation in housing prices varied across metropolitan areas, but were larger in local economies with important agriculture and energy sectors.

47 See D'Arista, "The Parallel Banking System."

Table 4.1. *Percentage of total assets owned by financial intermediaries, 1950–90*

	1950	1960	1970	1980	1990
Core intermediaries	88	78	74	70	56
Commercial banks	52	38	38	37	30
Savings & loans	6	12	14	15	10
Mutual savings banks	8	7	6	4	2
Credit unions	—	1	1	2	2
Life insurance cos.	22	20	15	12	12
Pension funds and other insurance	8	23	18	21	26
Private pension funds	2	6	9	12	14
State & local pension trusts	2	12	5	5	7
Casualty insurance cos.	4	5	4	4	5
Market-based intermediaries	4	8	9	9	18
Finance companies	3	5	5	5	7
Mutual funds	1	3	4	2	6
Money market funds	—	—	—	2	5

Source: Federal Reserve System, Flow of Funds Accounts, various years.

hold reserves against their shares, and information costs on open market securities (they acquire primarily bank CDs, government securities, and commercial paper) are low. Similarly, growth in the volume of funds raised through the commercial paper market has been propelled over the long run by the lower cost of commercial paper compared with bank loans; particularly rapid short-term growth occurred when open market interest rates rose above the interest rate ceilings on regulated deposits.

In the arena of business finance, the shrinking share of bank loans has been offset by the rising share of the commercial paper market and finance companies. The growing share of market-based intermediaries and the open money and security markets have not occurred entirely at the expense of commercial banks. Although commercial banks have lost shares of loan markets per se, they have also found new sources of revenue growth in the rise of market-based intermediaries, such as lending to finance companies and providing backup letters of credit for issuers of commercial paper.

While the commercial paper market is generally available only to large corporations with good credit quality, finance companies serve households and businesses with marginal credit quality (although this is not the only market they serve). Much of the direct lending performed by finance companies finances finished good inventories in the trade sector and purchases of equipment by businesses.[48] For the most part, larger finance companies are owned by manufacturing or retail corporations; of these, many are "captives," meaning that they finance only the sales or operations of their parents, while others provide finance to "third parties engaged in activities unrelated to the parent."[49]

In addition to inventory finance and asset-based finance, finance companies provide secured, revolving credit. According to Harris, "In [the] most common form [of revolving credit], a firm offers its accounts receivables as security . . . and credit is limited to 75–85% of eligible receivables. . . . The outstanding loan amount varies over time since extensions are tied to receivables and repayments are coordinated with receipts." Such finance involves intensive monitoring by the finance company and "is used to accommodate new businesses, small- and medium-sized firms experiencing relatively fast growth, and companies having temporary business difficulties."[50] The interest rate on such loans is "two to five percentage points and more above the prime lending rate," according to Harris, reflecting monitoring costs, lender's assessment of default risk, and the limited alternatives of borrowers.

The broader significance of the rise of market-based intermediation lies not in its implications for the profitability of the commercial banking industry in and of itself, but in its implications for the institutional context of lending decisions. With the declining role of commercial banks in the underwriting step of the lending process comes a loss of "relationship lending" in which the long-term profitability of the lender is tied to the long-term profitability of the borrower. In addition, as lending decisions are increasingly severed from deposit gathering, so is the link between the long-term profitability of the lender and the long-term viability of the local or regional economy which is the source of the lender's deposit base.[51]

48 See Harris, "Finance Companies as Business Lenders."

49 See D'Arista, "Parallel Banking System."

50 See Harris, "Finance Companies."

51 Another problem, one emphasized by D'Arista, is that as the share of lending

Financial deregulation

Regulatory restrictions on operations of core intermediaries were progressively relaxed between the 1960s and the early 1980s to help core intermediaries grow out of the problems of competition from the open market and interest rate risk. This discussion will be limited to the relaxation of two types of regulations, interest rate ceilings and asset restrictions.

The money center banks, with a customer base dominated by large corporate depositor-borrowers, were the first to face competition from the open market. The Federal Reserve Board of Governors, which had the authority to levy and change commercial bank interest rate ceilings, first relaxed interest rate ceilings in the early 1960s, when the ceiling on three-month negotiable CDs was repeatedly lifted as open market interest rates rose above the previous ceiling. Ceilings on three-month negotiable CDs were eliminated in 1970, followed by the elimination of ceilings on longer-term negotiable CDs in 1973.

Ceilings on smaller time deposits were amended in the 1970s, then eliminated altogether in the early 1980s. In the 1970s, a hierarchy of interest rate ceilings was created as higher ceilings were allowed for longer-term time deposits. The 1980 Depository Institution Deregulation and Monetary Control Act (DIDMCA) called for the "orderly phase-out" of deposit interest rate ceilings and allowed depository institutions (a then-new phrase reflecting the growing similarity of thrifts and commercial banks) to pay interest on personal transactions deposits. The Garn–St. Germain Act of 1982 authorized banks and thrifts to issue money market deposit accounts to respond to the competitive challenge from money market mutual funds, and in January 1983 Super NOW accounts were also authorized. Interest rates on these accounts were not regulated, allowing banks and thrifts to compete with the open market during the transition to full interest rate deregulation.

Commercial banks and thrifts were also authorized to acquire a broad-

of the less regulated "parallel banking system" rises, society's protection against lender imprudence, discrimination, and community disinvestment falls. Dymski, in "Is Intermediation Redundant in the U.S. Economy?" argues that with the loss of bank intermediation comes a loss of associated "spillover benefits" and asset devaluation, which will be felt in those communities that are most dependent on bank finance – communities of small businesses and working-class households.

er menu of earning assets. DIDMCA allowed federally chartered savings and loans to place up to 20% of their assets in consumer loans, commercial paper, and corporate debt, assets which were previously prohibited. The Federal Home Loan Bank Board, which regulated federal savings and loan associations, authorized variable-rate mortgages in 1979. The Garn–St. Germain Depository Institutions Act of 1982 (a "rescue operation" for the thrifts) made more radical changes in this area, allowing S&Ls to place up to 55% of their assets in a combination of three types of commercial loans – loans secured by commercial real estate (up to 40%), secured or unsecured commercial loans (up to 5%), and leases (up to 10%); in addition, thrifts were allowed to make real estate loans without any down payment.

Garn–St. Germain also loosened regulatory restrictions on national banks. It raised the limit on the percentage of capital and surplus that they could lend to any individual borrower from 10% to 25%.[52] In addition, the act removed loan-to-value ceilings on various types of real estate loans, ranging from loans on unimproved land (which had been set at 66.7%) to loans on improved structures (which had been set at 90%).[53]

Congress was concerned not only with enhancing core intermediaries' ability to compete with the open market, but also with improving the Federal Reserve's ability to control the money supply, which had been eroded by the exodus of commercial banks from the Federal Reserve System in order to avoid the attendant reserve requirements. The DIDMCA extended uniform reserve requirements to all depository institutions and mandated them to disclose information on money and credit aggregates to the Federal Reserve; access to this information was deemed essential for the new nonborrowed reserve-targeting approach of Federal Reserve monetary policy.

52 This increased the largest loan a national bank with a given amount of capital could offer, improving its competitive position vis-à-vis the open market.

53 See Litan, "Banks and Real Estate: Regulating the Unholy Alliance." Litan notes (pp. 195–96) that "at the beginning of the [1980s] the typical bank did not finance unimproved land; when it financed construction it did so only when a developer had a commitment for 'takeout' financing in hand; and commercial mortgages were provided only where developers put up at least 30% of the money. By the end of the decade, land loans were common, construction loans often were provided without advance takeout commitments, and many developers put up as little as 10% equity."

After the consequences of deregulation became clear over the course of the 1980s, the regulatory pendulum swung in the opposite direction in the early 1990s, to which we return below.

Adjustment strategies of core intermediaries

There were two kinds of strategies adopted by core intermediaries to adjust to their riskier macroeconomic environment and meet the competitive threat from market-based intermediaries: one was to seek high returns to compensate for previous losses by chasing risk; the other was to restructure operations in order to better protect the institution against future risk. In general, the high-risk strategy was taken by the minority of institutions which were insolvent or near-insolvent, and the low-risk strategy was taken by solvent institutions which had net worth to lose. The coexistence of these two strategies can be observed in both housing finance and business finance.

Adjustments in housing finance methods

The high-risk strategy in housing finance was taken by near-insolvent S&Ls following the Garn–St. Germain Act of 1982 which liberalized previous asset restrictions. These institutions pursued a policy of rapid growth of assets with high expected yields (loans for the acquisition and development of land, developed building lots, and unimproved land) funded with short-term managed liabilities (such forms of "hot money" as brokered, insured CDs, and repurchase agreements). The failure of this strategy for most thrifts led to the failure of the S&L insurance fund and the federal government "bailout" of depositors in and owners of failed S&Ls.

Thrifts following the low-risk strategy in housing finance have sought to restructure their portfolios in order to reduce their vulnerability to future increases in interest rates such as was experienced in the late 1970s. In general, thrifts (and commercial banks, whose share of residential mortgage originations grew in the 1980s) seek to hold to a minimum the percentage of their portfolio in thirty-year fixed-rate mortgages, to better balance that portion of their portfolio in fixed-rate mortgages with longer-term liabilities, and to use new hedging devices like financial futures.[54] They have accomplished this by substituting variable-rate mort-

54 A financial futures contract is an agreement between a seller and a buyer to

gages for fixed-rate mortgages, by promoting shorter-term fixed-rate mortgages, and by participating in the securitization of housing finance on both the liability and asset sides of their balance sheets.[55]

On the liability side, housing intermediaries issue mortgage-backed bonds with maturities that match long-term mortgages more closely than time deposits and money market certificates. On the asset side, housing intermediaries substitute mortgage-backed securities (which, like mortgages, have fixed interest payments but, unlike mortgages, have a secondary market) for the mortgage themselves. Some housing intermediaries, seeking to avoid holding fixed-rate assets altogether, have essentially become mortgage bankers, originating and underwriting mortgages, then packaging them in large bundles and selling them on the secondary market.

Federal agencies and federally sponsored agencies have played a central and essential role in the securitization of housing finance. In 1968 and 1970, the federal government redefined the role of federal intermediaries, focussing those agencies on the development of active secondary markets for both conventional and government-insured loans. As the chapter's first section explained, New Deal housing legislation advanced the development of a secondary market in insured (FHA and VA) mortgages only; the largest lenders in the insured segment of the market were life insurance companies and mutual savings banks, which generally did not originate the mortgages, but acquired them from mortgage bankers. The Federal National Mortgage Association's (FNMA) secondary market role was limited to providing liquidity to the insured mortgage market during tight money periods, and it was prohibited from performing any secondary market role for conventional mortgages.

In 1968, FNMA was privatized (although it retains "agency status" in the credit markets), its market support function was transferred to the Government National Mortgage Association (GNMA, created in 1970), and its secondary market-making functions were expanded to include issuing mortgage-backed securities, buying and selling FHA, VA, and

trade a specific financial instrument (e.g., Treasury bills) at a specified price to be paid at some specified future date. It can be used by financial intermediaries to offset the risk from holding an asset portfolio whose weighted-average term to maturity exceeds that of liabilities.

55 The securitization of housing finance refers to the creation of various types of mortgage-backed securities which are "similar to and competitive with other debt instruments in the [open] capital market." See Sellon and VanNahmen, "The Securitization of Housing Finance."

conventional mortgage loans, and guaranteeing private sector mortgage-backed securities. GNMA does not issue mortgage-backed securities; its primary role is to also guarantee repayment on such securities issued by mortgage originators (thrifts and mortgage banking companies).

The Federal Home Loan Mortgage Corporation (FHLMC), also created in 1970, has the primary purpose of creating a secondary market for conventional mortgages; to this end it engages in the same operations as FNMA, but for conventional mortgages only. FHLMC and FNMA are a key link between the bond market and the housing finance system; they issue long-term mortgage-backed securities, explicitly or implicitly backed by the full faith and credit of the federal government, and use the liquidity to purchase pools of mortgages from conventional and non-conventional mortgage lenders.[56] These two agencies are also actively involved in the development of new types of mortgage-backed securities.[57]

The securitization of housing finance proceeded at a rapid pace in the 1980s. Agency pass-through securities (see note 56) comprised over 30% of the total stock of residential mortgage debt in 1987, up from under 10% in 1980, and comprised 60% of mortgage originations in 1987.[58] Secondary mortgage market pools together owned 43.7% of the stock of residential mortgages in 1991, up from 17.1% in 1980; this growing share has taken place at the expense of that of thrifts, which fell from 50.1% in 1980 to 21.1% in 1991 (reflecting the shrinkage of the thrift industry and asset substitution by surviving thrifts).[59]

Adjustments in business finance methods

In business finance as in housing finance, one response to higher levels of interest rate risk and credit risk was to seek compensating yields and new

56 The dominant type of mortgage-backed security is the pass-through security, in which the mortgage originator (e.g., thrift institution) assembles a pool of mortgages conforming to the underwriting criteria defined by GNMA, FNMA, or FHLMC, and issues a security whose interest and principal repayments, guaranteed by the federal agency, derive from the pool of mortgages. Ownership of the underlying mortgages passes to the holders of the security.

57 See Sellon and VanNahmen, "Securitization of Housing Finance."

58 Ibid.

59 Statistics taken from Hester, "Financial Institutions and the Collapse of Real Estate Markets."

asset growth; the other response was to restructure operations so as to protect the institution from future risk.

It is worth noting that deregulation, which eliminated interest rate ceilings on banks' time deposits and authorized the issuance of interest-earning personal checking accounts, increased commercial banks' exposure to interest rate risk by making their average cost of funds more sensitive to fluctuations in the rate of interest. This change in the structure of bank liabilities amplified the higher interest rate risk in the macroeconomic environment in general, and increased the interest rate risk associated with longer-term, fixed-rate loans in particular. Earlier in the postwar period, when some portion of the deposit base carried no interest cost, a rise in interest rates entailed an opportunity cost for commercial banks, but it did not shrink the margin on the fixed-rate loan; when interest payments on deposits rise with interest rates, the profit margin on fixed-rate loans shrinks and can turn negative depending on how high and fast short-term rates rise.

Money center banks' experience with term loans in the early 1970s is illustrative of the transition to a high-interest-rate-risk world. At that time, money center banks had broken with their earlier fixed-rate pricing on term loans and offered term loans with an interest rate which floated up to a cap based on the historical peak in the prime rate; in 1974, the prime rate exceeded its previous peak, and banks lost net income because of their term loans.[60]

The commercial banking industry has taken a range of steps to protect themselves from higher levels of interest rate risk: substituting variable-rate loans for fixed-rate loans, shortening the maturity of term loans, securitizing loans, and using hedging devices like financial futures and interest rate swaps. By 1977, half of all commercial and industrial loans carried floating interest rates; by 1988, 70% of all term loans carried floating interest rates, and the average maturity of term loans was four years, down from the five- to twelve-year term loans booked in the early 1970s.[61] As with housing finance, securitization allows commercial banks to liquidate some of the longer-term loans in their asset portfolios. Markets for loan-backed securities developed in the 1980s for selected commercial loans (commercial mortgages, automobile loans, SBA loans,

60 See Hayes, *Bank Lending Policies,* 2d ed., p. 149.

61 See Wojnilower and the *Federal Reserve Bulletin,* various issues. The fixed-rate term loans were reserved for the primest of prime borrowers.

computer and truck leases, and finance receivables), but numerous barriers exist to the securitization of nonguaranteed commercial and industrial loans, most notably their extremely heterogeneous character.

The composition of insurance companies' portfolios has also changed in reaction to the qualitative shifts in demand for life insurance products (which have shortened the average term of life insurance companies' liabilities) and to the higher level of interest rate risk in the macroeconomic environment. The most rapidly growing segment of their assets in the 1980s has been in liquid assets, such as mutual fund shares, money market mutual fund shares, Treasury securities, and commercial paper; the share of assets in mortgages and policy loans have correspondingly declined. While the share of life insurance companies' assets earmarked for corporate bonds has stayed roughly constant at one-third (constituting roughly half of all outstanding corporate bonds), there has been a significant qualitative shift in life insurance companies' corporate bond holdings.

Historically, life insurance companies held half of their corporate bond portfolio as smaller-denomination private placement bonds, which have thin secondary markets and which are issued by "smaller, less well-known nonfinancial corporations that require flexible loan terms and special provisions."[62] By the mid-1980s, life insurance companies held only 25% of all corporate bonds as private placements. In addition, the average term to maturity of fully marketable corporate bonds fell from fifteen to twenty years before the late 1970s to under twelve years in the mid-1980s.

The risk-chasing approach in business finance manifested itself in the middle to late 1980s as medium-sized and large commercial banks moved into commercial real estate lending, particularly commercial mortgages and construction and development loans. This segment of the banking industry had lost commercial and industrial loan volume to the securities markets, unlike smaller banks, but had not suffered a comparable loss in deposits.[63] The result, in many metropolitan markets, was overbuilding and rising rates of commercial real estate loans in nonaccrual status, which were without doubt inflated by the shift in the regulatory climate after 1989.

62 See Curry and Warshawsky, "Life Insurance Companies," p. 244.
63 See Litan, "Unholy Alliance," p. 191.

Financial re-regulation

Concern about the solvency of the deposit insurance fund motivated the re-regulation of financial institutions, which was initiated with the Financial Institutions Reform, Recovery, and Enforcement Act (FIRREA). Among other things, FIRREA reduced the maximum loan a thrift could extend to any individual borrower from 100% to 15% of capital (and which in practice had the greatest impact on commercial real estate loans, the largest loans in thrifts' portfolios). Shortly after FIRREA was enacted, bank regulators became more conservative in their valuation of loans collateralized with real estate and of commercial loans more generally and in their requirements for loan loss reserves. Examiners started requiring banks "to carry loan loss reserves against loans on which borrowers were current in their payments but where the market value of the underlying real estate collateral had fallen so low as to wipe out any equity the borrower may once have had in the project."[64] In 1991, Congress passed the Federal Deposit Insurance Corporation Improvement Act, which defined five capitalization categories and stipulated corresponding corrective regulatory action for each.

Many observers believe that the shift in regulator attitude toward risk amplified the cyclical credit contraction of the early 1990s with a "capital crunch" in commercial lending. Tougher regulatory treatment of real estate and commercial loans reduced bank capital at the same time regulators adopted stricter capital–asset ratios; the "capital crunch" occurred as commercial banks rebuilt their capital–asset ratio by drastically shrinking their assets and contracting higher-cost managed liabilities.[65]

Conclusion

The financial landscape of the early 1990s is substantially different from that created by the New Deal legislation of the 1930s. Core intermediaries account for a smaller share of the finance provided to the real economy, and core intermediaries' asset portfolios increasingly reflect a desire, in part regulator-induced, to be more liquid and less exposed to

64 Ibid., p. 197.

65 See Peek and Rosengren, "Crunching the Recovery: Bank Capital and the Role of Bank Credit," and Wojnilower, "Discussion of Peek and Rosengren."

both interest rate and credit risk. Long-term financial intermediation, the basis of the New Deal system, is increasingly a financing form of the past.

5. IMPLICATIONS FOR CONTEMPORARY ECONOMIC PERFORMANCE

The institutional response of finance to the higher-risk macroeconomic environment is adaptive from the microeconomic point of view but maladaptive from the macroeconomic point of view. Financial institutions, assisted by financial market innovations, increasingly manage interest rate risk and credit risk in ways that create financial impediments to aggregate spending, particularly capital spending. This should not be seen as a fundamental source of economic decline, but rather as a factor which reinforces economic stagnation. The failure of finance to lead the U.S. economy out of stagnation can be seen in the responses of providers of housing finance, providers of business finance, and of the federal government in its capacity as overarching monetary and fiscal manager.

Housing finance

As explained in the previous main section, financial institutions have shielded themselves from interest rate risk by selling bundles of mortgages on the secondary markets (securitizing mortgages), by substituting variable-rate mortgages for fixed-rate mortgages, and by using hedging instruments like financial futures contracts, options, and swaps. All of these responses involve the creation of new forms of financial risk and/or the shifting of interest rate risk onto other financial firms or onto spending units.

Securitization removes most of the interest rate risk from mortgage underwriting, but shifts it into the holder of the fixed-rate mortgage-backed security, who is also exposed to a new kind of financial risk, prepayment risk.[66] The uncertainty of financing home purchases with variable-rate mortgages has the potential, particularly at the bottom of the interest rate cycle, to depress consumer spending insofar as borrowers' savings rates rise to prepare for the possibility of a large future increase in

66 This is a new kind of risk in the sense that it was not present with the previous institutional form of residential mortgage lending.

interest rates.[67] The new risk-transferring techniques and instruments, which multiplied during the 1980s, reduce risk for individual banks and thrifts while creating new, not well understood, forms of risk exposure for the financial system as a whole.[68]

The development of the secondary mortgage market has arguably prevented what would otherwise have been a wholesale withdrawal of financial institutions from the long-term fixed-rate amortized mortgage. In that sense, the federal housing intermediaries have played an important role in cushioning the effect of interest rate volatility on the housing sector by facilitating the development of the secondary mortgage market.

However, unlike their response to the housing finance crisis of the 1930s, the secondary market-making activities of the federal intermediaries do nothing to broaden access to home ownership and may restrict the availability of finance which would serve this end, thereby limiting expansion of residential construction and rehabilitation spending. Because of the imbalance between housing prices and wages, most potential first-time single-family home buyers do not qualify for mortgages according to FNMA's, GNMA's, and FHLMC's underwriting guidelines. To a large extent, meeting this market's unmet housing needs requires nontraditional ownership structures, alternative forms of finance, and, in many cases, public subsidies. Such customized finance stands in stark contrast to the standardized finance offered by the secondary market.[69]

67 As a possible counter to the uncertainty argument, one could argue that, unlike fixed-rate loans, debt service costs on variable-rate longer-term loans booked at the top of the interest rate cycle fall as short-term interest rates fall, freeing discretionary income and providing a potential stimulus to spending; while longer-term fixed-rate loans can be refinanced, but at non-negligible transactions costs. (This distinction matters only for longer-term loans. For shorter-term loans, debt service costs fall for both fixed- and variable-rate loans as interest rates fall and such loans are repaid or rolled over at lower rates.) Still, the possibility of a future rise in short-term rates (the "uncertainty" effect) will haunt the issuer of the variable-rate loan but not the issuer of the refinanced fixed-rate loan, potentially raising the propensity to spend out of freed discretionary income from the refinanced fixed-rate loan relative to that from the variable-rate loan.

68 See Carlson, "Debt Growth and the Financial System."

69 This problem is beginning to be addressed as political pressure to meet lower-income households' and communities' housing finance needs is brought to bear on the secondary mortgage market agencies.

Business finance

Commercial banks and insurance companies, which provided the bulk of debt finance for business in the postwar period, have responded to the higher level of interest rate risk by withdrawing from long-term fixed-rate forms of finance. By providing debt finance on shorter terms and/or with floating interest rates instead, financial institutions shift interest rate risk onto borrowers, narrowing the range of capital spending projects suitable for bank financing and, as on the housing side, introducing a greater element of uncertainty into capital spending decisions. Furthermore, variable-rate commercial loans elevate credit standards, since projects must be bankable even under high-interest-rate scenarios, and substitute credit risk for interest rate risk, since the possibility of a significant rise in interest rates increases the potential burden of debt on borrowers.[70]

In this way, the importance of credit risk in the business lending decision has been magnified at the same time that the macroeconomic environment, specifically the deepening of recessions and the slowing of long-run growth, makes the average borrower more credit-risky and less capitalized. This is particularly true for small- and medium-sized corporations, precisely the market historically served by commercial banks, since their retained earnings exhibit greater cyclical volatility than those of large corporations.[71] Furthermore, empirical studies indicate that the influence of internally generated funds on investment is stronger for those firms with relatively restricted access to external finance (smaller and newer firms).[72] This would suggest that as access to external finance tightens, cash flow exerts a stronger effect on investment. As a result, the combination of economic stagnation and financial institutions' methods of managing interest rate risk have worked to restrict small- and medium-sized corporations' capital spending and access to bank finance.

The growth of the finance company sector does not allay these con-

70 One way commercial banks protect themselves against credit risk is by placing a ceiling on a potential borrower's leverage (debt–equity) ratio; however, this can became a binding barrier to credit during times of slow economic growth, when the leverage-ratio ceiling tends to rise at the same time business equity accumulates more slowly.

71 See Vasan, quoted in Fazzari, Hubbard, and Petersen, "Financing Constraints and Corporate Investment," p. 148.

72 See Fezzari, Hubbard, and Peterson, "Financing Constraints and Corporate Investment," pp. 169–73.

cerns to the extent that finance companies impose restrictive terms of finance (high interest rates and high monitoring costs) on business borrowers. The rise of finance companies reverses the institutional direction set by the Reconstruction Finance Corporation, which sought to make the commercial banking system more accessible to smaller corporations. During the RFC regime, the commercial banking system became the first rung of the financial ladder for a segment of previously credit-rationed firms and, as such, the basis for gaining future access to the open securities markets. Given the relatively onerous terms of finance company lending, and the absence of an institutional relationship through which technical assistance can be transmitted, finance companies may be a poor substitute for commercial banks as the point of entry into the financial system and basis for future success.[73]

Finally, the previous main section noted that the open money and capital markets, notably the commercial paper market, grew in the 1980s at the expense of the commercial banking industry. As a result, there has been a relative expansion of the supply of finance to the largest corporations (which have access to the securities markets) and a relative contraction of bank finance available to medium- and small-sized corporations. Yet the cost and availability of external finance is a relatively insignificant factor in investment decisions for large, mature corporations with relatively abundant internal resources. Hence, that type of finance which is most available in the 1990s is that which has the least ability to positively affect business investment spending.[74]

73 L. Randall Wray, who is studying the activities of factors with Dimitri Papadimitriou and Ron Phillips in a Levy Institute study, believes that the same may not be true of factors, who are another rising source of nonbank small-scale commercial finance, in the form of credit services and market information to small firms.

74 Large corporations are taking advantage of the historically low nominal interest rates of the early 1990s by issuing long-term debt in record volumes; while there has been some broadening of access to public debt and equity markets in the 1980s, further study is needed to determine its extent and shape. In any case, that sector of firms excluded from the security markets but not from commercial banks is not benefiting from the low interest rates because commercial banks will not (or cannot) allow borrowers to lock into current low rates without creating excessive interest rate risk for themselves.

Pollin, in "Public Credit Allocation through the Federal Reserve," pp. 13–15, sees another problem in the relative expansion of capital markets as a source of finance as opposed to financial intermediaries. He argues that the U.S. capital market system "encourages a short-term focus on dividends and

Federal monetary and fiscal management

The federal government has failed to address the problem of systemic risk created by the macroeconomic environment and has, in fact, exacerbated that problem at at least three institutional levels: federal bank regulatory agencies, the Federal Reserve, and the federal budget.

Bank regulations adopted in the early 1990s seek stability (solvency of the bank insurance fund) through stagnation (overconservative bank-lending criteria). In this legislation, Congress mandates that federal bank regulators and deposit insurance fund managers act like private sector institutions, protecting themselves (e.g., taxpayers who are pledged to support the solvency of the bank insurance fund) by limiting the range of economic opportunities available to potential borrowers.[75]

The Federal Reserve's preoccupation with price level stability and protecting the international value of the dollar gives a deflationary bias to monetary policy which virtually guarantees – indeed, requires – continued stagnation. Many observers have noted that this approach to controlling the price level is self-defeating in the long run because it limits the growth of productive capacity.[76]

capital returns rather than a long-term focus on nurturing investment projects" and lacks an institutional framework for "encouraging the exercise of [stakeholders'] voice" in corporate investment decisions.

However, in the U.S. capital market system, stockholders (admittedly a subset of "stakeholders," which includes employees and local communities) *do* have an institutional mechanism for exercising voice – annual stockholders' meetings. Given the concentration of corporate equity that is owned by institutional investors such as pension funds, this is a potentially strong voice; the question then becomes why it isn't used to direct managers to work for long-run returns.

75 In his introduction to Bernard Shull's "The Limits of Prudential Supervision," Hyman Minsky goes even further, arguing (p. 10) that this legislation "assumes away the possibility that the occasional development of crisis-prone financial structures reflects a deep characteristic of our economy" and suggests that "it may not be worthwhile to constrain the developments that periodically make banking and other financial relations fragile . . . because the problems in banking arise after a period of exuberant economic performance . . ."

76 See Epstein, "Monetary Policy in the 1990's: Overcoming the Barriers to Equity and Growth," for a full discussion of the political and economic constraints on expansionary monetary policy in the U.S. See also Fazzari's and Galbraith's articles in *Transforming the U.S. Financial System* which discuss how contractionary monetary policy impedes long-run growth.

However, to the extent that sustained price level stability brings greater interest rate stability, this direction of Federal Reserve policy may in fact prove to reduce the systemic level of interest rate risk (barring destabilizing international conditions), but only by placing a monetary drag on economic growth and elevating the systemic level of credit risk. While this could weaken the contractionary chain of causation in which greater interest rate risk leads to financing techniques which emphasize credit risk at the same time that they constrain growth (thereby increasing systemic credit risk), it is difficult to argue that greater interest rate stability, in and of itself, will provide a significant stimulus to economic expansion.

Finally, the contractionary stance of fiscal policy at the outset of the 1990s, based on the constraint which the federal deficit is perceived (incorrectly) to place on budget policy, prevents the federal government from providing a stimulus to aggregate demand growth, which would ease business credit conditions to the extent that it enhanced business equity and expected cash flows.

Paths to economic prosperity

Structural reform of the financial system which addresses the supply-side constraints on capital spending discussed in this chapter will not, by itself, regenerate economic growth insofar as these constraints have arisen, as this chapter has argued, in response to macroeconomic problems with ultimately nonfinancial origins. Such reform may need to be undertaken, but will only be effective in coordination with measures which address the real-side origins of the growth slowdown. Possible components of such a plan are discussed briefly here.

On the real side of the economy, the federal government needs to play an active role in conversion from a military-centered economy to one oriented to civilian needs. This involves, at the most basic level, setting national priorities: identifying strategic sectors and instituting appropriate public supports for these sectors. While public support may entail the creation of alternative financial institutions to provide long-term developmental finance, reform of the Federal Reserve, and/or bank regulatory reform, the choice of public supports should follow from, not precede, the assessment of the developmental needs of strategic sectors.[77]

77 See Pollin, "Public Credit Allocation through the Federal Reserve," for the view that the Federal Reserve should pursue financial stability and economic growth by using tools of selective credit allocation.

A long-run conversion plan has a better chance of success if adopted in the context of expansionary monetary and fiscal policy, which requires that constraints in both political and economic institutions be overcome. The political-economic orthodoxies of reducing the federal deficit, controlling inflation with tight monetary policy, and letting private finance allocate capital and drive exchange rate movements must be challenged, in both academic and political life.

REFERENCES

Campagna, Anthony. *U.S. National Economic Policy, 1917–1985.* New York: Praeger Publishers, 1987.

Carlson, John B. "Debt Growth and the Financial System." Federal Reserve Bank of Cleveland, *Economic Commentary,* October 1986.

Cornwall, John. *Growth and Stability in a Mature Economy.* New York: John Wiley & Sons, 1972.

"Inflation as a Cause of Economic Stagnation: A Dual Model." In *Inflation and Income Distribution in Capitalist Crisis: Essays in Memory of Sidney Weintraub,* J. A. Kregel (ed.). New York: New York University Press, 1989.

Curry, Timothy, and Warshawsky, Mark. "Life Insurance Companies in a Changing Environment." In *Contemporary Developments in Financial Institutions and Markets,* 2d ed. Arlington Heights, Ill.: Harlan Davidson, Inc., 1987.

D'Arista, Jane W. "The Parallel Banking System." Working Paper, Boston University School of Law, March 1992.

Dickens, Edwin. "The Great Inflation and U.S. Monetary Policy in the Late 1960s: A Political Economic Approach." *Social Concept* 7 no. 1 (forthcoming).

Dymski, Gary. "Is Intermediation Redundant in the U.S. Economy?" Discussant's comments presented at Jerome Levy Economic Institute Conference on Financing Prosperity in the 21st Century, March 1993.

Earley, James, and Evans, Gary. "The Problem is Bank Liability Management." *Challenge,* January–February 1982.

Epstein, Gerald. "Monetary Policy in the 1990s: Overcoming the Barriers to Equity and Growth." In *Transforming the U.S. Financial System: Equity and Efficiency for the Twenty-first Century.* Armonk, N.Y.: M. E. Sharpe, 1993.

Epstein, Gerald, and Schor, Juliet B. "The Federal Reserve–Treasury Accord and the Construction of the Postwar Monetary Regime." *Social Concept* 7, no. 1 (forthcoming).

Fazzari, Steven. "Monetary Policy, Financial Structure and Investment." In *Transforming the U.S. Financial System: Equity and Efficiency for the Twenty-first Century.* Armonk, N.Y.: M. E. Sharpe, 1993.

Fazzari, Steven, Hubbard, R. Glenn, and Petersen, Bruce C. "Financing Constraints and Corporate Investment." *Brookings Papers in Economic Activity* 1988, no. 1.

Flannery, Mark J. "How Do Changes in Market Interest Rates Affect Bank Profits?" In *Contemporary Developments in Financial Institutions and Markets,* 2d ed. Arlington Heights, Ill.: Harlan Davidson, Inc., 1987.

Galbraith, James. "The Federal Reserve After Greenspan." In *Transforming the U.S. Financial System: Equity and Efficiency for the Twenty-first Century.* Armonk, N.Y.: M. E. Sharpe, 1993.

Goldsmith, Raymond W. *Capital Market Analysis and the Financial Accounts of the Nation.* Morristown, N.J.: General Learning Press, 1972.

Greider, William. *Secrets of the Temple.* New York; Simon & Schuster, 1987.

Harris, Maury. "Finance Companies as Business Lenders." In *Contemporary Developments in Financial Institutions and Markets,* 2d ed. Arlington Heights, Ill.: Harlan Davidson, Inc., 1987.

Hayes, Douglas A. *Bank Lending Policies,* 1st ed. Grand Rapids: Dean-Hicks Co., 1964; 2d ed. Ann Arbor: Division of Research, Graduate School of Business Administration, University of Michigan, 1977.

Hester, Donald D. "Financial Institutions and the Collapse of Real Estate Markets." In *Real Estate and the Credit Crunch,* Proceedings of a Federal Reserve Bank of Boston conference, September 1992.

Jackson, Kenneth T. *Crabgrass Frontier: The Suburbanization of the United States.* New York: Oxford University Press, 1985.

Klaman, Saul B. *The Postwar Rise of Mortgage Companies.* New York: National Bureau of Economic Research, Inc., 1959.

Kregel, Jan A. "Institutional Investors and Financial Markets in Britain, the U.S.A., and Germany." Unpublished manuscript, December 1992.

Lintner, John. "The Financing of Corporations." In *The Corporation in Modern Society,* edited by Edward Mason. New York: Atheneum, 1967.

Litan, Robert E. "Banks and Real Estate: Regulating the Unholy Alliance." In *Real Estate and the Credit Crunch,* Proceedings of a Federal Reserve Bank of Boston conference, September 1992.

Minsky, Hyman. "Introduction" to "The Limits of Prudential Supervision," by Bernard Shull. Public Policy Brief of The Jerome Levy Economics Institute of Bard College, No. 5., 1993.

Moore, Basil. "Wages, Bank Lending, and the Endogeneity of Credit Money." In *Money and Macro Policy,* edited by Marc Jarsulic. Boston: Kluwer-Nijhoff, 1985.

Pavel, Christine. "Securitization." In *Contemporary Developments in Financial Institutions and Markets,* 2d ed. Arlington Heights, Ill.: Harlan Davidson, Inc., 1987.

Peek, Joe, and Rosengren, Eric S. "Crunching the Recovery: Bank Capital and the Role of Bank Credit." In *Real Estate and the Credit Crunch,* Proceedings of a Federal Reserve Bank of Boston conference, September 1992.

Pollin, Robert. "Stability and Instability in the Debt–Income Relationship." *American Economic Review* 75, no. 2 (May 1985).

"Public Credit Allocation through the Federal Reserve: Why It Is Needed, How It Should Be Done." In *Transforming the U.S. Financial System: Equity and Efficiency for the Twenty-first Century.* Armonk, N.Y.: M. E. Sharpe, 1993.

Saulnier, R. J., Halcrow, H. G., and Jacoby, N. H. *Federal Lending and Loan Insurance.* Princeton, N.J.: Princeton University Press, 1958.

Schor, Juliet B. "Wage Flexibility, Social Welfare Expenditures, and Monetary Restrictiveness." In *Money and Macro Policy,* edited by Marc Jarsulic. Boston: Kluwer-Nijhoff, 1985.

Sellon, Gordon H., and VanNahmen, Deana. "The Securitization of Housing Finance." Federal Reserve Bank of Kansas City, *Economic Review,* July–August 1988.

Sherman, Howard. *The Business Cycle: Growth and Crisis Under Capitalism.* Princeton, N.J.: Princeton University Press, 1991.

Volcker, Paul, and Gyohten, Toyoo. *Changing Fortunes: The World's Money and the Threat to American Leadership.* New York: Times Books, 1992.

Wojnilower, Albert M. "The Central Role of Credit Crunches in Recent Financial History." *Brookings Papers on Economic Activity* 1980, vol. 2.

"Discussion of Peek and Rosengren." In *Real Estate and the Credit Crunch,* proceedings of a Federal Reserve Bank of Boston conference, September 1992.

Wolfson, Martin H. *Financial Crises: Understanding the Postwar U.S. Experience.* Armonk, N.Y.: M. E. Sharpe, 1986.

5

Industries, trade, and wages

JAMES K. GALBRAITH AND
PAULO DU PIN CALMON

Whether the American economy as a whole has been declining is, perhaps, more of a political than an analytical question. Pessimists point to budget deficits, trade deficits, slow measured productivity growth, job loss, and "deindustrialization." Optimists however can point to emerging technologies, strong aggregate growth as compared with, say, Europe, and the continuing market test of demand for immigration to the United States. There is no simple answer to a question for which no simple metric can exist.

Unquestionably, though, American society and economic life are changing. One change particularly stands out: after 1980 the distribution of income became much more unequal.[1] Tax reductions skewed to the wealthy, high interest rates, cuts in government services, and recessions affecting the poor all contributed to this change. But so, and importantly for an understanding of industrial change in America, did changes in the distribution of industrial wage income.

The nature of changing wage inequality is easier to describe than to explain. Numerous studies of worker characteristics have shown that, in general, the 1980s reinforced the association of education and earnings.[2] The relative wage of workers with high educational attainment rose, and that of those without such attainment declined. But why? Is this a matter of the productivity of workers, of the tools they work with, or of the occupations and industries in which they are employed?

In a recent article in the *American Economic Review,* John Bound and

1 See Krugman (1992) for a brief overview.

2 See, inter alia, Murphy and Welch (1988a,b).

George Johnson (1992) summarize one widely held view, perhaps the dominant one in the economics profession today:

> . . . the principal reason for the increases in wage differentials by educational attainment and the decrease in the gender differential is a combination of *skilled-labor-biased technical change* and changes in unmeasured labor quality. (p. 389, italics added)

This raises another question. What on earth is "skilled-labor-biased technical change"? The answer, as it turns out, is astonishingly simple. If the lay reader needs a one-word translation, here is the word, not perhaps a complete explanation but good enough to cover many phenomena: *computers.*

Bound and Johnson, along with a growing number of other economists,[3] argue that the computer revolution is fundamentally behind the big changes we observe in the American industrial wage structure. In part, they find this position attractive because it accords with the general predictions of mainstream economic theory. The argument holds that the use of computers both requires and indicates labor skill. The introduction of computers into production processes is therefore a technical change that favors skilled labor. According to Bound and Johnson, the fraction of all workers using computers rose from 25 percent in 1984 to 37 percent in 1989. Computers are more used by better-educated than by less-educated workers, and more by women than by men. Increased use of computers (and, to some extent, of other "high-tech" equipment)[4] is thus said to account for *both* the increase in the wage advantage accorded to higher educational attainment and the reduction in the gap between women's and men's wages.

As this analysis gains ground, several potentially competing explanations lose out. One is the idea that *demand* rose for products of industries employing highly educated labor. Alas for college professors and civil servants, such did not occur. Wages in education-intensive "industries" declined slightly faster in the 1980s even than in heavy-industrial blue-collar trades.

The other apparent loser is the idea that the differential competitive or technological performance of *industries,* on the cost or supply side, might

3 A recent paper by A. Krueger (1992), notably, reaches a similar conclusion.

4 Bound and Johnson specifically mention communications equipment, photocopy equipment, and instruments.

have led in some indirect way to increasing wages for educated workers. From a policy standpoint, this is more serious, for it cuts at the heart of the new arguments in favor of industrial policy. If there were no change in performance differentials across industries, or if such changing differentials existed without having any effect on wages, then surely much of the argument for organizing policies of all kinds along industrial lines, in particular for industrial, technology, and trade policies, must be dispensed with.

It is well established, of course, that there do exist large and unexplained wage differentials according to industry. Janitors in banks, for example, are paid more than janitors in schools; truck drivers for factories earn more, in general, than truck drivers for laundries. These differentials are known in the literature as *industry-specific labor rents*. They are presumed to arise mainly from the presence of monopoly power – and from the use of monopoly power to buy worker loyalty, labor peace, and higher levels of effort through higher wages.

Monopoly power, in turn, has many possible causes. Most of them are *static:* a barrier to entry or economy of scale that changes little from one year to the next. Static sources of monopoly can account for existing inter-industry wage differentials, without imposing an industrial explanation on the recent changes in the wage distribution. One cause of monopoly, however, is not static: the transitory advantage achieved through technological progress. The case for industrial policy rests, in essence, on the idea that these transitory advantages can be created, maintained for a time, and exploited for benefits in the form of higher wages and living standards.

It is also possible, in principle, that the pattern of industrial performance, and therefore of industry-specific labor rents, did vary systematically over the 1980s so as to raise the derived monopoly power of well-educated workers. If industries employing large fractions of highly educated workers gained cost advantages and therefore monopoly power, while those employing less-educated workers performed poorly, and if these differences in industrial performance translated into a larger industry wage differential, *then* the consequences would conform to the observed increases in the relative wages of the better-schooled. In that case, policies aimed at fostering the cost advantages and effective monopoly power of U.S. industries on world markets might prove an effective means of raising the American competitive position.

Bound and Johnson, however, specifically reject this possibility:

> It is clear that not very much of the wage changes of the 1980s can be explained – even with perhaps unrealistically favorable assumptions – by changes in the industrial wage structure. (p. 380)

Along the way, Bound and Johnson also reject the hypothesis that declining unionization or any other institutional change had a large effect on the relative wage structure. They return, in the end, to their computers, photocopiers (*photocopiers?*) and "skilled-labor-biased technical change." The implications for policy of these conclusions are straightforward. Workers seeking higher wages should go back to school. Governments seeking higher productivity and a more equal wage structure should foster better and more equal education and training – and more universal computerization. Unionization is unlikely to do much good. And, of particular interest here, *there is no useful role for industrial policy.* Education, training and computerization advance any one industry as much as any other. Nor should we worry, it appears, about such phenomena as the effect on American wages of competition with low-wage countries.[5] So long as we computerize faster than they do, evidently, our workers' position will be secure.

Appealing though this argument is, we shall contend here that it is implausible both in principle and empirically. Indeed, recent research into the wage structure, of which the Bound and Johnson article is just one prominent example, seems systematically to understate the importance of industrial change and of industry-specific influences. It consequently overstates, by an equal amount, the importance of generic influences, such as education, training and computerization, and of policies oriented to factor supplies as opposed to policies organized along industrial lines. These mischaracterizations stem, in the main, from casual use of the industrial classifications made available by the government – from a substitution of the coarse available data for meaning.

The problem lies in the fact that the standard industrial classifications do not provide an economically meaningful pattern of aggregation or set of "industries" on which to base an analysis of "industrial effects." Rather, they separate entities which are behaviorally linked and merge entities which are behaviorally distinct. When linked entities are kept separate, a variation that may be industrial must be attributed to a non-industrial

5 A subject, one might add, that one is hard pressed to find in published work on the wage structure.

cause. When distinct entities are merged and the aggregate is examined, variation that may be industrial is simply averaged out of the data. In both cases, information is lost, and the importance of industrial influences is undermeasured.

The upshot, to telegraph the conclusion of the analysis below, is that *industries do matter*. And if industries matter, then it is likely that trade performance also matters. Trade is an economic activity conducted along industrial and national lines. We buy automobiles and electronics (not "skilled-labor-intensive goods") from the Japanese, garments from China and Puerto Rico, and we sell aircraft and computers to the world. If changes by industry are importantly affecting wages, it may be that those industrial changes are importantly affected by trade.

If in fact industries and trade matter, then the policy conclusions mentioned above must be discarded, or at least the relation of priorities revised. Industrial policies may be necessary. Trade competitiveness of industries must be attended to. Education and training, on the other hand, may be less important for competitiveness than for other social functions. And computers may be viewed, once again, as merely the highly useful transistorized typewriters that in a high proportion of actual uses they actually are.

WHAT IS AN INDUSTRY?

The issue is whether industries are properly identified, and properly differentiated, in economic analysis of industrial influences on the wage structure. If so, one set of policies goes through. If not, another set must be considered.

A simple example may illustrate. Suppose an economy has four workers, Ann, Bill, Chuck and Diane. Ann makes computers. Bill sells computers. Chuck builds houses, and Diane paints houses. Ann and Bill earn $200 per week; Chuck and Diane earn $100 per week. Table 5.1 illustrates the setup.

Now, let us ask, What is the influence of "industry" on wages? This will depend on how we define an industry, which we have not yet done. Here we have two obvious choices.

One option is to divide our economy into "manufacturing" and "services." We can call this *horizontal stratification*. In this case, Ann and Chuck are in manufacturing, Bill and Diane in services. The average wage

Table 5.1. *An example of industrial classification and the wage structure*

	Computers	Housing
Manufacturing	*Ann* College $200	*Chuck* High school $100
Services	*Bill* College $200	*Diane* High school $100

in manufacturing is $150; that in services is also $150. Industry clearly does not matter to wages. An "industrial policy" that fostered manufacturing *per se* would have no effect on average wage levels.

Alternatively, we might define our industries as "housing" and "computers": *vertical stratification.* In this case, Ann and Bill are in computers; Chuck and Diane are in housing. Average wage in computers is $200, that in housing is $100. Now, industry clearly *does* matter to wages. An industrial policy that fostered the computer industry might eventually reduce (because of diminishing returns) the relative wage advantage of computer workers, but in the meantime it would raise the average level of wages.

To complicate matters, suppose Ann and Bill have college educations; Chuck and Diane went only to high school. Education is now clearly associated with earnings. But is this association independent of industry? If you defined industry horizontally, the answer would be yes; if vertically, the answer would be no. In the first decomposition, education stands out as the way to get ahead, irrespective of the activity you are in. In the second, the question is muddied. It may be that elements of industry-specific labor demand (the computer industry demands better-educated workers, in which case expanding the computer industry will generate better jobs) or job screening (the computer industry, flush with cash and able to discriminate in its hiring, insists on college graduates even though it doesn't actually need them), are at play.

Now, which definition of industry should one adopt? There is no single correct definition of an industry; the answer depends in principle on the research question one is asking. But if one is trying to confirm (as Bound

Table 5.2. *An industrial classification*

1.	Construction
2.	Durables/mining
3.	Nondurables
4.	Transport
5.	Utilities
6.	Wholesale trade
7.	Retail trade
8.	Finance
9.	Business services
10.	Personal services
11.	Entertainment
12.	Medical
13.	Hospitals
14.	Welfare
15.	Education
16.	Professional services
17.	Public administration

Source: John Bound and George Johnson, "Changes in the Structure of Wages in the 1980s: An Evaluation of Alternative Explanations," *American Economic Review,* Vol. 82, (June 1992) p. 381.

and Johnson and many other researchers have attempted to do) that industry *does not* matter to the wage structure, then one must test this hypothesis against the scheme of industrial classification that gives the *strongest* support to the counter-hypothesis that industrial performance does matter. It is always possible, by judicious misaggregation, to find some ordering or stratification or pattern of aggregations of the data according to which industries do not matter. But if industries truly do not matter, there should exist *no ordering* – or, at least, no economically meaningful ordering – according to which they do.

The classification scheme Bound and Johnson actually use – seventeen industries in total – is given in Table 5.2. It reflects, among other things, the limitations of industrial classifications in data from the Current Population Survey of the Census (CPS), and the large number of age/gender/skill divisions of the work force (thirty-two, in this case) that Bound and Johnson employ.[6] But, note that "horizontal" and "vertical" stratifications both appear in this listing. "Medical," "Transport," and "Construction" are classes of the vertical type; "Business Services" and "Personal Services" are of the horizontal type. In addition, the classification is very crude: virtually all of manufacturing, for instance, is squeezed into just three categories: Durables/mining, Nondurables (horizontal classes), and Transport (a vertical classification). Thus computers are mixed with coal mines, food with fuel, and airlines with ocean cruises.

Happily, it is possible to do better than this.

WAGES AND INDUSTRIAL CLASSIFICATION

In an important paper, Katz and Summers (1989) argue that most of the unexplained variation in factor compensation by industry accrues to labor. Industry-specific labor rents are substantial, whereas "capital rents" are not. The theoretical logic behind this conclusion is straightforward: compared to labor markets, capital markets are efficient. Therefore workers with organization-specific skills and competences enjoy an element of scarcity value that enables them to reap, in the long run, a measurable portion of the extra earnings that come from the technological or monopolistic advantages that a particular industry may enjoy. Profit rates tend to equalize in the short run, wage rates do not.

For its own reasons, much of the existing theoretical literature treats the industry wage structure as subject mainly to static forces, such as a degree of monopoly in product or labor markets. But there is no particularly good reason to maintain this restriction. Effective degrees of monopoly can vary with time and competitive conditions. If they do, and if the labor rents hypothesis is correct, then industry wage structures will change. And the pattern of change of average wages will, in many cases, provide an accurate barometer of industrial performance.

Working backwards from this observation, we can use changes in observed wage structures to develop a systematic method for aggregating across the standard industrial classifications. Suppose two industrial groups, say "women's undergarments" and "women's outergarments," experience identical *changes* in average wage levels over some long period

6 In a footnote, Bound and Johnson mention an unpublished analysis which divides industries into forty-five groupings. While an improvement, this evidently does not advance matters very far. Efforts to obtain this analysis from the authors were unsuccessful.

of time. Two possibilities exist. *Either* they are linked by some direct wage-coordinating mechanism, such as a labor contract, *or* they are identically affected by identical external forces. In either case, it makes sense to treat these two elements as parts of the *same industry*. For the purpose of analyzing wage change, no information can be lost, since the same track of wage change through time is being analyzed in both cases. Indeed it would be econometrically misleading to treat the two as distinct.[7] Correspondingly, if two industries normally classed together, say "automobiles" and "aircraft," show distinctly different patterns of wage change over time, it makes sense to keep them in different classes. To merge them is to rule out the possibility that their wages are responding to divergent forces *at the industrial level* – without any good evidence that this possibility should be excluded.

Procedures of numerical taxonomy known as cluster analysis can be deployed to group up three-digit Standard Industrial Classification (SIC) industries into a small number of groups exhibiting distinct patterns of wage change over time. We have settled, possibly *ad interim,* on a two-stage procedure using Ward's method of minimum variances. We start with ninety three-digit manufacturing industries for which we have continuous data over thirty years from 1958 to 1988. The analysis yields a scheme of six major groups and a dozen outliers or special cases, as shown in Table 5.3. Details of the procedure are provided in the appendix.

SIX INDUSTRIAL CLUSTERS

The first group we call Advanced Technology (AT) because it includes most of the industries normally described under that rubric: aerospace, communications, drugs, chemicals, special industrial machinery. It also includes a number of other industries that may be better described as producers of "Ricardo Goods" – paper, pulp, and foods – industries in which the United States happens to enjoy a strong history of comparative advantage. It also includes some industries, such as dairy, that benefit from substantial programs of price support and trade protection, and therefore enjoy a pattern of wage change comparable to the advanced sectors without, or perhaps in addition to, their technological edge.

7 The result in a regression using a panel data set will be spurious precision in the estimates of coefficients.

Table 5.3. *Industries clustered by the history of change in average hourly wages, 1959–88*

Outliers

201	Meat products
211	Cigarettes
239	Misc. fabricated textile products
253	Public building and related furniture
291	Petroleum refining
301	Tires and inner tubes
321	Flat glass
324	Cement, hydraulic
331	Blast furnace and basic steel products
333	Primary nonferrous metals
357	Computer and office equipment
373	Ship and boat building and repairing
374	Railroad equipment
382	Measuring and controlling devices
393	Musical instruments

Cluster 1: Advanced technology

202	Dairy products
204	Grain mill products
205	Bakery products
206	Sugar and confectionery products
208	Beverages
261	Pulp mills
263	Paperboard mills
264	Miscellaneous converted paper products
265	Paperboard containers and boxes
282	Plastic materials and synthetics
283	Drugs
284	Soap, cleaners, and toilet goods
285	Paints and allied products
327	Concrete, gypsum, and plaster products
341	Metal cans and shipping containers
342	Cutlery, hand tools, and hardware
355	Special industrial machinery
358	Refrigeration and service machinery
364	Electric lighting and wiring equipment
365	Household audio and video equipment
366	Communications equipment
372	Aircraft and aircraft parts
386	Photographic equipment and supplies

Cluster 2: Heavy industry

242	Sawmills and planing mills
322	Glass and glassware, pressed and blown
332	Iron and steel foundries
335	Nonferrous rolling and drawing
351	Engines and turbines
353	Construction and related machinery
369	Misc. electrical equipment and supplies
371	Motor vehicles and equipment

Cluster 3: Cotton textiles

221	Broadwoven fabric mills, cotton
222	Broadwoven fabric mills, manmade
227	Carpets and rugs
228	Yarn thread mills

Table 5.3. (*cont.*)

Cluster 4: General industry
223 Broadwoven fabric mills, wool
224 Narrow fabric mills
226 Textile finishing, except wool
229 Miscellaneous textile goods
252 Office furniture
254 Partitions and fixtures
271 Newspapers
275 Commercial printing
278 Blank books and bookbinding
307 Misc. plastic products
326 Pottery and related products
336 Nonferrous foundries (castings)
345 Screw machine products, bolts, etc.
347 Metal services, NEC
354 Metalworking machinery
356 General industrial machinery
362 Electrical industrial apparatus
363 Household appliances
385 Ophthalmic goods

Cluster 5: Light industry
259 Miscellaneous furniture and fixtures
273 Books
311 Leather tanning and finishing
325 Structural clay products
344 Fabricated structural metal products
361 Electric distribution equipment
367 Electronic components and accessories
384 Medical instruments and supplies
387 Watches, clocks, watchcases and parts
391 Jewelry, silverware, and plated ware
394 Toys and sporting goods
396 Costume jewelry and notions

Cluster 6: Garment trades
225 Knitting mills
231 Men's and boys' suits and coats
232 Men's and boys' furnishings
233 Women's and misses' outwear
234 Women's and misses' undergarments
236 Girls' and children's outwear
314 Footwear, except rubber
317 Handbags and personal leather goods
395 Pens, pencils, office and art supplies

Heavy Industry (HI) is a group centered on the automotive industry and related activities: construction equipment, engines and turbines, iron and steel foundries. Sawmills and planing mills are also in this group, reflecting a pattern of wage bargaining recognized by Eckstein and Wilson as long ago as 1962.

General Industry (GI), an unimaginative moniker, covers industries whose patterns of wage change cannot be distinguished from the average of American manufacturing as a whole: furniture, appliances, printing and bookbinding, general industrial machinery, metalworking of various kinds, and textiles except for cotton and cotton blends.

Light Industry (LI) covers two types of industry which appear to run parallel for distinct reasons. One is labor-intensive consumer-goods assembly, including electronic goods, toys, sporting goods, watches and clocks, jewelry and notions. The other is construction products, particularly structural steel items that are used in commercial building and larger engineering projects.

Cotton Textiles (CT) covers a small group of industries producing cotton yarn and cotton blends. Garment Trades (GT) cover the assembly of apparel.

Finally, major Outliers include ships, railroads, basic steel, flat glass, oil, computers, cigarettes, and meat. The fact that these are outliers means merely that they are special cases, groups of one, distinguished in several cases by specific years of wage gain or loss (the oil boom, the steel bust) not shared elsewhere in the economy. It does not imply that they are to be excluded from the analysis. To the contrary, the outliers constitute an important subset of industries, and their history is important to an understanding of the full story.

The outliers fall into two broad groups. One consists of industries whose wage histories reflect extraordinary developments that are, in substantial measure, unique to the industry. In the cases of meat, petroleum, computers, and steel, these hardly require explanation, while the exceptional wage performance of the cigarette industry can be associated with its extraordinary success in foreign markets. In other cases, the outliers simply occupy intermediate positions between two relatively well-defined clusters (Advanced Technology and Heavy Industry in the case of flat glass, for example).

Wage histories

Figure 5.1 presents pairwise comparisons of the wage histories of the clusters, which is to say the history of the average growth rate of wages in those industries making up each cluster. To facilitate comparison each cluster is presented in contrast with the wage history of the Advanced Technology group. Of course, in all cases the general trend of macroeconomic events, particularly inflation and recessions, can be discerned. What is interesting, however, is not how wage histories move together, but how they differ.

Heavy Industry
Compared to Advanced Technology

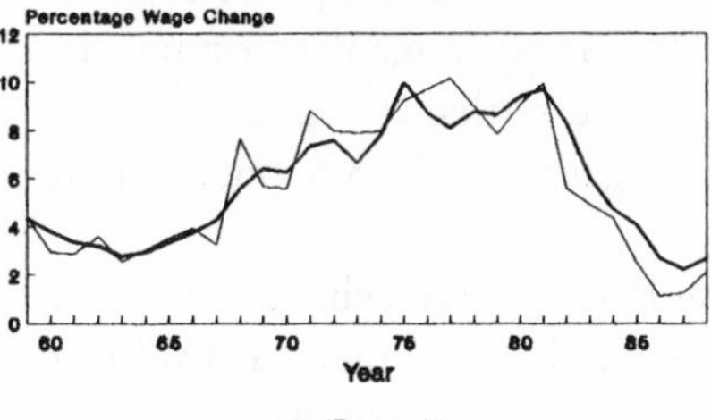

General Industry
Compared to Advanced Technology

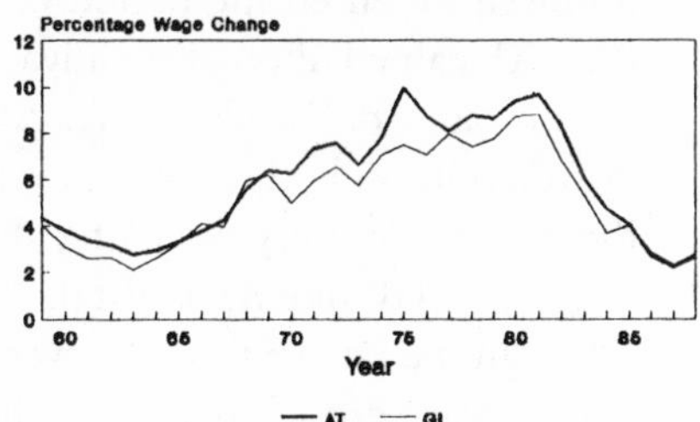

Light Industry
Compared to Advanced Technology

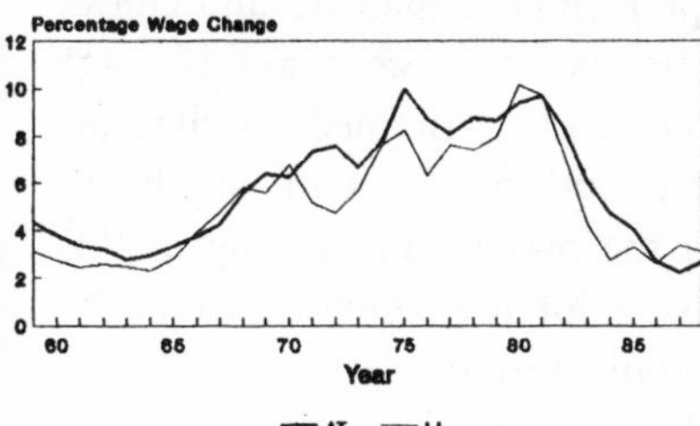

Cotton Textiles
Compared to Advanced Technology

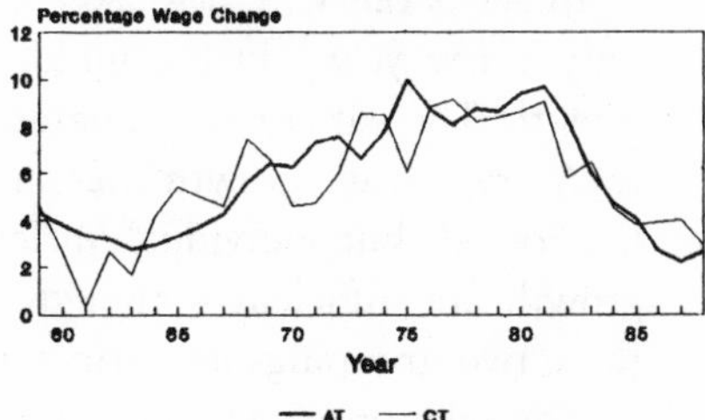

Garment Trades
Compared to Advanced Technology

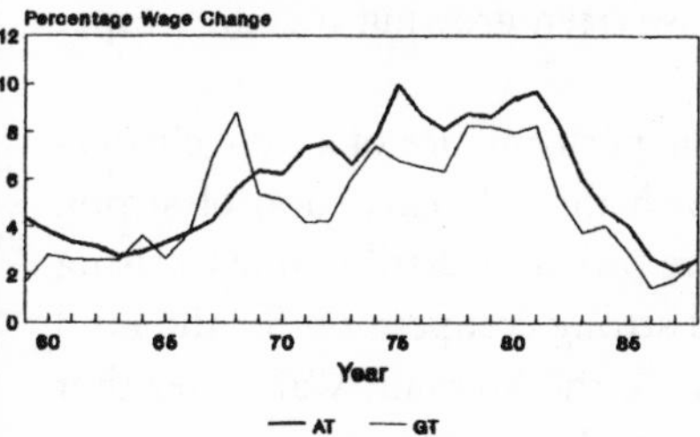

Garment Trades
Compared to Cotton Textiles

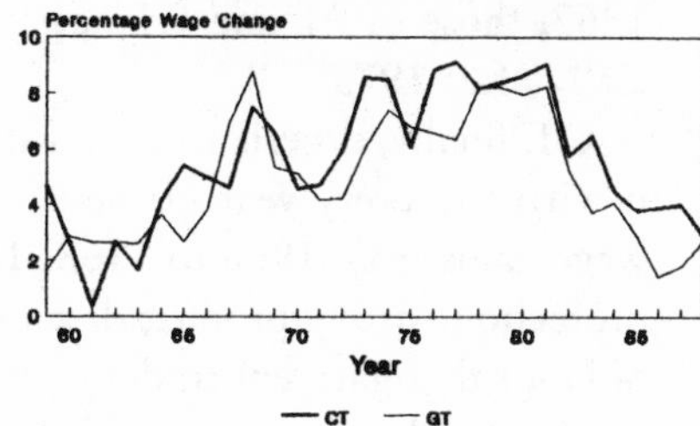

Figure 5.1. Change in hourly wages, 1959–88, by industrial cluster.

We see, for example, that Advanced Technology and Heavy Industry shared virtually identical patterns of smooth wage gains through 1967, followed by an erratic period of thirteen years in which at first HI and then AT gained alternating advantage. After 1980, wage performance in AT becomes decisively better. Although wage settlements decline (with disinflation) in both clusters, average wage gains in AT were higher than those in HI in every year after that date.

AT and GI, like AT and HI, show solidaristic wage behavior through 1967. In the late sixties, however, GI suffers a distinct downward shift in annual wage growth relative to that for AT, and experiences worse performance on the wage front in every subsequent year through 1984. Thus wages in GI must be falling through this entire period relative to those in AT.

LI starts out with a weaker average performance than AT and enjoys only a few years, in the middle and late sixties, of comparable wage growth. Thereafter the comparative decline of LI is sustained and dramatic. Average wage growth over the whole period for LI is quite similar to that of GI, but individual variations in the pattern and timing of this growth are sufficient – though only just – for the analysis to identify these two groupings as distinct and separate clusters.

The relation of AT and CT is notably different. Wage growth in CT fluctuates sharply about that of AT until the mid-seventies. After that, the patterns of wage growth in the two clusters grow more similar, and in the mid-eighties CT enjoys the same comparatively strong wage performance as does AT. Thus where the histories of AT and HI appear to diverge after 1967, those of AT and CT appear to have been growing together, especially after 1975.

GT, finally, experiences the worst wage performance of all the clusters in virtually every year of the sample, with the sole exception of strong wage gains from 1966 to 1968. These are probably attributable to rising protection, strong product demand, and strong competition for the kind of labor that garment trades employ, due to the Vietnam War. After that brief gain, the garment trades fare very poorly indeed.

Wage histories for five of the main outliers are presented in Figure 5.2, again against the benchmark of wage change in AT. We see that the outliers are distinguished by unusually erratic patterns of wage growth, or by specific years in which there occurred extraordinary events. Over the whole of the period, and particularly in the eighties, it is clear that the cigarette industry enjoys the strongest pattern of wage growth. Basic

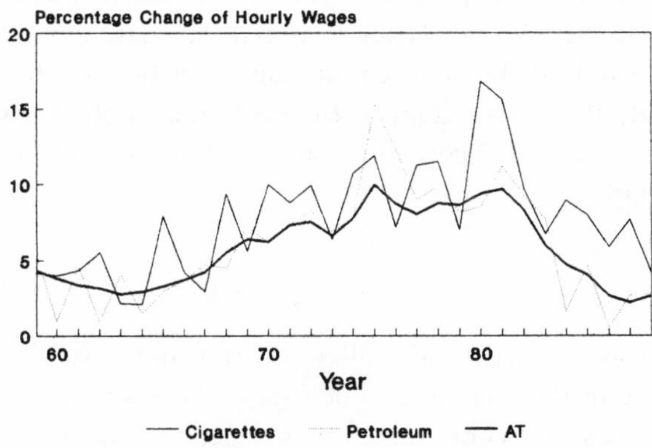

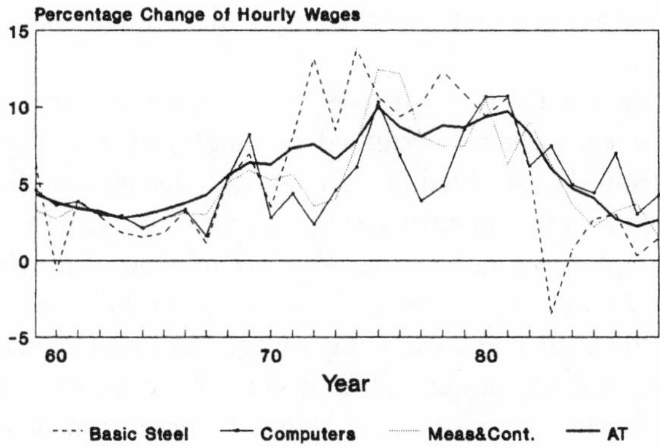

Figure 5.2. Main outliers: Wage Change, 1959–88.

steel's exceptional wage settlements in the early seventies stand out, as does the collapse of that industry in 1983. Wages in petroleum refining move, as one might expect, with the oil price. Computers, interestingly, suffer from relatively low average wage gains in the seventies. This appears to be a compositional effect, owing to the rapid growth of the industry and emergence of the computer as a mass-market commodity at the end of the decade.

In sum, cluster analysis succeeds in isolating distinct patterns of wage change over the twenty-nine years for which we have data, and in organizing industries into clusters that share these patterns, while segregating those few cases whose experience is unique. Of course, this tells us nothing about whether the industries so organized share any other characteristics, and indeed the cross-cutting character of some of the clusters might raise doubts. We therefore turn next to the question of whether the flocks we have identified contain, in any economically meaningful sense, birds of a feather.

Relative wage rates

A first dimension of structural similarity within and dissimilarity between clusters concerns the average level of wages. There is no obvious reason *a priori* why industries whose wages move together at the same percentage rates, and which are therefore associated with each other within clusters, should enjoy average wage levels which are the same or even close to each other. If they do in fact tend to share wage levels, that will tell us something about the nature of job clusters, and of wage solidarity, in the United States.

Figure 5.3a tells the tale. It shows the fractional deviation of the average wage for each cluster, weighted by employment in the underlying industries, from the weighted average hourly wage in manufacturing as a whole. We see that the range of average cluster wage rates, from nearly 30 percent above the average to about 40 percent below, is nearly as large as the range of wages happens to be in the industries themselves. Moreover, clusters can be clearly defined as high-wage (AT and HI), medium-wage (GI and LI), and low-wage (CT and GT). We can conclude that one dimension of wage contours in the United States is their delimitation by wage strata.

To what extent is this stratification due to differences in the characteristics of the workforce? We shall see shortly that our clusters do differ sharply along one easily measured dimension, namely the gender composition of their workforces. Detailed data are not available to help us determine what effect other differences in individual workers' characteristics might make. But we do know (from Katz and Summers 1989 and elsewhere) that correcting for differences in characteristics of workers where it can be done not only fails to explain very much about interindustry wage differentials, but does not even alter the relative positions of wages in any of the industries studied.[8] We therefore reject with confi-

8 Dickens and Katz (1988, cited in Katz and Summers 1989). Dickens and Katz

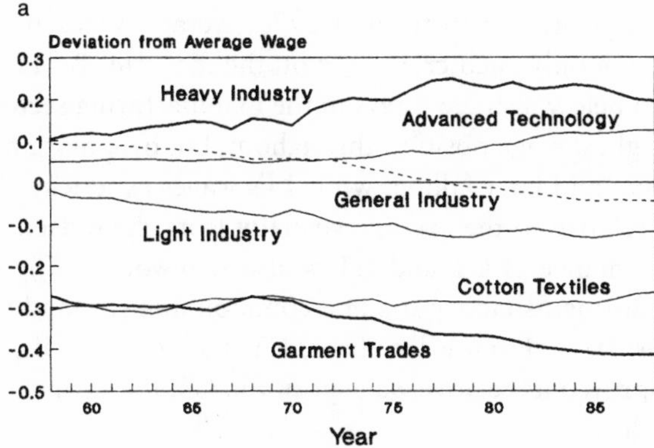

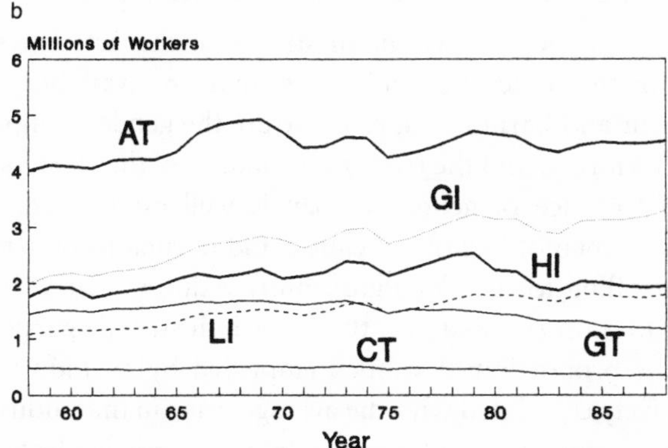

Figure 5.3. (a) Relative wages by industry type; (b) Employment by cluster.

dence the idea that the qualitative stratification we observe can be attributed to differences in individual worker characteristics.

Figure 5.3a also shows just how the industrial wage structure has changed over thirty years and just how far wrong are claims that it has been stable. We see that GI began the sixties with one of the two highest average wage positions. It has, however, suffered a continuing decline in its position ever since, a decline which accelerated after 1973. AT, mean-

report that in the CPS data only fifteen three-digit census occupations have large enough sample sizes to permit detailed estimation of industry wage differentials with extensive variables to control for observable differences in labor force characteristics.

while, began with wages only slightly above average and has been improving its relative position. Shortly after 1970, average wages in AT exceeded those in GI, the only such cross-over on the diagram. By 1980 wages in GI had fallen below average wages in the manufacturing sector. HI maintained the highest wage position throughout, but by a margin that was at first increasing and later falling, while LI's wages experienced a continuous decline relative to the average virtually from the outset.

The performance of CT and GT is also noteworthy. These begin the period as indistinguishable parts of a common industry and then diverge sharply after 1970. From a low base, CT, the cotton mills, maintained and then improved its relative wage position. GT, the garment trades, lost ground steadily.

Employment figures for the six clusters are presented in Figure 5.3b.

STRUCTURAL CHARACTERISTICS OF THE CLUSTERS

We present evidence on two major structural characteristics of our clusters, and of the underlying industries, that are available from the BLS Employment and Earnings tape. These are the gender composition of the cluster workforces, and the trade performance of the clusters themselves.[9]

The importance of gender to pay is well established. First, within industries women of like qualification and occupation are paid less than men; controlling for gender significantly reduces – though it and other controls do not eliminate – the inter-industry dispersion of wages. Second, the proportion of women employed by an industry is strongly and negatively correlated with the average wage in that industry. We stress that these are separate and (in principle) independent effects.[10] This point

9 We are completely persuaded that our clusters capture the major qualitative distinctions between types of industry as well. To sum up: AT industries are intensive in technology, energy and land; HI industries are materials and inventory intensive; LI and GT are labor intensive; CT is transitional between GT and AT; and GI is a residual grouping. However, to make this case requires not a footnote but a book. See the Report of the Policy Research Project on Wages and Competitiveness, LBJ School of Public Affairs, May 1991 (draft).

10 Katz and Summers document both of these facts. Note their independence: it would be possible to have a world where women's pay exactly equaled that of men in all occupations within any given industry, but where women were nevertheless predominantly employed in low-labor-rent industries and low-wage occupations. In such a world, controlling for the gender of workers within industries would not reduce the dispersion of inter-industry wages at all, but the women's wages would still be lower than men's because of the inter-industry effect.

is important, for it may be that labor market discrimination against women works primarily at the level of the industry rather than of the person – something which microdata that controls for industry will not reveal.

The left-hand panels of Figure 5.4 show the pattern of female employment and average weekly earnings by industrial cluster in 1960 and 1980. They show that the wage contours we have distinguished do, in fact, possess a clear structural underpinning along both of these dimensions. The right-hand panels present scatter plots for the underlying industries in the clusters; these confirm that the industries assigned to each do tend to cluster about their means in each dimension.[11]

We now turn to the trade question. Are the structural differences between industrial clusters in wage behavior and wage performance associated, in part, with differences in international trade performance? Do these relationships (if they exist) change as trade becomes more important to the U.S. economy after 1970? In a word, does trade affect wages, and, if so, how?

It would be highly useful for our purposes to have a single indicator of international trade performance, or competitiveness. Previous studies[12] have tended to follow official practice in treating exports and imports separately, measuring export performance by the ratio of exports to shipments and import performance by the ratio of imports to new supply. Then, typically, wage levels in high-export industries can be compared to wage levels in high-import industries. This procedure is useful at high levels of disaggregation, where intra-industry trade tends to be comparatively small and the two lists are therefore distinct. But it becomes less and less useful as industries are added together into industrial sectors. It will not do at all for our purposes, as we have clusters where (as will be seen) import and export ratios are nearly equal. Further, separate indices are cumbersome, since a decline in competitiveness may arise either from a fall in exports or a rise in imports; if one has classed an industry as high-export, a fall in competitiveness due to an import incursion may be overlooked, and vice versa.

We therefore propose a unified measure of competitiveness for industries, namely the complex fraction of exports-to-shipments over imports-to-domestic sales.[13] This fraction can be computed for any industry in

11 The policy implications of these panels, for women, at least, seem clear. In 1960, it did not pay to work. In 1980, it still didn't.

12 Including Katz and Summers (1989) and Galbraith (1989).

13 This measure is analogous to that proposed and discussed in Galbraith

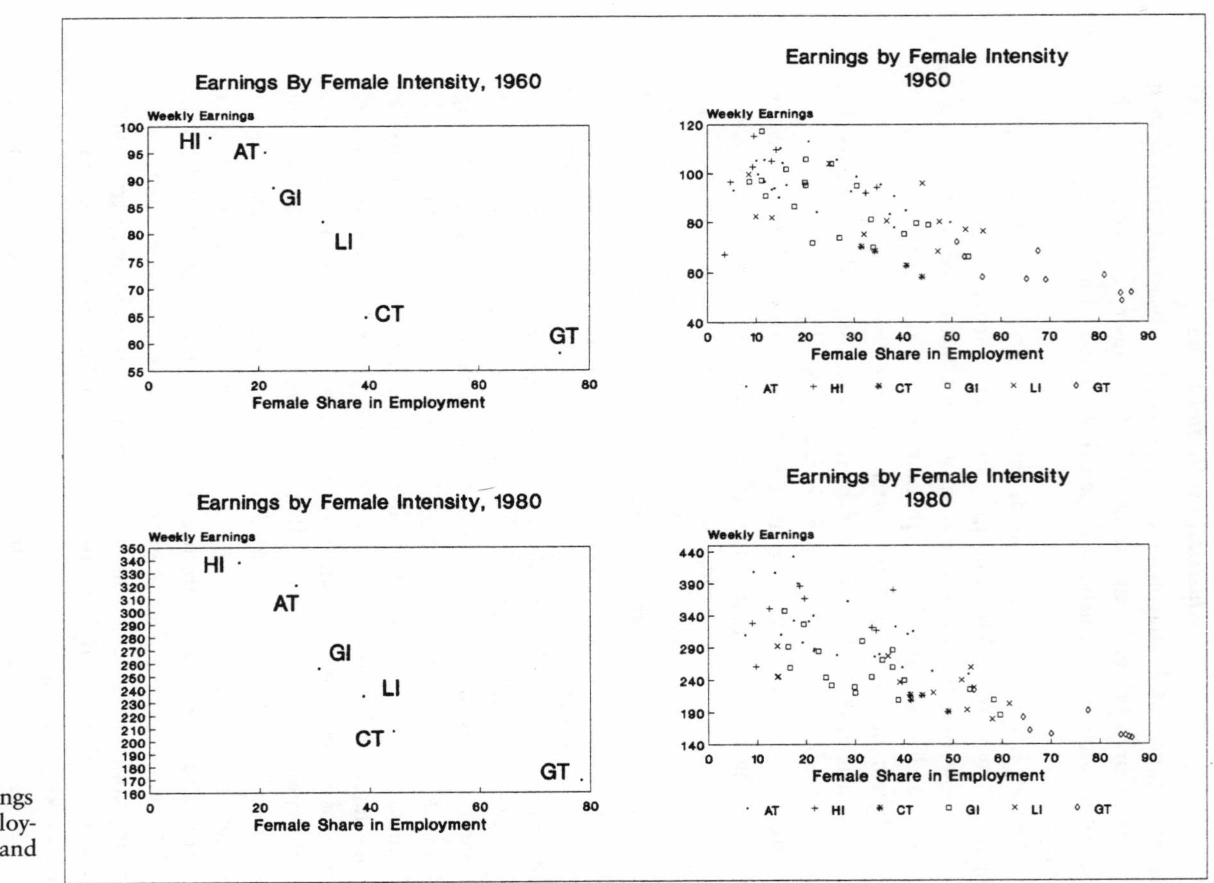

Figure 5.4. Earnings and female employment, 1960 and 1980.

any year from three numbers: total shipments (s), exports (e) and imports (i). Its value is:

$$C = \frac{(e/s)}{i/(s - e + i)}$$

The virtue of this index should lie in the relationship between movements of the index and the importance of international pressures on prices and costs.[14] It is the *proportionate* balance of trade within each industry that matters here. The level of our index will capture, as closely as one index can do and without reference to data from overseas sources (such as a comparison of unit labor costs would entail), whether an industry is oriented *more* toward competition in external markets, or toward competition from imports in the domestic market. The change in our measure will capture, we believe, whether an industry is becoming increasingly exposed to effective competition from foreign sources in *either* the external or the home market.[15]

Figure 5.5 presents basic data on C-ratings for the six clusters and for the industries they contain, built up by adding together import and export data for each of the underlying industries. Figure 5.5 also shows the evolution of C-ratings from decade to decade. Plots below the diagonal line indicate a decline in competitiveness; those above it indicate an improvement.

Overall, the degree of stratification is remarkable. Just as our clustering delivered industries grouped across the range of wage premia and female labor force memberships, so too it stratifies groupings across a

(1989, 123) for firms, but has the virtue that it can be measured from published data.

14 It should be noted also that this index does not distinguish between industries that are large and small traders, and therefore it is not necessarily the best one for an analysis of the balance of trade.

15 The index is centered on unity in several ways. In a hypothetical case, an industry which exports all of its output and imports all of its domestic sales has an index value of one. The same value will hold for any industry whose trade is balanced in this proportionate way, irrespective of the relative size of the two markets or the level of exposure to trade. In the special case where imports and exports are equal, the index also collapses to unity. The theoretical range of the index is from zero to infinity, and at the level of three-digit industries the upper tail is sufficiently long that a log transformation (centering on zero) is useful. At higher levels of aggregation the practical range of the untransformed index lies between zero and two.

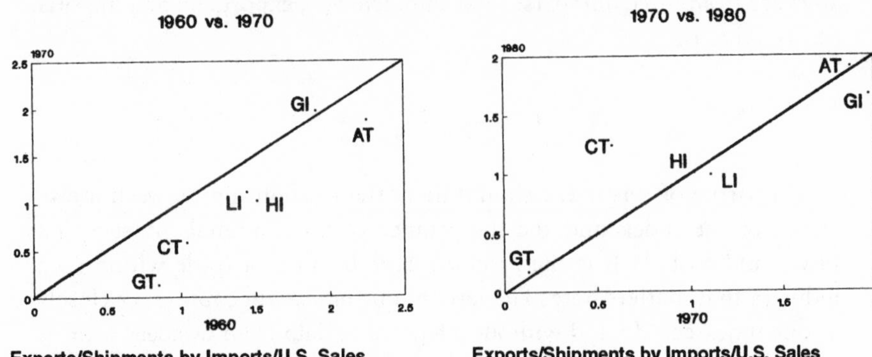

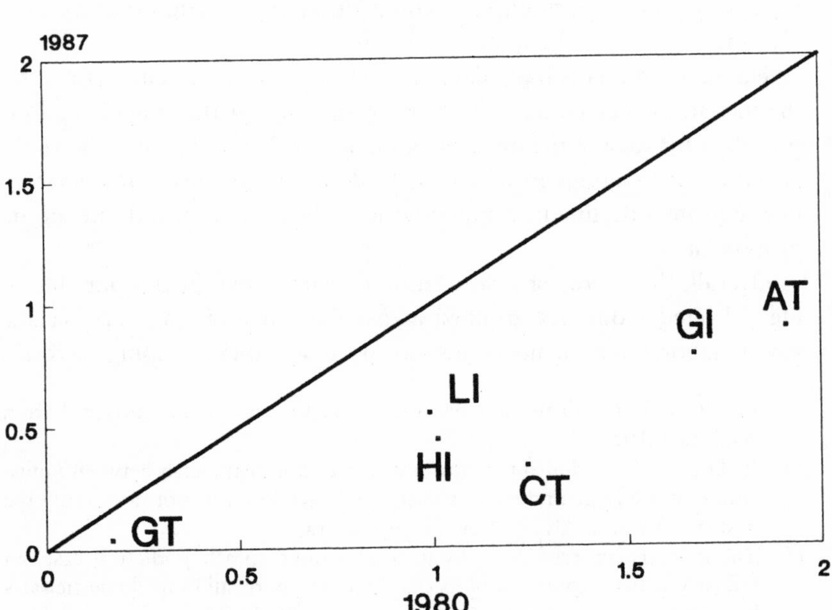

Figure 5.5. Competitiveness of clusters.

wide range of C-ratings. And the figure reveals the general pattern of changes in competitiveness across all industries over thirty years. Note that there is general decline in the 1960s, general stability from 1970 to 1980, and a sharp decline in the period from 1980 through 1987.

AT is the cluster with the highest rating overall, a strength which is derived from the strong export performance of the cluster in wheat, chemicals, machinery, communications, photographic equipment and (above all) aircraft. However, it contains several agricultural and tree-growing industries – dairy, sugar, beverages, pulp, and paper – whose C-ratings are very low. Clearly the tariffs, quotas, and subsidy programs affecting these sectors are partly responsible for their strong wage performance.[16]

HI is a mixture of high-wage, heavy industries, some of whom are highly competitive and oriented to exports, including construction equipment and engines and turbines. However, this sector also includes motor vehicles, where imports outweighed exports even in 1980 by about two to one.

CT suffered a collapse in its international position from 1960 to 1970, and then a full recovery by 1980, followed by a collapse again in 1981–83. The recovery of the 1970s appears to be associated with the pressure of modernization in the sector, which was fostered in part by a very aggressive program of federal occupational safety and health regulation.

GI is in transition in the other direction. It is a light trader overall, but in relative terms highly oriented toward exports. However, import penetration has been rising in this cluster since the late sixties, and GI's C-rating fell from 1970 to 1980 while that of AT and HI remained stable. A similar pattern holds for LI, but starting earlier, from a lower initial C-rating, and ending in a position where imports exceeded exports by 1980.

GT, finally, always the weakest trading sector, also suffered the most serious decline in trade competitiveness in the sixties. During the next decade, trade competitiveness in the garment trades remained approx-

16 Direct systematic evidence is available only on tariff protection. There is, however, no evident statistical relation between effective tariff levels, or the change in those levels, and wage changes in either decade we examine. We infer that direct subsidies (as in agriculture) and quota systems are the dominant means whereby government supports high wages in industries with low C-ratings. It is interesting that when dairy price supports were removed in 1981, wages in that industry fell out of line with the rest of AT.

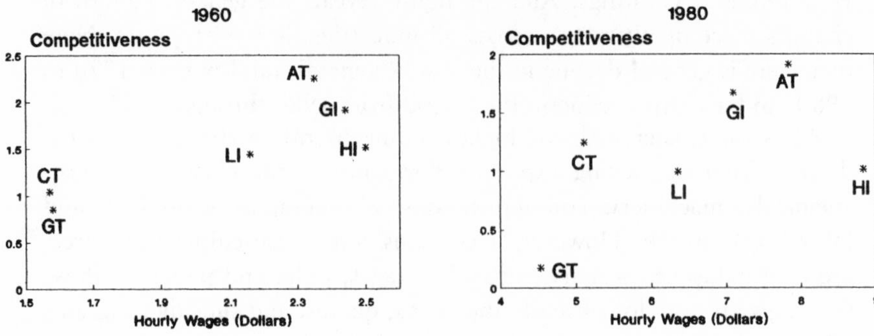

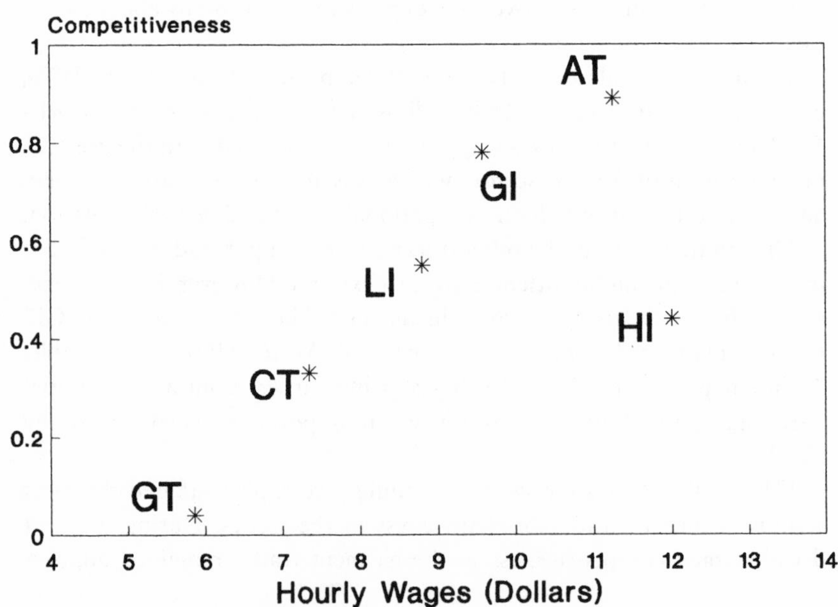

Figure 5.6. Wages and competitiveness.

imately stable, but imports overweighed exports in this cluster by six or seven to one. This ratio deteriorated still further in the 1980s.

Figure 5.6 presents the relationship between competitiveness and average hourly wages in 1960, 1980 and 1987. The figure shows that while in 1960 there was a loose association between wages and trade performance, this was owing mainly to the large differences between the clothing businesses and everything else; within high-wage manufacturing there was no such association. By 1987, however, the alignment of trade and wages had become remarkably precise. Only HI bucked the line, and this deviation is accounted for by the presence within that cluster of the automobile industry, whose high wages, poor trade performance, and protectionism all stand in contrast to the other members of the cluster.

INDUSTRIAL AND SERVICE WAGES

Do industrial wages matter? One evident limitation of this research lies in the fact that there are only some 20 million manufacturing workers in the United States, and our data cover only some 70 percent of those. Most of the action obviously lies in the service sector, and one may well ask whether the influences, notably of trade, that apparently do affect industrial wages can possibly be operating on the large mass of the population whose work does not bring them into direct contact with trade.

Mainstream theory would strongly suggest that they cannot. A service industry, virtually by definition, involves the lowest amounts of industry-specific capital equipment and presumably the lowest barriers to entry. If labor markets are efficient anywhere, they should be efficient in this part of the economy. And that means that wages in services should reflect worker productivities, not monopoly power. It would be extremely strange to find a pattern of industry-specific labor rents spilling over, so to speak, from goods production into related service activities.

This question can be approached through canonical discriminant analysis. Such analysis reduces our twenty-nine-dimensional observation vector on each industry to a low-dimensional approximation in the most efficient way, taking into account the imposed grouping structures.

Figure 5.7 presents a scatter of three-digit industries identified by cluster and plotted by their first and second canonical discriminant functions. The six-cluster grouping apparently provides a high degree of discrimination.[17] The outlier industries are plotted *post hoc,* using the weights computed for the clusters, and one can easily interpret the position of some of them. For example, blast furnaces and flat glass lie between the process-oriented advanced technology cluster, on the one hand, and the

17 All six cluster centroids are statistically distinct from each of the others at a 0.005 confidence level or higher. All five canonical discriminant functions proved statistically significant, but 73 percent of the information distinguishing the six clusters is contained in the first two, which are shown.

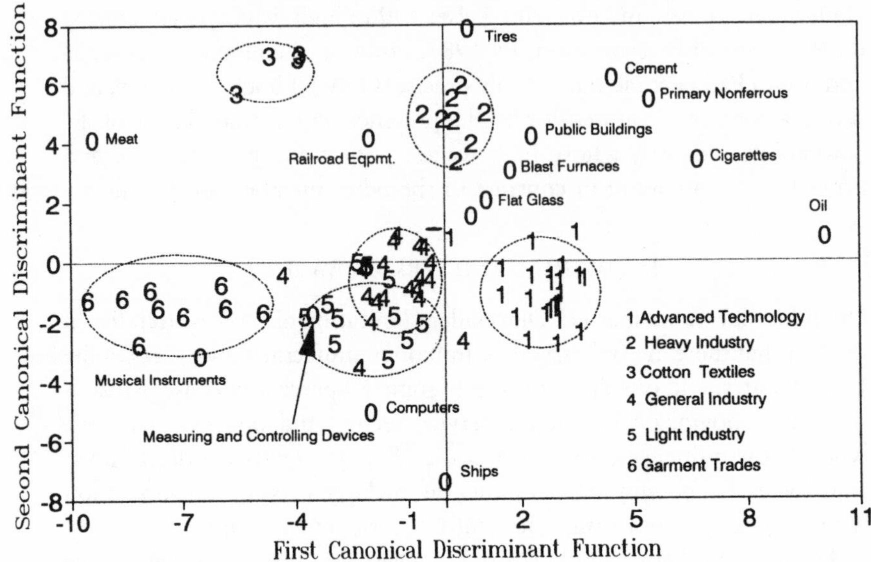

Figure 5.7. Cluster discrimination with outliers.

automobile-related heavy industry cluster, on the other. Note as well the closeness of tires to the HI cluster.

Figure 5.8 presents an application of the same canonical discriminant weights to twenty-nine-year wage paths in a number of service industries. The cluster locations are specified with labeled ovals, to improve the readability of the figure. What is particularly striking about this chart is the pattern of segmentation and perhaps industry-specific rent sharing in the service sectors that it apparently shows. For example, we see that wages in garment-related service trades, such as men and women's clothing, department stores and shoe stores, and even laundries, appear to move with wages in textiles (downward, for the most part), while wages in grocery stores move nearly alongside wages in bakeries and breweries (in the AT cluster), and wages among auto dealers move with wages among auto workers. The favored positions on the right of the chart are held by high-skilled service workers in sectors like telephones, utilities, and drug stores, whose industrial counterparts are to be found in the AT cluster. We can think of no model of a highly competitive service industry labor market that would plausibly produce this result, unless one allows for a very high degree of labor market segmentation. On the

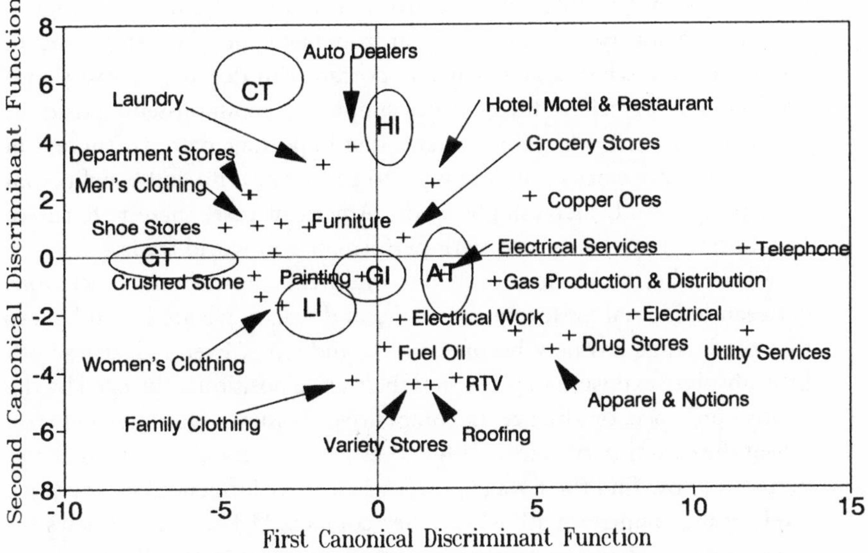

Figure 5.8. Service and manufacturing wages.

contrary, it would appear that the trail of influence from changes in the industrial wage structure, whatever their cause, stretches very far into the non-industrial reaches of the American workforce.

SUMMARY AND POLICY IMPLICATIONS

We find that the strategy of sorting industries by their wage histories produces clusters which span the range of American industrial experience with respect to both wages and trade performance. We are able, in particular, to distinguish clusters which are performing well, clusters which are performing badly, and those which are in transition in one direction and the other.

In this sense, we remain agnostic on the question of whether the American economy overall is or is not "in decline." Rather, we see weak sectors getting weaker, strong sectors getting stronger, and a range of problems emerging as a result of the increasing gap between the two.

Many of the strong sectors share, in our analysis, a common characteristic. For better or worse, industrial success in the United States is widely associated with a pattern of collaboration between the private sector and the state. Nothing we see suggests that the American state has lost its capacity to intervene effectively in industrial and technological matters. Obviously, the state role is far from being the whole story, and an argument over what is and is not important can degenerate easily into polemic. But we believe the evidence supports a common-sense position: in a country with a big government, one important path for success in private enterprise lies in finding ways to cooperate with and benefit from state power. And, increasingly in the American case, these patterns of collaboration are concerned with performance in world trade.

Where other studies have tended to find weak, amorphous associations between industrial performance, trade, and wages, we are led to believe that the linkage has now become strong and close. Even industries with little absolute exposure to trade find their wage position influenced by the relative presence, or absence, of competitive pressures. Our interpretation is that the causality runs from trade to wages, in particular that American industries now find their wage positions strongly influenced by the wage levels of the countries with whom they compete.[18] This is good news for advanced-technology sectors with competition only from fully-developed regions if at all (and strong state support in their competitive efforts), and very bad news for labor-intensive assembly operations.

Perhaps the most powerful message we have now concerns the role of wages in adjusting to the pressures of trade. At the level of the six large clusters, there are no cases of trade performance and wages moving in opposite directions.[19] That is, there is no case of rising relative wages in spite of falling trade performance – no case of manufacturing industry still inured, as many were in the sixties, to the pressures of international competition. And, perhaps more important, there was no case of falling wages alongside rising trade performance – no case of regaining advantage by cutting pay.

These results would appear to support, and rather strongly, the view

18 The question of *how* this channel operates remains to be decided. We note, without necessarily agreeing with it, the strong argument of Lawrence and Slaughter (1993) against a simple channel of price competition. It does not appear that foreign products produced with cheap labor are necessarily sold more cheaply on American markets.

19 We are aware, once again, that such divergent movements are found at the industry level. But if wages are determined at the cluster level, we repeat, it is appropriate to aggregate industries and observe patterns and movements of competitiveness at this more aggregate level.

that competition for advantage in trade is above all a matter of technological position, not of comparative pay. American industries can prosper in world and domestic markets, if and only if they maintain or indeed re-establish their technological edge. In that case, their wages will remain strong or indeed improve. AT and CT, covering between them about a quarter of manufacturing employment, are the proof. HI, covering an additional 10 percent of manufacturing workers, was also in this category at least as late as 1980.

Conversely, industries which fail to maintain or renew their advantage will gradually lose their ability to pay high wages. There is, unfortunately, no practical bottom to this process. Industrial wages in developing countries range as low as one-tenth of their U.S. equivalents, or lower, for labor that is nearly equivalent (and perhaps a good deal more docile). There is no way that cutting American wages can offset this cost advantage; only improved technology can do so. LI and GT are the proof of this proposition.

From the standpoint of workers, this result calls into question the wisdom of acquiescing in pay cuts that are (supposedly) justified by trade competition. The presence of growing competitive pressures signifies a *prima facie* need for renewal, or redeployment, of the capital stock. Wage givebacks not tied to capital renewal can forestall temporarily the loss of some jobs, but they cannot reverse competitive decline. Workers may better serve their industries, and their country, by fighting for their wages, and so forcing the choice between renewal and redeployment.

It is, of course, not possible for the United States to maintain an export advantage in all industries at once; as trade expands so the competitive position of some industries must erode as others gain. Nor can a decline happen to all U.S. industries at once. The critical question is, rather, whether the high-wage export-competitive sector can remain large enough, and grow rapidly enough, to support high wages for a large group of U.S. workers and the high import requirements of the society as a whole. And this question is very open.

What policies, then? The most compelling needs are for macroeconomic, financial and development policies that can support the trade position, the profitability and the expansion potential of the most successful U.S. industries. Some critical domestic changes, in particular, a prospective reduction of the budget deficit, have been made, and health care reform is in prospect. Lower interest rates and a lower dollar, though grudging and partial, have yielded significant results.

Going beyond these steps, attention must be paid to markets. Policy emphasis on opening Japanese markets to advanced technology products and on achieving faster growth in Europe is not misplaced. The North American Free Trade Agreement can be viewed with contingent optimism: it will help high-wage U.S. industries if it succeeds in restoring Mexico to a stable pattern of steady growth. But much more is needed. Final settlement of the Latin American debt on terms favorable to strong growth in the developing countries, a program to promote reconstruction and development in Eastern Europe, the former Soviet Union and other coordinated measures to raise the world growth rate are among essential steps not yet undertaken or even properly planned for.

On the industrial policy front specifically, our conclusions do not justify programs to expand output and employment in high wage industries *per se,* irrespective of their competitive condition and technological prospects. In this respect, we part company from a pure "labor rents" perspective on strategic trade policy. But the evidence does point to the cases of aircraft, computers, foods, drugs and cotton textiles, among others, as examples of the effects that governmental research and development programs, procurement policies, aggressive technological standard setting and even environmental and safety and health regulation can have. We believe there is no getting around this: the state has been, and will remain, a key player in the technological and therefore the competitive arena. The challenge for a new generation of industry policies must be to harness state powers to the needs of peace, social reconstruction and sustainable development.

APPENDIX: CLUSTER ANALYSIS AND INDUSTRIAL CLASSIFICATION

The problem of aggregation

Most expositions we have seen of changing patterns of wages in U.S. industry use industrial data[20] aggregated to the two-digit level of SIC classification. This reduces the manufacturing sector to a presentable number (usually twenty or so) of major industries. Studies based on the CPS are usually constrained to an even smaller grouping, because of limitations on the number of cases per industry once a large number of worker characteristics are also taken into account. Our analysis has con-

20 Or, in the case of microdata, industry dummy variables.

vinced us that aggregation of this kind is seriously misleading, especially after 1970, because it averages wage gainers with losers, and so imparts a false impression of stability to the industrial wage structure and obscures the effects of trade.

The problem evidently originates in the nature of the expansion of U.S. trade which began after 1965. This included very significant growth of trade with the developing world and with Japan, comprised of exports of capital equipment and advanced intermediates, followed by expanded imports of finished consumer goods. Much of this trade is defined as being intra-industry within the broad functional categories of the two-digit level. But it is in fact a case of the exchange of skill-intensive products for the fruits of comparatively cheap labor. Different groups of American workers even within a single two-digit classification feel radically different effects; those with skills are gainers, those without are losers.[21] To look only at shifts in trade across such classifications is therefore to lose sight of the most important trade-related transformations affecting American industry over the past twenty-five years. It is also to lose sight of the link between the observed gains of skilled workers and changes in the pattern of trade.

A typical example can be found in the textile industry, SIC code 22. Parts of that industry engaged in the production of cotton cloth experienced a major revival in their international competitive position between 1970 and 1980. Other parts, concerned with the production of wool and other fibers, did not. This divergent trade pattern was reflected in a divergent pattern of wage growth: high for cotton, lower for wool. To combine the cotton and wool mills, which are separate industries at the three-digit SIC level, into a single two-digit industry is to average together opposing patterns of trade and wage performance, and so to lose a vital piece of information. We find that similar problems arise in the aggregation of various metallurgical (SIC 33) and metalworking (34) trades, machinery (35), construction products (32), electrical equipment (36), and others.

Pitfalls of disaggregation

Analysts working with regression models avoid this pitfall by working at the lowest accessible level of aggregation, which may be the three- or four-

21 Murphy and Welch (1988a,b) demonstrate this point from the microdata.

digit SIC level. This leads to a great and fruitful multiplication of observations, resulting for example in the now widely confirmed finding (Lawrence and Lawrence 1985, Revenga 1989) that rising imports depress domestic wages. But disaggregation too has its drawbacks; what the analysis gains in degrees of freedom, it loses in specification. To the extent that a two-digit industry divides only into smaller clones of itself, no new information is being added, and the additional degrees of freedom are spurious.[22]

Moreover for expositional purposes disaggregation to the three-digit SIC level is unwieldy. There are more than a hundred manufacturing industries at that level, making qualitative and graphical assessments difficult. There is an evident need to reduce this mass of data to a small number of presentable categories, in a way that averages together divergent patterns to the least extent, and so preserves rather than destroys the evidence of changing patterns in the underlying data. But how?

Strategies of aggregation

One approach would be to compare structural characteristics of industries directly. Thus one would group together those that are most similar along the important dimensions, such as export share and import penetration. One could then ask about the wage performance of strong, average, and weak exporters, and that of strong, average, and weak importers, and so on. But such an approach, though quite commonly practiced, suffers from at least two serious difficulties. First, it requires assuming from the start that the specific measures of the structural characteristics chosen are the good ones; any change or improvement in the data or addition of new variables then requires reclassification and reaggregation of industries. Second, it forces an *a priori* decision about the relative weights of pertinent structural characteristics, some of which may be qualitatively of a different kind from others (e.g., measures of trade performance, the gender composition of the workforce, concentration indices for the industry, and so on). Yet there are no criteria for devising such weights, no theory to guide the construction of such an index.

22 The fact that three-digit industries are usually heterogeneous does not blunt this point; degrees of freedom are lost to the extent that any of the threes are clones of the twos. Does anyone really propose a model that will capture the differences of wage behavior in men's and boys' suits, as opposed to men's and boys' undergarments?

We solve the grouping problem in an entirely different and, so far as we know, novel way. Our approach is to group industries according to the similarity of the *behavioral variable*.[23] In our case, the pertinent behavioral variable is the rate of change of average hourly nominal wages in the industry, for which we have data for 90 three-digit SIC industries from 1959 through 1988. We thus group industries according to the similarity of the history of this variable, across industries, over time.

The idea is very simple. If wages in two separate industries grow in the same way, rising and falling together over an extended period of time, there are two possibilities. The industries may be linked, by an unobserved contract or even perhaps by an unobservable pattern of reference wage-change behavior, which will work to preserve over time the existing structure of relative wages between the two industries. Or the industries may share as yet unobserved structural characteristics, making them prone to react in a like way to events experienced in common. In the former case, the industries should be associated for the purpose of analyzing wage behavior, since changes affecting wages in one will *ipso facto* affect wages in the other. In the latter case, adding the industries together to form a group does no harm to the structural distinctiveness of the underlying observations. And one may then investigate the structural properties, as well as the time-dependent response patterns, of the group. It is a matter, in other words, of observing first which birds flock together, and then of investigating within-flock similarities and between-flock differences in their feathers.

Use of cluster analysis

The appropriate technique for achieving a grouping along these lines is cluster analysis.[24] Cluster analysis is a branch of numerical taxonomy, concerned with the appropriate assignment of objects to groups. It has

23 Note that this procedure is not at all akin to *sampling* on the dependent variable, something which would, in regression terms, lead to biased and inconsistent estimates. We are not sampling, but choosing an optimal level of aggregation.

24 Readers seeking a more detailed treatment are referred particularly to Sneath and Sokal (1973). Good brief discussions can be found in Bernstein (1988) and in Dillon and Goldstein (1984). Galbraith (1981) presents a discussion of the application of cluster analysis to the histories of growth rates, and an application to growth rates of federal expenditure by functional category.

enjoyed particular application in evolutionary biology, in some analytical chemistry, and in other fields where large numbers of (often diverse) characteristics must be compared. Cluster analysis provides a means to compute measures of similarity between objects, and thus criteria for assessing their closeness to each other.

The notion of "closeness" is telling, for in effect what is being computed is a measure of distance between objects, conceptualized in a space of high dimensionality where each distinct characteristic of the objects under investigation represents a different axis of measurement. Thus a collection of bird skeleta might be compared by measuring separately the length of wing, width of beak, separation of eyes, brain volume, and so on, and then constructing an index of similarity across specimens to help determine the underlying pattern of kinship between them.

Once measures of distance have been computed, cluster analysis proceeds in stepwise fashion, by associating first those objects which are evidently closest together, then those next closest, and so on. Thus one starts with a completely amorphous collection, and builds a hierarchical structure of association, until all the objects have been reduced to a single universal group. Many different rules for combining objects into clusters and clusters with each other are possible, including measurements of distance to the nearest edge of the nearest cluster, to the farthest edge, to the "centroid," and so on; each rule has its own pattern of bias, and there is no single best rule. Analysts typically proceed by choosing a rule that seems particularly appropriate to the task at hand, and then compare the results with those achieved by alternative algorithms to assess robustness.

After a structure of association has been produced, a final question concerns the appropriate level of clustering to report. There are, again, multiple approaches to this problem, of which perhaps the most rigorous is the "cubic clustering criterion," which seeks the level of clustering that most clearly distinguishes the pattern in the data from what a random draw on a uniform distribution of points in a hypercube of equivalent dimension might yield (Sarle, 1983). However, this technique is limited to those cases where the axes of dimensionality are strictly orthogonal. A more general and practical approach lies in the computation of a measure known as the "semi-partial R^2," which measures the change in the relative proportion of variance that is within clusters as compared with that between clusters at each step in the process of agglomeration. Since each step necessarily increases this relative proportion, while the object of the exercise is to group things which are broadly similar while keeping those that are broadly dissimilar apart, a good rule is to stop clustering at a point just before the semi-partial R^2 experiences a jump. (If no jump occurs, one may question whether the objects organize themselves into groups in any meaningful way.)

Cluster analysis has achieved little popularity among economists, for several reasons. First, it is often the case that changes in the scale of measurement of characteristics will affect the measures of similarity, and hence the composition of the clusters, if the various characteristic variables are correlated. Since any scheme of weighting variables is effectively a matter of scaling, the patterns of clustering appear dependent on an (effectively arbitrary) assignment of weights.

Kaufman et al. (1981) propose to solve this problem by computing the principal components of the matrix of characteristic variables and performing cluster analysis on the orthogonalized principal components rather than on the direct measures of characteristic variables themselves. This is an elegant solution, but it raises a further question, namely the theoretical basis for the choice of characteristic variables. Kaufman et al. are concerned with identifying major groupings in American industry, and they proceed by accumulating all descriptive data that are readily available, including information on sales, profitability, concentration ratios, capital intensity, advertising expenditure, exposure to regulation, productivity, and so on. The resulting clusters are interesting, but it is unfortunately unclear what they mean. And there is always the suspicion that a different collection of heterogeneous data (e.g., detailed data on labor force composition) might yield a different pattern of classification.

We solve both problems in a simple and general way, by choosing a matrix of characteristic variables that clearly measures the similarity in which we are interested, on the one hand, and that consists solely of homogeneous and unit-free numbers and is therefore immune to scaling and weighting difficulties, on the other. Our clustering criterion is purely behavioral; we form our clusters without any prejudicial reference to the qualitative characteristics of the industries being clustered. And then, after the clusters have been formed, we search for qualitative homogeneities within, and distinctions between, the clusters.

Our characteristic variable is the annual percentage rate of change of hourly nominal wages, from 1959 through 1988, for each of ninety three-digit SIC manufacturing industries. We thus rest our analysis on a triangular matrix of ninety rows and columns, each of whose elements is a euclidean distance in twenty-nine dimensions, one for each year, computed by pairwise comparison of annual rates of change of wages (w). The general formula for measuring the similarity of (distance between) two patterns of wage change over T years in industries X and Y is:

$$D = \sqrt{\sum_{t=1}^{T} (w_t^x - w_t^y)^2}$$

In order to achieve a tight and robust clustering, we followed a two-stage procedure, which involves the use of an initial clustering with a prespecified number of clusters to identify outliers (industries with highly unusual wage histories).[25] This is helpful since the inclusion of such industries can cause a distortion in the calculation of the centroids of clusters, and hence alter the sequence of agglomeration. With thirteen outliers excluded, we proceeded to the application of a full-scale agglomerative procedure to the remaining observations. We used Ward's minimum variance method, which proceeds by adding to clusters at each stage in such a way as to minimize the variance within (width of) newly formed clusters, relative to the variance remaining between clusters. We then used the semi-partial R^2 criterion to choose a point at which to stop. In our case, this criterion yielded two possible stopping places, the first at fourteen distinct clusters, the second at seven. We chose the latter, principally to simplify exposition of the results. Then, as one of the seven clusters was revealed to consist of only two industries, both quite small, we chose to treat them as separate outliers, reducing the final number of clusters to six. This expositional convenience does not alter any substantive conclusion.

REFERENCES

Bernstein, Ira H. (1988). *Applied Multivariate Analysis,* New York: Springer-Verlag, 357–363.

Bhagwati, Jagdish (1988). *Protectionism,* Cambridge, Mass.: MIT Press.

25 In principle, alternative clustering procedures can yield different results. In practice, our results are quite robust to alternative procedures, leading us to believe that we have in fact organized U.S. industrial wage behavior in an informationally efficient way. We have however discovered that a three-stage procedure, involving (1) isolation of outliers, (2) Ward's method to give an optimal number of clusters, and (3) K-means clustering, a non-hierarchical procedure, to find the best allocation of industries to that number of clusters, also yields an informative clustering that may be superior in some respects. Progress along these lines will be reported in future work.

Bound, John, and George Johnson (1992). "Changes in the Structure of Wages in the 1980s: An Evaluation of Alternative Explanations," *American Economic Review,* Vol. 82, June: 371–392.

Buchele, Robert (1983). "Economic Dualism and Employment Stability," *Industrial Relations,* 22, No. 3: 410–418.

Dickens, William T., and Kevin Lang (1988). "Why it Matters What We Trade: The Case for Active Policy," in Laura D'Andrea Tyson, William T. Dickens, and John Zysman, eds. (1988). *The Dynamics of Trade and Employment,* New York: Ballinger.

Dickens, William T., and Lawrence F. Katz (1988). "Further Notes on the Inter-industry Wage Structure," mimeo, Harvard University, August.

Dillon, William R., and Matthew Goldstein (1984). *Multivariate Analysis: Methods and Applications,* New York: John Wiley & Sons, 157–208.

Doeringer, Peter B., and Michael J. Piore (1971). *Internal Labor Markets and Manpower Analysis,* Lexington: Heath.

Eckstein, Otto, and Thomas A. Wilson (1962). "The Determination of Money Wages in American Industry, *Quarterly Journal of Economics* 76, No. 3: 379–414.

Galbraith, James K. (1981). "A Theory of the Government Budget Process," Ph.D. Dissertation, Yale University.

(1989). *Balancing Acts: Technology, Finance and the American Future,* New York: Basic Books.

Grunfeld, Y., and Zvi Griliches (1960). "Is Aggregation Necessarily Bad?" *Review of Economics and Statistics,* 42: 1–13.

Katz, Lawrence F. (1988). "Some Recent Developments in Labor Economics and Their Implications for Macroeconomics," *Journal of Money, Credit and Banking,* 20, No. 3 (August): 507–530.

Katz, Lawrence F., and Lawrence H. Summers (1989). "Industry Rents: Evidence and Implications," *Brookings Papers on Economic Activity: Microeconomics, 1989,* Washington: Brookings Institution, 209–290.

Kaufman, Robert L., Randy Hodson, and Neil D. Fligstein (1981). "Defrocking Dualism: A New Approach to Defining Industrial Sectors," *Social Science Research,* 10: 1–31.

Krueger, Alan (1992). "How Computers Have Changed the Wage Structure: Evidence from Microdata, 1984–89," mimeo, Princeton University.

Krugman, Paul, ed. (1987). *Strategic Trade Policy and the New International Economics,* Cambridge, Mass.: MIT Press.

"The Rich, the Right and the Facts" (1992). *American Prospect,* Fall: 19–31.

Lawrence, Colin, and Robert Z. Lawrence (1985). "Manufacturing Wage Dispersion: An End Game Interpretation," *Brookings Papers on Economic Activity,* 1: 47–116.

Lawrence, Robert Z., and Matthew J. Slaughter (1993). "Trade and U.S. Wages: Great Sucking Sound or Small Hiccup?" mimeo, Harvard University.

Murphy, Kevin, and Finis Welch (1988a). "The Structure of Wages," mimeo, University of Chicago.

(1988b). "Wage Differentials in the 1980s: The Role of International Trade," mimeo, University of Chicago.

Revenga, Ana (1989). "Wage Determination in an Open Economy: International Trade and U.S. Manufacturing Wages," mimeo, Harvard University.

Sachs, Jeffrey (1985). "The Dollar and the Policy Mix," *Brookings Papers on Economic Activity* 1: 117–97.

Sarle, Warren S. (1983). "Cubic Clustering Criterion," Cary, N.C.: SAS Institute, Inc., SAS Technical Report A-108, November 15.

Sneath, Peter A. H., and Robert R. Sokal (1973). *Numerical Taxonomy: The Principles and Practice of Numerical Classification,* San Francisco: W. H. Freeman.

6

A comparative analysis of the sources of America's relative economic decline

JEFFREY A. HART

Changes in international competitiveness since World War II have favored Germany and Japan over France, the United States, and Britain. This applies to competitiveness in general, but is examined here in three specific industries: steel, automobiles, and semiconductors. Explanations of changes in competitiveness often focus on economic and cultural variables, but an examination of the three industries shows that a better explanation can be found in the way in which each country organizes its state and society. State–societal arrangements influence competitiveness mainly through their impact on the speed of diffusion of new technologies. The disparate cases of Germany (strong business and labor, weak government) and Japan (strong business and government, weak labor) suggest that there is more than one path to competitiveness. The literature on competitiveness has focused too much on Japan, and therefore on state industrial policies, as the key to increasing competitiveness. The German case shows that increased competitiveness is possible with a relatively weak state, but only if there is a major commitment to upgrading the skill levels of the workforce.

INTRODUCTION

The main argument of this chapter and the larger research project from which it springs[1] is that variation in state–societal arrangements is a key

1 Jeffrey A. Hart, *Rival Capitalists: International Competitiveness in the United States, Japan, and Western Europe* (Ithaca, N.Y.: Cornell University Press, 1992).

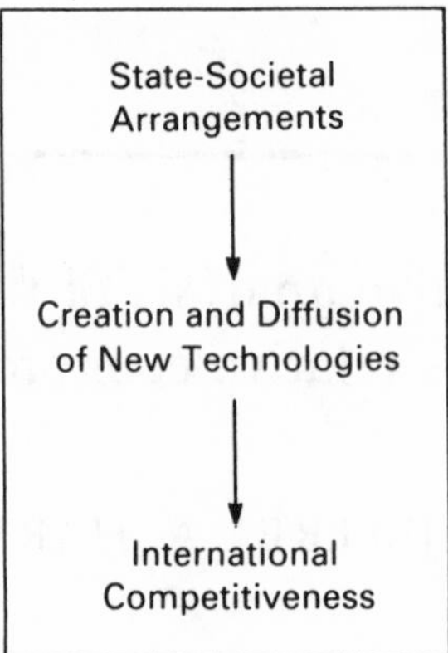

Figure 6.1. The main argument.

to explaining changes in the relative international competitiveness of the five largest capitalist countries since World War II. The reason that state–societal arrangements matter is that they can accelerate or impede the development and diffusion of technological innovations that are crucial for competitiveness (see Figure 6.1). This impact is felt most strongly during technological transitions such as the one we are currently experiencing.[2]

Because state–societal arrangements vary significantly among the major industrialized capitalist countries, there is likely to be very uneven growth during periods of technological transition. This uneven growth is the most important source of changes in the distribution of economic power, and therefore of military/strategic power.[3]

2 The idea of technological transition is taken from a variety of sources including: James Kurth, "The Political Consequences of the Product Cycle: Industrial History and Political Outcomes," *International Organization*, 33 (Winter 1979): 1–34; Michael J. Piore and Charles F. Sabel, *The Second Industrial Divide* (New York: Basic Books, 1984).

3 The key original works on hegemonial decline are: Charles Kindleberger, *The World in Depression, 1929–1939* (Berkeley: University of California Press, 1973); Stephen D. Krasner, "State Power and the Structure of International Trade," *World Politics*, 28 (April 1976): 317–47; Robert Gilpin, *U.S. Power and the Multinational Corporation* (New York: Basic Books, 1975). More recent discussions of the theory can be found in Robert Gilpin, *The Political Economy of International Relations* (Princeton, N.J.: Princeton University

State–societal arrangements are deeply rooted in the history of each country. Major upheavals connected with intense domestic social turmoil, the fighting of global wars, or drastic shifts in international competitiveness can result in changes in those arrangements. Despite some change in state–societal arrangements over time, there is little evidence that variance in arrangements has decreased. The decline in U.S. competitiveness and the rise in Japanese and German competitiveness has resulted in increasing conflict over international economic regimes in the last two decades.

All countries favor international economic regimes that are congenial to their internal state–societal arrangements. They would rather fight over international economic regimes than change their domestic arrangements. Economic hegemony permits one economically powerful country (e.g., Britain in the nineteenth century and the United States after World War II) to establish regimes that are highly consistent with its domestic arrangements. However, winning the consent of other countries to the establishment of these regimes requires compromises, and a certain amount of variation in state–societal arrangements will be tolerated as a result.[4]

As other countries grow in relative economic strength, and especially if the hegemony declines relative to one or more challengers, there will be increasing conflict over the content of preestablished regimes. There will also be debates over domestic arrangements in the major industrial countries, especially those suffering a relative decline (e.g., Britain and the United States), but also in those whose competitiveness has increased (e.g., Germany and Japan). Unless there is a major economic crisis or some other cataclysmic event (like a major war or revolution), these debates will result only in gradual changes in state–societal arrangements.

Press, 1987); and Michael C. Webb and Stephen D. Krasner, "Hegemonic Stability Theory: An Empirical Assessment," *Review of International Studies,* 15 (April 1989): 183–98.

4 I am taking, as a point of departure, the work on hegemonic stability by scholars like Robert Gilpin, Stephen Krasner, Charles Kindleberger, and Robert Keohane. The idea that variation in state–societal arrangements is tolerated is consistent with John Ruggie's idea of "embedded liberalism." See his "International Regimes, Transactions, and Change: Embedded Liberalism in the Post-War Economic Order," *International Organization,* 36 (Spring 1982): 379–415.

RESULTS OF EMPIRICAL ANALYSIS

These propositions were examined in the context of a comparative analysis of the role played by state–societal arrangements in changes in international competitiveness in the five largest industrial capitalist countries – the United States, Japan, the Federal Republic of Germany, France, and Britain – in three industries – steel, automobiles, and semiconductors – since World War II. These three industries were chosen to represent three distinct waves of innovation in industrial technology and to test the proposition that there is more consistency in state–societal arrangements within nations across industries than there is within industries across nations.

One of the key findings was that international competitiveness in steel, autos, and semiconductors has been strongly dependent on the diffusion of new technologies. In the case of steel, the new technologies were basic oxygen processing and continuous casting. In the case of autos, the new technologies were just-in-time (or *kanban*) production systems and, later, new forms of factory automation. In the case of semiconductors, the new technologies were the product and process technologies necessary to move from one generation of semiconductors to another (e.g., from transistors to integrated circuits and from integrated circuits to large-scale integrated circuits).

Those countries that were successful in innovating and diffusing these technologies earliest were most likely to increase their share of world production, to experience high rates of productivity growth, to maintain or increase employment, and to experience fewer financial crises. Overall, innovation was not as important as diffusion. Even if domestic firms were not first in commercializing a new technology, the national industries that widely adopted new technologies in a timely manner had a distinct competitive advantage over those that did not, independently of other presumably important variables like average wages.

DEFINING INTERNATIONAL COMPETITIVENESS

The definition of international competitiveness has proven to be controversial, but one proposed by the President's Commission on Industrial Competitiveness seems to satisfy many experts: "the degree to which a nation can, under free and fair market conditions, produce goods and services that meet the test of international markets while simultaneously maintaining or expanding the real income of its citizens."[5] This definition has three main elements which deserve some elaboration.

First, meeting the test of international markets means the ability to design, produce, and distribute goods and services at costs which are globally competitive. Factor costs and the application of leading-edge technologies enter in here most centrally. If factor costs are high or rising, application of technologies which increase the productivity of factors will be crucial for maintaining or increasing competitiveness. If a country's factor costs are low, the application of productivity-enhancing technologies can give an extra boost to its competitiveness.[6]

Second, there is the question of whether market conditions are free or fair. If they are not, then some countries will appear to be internationally competitive when they are not, because their domestic markets are sheltered or their firms are receiving large subsidies. Any country can have a simulacrum of competitiveness by adopting illiberal policies. Similarly, truly competitive countries will appear not to be competitive, because their unsubsidized and unprotected industries are forced to compete with subsidized or sheltered firms from other lands.

Third, there is the question of real incomes. If a country is experiencing a large increase in exports, but real incomes are declining, it may be inferred that workers and other citizens are subsidizing the nation's competitiveness. Any country can adopt labor market policies which reduce real wages in order to improve its position in world trade. This practice, however, should not be identified with genuine competitiveness.[7]

National competitiveness is not the same as the competitiveness of nationally owned firms. Firms which are multinational in operations frequently put large amounts of their productivity-enhancing technolo-

5 *Global Competition: The New Reality,* Report of the President's Commission on Industrial Competitiveness, Vol. II (Washington, D.C.: U.S. Government Printing Office, 1985), p. 6; see also *The Cuomo Commission Report: A New American Formula for a Strong Economy* (New York: Simon & Schuster, 1988), p. 19; and Stephen S. Cohen and John Zysman, *Manufacturing Matters: The Myth of the Post-Industrial Economy* (New York: Basic Books, 1987), p. 60.

6 For a much lengthier discussion of the variables which explain competitiveness, see Michael Porter, *The Competitive Advantage of Nations* (New York: Free Press, 1990), chap. 3.

7 "Competitiveness is associated with rising living standards, and an upgrading of employment." Cohen and Zysman, *Manufacturing Matters,* p. 61.

gies in foreign locations. Thus, it is possible for them to be internationally competitive without having much impact on the competitiveness of the home country. Indeed, encouraging the local presence of foreign firms which use state-of-the-art design, production, and distribution technologies can conceivably be a more effective way of enhancing national competitiveness than supporting domestic firms.[8]

It is not necessary to be competitive in all industries in order for a country to be competitive overall, but it *is* necessary to be competitive in a variety of industries. Countries which become overly specialized in the production of a small number of industrial goods tend to become overly vulnerable to external economic shocks, such as disruptions in the supply of vital inputs, sudden changes in the demand for specialized products, and predatory behavior on the part of foreign producers in upstream or downstream markets. More importantly, there are industries which are economically strategic in the sense that a failure to be competitive in those industries makes it impossible for a country to be competitive in a range of others, because participation in those industries is necessary to obtain access to generic technologies.[9]

MEASURING INTERNATIONAL COMPETITIVENESS

There are two basic levels at which to measure national competitiveness: economy-wide and industry-specific. Here the stress is on the latter, although there appears to be sufficient consistency across industries to suggest that an economy-wide approach is possible. The main reason to measure competitiveness at the level of specific industries it that data on specific industries is easier to interpret than data on the economy as a whole. Interpreting economy-wide data on competitiveness is complicated by a number of problems to be discussed below. In addition, if

8 This issue is discussed in Jeffrey A. Hart and Laura Tyson, "Responding to the Challenge of HDTV," *California Management Review,* 31 (Summer 1989): 132–45; Robert B. Reich, "Who is Us?" *Harvard Business Review,* January–February 1990: 53–64; and Laura Tyson, "They Are Not Us: Why American Ownership Still Matters," *American Prospect,* Winter 1991: 37–49.

9 See Hart and Tyson, "Responding to the Challenge," pp. 37–39. For a contrasting view, see Porter, *Competitive Advantage,* pp. 6–11. Here Porter argues that national competitiveness is either meaningless or simply a proxy for productivity. Porter does not accept the idea that some industries may be economically strategic. He notes, however, the tendency of firms in any given nation to be competitive in clusters of related industries.

technological innovation and diffusion is an important mediating variable, as hypothesized above (see Figure 6.1), it will be impossible to test this without looking at industry-specific data, since technologies vary widely from industry to industry. The competitiveness of an entire country cannot be measured by focusing on a small set of specific industries, however. A judicious combination of industry-specific and economy-wide indicators is the best way to measure national competitiveness.

Competitiveness at the level of the whole economy

International competitiveness can be measured on an economy-wide basis using such indicators as: (1) trade balances, (2) world export shares, (3) rates of productivity growth, (4) growth in real wages, and (5) price elasticities of imports.[10] Increasing trade balances and world export shares, high rates of productivity growth, rapidly growing real wages, and decreasing price elasticities of imports are all indicative of growing international competitiveness. Because productivity growth tends to be strongly correlated with growth in real income, and because sustained growth in productivity requires constant upgrading of production techniques, productivity growth is the most fundamental and reliable way of measuring national competitiveness.[11]

All of the economy-wide indicators are imperfect in some respect. Markets are often not free or fair. Trade balances and world export shares are subject to governmental manipulation of exchange rates and trade barriers. National production and export statistics usually do not reflect the ability of multinational firms to penetrate foreign markets through local production and licensing of technologies. Labor productivity grows rapidly during periods of massive layoffs; both labor and capital productivity increase sharply whenever aggregate demand surges. Nevertheless, the indicators listed above do a reasonably good job of measuring shifts in competitiveness over time.

A more accurate view of competitiveness is obtained by combining the separate indicators into a composite view. For example, a country which experiences growth in productivity, world export shares, *and* real wages

10 The logic behind this last measure is that quality differentials between domestic products and imports will be indicated by low price elasticities of imports. See *Global Competition: The New Reality*, p. 8; and Cohen and Zysman, *Manufacturing Matters*, pp. 61 and 68.

11 Porter, *Competitive Advantage*, p. 6.

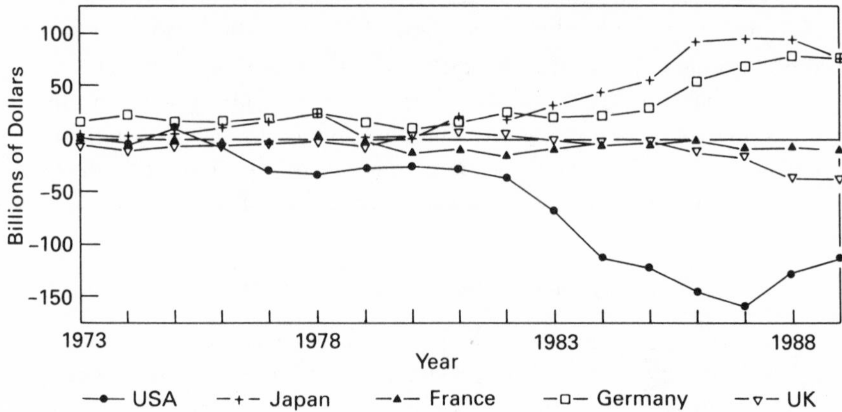

Figure 6.2. Balance of trade of the five countries. *Source:* International Monetary Fund, *International Financial Statistics Yearbook* (Washington, D.C.: 1990), p. 140.

(e.g., Japan) is clearly more competitive than one experiencing declining productivity, world export shares, and real wages (e.g., Britain).

Trade balances and world export shares

Between 1980 and 1987, Japan and Germany experienced increasing global trade surpluses, while the United States and Britain suffered increasing deficits (see Figure 6.2).[12] France suffered from chronic but relatively smaller trade deficits than both the United States and Britain in the 1980s.

World export shares in manufactured goods provide a similar picture. The United States and Britain both lost considerably in their shares of world manufactured exports between 1960 and 1982, although the United States started from a higher level. Japan rose rapidly, from around 6 percent of world exports to around 14 percent during the same period. Germany held steady at around 20 percent; France did the same at around 10 percent.[13]

12 The trade surplus from exports of petroleum in Britain (which ended in 1983) complicates using the trade surplus as a measure of the competitiveness of Britain.

13 Bruce R. Scott, "National Strategies: Key to International Competition," in Bruce R. Scott and George C. Lodge, eds., *U.S. Competitiveness in the World Economy* (Boston: Harvard Business School Press, 1985), p. 27.

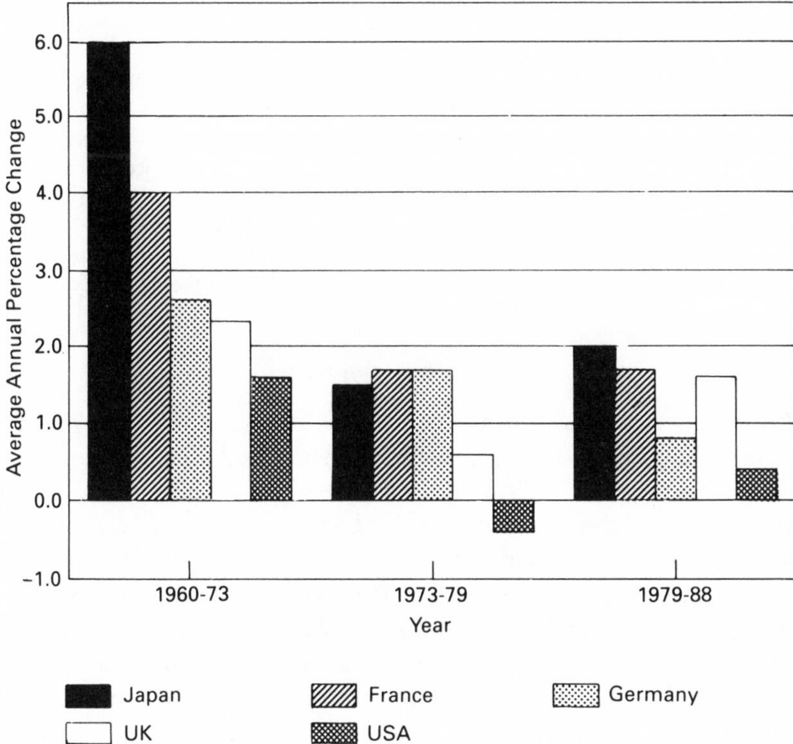

Figure 6.3. Growth in productivity in the five countries. *Source:* Organization for Economic Cooperation and Development, *OECD Economic Outlook,* No. 48 (December 1990), p. 120.

Productivity

Growth in productivity has been most rapid in Japan and least rapid in the United States since 1960. From 1966 to 1973, Japanese total factor productivity grew at 6.3 percent per year. U.S. total factor productivity grew at 1.5 percent per year from 1960 to 1973. French productivity growth has been somewhat more rapid than that of both Germany and Britain, but all three have experienced more rapid productivity growth than the United States (see Figure 6.3).

Prior to the late 1960s, labor productivity in manufacturing in the United States grew at around 3 percent annually. Between 1973 and 1979, it grew at only 1 percent annually. Labor productivity growth increased to 3 percent between 1979 and 1986. But the authors of the

MIT study *Made in America* warn against interpreting this as a return to economic health:

> A significant fraction of the productivity gains in manufacturing were achieved by shutting down inefficient plants and by permanently laying off workers at others. Employment in U.S. manufacturing industry declined by 10 percent between 1979 and 1986, and that loss of jobs accounted for about 36 percent of the recorded improvement in labor productivity. Another reason for caution is that the productivity recovery spanned a deep recession; productivity growth always accelerates following a recession as factories increase their output and take up the slack in the economy.[14]

Growth in real wages

Real wages rose steadily in all five countries between 1960 and 1989. The largest increases in real wages during that period were in France and Britain (see Figure 6.4). The smallest increases were in Germany and the United States, which started the period with higher absolute wages than the other three. The fact that real wages in Japan and Germany grew slower than those in France and Britain, while the former two countries outperformed the others in trade and productivity, suggests strongly that wage restraint was an important factor in their increased overall competitiveness. The slow growth of U.S. real wages combined with its poor trade, profits, and productivity performance suggests a general decline in competitiveness. The British pattern, as usual, is the worst: bad trade and productivity performances and rapidly increasing real wages.

Price elasticity of imports

The price elasticity of imports in the United States increased in the 1970s and 1980s, as U.S. buyers no longer were willing to pay a premium for U.S.-made products because of perceived differences in quality.[15] Price elasticity of imports has never been particularly high in Japan because of a generally low propensity to import (which has a lot to do with the Japa-

14 Michael L. Dertouzos, Richard K. Lester, Robert M. Solow, and the MIT Commission on Industrial Productivity, *Made in America: Regaining the Productive Edge* (Cambridge, Mass.: MIT Press, 1989), p. 31.

15 Cohen and Zysman, *Manufacturing Matters,* p. 67. Cohen and Zysman cite the following source: Elizabeth Kremp and Jacques Mistral, "Commerce extérieur americain: d'où vient, où va le déficit?" *Economie prospective internationale,* 22 (1985): 5–41.

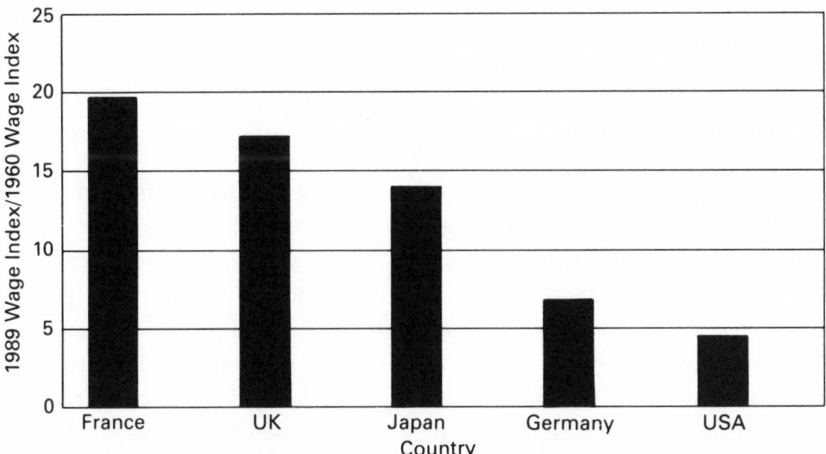

Figure 6.4. Growth in real wages in the five countries, 1960–89. *Source:* International Monetary Fund, *International Financial Statistics Yearbook* (Washington, D.C.: 1990), pp. 112–13.

nese distribution system). Nevertheless, Japanese consumers began to buy consumer products from abroad as their affluence rose in the 1980s: especially luxury goods from Europe and low-end standardized products from Asian developing countries. The increased imports from Asia were partly the result of perceptions of decreasing quality differentials, while the imports from Europe were the result of continued perceptions of quality differentials in favor of European goods. In producer goods, with a few exceptions, Japanese buyers remained convinced of the superiority of Japanese products. Consumers in Britain and France have behaved more like those in the United States in recent years; consumers in Germany more like those in Japan.

Summary of economy-wide indicators of competitiveness

In summary, the economy-wide data on competitiveness indicate increased competitiveness across the board in Japan and Germany, decreased competitiveness in the United States and Britain, with France somewhere in the middle. Japan does particularly well in trade and productivity; but Germany remains a close second. The United States and Britain both suffer a decline in competitiveness, but the United States starts from a much better initial position. The French do remarkably well until the 1980s, when they begin to experience chronic trade deficits and decreased productivity growth, while wages remain on a steep upward trajectory.

COMPETITIVENESS IN SPECIFIC INDUSTRIES

Useful indicators for national competitiveness in specific industries are: (1) growth in national shares of global production; (2) growth in employment of production workers; (3) growth in revenues and profits of firms in the industry; and (4) the frequency of industrial crises. In a specific industry, if a country is increasing its share of global production, increasing (or decreasing relatively slowly) its level of employment, increasing its revenues and profits, and experiencing very few industrial crises relative to other countries, then that country has increased its international competitiveness. Although it will be impossible to present statistical evidence for all these indicators here, it will still be possible to show that the available industry-specific data reinforce the message conveyed by the economy-wide data: that is, that Japan and Germany have increased their international competitiveness relative to the United States and Britain, while France lies somewhere in between.

Production shares

Global production of steel was 313 million metric tons in 1956. By 1985, this had increased to 793 million metric tons. The average annual growth of steel production by volume during that period was 3.4 percent. The share of U.S. production in this total dropped from 37 percent to 11 percent (see Figure 6.5). The absolute level of U.S. production remained near the 1956 level through the beginning of the 1980s – averaging around 120 million metric tons. The mid-1950s were a relatively high point in the U.S. share of global production because of the sales of iron and steel to a Europe not fully recovered from the damages of World War II, and because of a defense industry that had grown enormously during the Korean War.

The European share of global steel production rose substantially from the mid-1950s to the early 1970s, finally overtaking U.S. production in 1968, and then dropped off to a plateau of 130–140 million metric tons. The Japanese, also recovering from World War II, increased their share of global production from 4 percent in 1956 to around 15 percent in the late

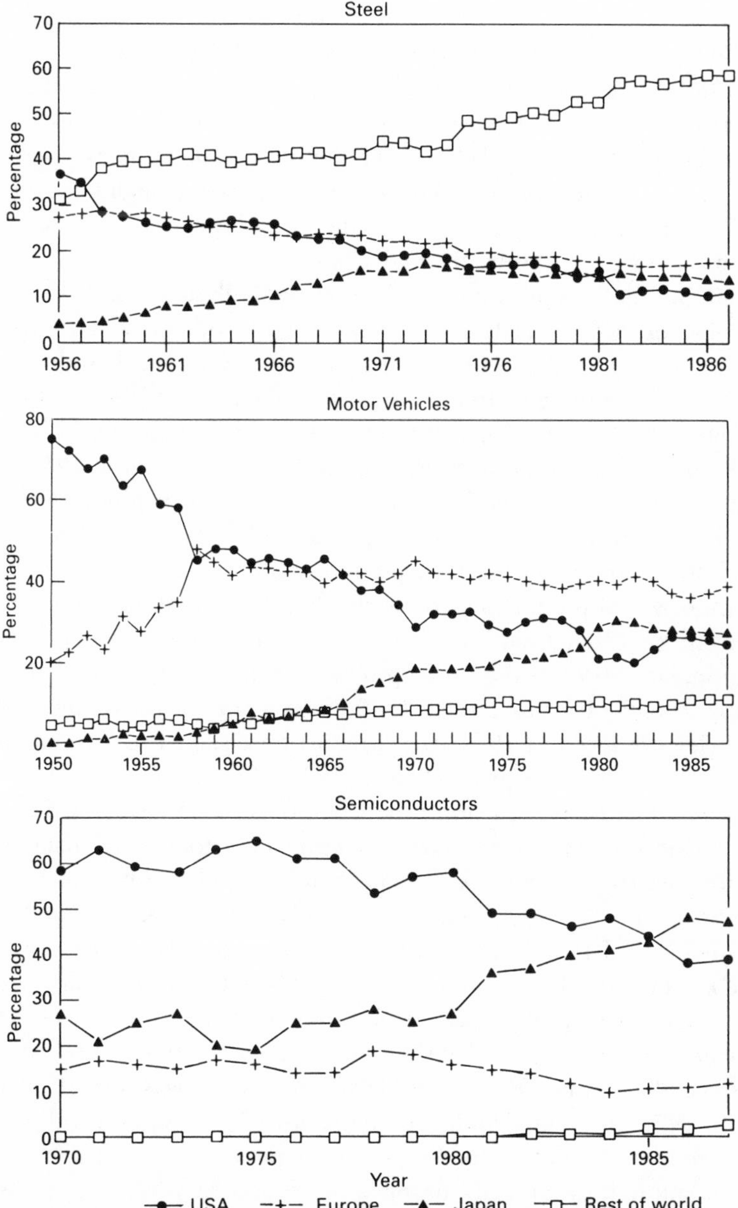

Figure 6.5. World production shares in steel, motor vehicles, and semiconductors. Dataquest statistics for semiconductor production include estimates of captive production of semiconductors by large firms like IBM and AT&T. *Sources:* American Iron and Steel Institute, *Annual Statistical Report* (Washington, D.C.: various years); Motor Vehicle Manufacturers Association, *Motor Vehicle Facts and Figures* (Detroit: various years); and Dataquest.

1970s. Japanese steel production only surpassed that of the United States in 1980, but it should be recalled that the gross national product (GNP) of Japan was about half the GNP of the United States at that time. Japanese production levels hovered around 115 million metric tons after 1975. U.S. production, in contrast, never regained its high point of 151 million metric tons (in 1973), but rather sank lower and lower to below 90 million metric tons by the mid-1980s.

Global motor vehicle production grew rapidly after the 1950s. The number of motor vehicles manufactured worldwide grew at an average annual rate of 5.1 percent between 1956 and 1985. Global production of motor vehicles doubled from 10 million in the early 1950s to 20 million in the mid-1960s and doubled again to 40 million in the late 1970s. The U.S. share of global production dropped from 75 percent in 1950 to 26 percent in 1985. Europe increased its share of global production from about 20 percent in 1950 to almost 50 percent in the late 1960s, but fell back to less than 40 percent by the end of the 1970s. Japan increased its share of world production from virtually zero in 1950 to more than 30 percent by 1981. Even though Europe remained the largest producing region, Japan became the largest producing country – Japan took the lead away from the United States in 1980. From a peak of 12.9 million motor vehicles produced in 1978, U.S. production declined to 7.0 million in 1982 (lower than the production level of 1962), recovering to 11.7 million in 1985. In 1987, world production of semiconductors was around $39 billion and of integrated circuits (semiconductor devices that contain entire electronic circuits on a single chip) around $29 billion. Between 1970 and 1987, world production of semiconductors grew at an average annual rate of 18.8 percent. The share of discrete devices (devices which are *not* integrated circuits) in the overall market for semiconductors has been declining steadily since the invention of integrated circuits in 1958. Integrated circuits were slightly over 30 percent of world production of semiconductors in 1970; by the 1980s, this figure was over 70 percent.

In 1975, the United States accounted for 65 percent of world production of semiconductors and 76 percent of integrated circuits. The corresponding figures for 1987 dropped to 39 and 41 percent, respectively. Japan's share of world semiconductor production increased from less than 20 percent in 1975 to 47 percent in 1987. Its share of world integrated circuit production increased from 14 percent in 1975 to 48 percent in 1987. It was in 1986 that Japanese production surpassed that of the United States in both semiconductors and integrated circuits.

The increase in the Japanese share of world production is remarkable, but perhaps more important is its domination of markets for the more advanced integrated circuits and especially CMOS (complementary metal oxide silicon) devices and the latest generation of random access memories (RAMs). By the end of 1979, the Japanese firms controlled 43 percent of the U.S. market for 16-kilobit (16K) dynamic RAM (DRAM) devices.[16] By the end of 1981, they supplied almost 70 percent of 64K DRAMs in the open part of the U.S. market.[17] In 1984, Japanese firms introduced 256K DRAMs before a number of major U.S. firms did so. The same thing happened in 1987 with 1-Megabit DRAMs. Japanese firms controlled over 90 percent of both 256K and 1-Megabit DRAM markets after 1986, and, on average, 75 percent of total DRAM markets between 1985 and 1987.[18]

Employment

Employment in the British steel industry fell from over 270,000 in 1972 to around 52,000 in 1981. This was the largest percentage drop in steel employment in the five countries, but the largest absolute decline in steel employment was in the United States. U.S. employment in steel dropped from 478,000 in 1974 to 170,000 in 1988. Although there were major reductions in jobs in the Japanese and German steel industries after 1973, they were not as large as the declines in the United States and Britain (see Figure 6.6).[19]

Employment in the British auto industry fell from 184,000 in 1972 (a peak year) to 78,000 in 1985 (see Figure 6.6). U.S. auto employment dropped from 304,000 in 1978 to 194,000 in 1982, but rose again to around 250,000 in 1984 and 1985 (due to the recovery of the U.S.

16 Michael Borrus, James Millstein, and John Zysman, *International Competition in Advanced Industrial Sectors: Trade and Development in the Semiconductor Industry* (Washington, D.C.: Joint Economic Committee of Congress, 1982), p. 106.

17 Gene Bylinsky, "Japan's Ominous Chip Victory," *Fortune*, December 14, 1981, p. 55.

18 Dataquest data presented by Andrew A. Procasssini, President of the Semiconductor Industry Association, at Stanford University, on October 21, 1988.

19 All data cited in this paragraph are from the *U.S. Industrial Outlook* (Washington, D.C.: United States Government Printing Office, 1988 and 1989).

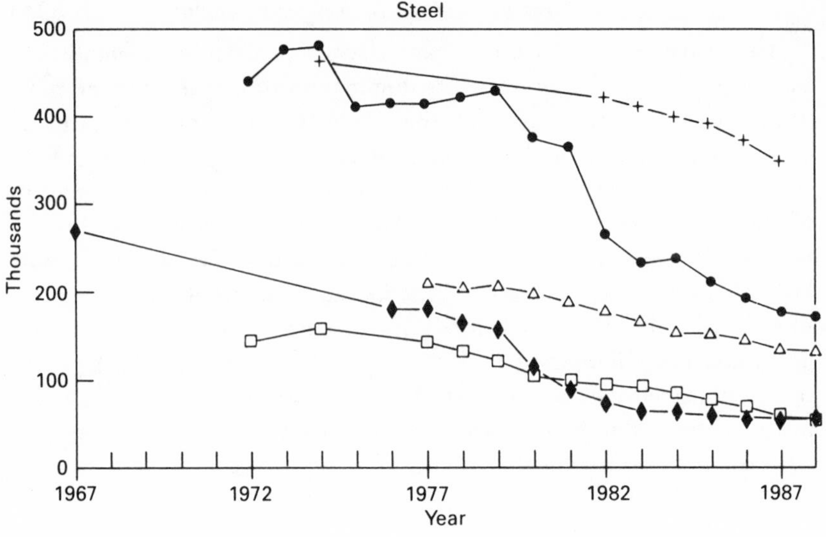

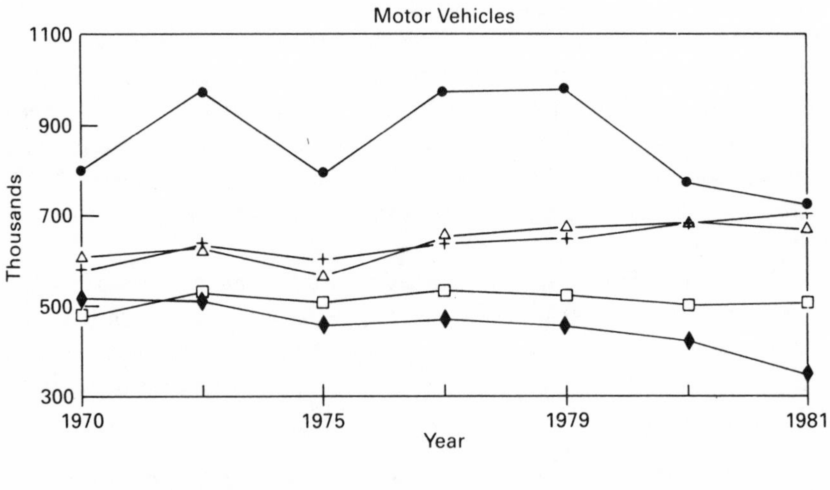

Figure 6.6. Employment in steel and motor vehicles. *Sources:* Louka Tsoukalis and Robert Strauss, "Crisis and Adjustment in European Steel: Beyond Laissez-Faire," in Yves Mény and Vincent Wright, eds. *The Politics of Steel: Western Europe and the Steel Industry in the Crisis Years* (New York: Walter de Gruyter, 1986), p. 208; Statistical Office of the European Community, *Iron and Steel Yearbook* (Luxembourg: Eurostat, 1989), p. 24; *U.S. Industrial Outlook* (Washington, D.C.: United States Government Printing Office, various years); and Alan Altshuler, Martin Anderson, Daniel Jones, Daniel Roos, and James Womack, *The Future of the Automobile: The Report of MIT's International Automobile Program* (Cambridge, Mass.: MIT Press, 1984), p. 201.

economy and the Voluntary Export Restraint [VER] agreement with Japan). The French and German auto industries created new jobs in the 1960s and 1970s, but the French industry began to shed jobs in the 1980s. German employment in automobile production stabilized during the 1980s, possibly at the expense of needed rationalization.

Accurate and fully comparable statistical data on employment in the semiconductor industry are hard to find for the countries in this study. Most countries have only recently begun to report figures on employment in the semiconductor industry. Several countries lump data on employment in semiconductors together with data on employment in electronics or data processing. With these caveats in mind, I will report my findings.

Employment in semiconductor production in the United States rose from 234,000 in 1972 to 375,000 in 1984, and then fell to around 320,000 in 1986–87.[20] Employment in electronics in Japan was exceedingly buoyant from the early 1970s on, increasing from 948,000 workers in 1982 to 1,212,000 workers in 1986.[21] Employment in the production of monolithic integrated circuits remained flat at around 50,000 workers in France, Britain, and Germany between 1983 and 1989. Employment in hybrid integrated circuits increased in Germany from 58,000 to 103,000 workers and in France from 80,000 to over 150,000 workers during the same period; British employment in this area declined slightly from 182,000 to 164,000 workers.[22]

Profitability

Firms in all five countries experienced financial difficulties during global recessions, but Japanese and German firms tended to do better during these periods and to emerge from them in better shape than American, British, and French firms. Both Japanese and German steel firms suffered financially from the stabilization in demand for steel after 1973. In contrast, the larger automobile firms of both countries did remarkably well

20 Ibid.

21 MITI data from the census of manufacturers as cited in *Facts and Figures on the Japanese Electronics Industry* (Tokyo: Electronic Industries Association of Japan, 1988), p. 29. These figures include employment in the manufacturing of all types of electronic components and systems and not just employment in semiconductor manufacturing.

22 Eurostat, *Industrial Production: Quarterly Statistics* (Luxembourg: Eurostat, Third Quarter 1990), p. 173.

financially for the entire period. There were exceptions, of course, such as the financial problems of Mazda and Volkswagen in the mid-1970s. But these were generally short-lived. Smaller firms which had financial problems were either acquired by larger firms or became linked to larger firms through various forms of interfirm cooperation. The profits of the Japanese semiconductor industry have been very strong, especially since 1986, while the profits of the semiconductor operations of Siemens, Germany's largest producer, have been relatively small compared with its main source of profits: large central-office switches for public telecommunications networks.

French firms did less well financially than the German and Japanese firms, especially during the 1980s, after steady growth in revenues and profits in the 1960s and 1970s. The French steel firms were unprofitable from the late 1970s until the late 1980s. The two main French auto firms suffered losses from 1980 until 1986–87, although Renault's losses were deeper and longer lasting than those of Peugeot. The only major French producer of semiconductors, Thomson, was not making much money in that business during the entire 1980s.

British financial performance mirrored the stop-and-go pattern of the British economy, but British profits took a turn for the worse in the 1970s and 1980s. British Steel Corporation and British Leyland, the national champions in steel and automobiles, suffered deep and prolonged losses in the 1970s and 1980s, even during periods of economic recovery. British semiconductor firms were marginally profitable, but profits were contingent upon the continued funding of defense programs which provided the main source of demand in Britain for application-specific integrated circuits (ASICs). British firms, with the exception of a small firm called Inmos, did not produce high-volume, standardized semiconductor devices.[23]

American financial performance was reasonably strong in all three industries until the 1970s. The profits of the American auto industry generally depended on levels of domestic demand and were highly cyclical as a result. The huge losses of Chrysler and the lower profitability of Ford and GM beginning in the late 1970s were ended artificially with the negotiation of the voluntary export restraint with Japan in 1981. The semiconductor industry seemed recession-proof until the global semicon-

23 Inmos was sold to SGS-Thomson, a Franco-Italian semiconductor firm, in 1989.

ductor slump of 1985. Firms such as Intel and Motorola sprang back quickly when demand increased again, while others, such as AMD and National Semiconductor, never fully recovered from the shock.

Thus, profitability data reinforce the notion that Germany and Japan experienced increased international competitiveness during the period, while the United States and Britain suffered from competitive decline. The French experience was mixed: profits were generally up until 1980; the losses of the mid-1980s were followed by a general turnaround in the late 1980s.

Industrial crises

Table 6.1 below lists forty-seven industrial crises in the five countries in steel, automobiles, and semiconductors between 1960 and 1989. The main criterion for selection is the broad perception of the potential for financial collapse of a firm or industry and major possible consequences in increased unemployment, national or regional, and negative effects for important downstream industries.[24] Connected with each crisis is a combination of government, business, and labor responses and a variety of outcomes – including bankruptcies, liquidations, acquisitions and mergers, and government rescues.

Japan experienced the fewest industrial crises during the period, and only one after 1973. Most of the crises it suffered were limited in scope, dealt with quickly, and did not recur. In contrast, Britain and France suffered the most crises, but the British crises were deeper than the French and more prone to recur. French crises were often provoked by the breakdown of bargaining between business interests and the state and are not, therefore, always good indicators of changes in competitiveness of firms or industries. Even though the United States suffered relatively few industrial crises, when they occurred they tended to be industry-wide. The management of industrial crises in the United States was much more likely to involve government imposition of trade barriers than in the other four countries.

One surprise in Table 6.1 is the frequency of German industrial crises.

24 For a more complete description and analysis of these data, see Jeffrey A. Hart, "Crisis Management and the Institutionalization of Corporatist Bargaining Mechanisms," paper delivered at the Conference of Europeanists of the Council for European Studies, Washington, D.C., October 18–20, 1985.

Table 6.1. *Industrial crises since 1960 in the five industrial countries in steel, motor vehicles, and electronics*

Country	Steel	Motor vehicles	Electronics
United States	1968	1970 Chrysler	1985 semiconductors
	1977	1979 Chrysler	
	1981	1980	
Japan	1964	1966 Prince	
		1968 Isuzu, Mitsubishi	
		1977 Toyo Kogyo (Mazda)	
Germany	1962	1965 Auto Union	1980 AEG-Telefunken
	1977 Saar	1967 BMW	1982 AEG-Telefunken
	1982 Ruhr	1969 NSU	
		1974 VW	
France	1965	1963 Simca	1964 Bull
	1976	1974 Citroen	1968 CSF
	1983 Creusot	1978 Chrysler	1970 Bull/GE
		1980 Renault	1975 CII
		1984 Citroen	1977 Sescosem
Britain	1967	1964 Rootes	1964 ICL
	1977 BSC	1967 Triumph, Talbot	1980 ICL
	1982 BSC	1974 Chrysler	1984 Inmos
		1977 Chrysler	1989 Inmos
		1981 BL	
		1982 DeLorean	
		1986 BL/Rover	

Note: Each crisis is identified by its initial year. If no specific firm or region is mentioned after that date, the crisis affected the whole industry in all regions.
Source: Jeffrey A. Hart, "Crisis Management and the Institutionalization of Corporatist Bargaining Mechanisms," paper delivered at the Conference of Europeanists of the Council for European Studies, Washington, D.C., October 1985.

It should be noted, however, that the biggest crises were in steel and that the others were relatively limited in scope and time. The German system was able to manage most of its crises without resort to governmental intervention. Indeed, the propensity of the federal government to avoid industry-specific interventions is a key factor in the generation of German industrial crises.

Summary of industry-specific indicators of competitiveness

Industry-specific measures of competitiveness provide evidence for the increased competitiveness of Japan and Germany and the decreased competitiveness of Britain and the United States. French industry-specific competitiveness rises until the late 1970s, and then declines in the 1980s. While some anomalies exist in specific indicators, the general pattern is clear and is highly consistent with that suggested by the economy-wide indicators discussed above.

STATE–SOCIETAL ARRANGEMENTS

State–societal arrangements are defined as the manner in which state and civil society are organized and how state and society are institutionally linked. The state consists of a set of institutions mostly associated with the government but also including such actors as tripartite (government–business–labor) boards and commissions, state-owned business enterprises, and other parastatal organizations. Civil society is the domestic social environment in which the state operates. In contemporary advanced industrial countries, it makes sense to focus on only two groups in civil society, business and organized labor, especially when the issue to be examined is competitiveness in manufacturing industries.[25]

The state–societal dichotomy, which has deep roots in liberal political philosophy, is premised on the notion that the power of the state should be and will be limited to prevent undue interference in the actions of individuals and selected collectivities.[26] In an ideal, free-enterprise economy, all business corporations would be private and relatively au-

25 For a convincing argument that agricultural groups need to be included in descriptions of social dynamics in earlier historical periods, see Ronald Rogowski, *Commerce and Coalitions: How Trade Affects Domestic Political Alignments* (Princeton, N.J.: Princeton University Press, 1989).

26 The discussion of the concepts of state and civil society in this work must, by necessity, be brief to the point of caricature for those who are familiar with the vast literature on this subject. For more lengthy discussions, see Bertrand Badie and Pierre Birnbaum, *Sociologie de l'Etat* (Paris: Bernard Grasset, 1979); Martin Carnoy, *The State and Political Theory* (Princeton, N.J.: Princeton University Press, 1984); Eric A. Nordlinger, *On the Autonomy of the Democratic State* (Cambridge, Mass.: Harvard University Press, 1981); Reinhard Bendix, ed., *State and Society* (Boston: Little, Brown, 1968); Charles Tilly, ed., *The Formation of National States in Western Europe* (Princeton, N.J.: Princeton University Press, 1975); John A. Hall and G. John Ikenberry, *The State* (Minneapolis, Minn.: University of Minnesota Press, 1989); and Alfred C. Stepan, *The State and Society: Peru in Comparative Perspective* (Princeton, N.J.: Princeton University Press, 1978).

tonomous from state agencies, and therefore would be part of civil society. All private individuals would also be members of civil society, except when they are holders of state offices. All capitalist countries fall short of the liberal ideal, using state-owned enterprises to perform certain functions of government and limiting the autonomy of private firms through a variety of regulations.

The liberal ideal is not the only one that has been defined for state–society relations. The communist ideal subordinates the state to the interests of one class in society – the proletariat – so that the state may eventually wither away in a classless society. The social democratic ideal gives the state sufficient power to reduce the inequities between classes that is created over time by capitalism, but tries to keep it accountable by maintaining a representative form of government.[27] The fascist ideal gives the head of state extraordinary powers and organizes societal interests from above, while at the same time prohibiting the formation of autonomous groupings which might resist state leadership.[28] The neocorporatist ideal is the concertation of the state and privileged groups – especially business and labor – to determine national policies.[29]

None of these ideals has ever been fully realized. Yet their very existence has obviously had a major impact on national and international politics in the twentieth century. National debates over state–societal relations tend to be defined in terms of the alternative ideals discussed above. Not only do these debates become an important element of partisan politics, they become highly salient during and after major international wars, domestic social conflicts, and deep economic crises. At key moments in a nation's history, changes in state–societal arrangements

27 See David Held and Joel Krieger, "Theories of the State: Some Competing Claims," in Stephen Bornstein, David Held, and Joel Krieger, eds., *The State in Capitalist Europe: A Casebook* (Winchester, Mass.: Allen & Unwin, 1984).

28 I owe this formulation of the fascist ideal to Gregory Kasza, *Administered Mass Organizations* (forthcoming).

29 A very clear statement of this ideal is in Wolfgang Streeck and Philippe C. Schmitter, "Community, Market, State – and Associations? The Prospective Contribution of Interest Governance to Social Order," in Wolfgang Streeck and Philippe C. Schmitter, eds., *Private Interest Government: Beyond Market and State* (Beverly Hills, Calif.: Sage, 1985), p. 10. See also Gerhard Lehmbruch, "Introduction: Neocorporatism in Comparative Perspective," in Gerhard Lehmbruch and Philippe C. Schmitter, eds., *Patterns in Corporatist Policy Making* (Beverly Hills, Calif.: Sage, 1982).

may be embodied in new political, social, and economic institutions which are designed to settle, for a time, the domestic debates.[30]

The way state and society are organized and how state and society are linked will therefore vary significantly from country to country. The key reasons for these variations are historical and contextual. Different institutions are inherited from the past. Some states have more centralized bureaucratic systems than others, often combined with a pattern of recruitment from elite colleges and universities. Some states are more inclined to structure civil society than others through the exercise of state authority and, at times, direct intervention in the economy.[31]

SYSTEMATIC OBSERVATION OF STATE–SOCIETAL ARRANGEMENTS

State–societal arrangements will vary across countries and across time. They may even vary across specific industries, although the empirical cases presented here suggest that this type of variation is not very important. The following approach was adopted to observe state–societal arrangements in the area of industrial competitiveness: for each country examined in this study, the following questions were asked.

1) *How is the government organized?* Specifically, how centralized and influential are the bureaucracies dealing with industry-specific policy making? What sorts of policy instruments are available to the government for the making of industrial policies? How inclined is the government to use these instruments? How successful is the government in getting its way with business or labor in conflicts over industrial policies?

2) *How is the business sector organized?* How powerful are business

30 On this subject, see G. John Ikenberry, "Conclusion: An Institutional Approach to American Foreign Economic Policy," in G. John Ikenberry, David A. Lake, and Michael Mastanduno, eds., *The State and American Foreign Economic Policy* (Ithaca, N.Y.: Cornell University Press, 1988), pp. 223–25; and Stephen Krasner, "Approaches to the State: Alternative Conceptions and Historical Dynamics," *Comparative Politics,* 16 (January 1984), p. 234.

31 The works that inspired this formulation are Andrew Schonfield, *Modern Capitalism* (London: Oxford University Press, 1965); Peter Katzenstein, ed., *Between Power and Plenty* (Madison, Wis.: University of Wisconsin Press, 1978); John Zysman, *Governments, Markets, and Growth; Financial Systems and the Politics of Industrial Change* (Ithaca, N.Y.: Cornell University Press, 1983); and Peter Hall, *Governing the Economy: The Politics of State Intervention in Britain and France* (New York: Oxford University Press, 1986).

peak associations?[32] Do individual firms or subgroups have the ability to lobby successfully for policy changes outside of business associations? Is there a system of "industrial families" (loose horizontal groupings) in the business sector? What is the role of the financial sector in underpinning these arrangements? Are the articulated interests of business in the country so diverse that there is insufficient unity to influence governmental policies or legal regimes that affect business–labor relations?

3) *How is labor organized?* How powerful are labor peak associations? What percentage of the workforce is unionized? Are unions organized on an enterprise or industrial basis? Can unions successfully block undesired governmental policies or managerial decisions?

4) *What sorts of institutions link state and society?* In particular, are individuals recruited for top positions in the governmental bureaucracy from elite colleges and universities? What role does the state play in financing those institutions? Does the government own major business enterprises or does it closely supervise the operations of "private" firms? Does the government help to organize and fund consortia of businesses for the purpose of advancing industrial technology? Are there special institutions for transmitting abstract knowledge from universities to the business sector? What role do the state and business sectors play in providing training for workers? What sorts of parastatal institutions exist – especially those involving neo-corporatist concertative mechanisms – and how important are they in specific policy realms?

Some state–societal arrangements are conducive to the creation and diffusion of new technologies and others are not. The distribution of power among government, business, and labor is the simplest way of summarizing the differences in the state–societal arrangements among the five major industrial countries selected for examination here: the United States, Japan, Germany, France, and Britain. I will argue below that the distribution of power among those three social actors is the basic underpinning of state–societal arrangements.

32 A peak association is an association that aspires to represent all organizations of a certain type (e.g., businesses or labor unions) in a given society. Examples of business peak associations are the U.S. Chamber of Commerce, the Japanese Keidanren, and the German Bundesverein der Deutschen Industrie. Examples of labor peak associations are the U.S. AFL-CIO and the German Deutsche Gewerkschaftsbund.

THE ROLE OF TECHNOLOGICAL INNOVATION AND DIFFUSION IN COMPETITIVENESS IN THE THREE INDUSTRIES

Technological innovation played a pivotal role in all three industries in determining which firms and which countries would come out on top in international competition. State–societal arrangements strongly influenced the creation and diffusion of new technologies. Therefore, state–societal arrangements had a major effect on international competitiveness through their effects on innovation. While these rather bold statements need to be qualified somewhat in specific cases, nevertheless they provide a better explanation of changes in international competitiveness than alternative explanations. Let us start by making the case for the crucial role of technological innovation and consider afterwards the claims of competing explanations.

The steel industry

In the steel industry, the most important technologies introduced after World War II were basic oxygen furnaces and continuous casting. The replacement of other types of furnaces with basic oxygen furnaces on a major scale occurred first in Japan, spread quickly to Germany, and diffused more slowly to the rest of Europe and the United States. In 1960, 11.9 percent of Japanese production was basic oxygen, compared with 3.4 percent in the U.S. In 1970, 79.1 percent of Japanese production was basic oxygen, while U.S. production was still only 48.2 percent basic oxygen.[33] The larger German companies were also quicker to adopt basic oxygen furnaces than most U.S., French, and British firms.

The basic oxygen technology was invented in Austria – the Japanese licensed the necessary patents from Canadian firms. The Japanese government played a key role in encouraging the major Japanese firms to adopt this technology. One of the more important reasons why the government encouraged the firms to adopt the technology was to lower their dependence on imported scrap iron and steel, a dependence which figured importantly in U.S.–Japanese relations in the years prior to the

33 Leonard H. Lynn, *How Japan Innovates: A Comparison with the United States in the Case of Oxygen Steelmaking* (Boulder, Colo.: Westview, 1982), p. 23.

attack on Pearl Harbor.[34] But the firms themselves had an interest in lowering their dependence on imported scrap, as scrap prices had been controlled by the large U.S. firms and had been set just high enough to discourage competition.

The basic oxygen technology was risky because it was unproven. No one had "scaled up" the technology to the size required for realizing production cost advantages over the Bessemer technology. The U.S. producers might have converted their plants to basic oxygen furnaces in the 1950s when they made major investments to upgrade their facilities. Instead, they passed up the opportunity, either because they did not see the future of the basic oxygen technology or because their major investors were unwilling to assume the risks involved in adopting the new technology.[35]

While bad management or risk-averse financial institutions may have been to blame in slowing the adoption of basic oxygen technology in France, Britain, and the United States, one needs to consider other explanations for the slowness with which the technology was adopted after it became clear that it was the more efficient technology. One important source of slow diffusion in the United States was the problem of amortizing investments made in the 1950s on the now obsolete older technologies. The mistakes of the 1950s, in essence, haunted the U.S. steel industry for the next three decades. Nevertheless, by the mid-1970s the U.S. industry had caught up with the rest of the world in the diffusion of oxygen furnaces (see Figure 6.7).

U.S. industry remained far behind Japan and Europe in the adoption of another technology: continuous casting. Prior to the introduction of continuous casting, steel ingots or slabs were cast in separate plants and then reheated in another location so that they could be formed or rolled into their final shapes. With continuous casting, the molten steel is poured from the steelmaking furnace directly onto a processing line which produces the required shapes. The savings in the energy required to reheat the cooled steel ingots and slabs are substantial, as are the savings in processing time and handling. Continuous casting requires relatively so-

34 Together with Britain and the Netherlands, the United States imposed an embargo of iron ore and scrap exports to Japan in July 1941 after the takeover of Indochina. See Paul Kennedy, *The Rise and Fall of the Great Powers* (New York: Random House, 1987), p. 303.

35 Interview materials.

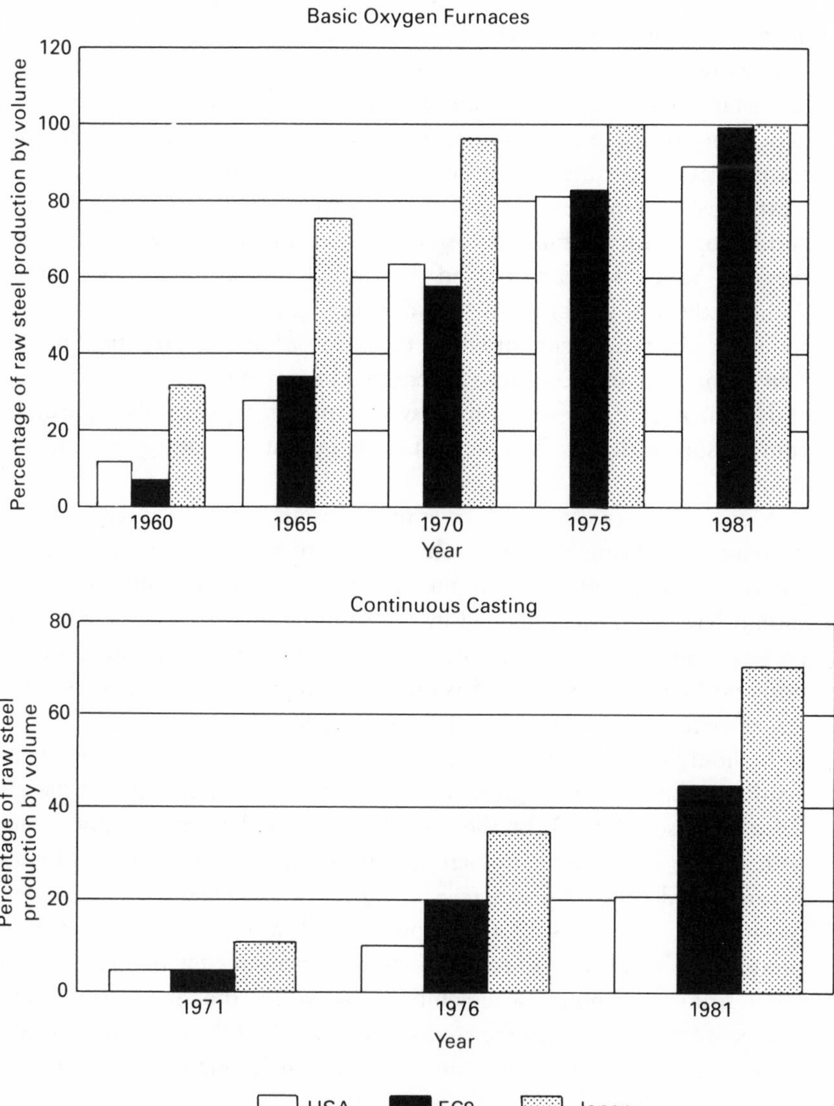

Figure 6.7. Diffusion of new production technologies. *Source:* Donald Barnett and Louis Schorsch, *Steel: Upheaval in a Basic Industry* (Cambridge, Mass.: Ballinger, 1983), p. 55.

phisticated scheduling, however, which has become easier with the introduction of computer-controlled production lines.

Having the opportunity to build new plants on large sites was an important advantage held by the Japanese in adopting continuous casting. Many of the plants built in the 1960s in Japan were "greenfield" plants – as opposed to the "brownfield" plants of the U.S. and Europe.[36] Nevertheless, some new integrated plants were built in the United States and Europe with continuous casters. The steel plants of Britain, France, the Saar Valley in Germany, and the United States, however, were predominantly in traditional steel-producing regions where there was little room for plant expansion or where the costs of building greenfield plants were so high as to discourage the required investment. Higher labor costs and environmental restrictions played a minor role in this regard, in comparison with the factors militating against upgrading production technologies.

Major mistakes were made in France, Britain, and the United States in delaying the phasing out of obsolete production facilities. In Britain, the major expansion of steel production in the 1970s in modern plants should have been accompanied by the shutting down of obsolete plants, especially in light of the weakening of demand for both domestic production and steel exports. The British paid a high price for this error. Similar errors were made in France and the United States.

It should be noted that no national steel industry had strong financial results in the absence of growth in steel demand which followed the oil price increases of 1973. By the early 1980s, even the traditionally strong firms of the Ruhr Valley in Germany were experiencing financial losses because of depressed prices in a European market glutted with excess production. Nippon Steel also experienced lower than average rates of profitability and began to redeploy its idle workforce by loaning them to other firms. The point to remember, however, is that the German and Japanese firms weathered the recessions better than the firms of the other three countries; steel employment decreased in Germany and Japan, but not as much as in the other three countries.

36 "Greenfield" means that no previous facility was on the site. "Brownfield" means that a previous facility was modernized or renovated. For a discussion of this issue, see Ira C. Magaziner and Robert B. Reich, *Minding America's Business: The Decline and Rise of the American Economy* (New York: Vintage Books, 1983), chap. 13.

The auto industry

In the automobile industry, technology played a vital role in the rise of the Japanese industry as well. Both product and process innovations were important. In the 1950s and 1960s, the Japanese firms played the game of catching up to the product and process technologies of the U.S. and European industries. Initially, the Japanese firms imported new product technologies through licensing and co-production agreements with Western firms. By the mid 1960s, however, they began to produce their own car models and to compete intensively with one another for domestic market shares.

Toyota invented an entirely new way to produce motor vehicles. Toyota redesigned the assembly process to reduce the total man-hours required for producing a single unit. Part of this redesign was the shift to *kanban,* or just-in-time production, under which inventories of components and parts were kept to a minimum, and suppliers were required to make early morning deliveries of only those parts needed for the day's production schedule. Suppliers had to locate quite close to the main factory for this system to be feasible – in marked contrast with the wide distribution of suppliers in both the U.S. and European systems.[37]

By the 1970s, the Japanese auto firms began to respond to increasing domestic wage rates by automating production and assembly with an increased use of robots, computer-controlled machine tools, and computerized assembly lines. The new process technologies adopted by Japanese firms allowed them to increase worker productivity in the face of increased wages, while at the same time improving the quality of vehicles produced. Products were redesigned around the new processes, both to make the new processes work more efficiently and to improve the reliability of the products. The new generation of Japanese models that resulted were able to compete overseas with the generally higher-quality vehicles produced in the United States and Europe. Computerized automation reduced retooling "downtime" – the amount of time production

37 See C. S. Chang, *The Japanese Auto Industry and the U.S. Market* (New York: Praeger, 1981); Michael A. Cusumano, *The Japanese Automobile Industry* (Cambridge, Mass.: Harvard University Press, 1985); Yasuhiro Monden, *Toyota Production System* (Norcross, Ga.: Industrial Engineering and Management Press, 1983); and Richard J. Schonberger, *Japanese Manufacturing Techniques* (New York: Free Press, 1982).

had to stop for the retooling that accompanied the annual changes in models – resulting in major efficiency gains for Japanese firms.

It needs to be acknowledged that the product and process innovations pioneered by the Japanese might not have resulted in such dramatic increases in exports, had it not been for the added effect of the increased oil prices on the demand for small cars – especially in the huge North American market. Had the U.S. producers been able to match Japanese innovations in small car production, the opportunities for Japan in that market would have been greatly diminished.

While U.S. product and process technology lagged seriously behind that of Japan, especially in small cars, European technology followed at a somewhat shorter lag. European production was more similar to that of Japan in servicing demand for small cars; and many of the product innovations introduced in Japanese models either originated in Europe or were quickly copied by European producers. Some European firms were slower than others in this regard, of course. British Leyland (now called the Rover Group) suffered the most from its inability to match Japanese product and process innovations – a suffering accentuated by its overmanning with high-wage labor. French and Italian producers were lulled into a false sense of security by traditional tariff and nontariff barriers and, in the case of France, the availability of less expensive North African and Turkish workers. Even Volkswagen suffered diminished export demand as a result of more intense competition from Japan and problems in making the transition to multi-model production in the mid-1970s.

One consequence of the increased challenge from Japan in Europe was the accelerated diffusion of computerized automation in the major firms. Firms like Volkswagen, Renault, and Fiat rapidly introduced new flexible manufacturing systems that allowed them to produce more than one model on a single production line. Automation was used also as a tool of management to ensure reduced worker militancy by eliminating workers from processes that were particularly vulnerable to work stoppages.[38] Both European and U.S. manufacturers also responded to the Japanese challenge by moving some production to lower-wage countries.

The issue of offshoring production comes up again in the case of semiconductors. The Japanese firms in both autos and semiconductors

38 See, e.g., Wolfgang Streeck and Andreas Hoff, "Industrial Relations and Structural Change in the International Automobile Industry," working paper, International Institute of Management, Berlin, August 1981.

acted as if they did not have the option to locate labor-intensive production processes overseas, thus forcing themselves to use automation to compensate for increasing wages. U.S. and European firms, in marked contrast, used a combination of offshoring and less expensive foreign workers to compete with Japanese firms. Even after Japanese wage rates began to increase in the 1960s and 1970s, U.S. and European firms – with few exceptions – continued to believe that differences in wage rates were the most important reason for the lower prices of Japanese cars. Only when those firms began to perceive that Japanese innovations in process technology were compensating for rising labor costs did they make the necessary investments in production technology. By and large, the Europeans and the European subsidiaries of U.S. firms were faster in doing this than the U.S. firms in their North American operations.

The semiconductor industry

Very rapid rates of technological innovation, in both product and process technologies, characterized the semiconductor industry from the invention of the transistor in the late 1940s. The jump from integrated circuits to large-scale integrated (LSI) circuits in the mid-1970s was made possible by the invention of a new process involving the use of photographically produced masks to create an electronic circuit of thousands of transistors, resistors, and capacitors on a small portion (chip) of a wafer of silicon. This new process made possible a series of product innovations, including the calculator chips that were responsible for the rapid rise in the fortunes of companies like Texas Instruments and National Semiconductors. The next generation of products, very-large-scale integrated (VLSI) products, in the late 1970s was made possible by another process innovation – the wafer stepper. Wafer steppers allowed manufacturers to accurately etch hundreds of copies of a single circuit design on a silicon wafer.

Photolithography and wafer steppers alone were not sufficient to make it possible to move from one generation of integrated circuits to another. They had to be supplemented with a variety of new technologies that made it possible to produce wafers with fewer and fewer impurities and with very smooth surfaces, so that smaller and smaller line widths could be etched on the silicon. A variety of chemical baths evolved to make the etching process cheaper and more reliable. Clean-room technology had to evolve also to make the chip yields per wafer high enough to allow new generation products to compete with older generation products in price. Finally, the processes by which circuit designs were converted into masks had to be improved as line widths got smaller. But the transition from generation to generation would have been impossible without advances in photolithography and the introduction of wafer steppers.[39]

Japanese firms were not competitive with U.S. firms in integrated circuits until the transition from LSI to VLSI circuits. In previous generations, by the time the Japanese firms began to get manufacturing costs down to U.S. levels, the U.S. firms had begun to produce the next generation of circuits. U.S. firms were driven to innovate in semiconductors at first by the rapid growth of demand from the military and space programs, and later by the enormous growth of the computer industry. Japanese firms were limited in their innovative potential by having to focus on supplying the demand for consumer electronics circuitry.

In the transition to VLSI, however, it became the policy of both the major firms and the Japanese government to beat the Americans in process technology so as not to be dealt out of the competition in VLSI products. The government committed itself to this enterprise not just because it was concerned about semiconductors, but also because it believed that overtaking the U.S. in semiconductors was the key to improving Japanese competitiveness in all major downstream industries such as consumer electronics, computers, and telecommunications equipment. Thus, in the transition from LSI to VLSI in semiconductors, the connection between state–societal arrangements and technological innovation was extremely clear.

Technological innovations were very important, in some cases crucial, factors explaining the rise in the international competitiveness of Japanese firms in steel, automobiles, and semiconductors and the continued or enhanced competitiveness of German steel and automobile firms. Almost every decline in competitiveness in the three industries can be traced back to a failure either to invent or to incorporate a new product or process

39 The best sources of information on these matters are: Ernest Braun and Stuart Macdonald, *Revolution in Miniature: The History and Impact of Semiconductor Electronics,* Second edition (New York: Cambridge University Press, 1982); Michael Borrus, *Competing for Control: America's Stake in Microelectronics* (Cambridge, Mass.: Ballinger, 1988); and George Gilder, *Microcosm: The Quantum Revolution in Economics and Technology* (New York: Simon & Schuster, 1989). Gilder provides an excellent bibliography on this subject on pp. 385–402.

technology. The technological explanation is not always sufficient to explain all individual cases of rises and declines in competitiveness, of course. But as a general explanation it is superior to its main competitors.

VARIATION IN STATE–SOCIETAL ARRANGEMENTS

Figure 6.8 summarizes information concerning the organization of state, business, and labor in the five industrial countries. It places the five countries on the faces or vertices of a triangle that represents the influence of the government, business, and labor embodied in state–societal arrangements. A country on the labor vertex has strong labor, weak government, and weak business. A country on the business vertex has strong business, weak labor, and weak government. A country between the labor and business vertices has strong labor and business, and weak government. Each country has a distinctive pattern. That is, Japan has a pattern of high influence for the state and business but low influence for labor; Germany has a pattern of high influence for business and labor but low influence for the state (although here the qualification has to be made that the federal government is in a weaker position than the provincial governments in matters dealing with specific industries).

Some of the judgments implicit in Figure 6.8 need to be qualified because of important changes that have occurred since World War II. For example, the influence of labor in Britain was greatly reduced during the Thatcher administration – that is, from 1979 to 1990 – and the state became more assertive if only to carry out its program of privatization. Similarly, labor in Germany had somewhat less influence under the Kohl administration than it had in previous SPD governments. Labor may have

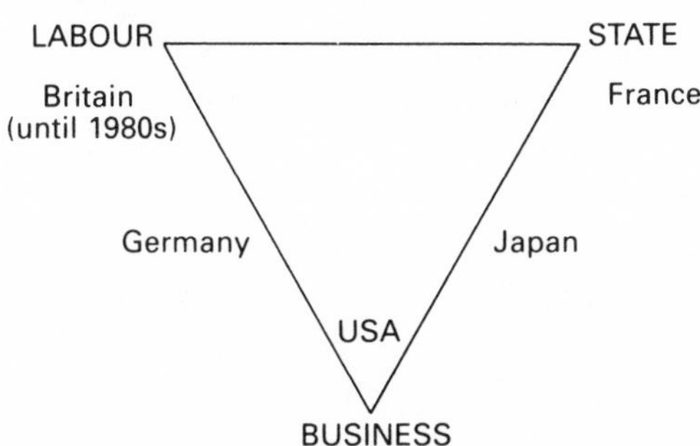

Figure 6.8. State–societal arrangements in the five countries.

gained some influence in Japan with the unification of the *Sohyo* and *Domei*. Labor was temporarily influential in France immediately after the strike in 1968 and had greater say in French politics during the Mitterrand presidency than under previous presidents.

In Britain, both the degree of centralization and the influence of the state increased markedly after the institutional changes introduced by the Conservatives in 1972, but both remained low in comparison with that of France and Japan. In the United States, the trend toward greater use of governmental resources to support civilian industries in the late 1980s is not reflected in Figure 6.8, nor is the move away from the use of state enterprises in France and Britain under the Thatcher and Chirac governments.

The influence of business increased in Japan during the period in question, but it has been high relative to the other industrialized countries for the entire period thanks to the *keiretsu* form of organization. The influence of business has fluctuated substantially over time in both the United States and Germany, but again relative to other countries it must be considered to be high throughout the period. In Britain, the influence of services and financial interests has always been substantial, while manufacturing has had its ups and downs. Thus, the influence of business as a whole has been weakened by its diversity and lack of a single voice.

Business in Britain and the United States has fewer incentives to create centralized peak associations because of the fragmented nature of the state. It is not necessary to centralize in order to influence public policies, and may even be counterproductive. In Germany, business is centralized primarily as a counterweight to centralized labor, but is also partially a consequence of the large role played by the "big three" universal banks in the financing of industrial activities. The centralization of German business organization stems also from a legal environment that creates national forums for tripartite bargaining among government, business, and labor for wages and other labor market issues.

France like Britain scores low on business influence because of the high dependency of French firms on governmental policies. Because most French firms never achieved the global competitiveness enjoyed by Japanese firms, they were not able to rival the influence of the state. While France has industrial families, they have never played the role of the *keiretsu* in Japan in creating high levels of domestic competition. The high centralization of French business reflects the high concentration of ownership in most industries and their need to deal with the government in a relatively unified way: it stems from their relative weakness and is not (as in Japan and Germany) a source of strength.

In short, the relative influence of government, business, and labor in the five countries creates a distinctive pattern for each country which has a certain logic of its own. The least successful pattern was that of Britain: that is, low government and business influence combined with highly influential labor. Japan and Germany, with very different state–societal arrangements, both increased their international competitiveness. The state-dominant pattern of France performed well until the late 1970s, which suggests that this pattern is not well suited for the technological transition connected with innovations in microelectronics. The business-dominant pattern of the United States also does poorly when compared with all the other large industrial countries except Britain.

THE LINKAGE BETWEEN STATE–SOCIETAL ARRANGEMENTS AND THE CREATION/DIFFUSION OF TECHNOLOGIES

The relative power of the state, business, and labor in the domain of industrial policy is closely linked with the creation and diffusion of new technologies. Labor must be receptive to the introduction of new technologies at the workplace, business must be prepared to adopt new technologies in a timely manner, and the state must be able to work with both business and labor to maximize the probability that new technologies will be created and diffused rapidly.

The receptivity of labor to the introduction of new technologies in the workplace depends on the confidence of labor that it will receive higher wages when productivity increases. This confidence depends very much on the political power of labor in the system, which in turn seems to depend on the level of skills possessed by the average laborer. In the absence of political power, labor may still accept new technologies if guaranteed job security and opportunities for training, but the upgrading of production technologies will be limited by a lower average level of skills in the workforce.

The ability of business to rapidly adopt new technologies depends on its access to information about technological change, which can be positively affected by the direct actions of an influential state (as in Japan) or by the transmission of this information by institutions, especially educational ones, that link state and society (as in Germany).

In Japan, the close working relationship between government agencies and the larger firms, which is partly a function of the weakness of organized labor, but also of the long dominance of the Liberal Democratic Party in Japanese politics, allows Japan to combine private and public resources in order to pursue technological and economic priorities established jointly by government and business. The main payoff to labor has been job security and steadily increasing wages. A societal commitment to upgrading the skills of workers has also been part of the arrangement, but this commitment is not as deep in Japan as it has been in Germany. The big loser under the Japanese system is the average consumer (who is also the average worker), because the Japanese consumer tends to pay higher prices than those in other industrialized countries for equivalent consumer goods and receives lower interest on personal savings and investments. This set of arrangements – which could be upset in the future if labor and consumer interests are able to organize effectively – has been the basis of the dominance of the Liberal Democratic Party in Japanese politics since the 1950s.

The Japanese system is well organized for joint state and business efforts to bring Japan to the technological frontier in strategic industries and keep it there. There is very little room for resistance on the part of labor to the introduction of new product and process technologies. So far, these innovations have benefited labor as a whole, because of their effect on employment and wages. Business can block government measures that they perceive are against their interests, and especially measures that appear to favor a limited number of *keiretsu* over others, but they have enough weight in government–business forums to assure that government initiatives in technology creation enhance their individual and collective competitiveness.

In Germany, government plays a much less important role than in Japan, while labor plays a much more important role. The strength of the German system is built on the high skill level of German workers. Those skills are the end result of educational efforts that can be traced back to Wilhelmine Germany. After World War II, the traditional power of skilled labor in the workplace was reinforced by the growing power of organized labor in the political system and the embodiment of that power in legal institutions that guaranteed labor a voice in important policy-making forums.

The high influence of labor in the German system, combined with its higher than average level of skills, has meant strong support for technological improvements in established industries as a way of guaranteeing continued growth in wages. German labor has been somewhat less enthusiastic about encouraging the growth of new industries such as microelectronics because they are concerned that new process technologies will replace labor with machines. Nevertheless, increasing competition within the European Community and from the newly industrializing countries has made it clear to both business and labor that the rapid introduction of technological innovations is the key to continued German competitiveness.

While the government plays a minor role relative to other governments, it still has some important instruments. For example, the government is responsible for the educational system which transmits skills to the workforce. In addition, the government funds many of the activities of universities and the Fraunhofer Institutes, which help to assure the transmission of university-created knowledge to businesses. Finally, the German government, like that of Japan, has created a stable macroeconomic climate for business investments. Thus, the German system has worked nearly as well as the Japanese system because it encourages the creation and diffusion of technologies.

In sharpest contrast, the British system has not encouraged the diffusion of technologies, despite the continued importance of Britain in the creation of new technologies. The uncertainties created by fluctuating political and macroeconomic climates has clearly played an important role in delaying diffusion of new technologies. The relative weakness of both government and business in the face of a relatively unified and militant labor movement has added a further disincentive. Britain's competitive decline is partly, but not wholly, a function of poor management. But even wise management was confronted with important constraints that were not present in other industrial countries.

In the United States, the political weakness of labor, closely connected with the low average level of skills of the workforce, has impeded the diffusion of new production technologies. The fragmentation of the American state makes it difficult for the state to play the role of partner with business in the creation of new technologies, especially if those technologies have no possible military application. Business may impose its wishes on both the government and organized labor in the United States, but it is strongly constrained in the types of competitive strategies it can adopt as a result.

In France, the main impediments to the creation and diffusion of new technologies have been the lack of domestic competition in important markets and the marginalization of French labor. The lack of domestic competition will become less important as French firms deal with the problem of surviving in the increasingly open European market, but they will still have to grow out of their current dependence on the tutelary relationship with the powerful French state. The state has learned the lesson of being overly dependent on one or two national champions per industry. But the political fragmentation of organized labor is likely to continue, and there seems to be no major move toward upgrading the skills of the workforce. Nevertheless, state–societal arrangements have not been as much of a handicap to making the technological transition in France as they have been in Britain and the United States.

WHERE DO WE GO FROM HERE?

The two countries that experienced increased competitiveness in the last two decades – Japan and Germany – are not on the vertices of the state–business–labor triangle in Figure 6.8 but on the sides linking the state and business and business and labor respectively. The country that experienced the greatest decline in competitiveness – Britain – is on the labor corner, which suggests that this is a position to avoid in the future if possible. There is no example of a country on the side linking state and labor, although we might think of this as an option in countries undergoing a "populist" phase (e.g., Brazil under Goulart or Poland after the election of the Solidarity government). Neither populism nor full-fledged tripartite concertation appears to have been an option for large industrialized capitalist countries during the postwar period.

It seems reasonable to argue that it is easier to move from a corner of the state–business–labor triangle to an adjacent side or from a side to an adjacent corner than to a nonadjacent position. A move to a nonadjacent position means removing one societal grouping from a position of influence and replacing it with at least one other grouping. Such a change would probably involve a rather lengthy and perhaps violent struggle. If one assumes that Japanese- and German-style state–societal arrangements are likely to continue to be connected with increasing competitiveness in the world economy (this assumption will be reexamined below), then each of the other three countries faces a different set of choices about which of the two models to emulate in reforming its domestic institutions.

If the assumptions in the previous paragraph are correct, then the main option for France is to emulate Japan and for Britain to emulate Germany. To do this, France will have to build a much more competitive domestic market around competing industrial families. Given the position of France in the European Community, it is likely that the "Frenchness" of those industrial families will be even more broadly defined than it is at present. In addition, the French state will have to give up some of its prerogatives in the allocation of credit and focus more of its efforts on promoting the creation and diffusion of new technologies outside of the charmed circle of champion firms. Finally, the French state will have to work with business to create a more stable macroeconomic climate.

In Britain, there will have to be major efforts to increase the skills of the workforce. A major overhaul of the educational system will be required, with heavy involvement of both business and labor. New investments in British manufacturing will be required, and the most likely sources of new capital will be Japan and Germany. The government will have to focus its efforts on assuring that state-funded universities are creating technologies oriented toward manufacturing and can transfer those technologies to business, a task already begun under the Thatcher government. A new political coalition would have to form around the joint interests of business and labor, which would mean a centrist party of some sort and an avoidance of either the Thatcherism or laborism of the recent past.

The United States is fortunate in having a choice between the Japanese and German models. If it chooses the Japanese model, there will have to be a major upgrading of governmental agencies and a centralization of industrial policy making in a single agency. At the very minimum, there will have to be a civilian equivalent to the role of the Department of Defense in supporting the development of defense-related products and technologies. If the United States chooses the German model, there will have to be a major upgrading of the role of unions in government policy making and in labor–management relations. A significantly increased commitment to the training and retraining of workers will also be involved in such a choice. While the transition to the German style of state–societal arrangements will take longer, because of the need to narrow the gap in skill levels between the United States and Germany, a transition to a Japanese style would encounter strong resistance from those Americans (the vast majority) who are suspicious of strong central government.

SUMMING UP

How can we explain changes in international competitiveness among the major industrial nations in the last twenty years or so? The answer lies in the political and social institutions that establish the fundamental relationships among government, business, and labor in each society. These state–societal arrangements vary substantially from country to country. Variations in state–societal arrangements affect competitiveness mainly through their impact on the creation and diffusion of new technologies.

It is ironic that systems with only one major dominant social actor in the realm of industrial policy (Britain, France, and the United States) have tended to do worse in postwar international competition than systems with two (Germany and Japan). A coalition of either the state and business (Japan) or business and labor (Germany) seems to be more conducive to the diffusion of new technologies than one-actor dominance. One might think that a business-dominant system like that of the United States would be ideal for maintaining competitiveness, but that is not so. In a technological age, when the weakness of labor is the result of a low societal commitment to raising the level of skills in the workforce, there will be extensive resistance to the introduction of new technologies in factories and offices. Similarly, one might think that systems with state dominance, such as France, would do well in international competition. But a strong state acting alone without strong allies in the private sector will be quite limited in its ability to anticipate shifts in markets and to respond correctly to them.

Thus, we are left with a choice between two "models" – currently embodied in the German and Japanese systems. I have argued here that the United States and Britain should opt for a German-style system, while France might pursue a Japanese-style approach. The United States seems to be torn between the Japanese and the German models. Illinois Republican Senator Adlai Stevenson III was the first to explicitly propose a U.S. version of MITI. This proposal was not well received by either political party. The Reagan and Bush administrations leaned very tentatively toward the Japanese approach, but the Bush administration later denied itself the right to pursue explicit industrial policies even in the Pentagon. President Bush lost the support of important segments of the business community by taking a dogmatic stand on this issue.[40] The Clinton administration harbors a number of individuals, like Secretary of Labor Robert Reich, who favor the German model. Their advisers from Silicon Valley sometimes appear to favor the Japanese approach. But the prevailing mentality is one of confusion about what the options really are. In light of this, one cannot be very optimistic about the prospects for major institutional changes in the United States.

40 For evidence, see Jeffrey A. Hart, *The Politics of HDTV*, forthcoming.

I have indicated that certain problematic features remain in both the German and Japanese approaches. Neither Germany nor Japan are standing still in their state–societal arrangements. The unification of Germany and the recent defeat of the Liberal Democratic Party by a coalition of smaller parties have created opportunities for change. Unification has created economic pressures that have led to the rise of new right-wing political forces and violent demonstrations against German immigrants. Germany seems now more willing to accept higher levels of inflation in order to create jobs for the workers displaced by unification. This, combined with increasing problems of competing with the United States and Japan in high technology, have shaken many people's confidence in the robustness of the German model. The new coalition government in Japan has already begun to attack the elite bureaucracy and has pledged itself to rapidly reduce Japan's trade surplus. Whether these are temporary aberrations remains to be seen.

In any case, I expect state–societal arrangements in the big five industrialized countries to remain reasonably close to the pattern illustrated in Figure 6.8 for the foreseeable future. If that is so, we should continue to see Germany and Japan outperforming the other three countries in overall productivity growth and in world trade performance. There are really only three ways to diffuse the tensions among the industrialized countries that will result: (1) extensive institutional change in the three weaker countries; (2) a shift in international arrangements to reflect the growing economic leadership of Germany and Japan including, among other things, the completion of a new round of the GATT, further moves toward European unity, the creation of a stronger North American trading bloc through NAFTA, the building of an Asian trading bloc through APEC, and a seat on the U.N. Security Council for the two countries; and (3) growing levels of overt conflict among the industrialized countries with economic disputes spilling over into military/strategic issues. The first of these is probably the most desirable and the last is certainly the least. The second is a sort of multilateral muddling through, not very pretty but better than open conflict and easier than domestic change.

Policy perspectives

It has been commonplace for over two decades now to argue that contemporary difficulties in the American economy derive from Keynesian-style policy commitments dating from the early 1960s. The extremely poor macroeconomic performance of the 1970s, in fact, prompted a wholesale revision of federal economic practice known as "supply-side economics." By the late 1980s, however, and now in the 1990s, it has become increasingly clear that many of the nation's current economic problems are the direct result of the imposition of supply-side policy regimes.

This part is concerned with the policy-driven causes of contemporary American economic decline. David M. Gordon, Thomas E. Weisskopf, and Samuel Bowles survey the failures of the conservative economic policies pursued during the 1980s. The many contradictions of the new policy making that has emanated from Washington are further explored by Robert A. Blecker.

7

Right-wing economics in the 1980s: the anatomy of failure

DAVID M. GORDON
THOMAS E. WEISSKOPF
SAMUEL BOWLES

The Right in the United States sought to wage economic revolution during the 1980s, capitalizing on its twelve-year run during the Reagan and Bush administrations. By the end of its reign, right-wing economics had apparently failed – with the attendant economic malaise helping Bill Clinton defeat George Bush in the presidential election of 1992. This chapter traces the anatomy of that policy failure.

This task is not entirely straightforward, since different observers obviously have different views about the effects of right-wing economics. The wealthy loved it, for example, while many suffered serious deprivation. Whether between winners and losers or between economists of differing political stripes, however, the debate is often marked by a myopia which we will seek here to avoid. The record of right-wing economics cannot be evaluated by looking at a single year or even a couple of years, such as the sharp recession at the beginning of the 1990s – the right-wing era saw its share of both good and bad years.

In order to try to avoid misleading comparisons, we will consider changes between years that are similar in their position within the business cycle. Preferring to evaluate business cycles from one peak to the next, we begin our analysis with the cyclical peak year 1979, when Paul Volcker took control of the Fed and steered economic policy to the right.

This essay is reproduced, by permission, from *After the Waste Land*, by Samuel Bowles, David M. Gordon, and Thomas E. Weisskopf (Armonk, N.Y.: M. E. Sharpe, 1990). No significance attaches to the order in which the authors' names are presented here.

We conclude with the peak year 1989, capping the long economic expansion which began in 1983.[1] Our assessment of right-wing economics will thus be based on how the U.S. economy performed during the complete business cycle from 1979 through 1989, largely setting aside the effects of the sharp recession which took hold at the end of the Reagan–Bush era in 1990.

Why call it "right-wing" economics? The economic program of the right has gone by many names. George Bush called it "voodoo economics" during the 1980 campaign for the Republican presidential nomination. More typically, and more neutrally, many have called it "Reaganomics." We avoid this term since it is tied too closely to a single administration. Many have also labeled it "conservative" economics. But this conveys a false impression. As we shall see below, the right-wing program did many things, but it hardly "conserved" our economy. Instead, it squandered our natural environment, our human resources, and our public capital stock, and it plunged the U.S. economy into massive debt. "Trickle-down economics" would seem to be more apt, since it points to one of the major priorities of the right – to put more money in the hands of the corporations and the rich, with the promise that through their saving and investment decisions some benefits would eventually dribble down to the vast majority. But the "trickle-down" label ignores many other important aspects of the right's program, such as deregulation, militarization, and its attack on labor. On balance, the generic and encompassing term "right-wing" seems to us the best available designation.

We review here, in four major sections, the logic, the human costs, the macroeconomic effects, and the internal contradictions of right-wing economics.

THE LOGIC OF RIGHT-WING ECONOMICS

> We had, Reagan suggested, lost or forgotten the principles through which we had become the most productive, the most prosperous, the

1 We identify business cycle peak years by looking at the ratio of actual GNP to potential GNP; this ratio reaches its cyclical peak at the stage of an expansion when the economy's productive capacity is most fully utilized. For full justification of this measure, see Samuel Bowles, David M. Gordon, and Thomas E. Weisskopf, *After the Waste Land* (Armonk, N.Y.: M. E. Sharpe, 1990), Ch. 4.

strongest and the most respected nation on earth. . . . [T]he lost or forgotten principle which had to be rediscovered and reanimated in this area was to promote economic growth through the encouragement of investment, enterprise, risk and the quest for wealth. In a word: capitalism.

– Norman Podhoretz, editor of *Commentary*[2]

Policy initiatives

The right-wing offensive in economic policy began several years before Ronald Reagan rode into Washington and took control of the White House. Almost all of the key initiatives of the pro-business policy revolution began in the late 1970s, during the later years of Jimmy Carter's presidential administration. Since the history of the right-wing regime is by now familiar to most readers, we skeletally summarize its initiatives. Five main policy thrusts fueled the right-wing economic juggernaut:

Tight money. The first initiative involved using tight monetary policy to generate high interest rates – initially to plunge the economy into the cold bath of recession during the early 1980s, and subsequently to restrain growth in order to avoid the labor shortages which might fuel wage increases and inflation. Real interest rates in the 1980s reached their highest levels in the postwar period.[3]

Zapping labor. The second initiative involved attacking labor unions and intimidating workers through high unemployment, a hostile legal and public policy environment towards unions, and anti-labor ideological campaigns. The decline in union's share of the labor force accelerated during the 1980s as a result.[4]

2 Norman Podhoretz, "The Neo-Conservative Anguish Over Reagan's Foreign Policy," *New York Times Magazine,* May 2, 1982, p. 31.

3 The real interest rate for these purposes is defined as the nominal Federal Funds rate adjusted for the expected rate of inflation. Data for the Federal Funds rate are taken from *Economic Report of the President, 1991* (Washington, D.C.: U.S. Government Printing Office, 1991), Table B-71. The expected rate of inflation is measured by the expected rate of change in the GNP implicit price deflator predicted by a distributed lag on its past three years. Data for the GNP implicit price deflator come from ibid., Table B-3.

4 See Michael Goldfield, *The Decline of Organized Labor in the United States* (Chicago: University of Chicago Press, 1987), Tables 3 and 8.

Deregulation. The right-wing regime also promoted government deregulation of business, with the effect – *inter alia* – of rolling back environmental and other citizen efforts to curb business profligacy. Having increased dramatically during the 1970s, federal government spending on and staffing for regulation of business declined significantly during the early to mid-1980s.[5]

Tax breaks for the wealthy and corporations. The right-wing regime also used tax policy to shift income away from the vast majority and toward the accounts of the wealthy and the corporations. The effective corporate profits tax rate fell, for example, from 54 percent in 1980 to 33 percent in 1986.[6]

Remilitarization. Seeking to regain international economic advantage, the right also promoted remilitarization and an aggressive gunboat diplomacy. Many associate the resurgence of militarism in the U.S. with the Republicans' conquest of Washington, D.C., in 1981. But, like the rest of the right-wing economic agenda, remilitarization began earlier, in 1978–79, during the Carter administration. Defense spending as a share of GNP increased from 4.8 percent in fiscal year 1979 to 6.4 percent in 1987.[7]

Logical foundations

The right-wing economic initiatives which gathered momentum in the late 1970s and steamrollered through the 1980s were not simply a collection of policies favored by the well-to-do in their own immediate self-interest. Had these right-wing policies been simply a gravy train for the

5 Data on spending and staffing from Ronald J. Penoyer, *Directory of Federal Regulatory Agencies* (St. Louis: Center for the Study of American Business, 1981), Tables 1 and 2; and Melinda Warren and Kenneth Chilton, "1989 Federal Regulatory Budgets and Staffing: Effects of the Reagan Presidency," Center for the Study of American Business, Occasional Paper No. 69, April 1988, Tables 3A and 4.

6 This is measured as the ratio of corporate profits tax liability to total before-tax profits (corrected for inventory valuation and capital consumption adjustments). *Economic Report, 1991,* Table B-12.

7 Data for national defense outlays as a share of GNP from *Statistical Abstract of the United States 1989* (Washington, D.C.: U.S. Government Printing Office, 1990), Table 526.

rich, indeed, it would be hard to account for their widespread popularity. Instead, these right-wing initiatives were based on a theory of the capitalist economy which, to many, looked good on paper. Right-wing economics seemed plausible in part because it was based on widely believed economic theory. This theory builds on what we call the "logic of right-wing economics." It may be summarized by four basic principles:

Trickle-down economics. The essential idea of trickle-down economics is simple: it argues that the best way for the majority of the people to improve their standard of living in the long run is to provide rewards for productive economic behavior to those at the top. As they prosper, according to this logic, the economy will also prosper, and the benefits of that prosperity will eventually trickle down to everyone below.

The discipline of the whip. Workers may be motivated by positive incentives, such as a good working environment and high wages, or by negative sanctions, such as the threat of job loss. The discipline of the whip refers to the use of negative sanctions to elicit worker effort on the job. It calls for the removal of the kind of job protection and grievance provisions negotiated by unions, and for the reduction of unemployment compensation and other benefits available to workers who have lost their jobs, in order to reduce the availability and desirability of any alternative to disciplined performance on the job.

The invisible hand. The invisible hand is what guides private individuals, reacting to market prices while interacting in competitive capitalist markets, to undertake those activities which are supposed to lead to the greatest benefit for all. As an element in right-wing economics, this principle counsels reliance on market price signals as guides to appropriate economic activity. It further serves to generate suspicion of any effort – whether by government or by unions – to intervene in the operation of markets. Economists know that this theory is, strictly speaking, wrong – prices do not measure real costs and benefits where there are environmental costs not taken into account by businesses, for example. But right-wing economists accept the laissez-faire prescription implied by the invisible hand logic as a rough-and-ready rule of thumb for economic policy affecting resource allocation.

The global big stick. There is one important arena, however, where conservatives are reluctant to rely on the market. This is the global arena.

The exercise of power on a world scale can potentially boost profits in the U.S. both by allowing the U.S. to buy cheap and sell dear in the global marketplace and by providing U.S. corporations with safe international havens in which they can do business under favorable conditions.[8] Should adverse foreign government policies or political instability threaten the far-flung profits of these corporations, help from the U.S. State Department or U.S. armed forces stands just a telephone call away. The global big stick thus displays a kind of double standard analogous to right-wing provision of a carrot for the rich and the stick for everyone else: it favors laissez-faire policies for domestic markets while promoting a military buildup and aggressive foreign policy to back up the big stick internationally.

These four principles underlie the five central policy initiatives of the right-wing regime summarized above. Tight monetary policy and the attack on labor unions were intended to subject workers to the discipline of the market and to redistribute income from wages to profits. Deregulation aimed to unleash the invisible hand and to restore the force of an unfettered market mechanism. Tax breaks for the wealthy sought to shift resources from the poor and middle-income groups to the rich to reduce the impact of taxes on market signals as guides to allocation. And the expansion of the U.S. military establishment was expected to cause other governments to think twice before challenging the desired international hegemony of profitability and the market mechanism. We must build profits, brandish the whip, follow the market, and remilitarize, the conservatives argued, or condemn ourselves to further stagnation and decline. Did this strategy work?

RIGHT-WING ECONOMICS: THE HUMAN COSTS

> Economic violence is the critical issue of our day. When plants close on workers without notice – that's economic violence. When merger maniacs make windfall profits and top management is given excessive bonuses – that's economic violence. When two to three million Americans are on the streets and homeless – that's economic violence. When children are victimized by poor health care, poor educa-

8 Evidence supporting this hypothesis is provided in Samuel Bowles, David M. Gordon, and Thomas E. Weisskopf, "Power and Profits: The Social Structure of Accumulation and the Profitability of the Postwar U.S. Economy," *Review of Radical Political Economics*, Spring–Summer 1986, 132–67.

> tion, poor housing, poor diets and more – that's economic violence against our children and it must stop.
>
> – Rev. Jesse Jackson, 1988[9]

In the early 1980s the American people wanted relief. But relief was not spelled "right-wing economics." Viewing the human costs of right-wing economics in retrospect, it is stunning how many people in the United States took it on the chin.

As argued in Gordon's earlier essay in this volume, two trends hold the key to the economic well-being of the vast majority of U.S. households: the value of the hourly take-home pay of those – the vast majority – who depend on wage-and-salary income for a living, and the number of hours they work to support themselves and others in their families.

Figure 7.1 traces these two series for the postwar period through 1989. Real spendable hourly earnings did not recover from its declines during the late 1970s, dropping sharply from 1979 to 1981 and then remaining almost exactly flat from 1981 through 1989; by 1989, workers' real take-home pay had fallen back to below the level previously achieved in 1965. And, continuing earlier trends, hours worked per capita followed their upward course, rising from 742 in 1979 to 790 in 1989. People were working more hours, on average, and taking home less (per hour) than before.

These two trends are important, but they hardly exhaust the standards by which we should judge the impact of right-wing economics on the lives and livelihoods of the vast majority in the United States. We have assembled in Table 7.1 a number of additional measures of economic well-being, inequality, and insecurity. For each measure, in order to abstract from business cycle fluctuations, we indicate its level at the respective business cycle peaks since the mid-1960s – 1966, 1973, 1979, and 1989. For each of these measures we ask the same basic question: did right-wing economics succeed in reversing the earlier decline in people's well-being (tracked in Gordon's earlier essay), or did it extend or perhaps even exacerbate that decline?

Row 1 extends data on real median family income (in $1989) through the 1980s. Facing declining real spendable earnings and by working more hours (per capita), households simply succeeded in racing to stay in place: real median household incomes remained essentially flat (in $1989) dur-

9 Frank Clemente, ed., *Keep Hope Alive: Jesse Jackson's 1988 Presidential Campaign* (Boston: South End Press, 1989), p. 63.

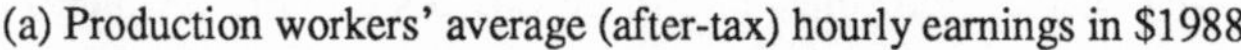

(a) Production workers' average (after-tax) hourly earnings in $1988

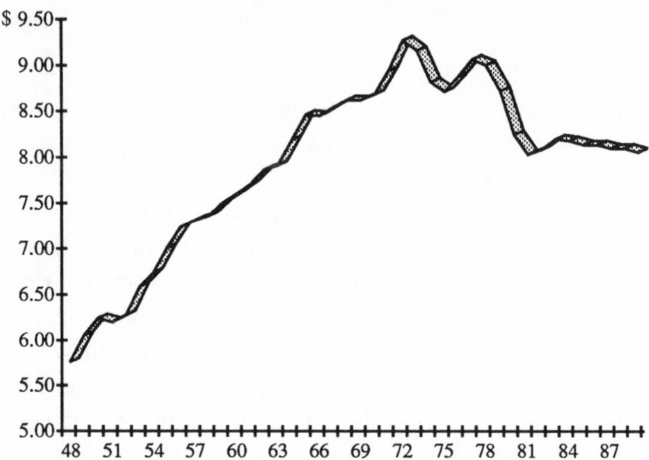

(b) Average annual hours of work (excluding unpaid family labor) per capita

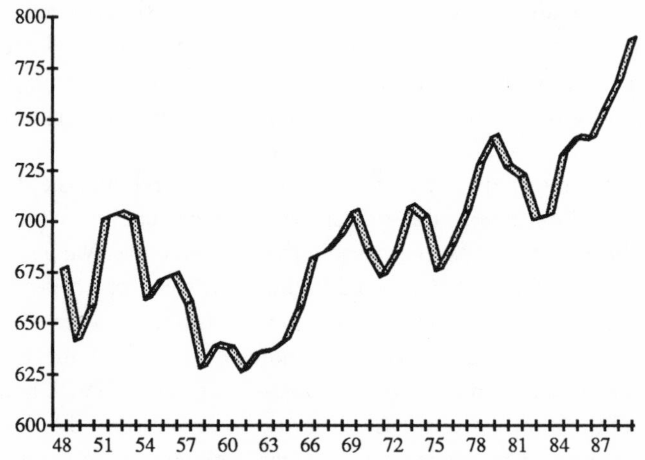

Figure 7.1. Deepening symptoms of stagnation: (a) Real spendable hourly earnings; (b) hours per capita. *Sources:* See source notes for Table 2.2 in this volume, rows [1] and [2].

ing the entire period from 1973 through 1989, moving from $33,656 in 1973 to $33,454 in 1979, to $34,213 in 1989. Because after-tax wages were down, it simply took longer in the late 1980s to gain a given standard of living than it had in the 1970s.

We turn next to the employment record. People worked more hours

Table 7.1. *The human costs of right-wing economics*

	Level at Cycle Peak			
	1966	**1973**	**1979**	**1989**
[1] Real median family income ($1989)	29,202	33,656	33,454	34,213
[2] Unemployment rate (%)	3.8	4.9	5.8	5.3
[3] Inflation rate, consumer prices (%)	3.5	8.7	13.3	4.6
[4] Family income inequality (ratio)	0.87	0.89	0.94	1.18
[5] Ratio, black/white median incomes: males	0.55[a]	0.60	0.62	0.60
[6] Ratio, black/white median incomes: females	0.76[a]	0.90	0.91	0.80
[7] Ratio, female/male median earnings	0.58	0.57	0.60	0.69
[8] Private sector debt burden (as fraction of GNP)	0.84	0.88	0.92	1.10
[9] Business failure rate (per 10,000 enterprises)	52	36	28	98

[a] Figure is for "black and other races."

Sources: ERP refers to *Economic Report of the President*, 1991; *CPR* refers to *Current Population Reports*; *SA* refers to *Statistical Abstract*.

[1] Real median family income ($1989): *ERP*, Table B-30. (1966 figure from *CPR*, Series P-60, no. 160, Table 11 [in $1989]).

[2] Civilian unemployment rate: *ERP*, Table B-322.

[3] Consumer price index, all items, December-to-December rate of change: *ERP*, Table B-62.

[4] Ratio of income share of top 5 percent of income distribution to share of bottom 40 percent: *CPR*, Series P-60, no. 172, July 1991, Table B-5.

[5] Ratio of black to white median earnings, all employees, for males and females separately: *ERP*, Table B-30; 1966 figure from *CPR*, Series P-60, no. 160, February 1989, Table 11.

[6] Same as for [4].

[7] Ratio of female to male median earnings, year-round full-time workers: *ERP*, Table B-30; 1966 figure from *CPR*, Series P-60, no. 160, February 1989, Table 11.

[8] Ratio of (corporate + household + farm) debt to GNP: Flow of funds accounts, unpublished historical tables; and *Federal Reserve Bulletin*, statistical tables.

[9] Business failure rate per 10,000 listed enterprises: *ERP*, Table B-94.

per capita, as we have already seen, but the problem of unemployment was hardly eradicated. After reaching an officially measured unemployment rate of 9.5 percent in the depths of the 1980–82 recession, the long expansion from 1983 to 1989, for all of the vaunted increases in employment accompanying the "U.S. employment miracle," succeeded in bringing the unemployment rate (row 2) down to only 5.3 percent in 1989 – barely below its level at the business cycle peak of 1979.

To its credit, the right-wing program did indeed slay the dragon of inflation. As row 3 shows, the inflation rate in 1989 was dramatically lower than at the previous peak in 1979. Even though right-wing economics simultaneously butchered wages and incomes so much that real living standards fell *in spite of the sharp declines in inflation rates,* many people appear for a time to have paid relatively more attention to the slain dragon than to their own butchered living standards. As the Clinton victory in 1992 attests, however, this "money illusion" was punctured soon enough.

Not only did most people fail to reap the fruits of right-wing economic policy, but those who began the 1980s with the most severe disadvantages fell further behind.

One useful measure of inequality is an index of family income inequality (row 4), measuring the ratio of the income share of the top 5 percent to the income share of the bottom 40 percent of the income distribution. This index of income inequality had risen only slightly from the mid-1960s through the late 1970s, but then increased sharply as the wealthy feasted at the banquet table during the roaring eighties. In 1989 the top five percent of the income distribution received considerably more than the bottom 40 percent.

In large part as a result of these trends, there was also a substantial increase in the inequality of the distribution of personal wealth in the United States. The data are subject to significant error because they rely heavily on the accuracy of sampling from a tiny base of the wealthiest 0.5 percent of U.S. households. But it appears that the share of personal wealth controlled by the wealthiest 1 percent of households – representing somewhat more than 800,000 households – increased significantly from the early 1970s to the mid-1980s. In 1976 that group of the superrich controlled roughly 19 percent of total net personal wealth, down from the postwar peaks in wealth inequality in the mid-1960s. By 1983, this equalizing trend had been reversed. The share of the wealthiest 1 percent of households had increased by 25 percent over its 1976 levels – apparently increasing further, by small margins, through 1986.[10]

The halting progress toward greater racial equality experienced during the late 1960s and early 1970s also moved into reverse. Data on the median income of black and white workers confirms the impression that the right-wing economic agenda turned its back on racial equality. As rows 5 and 6 of Table 7.1 show, the ratio of black to white incomes rose somewhat between 1973 and 1979 for both men and women, but the racial income gap widened after 1979; for males, earnings equality declined by 3 percent while for females it fell by 10 percent.

There is one – and apparently only one – respect in which the distribution of income became notably more equal during the 1980s: the income of employed women relative to that of employed men rose substantially. Row 7 traces the ratio of median earnings for full-time female to full-time male earnings; by this measure, gender earnings equality improved by 15 percent between 1979 and 1988. Yet, even after this improvement, the median earnings of full-time women workers was only two-thirds that of their male counterparts.

Missing thus far from our assessment of the effects of right-wing economics is the anxiety and economic insecurity that so many felt in the face of plant shutdowns, overextended debt, business failures, financial panic, and mortgage foreclosures. We select only two among many potential measures of the economic vulnerability of households and small businesses to complete Table 7.1:

- The private sector debt burden (row 8) measures the outstanding debt owed by families and businesses (including farms) as a percentage of gross national product. It captures the weight of indebtedness relative to the economy's capacity to sustain it. This index of debt burden rose sharply during the 1980s as families, farms, and firms alike borrowed to try to stay afloat. Having increased by only 5 percent from 1973 to 1979, the private sector debt burden jumped by 20 percent from 1979 to 1989.
- The business failure rate (row 9) similarly measures the vulnerability of small businesses to a stagnant economy and record-high real interest

10 Edward N. Wolff, "Changing Inequality of Wealth," *American Economic Review*, May 1992, 552–58.

rates. Having declined during the 1970s, the business failure rate soared during the 1980s. In 1989 it was more than twice as high as in 1979. The failure rate in 1986, well into the business cycle expansion, was the highest recorded since the pits of the Great Depression in 1931.[11]

MACROECONOMIC EFFECTS

> Vaclav Havel, the playwright President of Czechoslovakia, counseled his people that the highest patriotism is the frank admission of serious problems. For Ronald Reagan and, so far, for George Bush, the idea has been to throw a coat of fresh paint over a house with rotting beams.
>
> – Ralph Nader and Mark Green, 1990[12]

Judged by its impact on people's income and economic well-being, the scorecard on right-wing economics is clear. For the richest families it worked; for just about everyone else it did not.

But defenders of the right-wing program asked us to focus on the macroeconomic record rather than the immediate impact on people's well-being. They argued that the medicine was tough to swallow, but that the economy itself was much healthier as a result.

In order to place the 1980s in historical perspective, we compare the recent period of business ascendancy with the three previous periods of the postwar era: the boom, running from 1948 to 1966; the first period of stagnation, from 1966 to 1973, and the period of full stagnation and political stalemate, 1973 to 1979.[13] This analysis thus extends through the 1980s the discussion of macroeconomic performance introduced in Gordon's earlier essay.

The measures selected for presentation in Table 7.2 represent those which economists conventionally emphasize as indicators of macroeconomic performance – the growth of real gross national product, the growth of the real capital stock, and the growth of productivity. In addition we have included three widely discussed measures which we consider to be symptoms of macroeconomic health or illness: the federal budget deficit, the international trade deficit, and the net national saving rate.[14]

11 For historical data, see *Historical Statistics of the United States* (Washington, D.C.: U.S. Government Printing Office, 1976), p. 913.

12 "Passing on the Legacy of Shame," *Nation*, April 2, 1990, p. 446.

13 For detailed discussion of the differences among these periods, see Bowles, Gordon, and Weisskopf, *After the Waste Land*, Chs. 4–6.

14 Since we have already considered the success of the right-wing program in

Table 7.2. *The deteriorating performance of the U.S. postwar macroeconomy*

	Phase Averages			
	1948-66	**1966-73**	**1973-79**	**1979-89**
[1] Real GNP growth rate (%)	3.8	3.1	2.5	2.6
[2] Rate of capital accumulation (%)	3.6	4.4	3.5	2.6
[3] Real productivity growth rate (%)	2.6	1.8	0.6	1.0
[4] Federal deficit as percent of GNP	-0.2	-0.6	-1.2	-2.5
[5] Trade balance as percent of GNP	0.4	0.1	0.0	-1.8
[6] Net national savings rate (%)[a]	9.6	10.8	8.5	3.2

[a] Figure is for peak year at end of cycle rather than for cycle average.

Sources: Growth rates are annual rates, calculated as logarithmic growth rates. Levels are calculated as average annual levels. *ERP* refers to *Economic Report of the President,* 1991.

[1] Rate of growth of real GNP ($1982): *ERP,* Table B-2.

[2] Rate of growth, net fixed NFCB nonresidential capital stock: Dept. of Commerce, *Fixed Reproducible Tangible Wealth in the United States, 1925–85* (Washington, D.C.: U.S. Government Printing Office, 1987), A6; *Survey of Current Business,* Aug. 1991, Table 7.

[3] Rate of growth of output per hour of all persons, nonfarm business sector (1977 = 100): *ERP,* Table B-46.

[4] Federal surplus (+) or deficit (-) as percent of GNP: *ERP,* Tables B-79, B-1.

[5] Trade surplus (+) or deficit (-) on current account, as percent of GNP: *ERP,* Tables B-102, B-1.

[6] Personal, business, and government savings (net of depreciation) as percent of net national product: *ERP,* Tables B-26, B-22.

Even a cursory glance at Table 7.2 reveals the main message of the data. The leaders of the right-wing economic program inherited an economy which had been in serious trouble since the mid-1960s and promised

bringing down the rate of inflation (Table 7.1), and since it is growth in real (inflation-corrected) output, capital stock, and productivity – not inflation as such – which is generally regarded as the key to long-term economic performance, we do not include the rate of inflation in this assessment of economic performance.

to reverse its decline; but they failed to deliver on that promise. It *was* broke, and they did not fix it. If anything they hastened its deterioration.

We begin (row 1) with the rate of increase of real GNP, a common encompassing measure of aggregate economic performance. Despite seven years of expansion in the 1980s, the average real GNP growth rate from 1979 to 1989 was essentially the same as during the previous business cycle – and far below its pace during the long postwar boom.

Many right-wing economists set their sights on supply-side performance, hoping to reinvigorate productive investment by revitalizing corporate profits. Row 2 casts doubt on the success of this enterprise. The rate of growth of the real net capital stock, a measure of the economy's success at expanding its productive capacity over time, continued to fall. The supply-siders promised us a rose garden of blooming investment; instead, capital accumulation got stuck on the thorns, with its pace declining by nearly a quarter from 1973–79 to 1979–89.

The story of productivity growth is slightly more encouraging, but few would call it a triumphant success. After the long period of decline through the late 1970s, the rate of growth of real nonfarm hourly output picked up slightly during the 1980s. But it was still limp, averaging only about two-fifths of its pace during the long expansion from 1948 to 1966. And U.S. productivity growth during the 1980s lagged far behind its pace in leading competing economies. Among the seven major advanced economies (the U.S., Japan, Germany, France, the U.K., Italy, and Canada) during the 1980s, average annual productivity growth in the U.S. ranked dead last, averaging one-third the pace in Japan and only three-fifths the average of the remaining five.[15]

The final rows of the table present the most notorious symptoms of this shaky macroeconomic record: the "twin deficits" and the net national saving rate. The federal budget deficit as a percent of GNP climbed sharply, more than doubling from a deficit burden of only 1.2 percent of GNP in 1973–79 to 2.5 percent in 1979–89. And the U.S. current account trade deficit soared to new heights. After a slight trade surplus during the long boom and a rough balance from the mid-1960s through the late 1970s, the trade deficit increased to 1.8 percent of GNP in the 1980s.

Net national saving is defined as the sum of personal saving, business saving, and government saving, minus the level of saving necessary to

15 Bowles, Gordon, and Weisskopf, *After the Waste Land,* Table 1.2.

maintain the capital stock. Since government saving is equal to the government budget surplus, it is negative whenever there is a deficit (as there had been throughout the 1980s). The level of net national savings represents the level of net investment which could be undertaken from domestic sources – without borrowing from abroad. The extent of the U.S. saving problem is indicted by the fact that in 1989 net national saving constituted barely more than 3 percent of net national product – considerably less than the level of net foreign investment in the U.S. economy.[16] As the last line in Table 7.2 shows, the collapse of national saving is a relatively recent development.

Living on borrowed time

As the data on investment and saving suggest, the U.S. economy was being managed as if there were no tomorrow – generating less and less saving and investment for the future. This judgment becomes even more strongly grounded if we probe beneath the surface of conventional economic statistics. We then discover that much of the economic growth recorded during the long expansion of the 1980s was achieved by borrowing against the future, sacrificing our children's long-term economic welfare for our own generation's short-term gain. The assets on which the long-term productive potential of the U.S. economy depends were being steadily depleted; we incurred huge debts to the rest of the world while at the same time running down our own public capital infrastructure, our human resources, and our natural environment.

In debt to the rest of the world. Because the U.S. economy ran such persistently large trade deficits during the 1980s, right-wing economics succeeded in converting the U.S. economy from the world's biggest creditor nation to its biggest debtor nation in the space of less than a decade. This deterioration in the U.S. international investment position means that the observed growth of U.S. real GNP in the 1980s overstates the extent to which people in the United States have really increased their spending capacity. The problem is that we could not go on forever borrowing from foreigners – and thereby increasing U.S. international debt – in order to sustain our potential domestic spending.

16 We measure the flow of net foreign investment into the United States by the change in the net international investment position of the United States. Data are from *Economic Report,* 1991, Table B-102.

Running down the environment. When statisticians measure the U.S. net national product, they subtract from GNP an amount of output representing what is necessary to maintain the nation's stock of productive equipment. This subtraction is termed capital consumption or depreciation. But the statisticians do not subtract anything when stocks of mineral resources are used up, when the quality of the soil is diminished, or when air and water are polluted. Yet we depend on the natural environment for our productive potential in the same way that we depend on produced capital assets such as machinery and buildings: without those natural resources, we could produce much less with our own labor.

If statisticians had been keeping track of the depletion of these stocks of natural resources, our true macroeconomic record during the 1980s would have looked worse still, for in recent years we have squandered the environment on a massive scale. "Since mid-century," Lester Brown of the Worldwatch Institute reports, "the world has lost nearly one fifth of the topsoil from its cropland, a fifth of its tropical rain forests, and tens of thousands of its plant and animal species."[17]

Running down our human resources. Similar shortsightedness may be affecting our stock of human resources. Our capacity to grow in the future depends substantially on a growing base of "human capital," of skills embodied in our present and future productive workers. This requires continual upgrading of our educational system, of our technical training, of our commitment to future human resource development.

But the priorities of right-wing economics during the 1980s – the military buildup combined with cuts in domestic social programs – diverted resources away from this productive investment. Real government expenditures on education, in constant 1982 dollars, grew at an average annual rate of 7.2 percent a year during the long expansion years from 1948 to 1966. During the 1980s, real educational expenditures grew at only 1.3 percent a year. Public educational expenditures as a percentage of GNP fell as a result, dropping from an average of 4.7 percent in 1973–79 to only 4.0 percent in 1979–89.[18]

17 Lester R. Brown, "The Illusion of Progress," in Lester R. Brown et al., *State of the World, 1990* (New York: W. W. Norton, 1990), p. 3.

18 Data on total government expenditures on education from *Historical Statistics,* p. 340; *Statistical Abstract,* 1992, Table 560 and earlier years; the figures for 1971–74 were estimated by linear interpolation.

A deteriorating infrastructure. Last, but hardly least, we were running down our physical infrastructure – the bridges, roads, electrical systems, and water systems which provide the necessary foundation for production and distribution. And the alarm was being sounded from all points on the political compass. Invoking the wisdom of Adam Smith that public works are essential to "facilitate the commerce of society," David Aschauer of the Chicago Federal Reserve Bank concluded that "current public capital expenditures are too low."[19] One careful study of government infrastructural investment found that real government investment in highways and other infrastructure averaged $3.8 billion a year (in constant 1982 dollars) during the 1973–79 business cycle, but fell to an average of $2.8 billion a year during the 1980s (through 1986); real infrastructural investment reached $4.0 billion in 1979. By 1986, after the devastating impact of continuing government cutbacks, it had fallen to $2.1 billion.[20]

THE CONTRADICTIONS OF RIGHT-WING ECONOMICS

> The economic ills we suffer have come upon us over several decades. They will not go away in days, weeks, or months, but they will go away.
>
> – Ronald Reagan, First Inaugural Address, 1981[21]

Whether in its devastating impact on the lives of the vast majority of people in the United States, its lackluster macroeconomic record, or its buy-now/pay-later character, right-wing economics failed. Why?

There can be little doubt that the right-wing agenda was implemented to a substantial extent. Indeed, the right won almost all of its significant political battles through much of the previous decade. The monetarists drove up real interest rates. No one in the labor movement could deny the toll which right-wing economics exacted from workers. The free-marketeers trimmed the government's regulatory nails. The supply-siders achieved dramatic reductions in tax rates for the wealthy. And the hawks produced soaring military expenditures. But if they won all the battles, how could they have lost the war?

19 "Is the Public Capital Stock Too Low?" *Chicago Fed Letter,* October 1987, number 2, 1–4.

20 Congressional Budget Office, *Trends in Public Investment* (Washington, D.C.: Congressional Budget Office, 1987), Table 3.

21 Quoted in *Economic Report,* 1989, pp. 7–8.

There are two ways to answer this question. The superficially most obvious answer is that they may not have been fighting the war they had proclaimed. The right may not have even cared about the long-term health of the U.S. economy or the well-being of the majority of its people. They may have sought, instead, to concentrate power and wealth in the hands of the wealthiest families and the major U.S. corporations – preferring a larger slice of a smaller pie – rather than taking their chances with the kinds of policies which would have been required to revitalize the U.S. economy. If redistribution was their objective, the battles which they fought – for higher interest rates, for weaker unions, for less regulation of business, for lower taxes on the affluent, and for larger military expenditures – were not won in vain. This answer has simplicity to recommend it: it assumes that the right-wing forces knew what they were doing, and that they got for their troubles more or less what they set out to get. They won their war.

A quite different answer – and the one toward which we incline – is that they did indeed seek to reverse the economic decline which they inherited from the 1960s and 1970s, but that they failed in this objective because the policy package they adopted was ill-suited for the job. Whatever the objectives of the leaders of right-wing economic policy, their dismal macroeconomic record, and its buy-now/pay-later character may be attributed to a number of important shortcomings. These shortcomings suggest that the logic of right-wing economics outlined in the first section – with its reliance on trickle-down economics, the discipline of the whip, the invisible hand, and the global big stick – was fundamentally flawed. Superficially, at least, there are some intuitive grounds for suspecting the sources of these flaws.

For example, the right-wing attachment to the discipline of the whip – the top-down approach to labor relations – is out of date; an outmoded hierarchical and conflictual system of labor relations lies at the root of the continuing inability of the U.S. to solve the productivity problem. During the 1980s the U.S. was consistently outpaced on the productivity front by nations which have adopted more meaningful forms of worker participation in decision making, job security, and collective bargaining. In the United States, the right-wing approach to the problem – relying on the threat of unemployment and intensive workplace supervision to keep workers on their toes – has prevailed. As our relative international standing attests, this strategy doesn't seem to work very well.

Similarly, the right-wing ideological commitment to the invisible hand is simply out of step with the way the world now works. Even setting aside the economic injustice fostered by the laissez-faire approach, to leave economic decision making entirely to private profit-and-loss calculations is just not a smart way to run an economy. A passive, noninterventionist government simply cannot cope with the unfolding environmental crisis, nor can it provide the needed guidance and support for the basic research and human resource development essential to future economic well-being.

But shouldn't the right-wing strategy at least have managed to stimulate investment rather than dampen it (see row 2 of Table 7.2)? This is perhaps the most surprising failure of the right-wing strategy. One might have thought that lower taxes, weaker unions, and a free hand to pursue profits while ignoring the social or environmental consequences would be just what the doctor ordered to revive ailing private investment. And this was exactly what the right-wing supply-siders promised at the beginning of their reign. Unraveling the puzzle of their unfulfilled promise will take us to the heart of the right-wing failure.

Profitability and investment

The right-wing economists were not mistaken in their emphasis on the connection between after-tax profitability and private investment. Extending data presented in Gordon's earlier essay, Figure 7.2 graphs annual values for these two supply-side indicators, tracking the rate of accumulation (the rate of growth of the net private capital stock) and the after-tax corporate profit rate. Because it is the profit rate which stimulates investment, movements in the former precede movements in the latter. For this reason we have graphed the profit rate prevailing two years earlier than the date shown; the profit rate indicated for the year 1966, for example, is the actual profit rate in 1964, the year in which the decision was taken to build the new investment goods which were actually installed in 1966. Evidently the after-tax profit rate and the rate of accumulation are not only closely related, but – equally important – the profit rate appears to lead the investment rate by two years.

As the investment boom of the 1960s was a response to a profit surge, so the stagnation of investment in the 1980s is clearly related to the surprisingly lackluster performance of the after-tax profit rate. But the data for 1986 through 1989 suggest that the poor showing of after-tax profits during the 1980s may not be the whole story. Profitability was

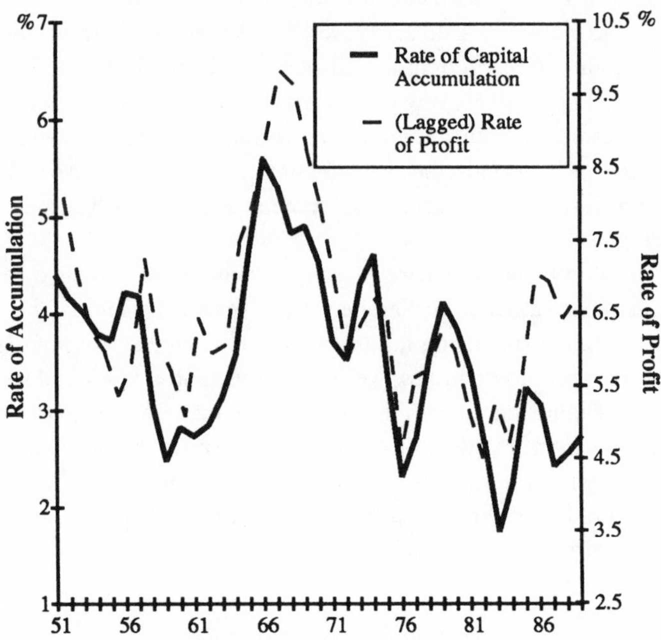

Figure 7.2. Profitability and accumulation in the U.S. economy. Rate of growth of real net fixed nonresidential capital stock and net after-tax rate of NFCB profit (lagged two years). *Sources:* See source notes for Table 7.2, row [2], and Table 7.3, row [1].

relatively strong during these years, yet investment continued to falter nonetheless.

We are left with two questions: why did after-tax profits respond so weakly to the political victories scored by the right-wing program? And why did the profit surge after the recession of 1983 not set off a correspondingly resurgent investment boom? In Table 7.3 we present data which will help us answer these two questions.

We begin by tracking average after-tax corporate profitability in row 1, the same variable graphed in Figure 7.2. It did improve slightly in 1979–89, as compared with the previous cycle, but it still remained substantially below its levels in the 1950s and 1960s.

To work toward an understanding of this sluggish recovery of after-tax profitability, it is helpful to distinguish between the profit *share* of output (or profits divided by total output) and the profit *rate* (profits divided by the capital stock). The profit rate is equal to the profit share times the level of output per unit of capital stock; this relationship is simply an

Table 7.3. *Tracing the contours of macroeconomic failure*

	Phase Averages			
	1948-66	**1966-73**	**1973-79**	**1979-89**
[1] After-tax profit rate (%)	6.9	7.0	5.5	6.0
[2] % change, real wages/hourly output	-0.2	0.6	0.1	-0.4
[3] % change, relative import price	-1.4	-0.3	5.2	-1.7
[4] Effect rate of profits taxation (ratio)	0.49	0.46	0.49	0.40
[5] After-tax profit share (%)	9.4	9.3	8.5	9.2
[6] Rate of capacity utilization (ratio)	0.98	0.99	0.96	0.94
[7] Real interest rate (%)	-0.3	1.7	0.8	4.8

Sources: Levels are calculated as average annual levels. *ERP* refers to *Economic Report of the President*, 1991.

[1] Rate of net after-tax profit, nonfinancial corporate business sector (NFCB), defined as (adjusted profits - profits tax liability + net interest)/(net capital stock + inventories): Numerator from *ERP*, B-12; capital stock same as Table 7.2, row [2]; inventories from unpublished tables, Bureau of Economic Analysis.

[2] Average annual rate of change of ratio of real hourly earnings to real hourly output, all employees, nonfarm business sector: *ERP*, B-44.

[3] Average annual rate of change of ratio of import price deflator to GNP price deflator: *ERP*, Table B-3.

[4] Ratio of profits tax liability to adjusted before-tax profits: *ERP*, B-12.

[5] Net after-tax profit share of NFCB domestic output, defined as (adjusted profits - profits tax liability + net interest)/(NFCB gross domestic product): *ERP*, B-12.

[6] Ratio of actual output to potential output, private business nonresidential sector: for method and sources, see Samuel Bowles, David M. Gordon, and Thomas E. Weisskopf, "Business Ascendancy and Economic Impasse: A Structural Retrospective on Conservative Economics, 1979–87," *Journal of Economic Perspectives*, Winter 1989, pp. 107–134, Data Appendix.

[7] Federal funds rate minus expected rate of inflation: federal funds rate from *ERP*, Table B-71 (with N.Y. Fed discount rate used for 1948–54); expected rate of inflation calculated from three-year distributed lag on past rates of change of GNP price deflator, *ERP*, B-1.

algebraic identity, with the output–capital ratio establishing a bridge between the profit share and the profit rate. One of the main determinants of the output–capital ratio is the level of capacity utilization in the economy: the higher the rate of utilization of existing capacity, the higher will be the ratio of output to capital and the higher, consequently, will be the ratio of the profit rate to the profit share.

Holding other things constant, the after-tax profit share of output will rise when the ratio of real wages to real hourly output falls (since the unit labor costs of producing output decline); when the real price of imports – the ratio of import prices to domestic prices – declines (since this allows firms to purchase foreign-produced inputs at relatively lower prices); and when the effective rate of taxation of before-tax profits falls.[22]

Each of these three determinants of the after-tax profit share had increased markedly in the 1973–79 cycle, moving adversely to corporate profitability and therefore cutting into the after-tax profit share. During the 1980s, these trends were reversed. After having increased for the previous two business cycles, the ratio of real wages to real hourly output declined (row 2). At the same time, the rise in the value of the dollar reversed the sharp upward trend in relative imports prices (row 3), while the effective corporate profit tax rate fell (row 4). These trends considerably bolstered the after-tax profit share (row 5), also reversing its sustained drop from 1948–66 through 1973–79.

Offsetting these gains for profitability, however, was a decline in the rate of capacity utilization which prevailed in the U.S. economy during the 1980s (row 6). We are thus in a position to answer our first question: given the favorable trends in the profit share, the rate of profit would have risen much more rapidly during the 1980s than it did (row 1) had it not been for the decline in the rate of capacity utilization (row 6).

Indeed, the low level of capacity utilization in the 1980s does double duty as a culprit in our story. Not only does it help explain the disappointing profit-rate record, as shown in Table 7.3, but it also played a leading role in discouraging private investment – even when the profit rate was doing well, as in the mid-1980s. To see why, we need to understand what determines the rate of private investment.

22 A more thorough analysis of the factors affecting the after-tax profit share is provided in our article, "Power and Profits: The Social Structure of Accumulation and the Profitability of the Postwar U.S. Economy"; see especially the Appendix to that article.

We have already seen (in Figure 7.2) that the after-tax profit rate has a strong influence on the net accumulation rate. The fit between these two variables is nonetheless far from perfect. Two other variables appear to have a significant influence on private investment. The rate of capacity utilization influences the decision to invest for the simple reason that, when a substantial portion of the nation's factories, equipment, and offices are idle, their owners and other potential investors have little incentive to invest in new productive equipment and thereby expand already underutilized productive capacity. Further, the decision to build new capacity is always made with the costs and alternative uses of funds in mind; when the real interest rate is high, the costs of borrowing for the purpose of investment may cancel an otherwise attractive project. High interest rates also act as a lure for the wealthy to use their funds not in building new capacity, but to retire their own corporate debt, or to loan their funds to others, or to engage in financial speculation and corporate mergers.

Taking account of all three determinants of private investment — the after-tax profit rate, the rate of capacity utilization, and the real interest rate – the poor performance of investment in the 1980s now appears as unsurprising. As can be seen from Table 7.3, rows 7 and 6, respectively, real interest rates were unprecedentedly high (the consequence of monetarist tight money policies) and, partly as a result, the level of capacity utilization dipped to its lowest average among the four phases of the postwar period. The slightly higher after-tax profit rate during the 1980s simply was not enough of a boost to offset these two negative influences on investment.

Are we to conclude, then, that the failure of the right-wing program to jump-start the stalled accumulation process was simply a mistake, the result of ill-conceived economic policies based on a misunderstanding of what it takes to stimulate private investment? It would be nice if the answer were yes, for a mistake as simple as this could easily be corrected. But, as we will see, the truth lies elsewhere: the right-wing program failed to stimulate investment because under conditions prevailing in the 1980s there was no way that all three of the determinants of investment – the after-tax profit rate, the real interest rate, and the rate of capacity utilization – could be made to move in the right direction at the same time. Thus, the failure was not a mistake; it was a result of the bind that eventually straight-jacketed the right-wing strategy.

Capitalist power and economic activity

There are two ways in which we can analyze the contradictions of right-wing economics. One uses the language of mainstream economics to focus attention on several critical trade-offs facing macroeconomic decision makers. The other uses the language of institutions and power, in a manner less familiar to mainstream economists. We investigate the internal tensions characterizing the right-wing agenda in each of these ways in turn.

Critical trade-offs. The contradictions of right-wing economics result from the fact that policies which support a high profit *share* are generally inconsistent with policies which promote high levels of capacity utilization and policies which promote low interest rates. But, as we have already seen, raising the profit share will not secure a high profit *rate unless* it is also accompanied by a high level of capacity utilization. Worse still, it will not generate a high level of investment *unless* it is also accompanied by low interest rates.

There are thus two critical trade-offs that generate contradictions for right-wing economics. The first involves a conflict between (1) the desirability of having a high level of capacity utilization to translate a high profit share into a high profit rate and to stimulate investment and (2) the desirability of having a low level of capacity utilization to sustain high unemployment as a way of maintaining labor discipline and thereby contributing to a high profit share. The second involves a conflict between (1) the desirability of having a low real interest rate to promote investment and (2) the desirability of having a high real interest rate to maintain the value of the dollar as a way of lowering the real price of imports and thereby contributing to a high profit share. We explore each of these two sources of tension in turn.

In the U.S. economy, the threat of unemployment plays a crucial role in keeping wages down, promoting the labor discipline necessary to enforce high levels of work effort, and thus supporting a high profit share. For the threat of unemployment to have teeth, however, the loss of a job must cost the worker a substantial amount in lost income, involving what we have termed a high cost of job loss. When jobs are plentiful, this threat does not have much bite.[23]

23 For more on this argument, see Bowles, Gordon, and Weisskopf, *After the Waste Land,* Chs. 5–7.

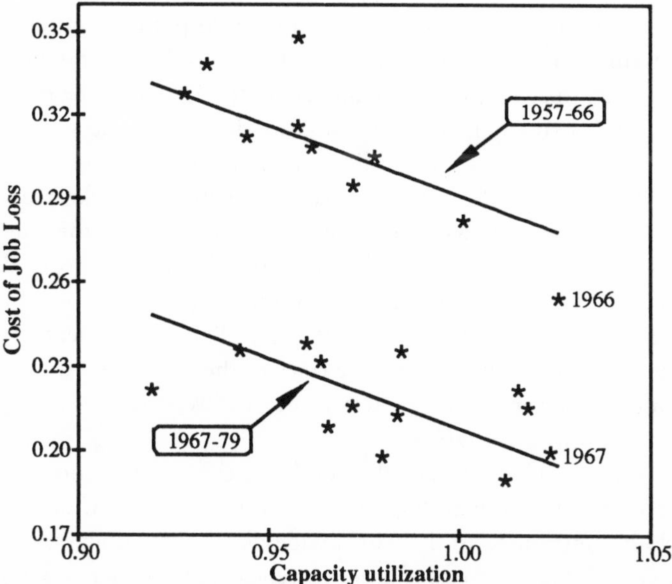

Figure 7.3. Critical trade-off I: Cost of job loss and capacity utilization. The trade-off between the cost of job loss and capacity utilization shifts inward, 1957–66/1967–79. *Sources:* See source notes for Table 2.5 in this volume, for [5], and for Table 7.3, row [6].

But that is just the problem: when capacity utilization is high, jobs are also plentiful and the threat of job dismissal is correspondingly low. The result is a trade-off between the level of capacity utilization and the cost of job loss. Increases in each would raise the profit rate. However, the economy can have high levels of capacity utilization, or it can have a high cost of job loss, but it cannot generally have both at the same time.

Figure 7.3 illustrates the trade-off between the cost of job loss and the rate of capacity utilization, mapping the levels of capacity utilization which actually prevailed in the U.S. economy between 1957 and 1979 against the actual levels of the cost of job loss. The straight lines represent the slopes of regression lines we have fit through these data. The regression lines clearly reveal both the trade-off itself – a downward slope in the lines indicates that higher capacity utilization is associated with a lower cost of job loss – and an inward shift of this trade-off after the mid-1960s. Combinations of capacity utilization and cost of job loss which were possible during the 1960s were unattainable during the seventies.

The shift in the trade-off line reflects the erosion of the social structure of accumulation which made sustained high corporate profitability and rapid accumulation during the postwar boom, and it sharply limited the options open to economic policy makers in the 1970s.[24] The recession of the mid-1970s greatly raised the cost of job loss, but it did so at a cost of even lower levels of capacity utilization. The cold bath recession of the early 1980s was no different: the price of a frightened workforce was idle factories. For the right-wing economic strategy to escape this bind, their policies would have had to shift the trade-off line outwards, allowing more favorable levels of both capacity utilization and the cost of job loss to be attained. And, despite greatly reduced unemployment insurance coverage, they failed to do this: the rules of the economic game defining the options open to policy makers in the 1980s were in this respect no different than in the 1970s.[25]

The second critical trade-off underlying the contradictions of right-wing economics is similar. High real interest rates in the United States in the 1980s contributed to the world-wide demand for dollars, driving up the price of dollars in terms of other currencies. The higher exchange rates which flowed from this rising dollar value meant that imports into the U.S. economy were cheaper. And cheaper imports – particularly imports of materials and other goods used in production – raised the profit share.

Taken by itself this should have contributed to a higher profit rate and subsequently to a rapid accumulation of capital. But here's the rub: the higher real interest rates also discouraged private investment and depressed consumer borrowing below what they would have been otherwise. The negative effect of high real interest rates on investment lands a one-two punch; not only do high rates directly depress investment, but the lower level of consumer demand reduces capacity utilization, further dampening the incentive to invest.

To illustrate this trade-off we graph in Figure 7.4 the real interest rate against the real price of imports. Because the exchange rate was fixed under the Bretton Woods system (in force until 1971), and because the flexible exchange rate system which followed was not fully in place until

24 For introduction to the concept of a social structure of accumulation, see ibid., Ch. 1.

25 Formally, one tests for this kind of shift by adding a dummy variable to the same regression equation used to estimate the shift of the trade-off line represented in Figure 7.3. When this equation is estimated on data through 1988, a dummy variable for the 1980s is not significant.

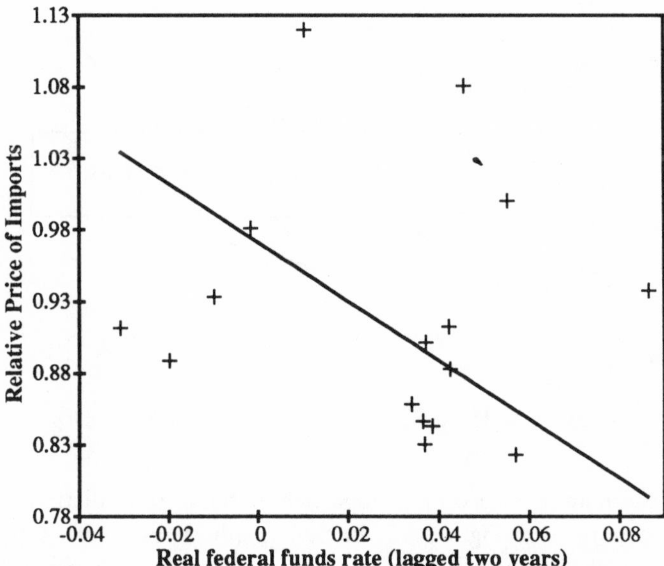

Figure 7.4. Critical trade-off II: Import prices and real interest rates. The trade-off between the relative price of imports and the real federal funds rate (lagged two years), 1974–89. *Sources:* Relative price of imports, import price deflator divided by GNP price deflator, *Economic Report of President*, 1990, Table C-3; real federal funds rate, see source notes for Table 7.3, row [7].

the end of the Nixon administration's "New Economic Policies" in 1973, our exercise begins in 1974. What is needed to stimulate investment is a combination of low real interest rates, which directly boost investment, and low real import prices, which indirectly spur investment through their favorable impact on profitability. But the data for Figure 7.4 make clear that the menu of real world choices facing policy makers did not include this auspicious combination: one could have low real interest rates and high import prices, as in the late 1970s, or high real interest rates and low import prices, as in the mid-1980s. One could not enjoy both at once.[26]

26 Worse still, changes in the economic environment appear to have made it even more difficult for policy makers to achieve the right combination of exchange rates and real interest rates. When we add a dummy variable for the 1980s to the equation estimated to generate the graph in Figure 7.4, that dummy variable has a significant and positive coefficient, indicating that the trade-off curve shifted outward and rightward during the 1980s. This sug-

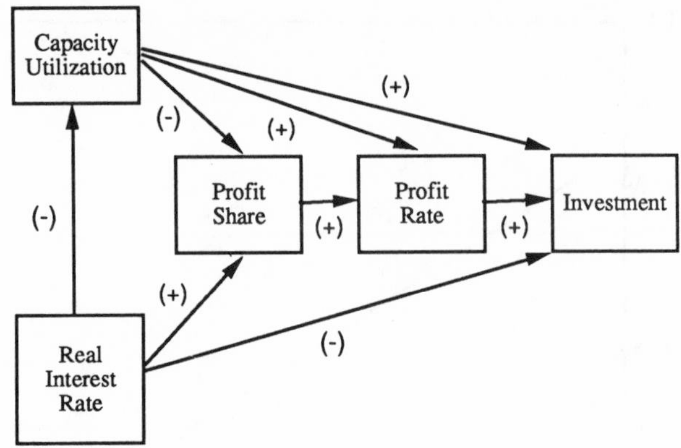

Figure 7.5. The contradictions of right-wing economics.

We summarize the economic logic behind these contradictions of right-wing economics in Figure 7.5. In that graph, arrows with a plus sign indicate a positive causal relationship; arrows with a negative sign indicate a negative causal relationship. When capacity utilization rises, for example, the profit share falls. The top part of the figure presents the tension flowing from the trade-off between the rate of capacity utilization and the cost of job loss, while the bottom part illustrates the tension resulting from the trade-off between the real interest rate and the real price of imports.

We can now see why the right-wing attempt to stimulate private investment failed. The high unemployment rates, high real interest rates, and high value of the dollar – all of which were key weapons in the right-wing arsenal – did indeed hit their targets. Wages were kept down, labor discipline was tightened, and U.S. firms were able to buy cheap and sell dear on a global scale; thus, the profit *share* rose. But these weapons also backfired, keeping capacity utilization low, keeping the profit *rate* lower than it would have otherwise been, and discouraging private investment. The game plan which evolved during the late 1970s, and which was masterminded from the White House after Ronald Reagan's inauguration, failed to escape the contradictions of right-wing economics.

gests that it took even higher levels of the real interest rate to achieve a given level of relative import prices during the 1980s than during the 1974–79 period, further tightening the constraints on the options available to right-wing policy makers.

In short, the right-wing economic program had indeed gained the upper hand for U.S. business. But it had done so at a price so heavy that the victory was nothing to celebrate, even for the winners.

Institutions and power

The same story of the contradictions of right-wing economics can be told in somewhat less familiar political and institutional terms.

We have argued at length elsewhere (see Gordon's earlier essay in this volume for a summary) that the long postwar boom built upon a new social structure of accumulation in the postwar period and that this new SSA was supported by four buttresses of capitalist power – the capital–labor accord, *Pax Americana,* the capital–citizen accord, and the moderation of inter-capitalist rivalry.[27] In related work we have been able to generate quantitative indicators of (relative) capitalist strength along these four SSA power axes. That exercise allows us, as well, to combine these individual indices of capitalist power into a single composite index of capitalist power, which we label **P**.[28] We can use this index to trace for the postwar period movements in the relative power of capitalists over workers, citizens, and foreign buyers and sellers – with that relative power measured in units expressing its favorable impact on the corporate after-tax profit rate.

Framed in these terms, the exercise conveys a clear message: the profit rate could be increased if it were possible to improve capital's power along the four SSA power axes without incurring losses on other profit rate determinants. And this was certainly one of the principal hopes spurring right-wing economic initiatives.

But, for reasons already explored in the previous section, wielding power in the interest of profits is expensive. The reason, in a nutshell, is that effective use of the main instruments of capitalist power (such as the tools for disciplining labor and obtaining relatively inexpensive inputs

27 Bowles, Gordon, and Weisskopf, *After the Waste Land,* Ch. 5.

28 **P** is estimated by weighting each of six quantitative indices of separate dimensions of capitalist power by their respective coefficients in an econometric estimate of the equation explaining annual variations in the rate of profit. For details, see Samuel Bowles, David M. Gordon, and Thomas E. Weisskopf, "Business Ascendancy and Economic Impasse: A Structural Retrospective on Conservative Economics, 1979–87," *Journal of Economic Perspectives,* Winter 1989, Table 3 and subsequent discussion.

from abroad) entail operating the economy at low levels of output and with high real rates of interest. Over the relevant range of economic activity and public policy established by the institutional condition of a prevailing SSA, capitalist power may be increased – but only at the cost of movements in capacity utilization and/or the real interest rate adversely affecting either profits or investment.

This leads us to want to distinguish between the *apparent* level of capitalist power prevailing at any moment in the economy and the *underlying* or *structurally determined* level of capitalist power, where underlying capitalist power is measured at constant levels of macroindicators like capacity utilization and the real interest rate. We would like to be able to distinguish, that is, between increases in capitalist power which result simply from less favorable macroeconomic circumstances, on the one hand, and those which result from a real shift in the underlying political and institutional environment conditioning the rate of profit and accumulation, on the other. In terms of Figures 7.3 and 7.4, we would like to distinguish between increases in capitalist power which result simply from movement up along one of those negatively sloped curves – increasing one or another dimension of capitalist power at the expense of less favorable macroeconomic conditions – and increases in capitalist power which result from an outward/rightward shift in one of those curves – political and institutional shifts favorable to capital which do *not* come at the expense of the macroeconomic environment.

We have been able to forge such a distinction through an additional empirical exercise, which allows us to generate indices of "underlying capitalist power."[29] Having estimated them, we can also combine them

29 We have taken our various quantitative measures of capitalist power, the individual components of the index of apparent capitalist power **P**, and statistically "purged" them of their association with movements in the level of capacity utilization or the real rate of interest. This "purging" process simply involves subtracting from those "observed" power indices the variations in their levels which can be attributed to movements along the curves illustrated in Figures 7.3 and 7.4 – movements which are associated with changes in macroeconomic conditions – and retaining only those portions of their fluctuations which could by the process of elimination represent upward/rightward or downward/leftward movements of those curves at any constant or benchmark index of the health of the economy; the latter shifts are therefore independent of shifts in the state of the macroeconomy. More technically, this exercise involves regressing the indices of apparent capitalist power on either capacity utilization or the real rate of interest and then

into a single composite index of "underlying capitalist power," **P***.[30] Given the structure of our analysis, variations in **P*** represent literally the variations in capitalist power affecting corporate profitability which are *not* associated with either favorable or unfavorable shifts in macroeconomic conditions.

What does our index of underlying capitalist power **P*** tell us about the long-term dynamics of the power economy? We present in Figure 7.6 a graph of **P*** from 1952 through 1988.[31] Also shown is a corresponding summary index of apparent capitalist power **P**.

The rising level of **P*** from the mid-1950s to the mid-1960s, followed by a long declining trend through the late 1970s, provides quantitative support for our institutional history of these decades. The institutional structure of the postwar social structure of accumulation in the United States was consolidated in such a way as to enhance the political-economic power of the capitalist class in the first two decades after World War II. Beginning in the mid-1960s, however, a series of challenges – from workers, Third World raw material suppliers, and citizens' movements – as well as an increase in inter-capitalist competition began to undermine the SSA and erode the power of the U.S. capitalist class. (See Gordon's earlier essay in this volume for a brief summary of these trends.)

The differences between the apparent and underlying power indices also tell an interesting story. Deviations of **P*** from **P** reflect variations in capacity utilization and the real interest rate. While the measured power of U.S. capital recovered strongly during the late 1970s and 1980s, according to Figure 7.6, its underlying power did not. The improvement in the apparent power indices was achieved primarily through variations in the level of capacity utilization and the real interest rate, reflecting move-

subtracting from the dependent variable the linear measure of its covariation with the independent variable represented by the regression coefficient times the value of the independent variable. This amounts to "residualizing" the power indices on the macroindices – and thus "purging" them of their covariation with those macroindices. For further detail, see ibid.

30 Here too, as in the construction of the composite index **P**, **P*** is estimated by weighting each of the six quantitative indices of underlying capitalist power by their respective coefficients in an econometric estimate of the equation explaining annual variations in the rate of profit, where in this case the equation includes the indices of "underlying" rather than "apparent" capitalist power. See ibid.

31 The graph presents smoothed values for the index, using three-year centered moving averages, in order to clarify the pattern of its trend variations.

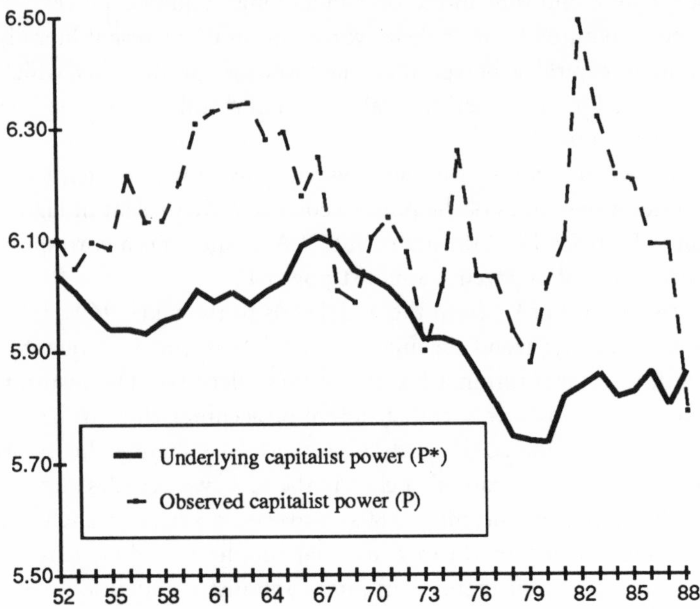

Figure 7.6. Trends in capitalist power. Indices of underlying and observed capitalist power, 1952–88. *Sources:* See text and notes 28–30.

ments along the kinds of curves traced in Figures 7.3 and 7.4 rather than outward shifts in the frontiers themselves. While those utilization and interest rate effects resulted in higher values for measured capitalist power, they were nonetheless consistent with a continuing decline in our index of underlying capitalist power.

Did the reign of conservative economics during the 1980s reverse the decline in the vitality of the postwar U.S. social structure of accumulation? We have already seen that while the measured power of U.S. capital rose dramatically in the 1980s, underlying power did not, indicating the absence of a favorable shift in the kinds of capitalist-power frontiers depicted in Figures 7.3 and 7.4. Meanwhile, hardball economics resulted in low rates of capacity utilization (on average) and high real rates of interest throughout the 1980s. The combination was deadly for the prospects of the right-wing macroeconomic agenda.

How, then, are we finally to evaluate right-wing economic policy in the 1980s? Given the ambitious nature of the right-wing economic agenda and its focus on institutional change, it is surely too soon to offer a definitive reckoning. An evaluation of the New Deal a decade after Roosevelt's first inauguration would doubtlessly have undervalued many of the institutional changes which were to bear fruit only much later. But from the vantage point of what appears to be the first completed business cycle under the right-wing umbrella, the following conclusions appear warranted.

First, the disappointing performance of the U.S. economy under right-wing tutelage reflects a long-term deterioration of conditions governing profitability and investment, exacerbated in the 1980s by the deleterious effects of right-wing economic policy.

Second, the reign of right-wing economics failed during the period of its ascendancy to alter the underlying structural relationships of the U.S. economy in a manner favorable to rapid accumulation.

The apparent paradox of this failure – that the right-wing agenda was largely adopted and highly successful in its particulars, yet failed to achieve a durable structural victory – can be readily resolved. The undeniable increase in the power of U.S. capital over the economic agents with which it deals – over workers, external buyers and sellers, and those who would use the state in ways contrary to the interests of business – was won at a prohibitive cost. Ironically, the economic doctrine which focused attention on improving profitability and investment through supply-side interventions appears to have won its only battles on the demand side, but with a decidedly non-Keynesian flavor – for it was demand contraction, not expansion, which was its most effective weapon.

It does remain possible that underlying power relationships in the United States have begun to shift in favor of capital in recent years. We cannot rule out the possibility of a more enduring victory for U.S. capital in the 1990s. It is clear, however, that the widespread perception of such a turnaround in the 1980s – as reflected in our index of apparent power **P** – was largely the artifact of low levels of capacity utilization and high levels of real interest rates, for which we paid a heavy macroeconomic price.

When all is said and done, it may turn out that the only sustained transformations effected by the right-wing economic program will have been the sectoral changes in the U.S. economic structure brought about by the military buildup and high real interest rates of the 1980s, and the regressive redistribution of wealth and income brought about by the inequitable tax and social policies of the Reagan administration. Nothing more of lasting effect may have been achieved. What may be best remembered from this episode of triumphant greed and jingoistic nationalism is the monumental waste and suffering which it bequeathed at the close of the twentieth century.

8

The new economic stagnation and the contradictions of economic policy making

ROBERT A. BLECKER

When World War II ended in 1945, it was widely feared that the U.S. economy would sink back into a state of stagnation, if not another Great Depression. New Keynesian economic theories seemed to imply that, once the stimulus of wartime deficit spending was removed, private consumption and investment demand would falter and economic growth would again grind to a half. Of course, the reality turned out quite differently. While there was a downturn in the late 1940s, the economy soon took off on a two-decade period of unparalleled growth and prosperity, interrupted by only brief and mild recessions, which has since been dubbed the "Golden Age" of American (and global) capitalism.[1]

Propelled by Cold War–related government spending, but also aided by the widespread diffusion of new technologies as well as by buoyant exports to the recovering economies of Europe and Asia, the U.S. economy marched along in fairly harmonious fashion from the late 1940s until the late 1960s. Inflation, while a subject of concern at the time (in a country that had never experienced sustained peacetime inflation before), was still moderate by later standards or in comparison with other countries. Real wages kept pace with productivity growth, so that workers shared in the benefits of improving technology. Unemployment generally remained low, and inequality in the distribution of income was reduced. The traditional working class apparently disappeared into the broad "middle class." Expectations of continuous increases in living standards from generation to generation became embedded in the American con-

1 See Stephen A. Marglin and Juliet B. Schor, eds., *The Golden Age of Capitalism* (Oxford: Oxford University Press, 1990).

sciousness. Even the movements for greater rights among African-Americans, women, and other disadvantaged groups can be understood, in part, as efforts to win broader participation in the American Dream.

The country then suffered a rude awakening from this golden economic dream starting in the late 1960s. First Vietnam War–era inflation, followed by oil price shocks, high interest rates, a volatile dollar, and finally the so-called "twin deficits" (budget and trade) upset the domestic equilibrium. In the intervening years we have experienced slower growth of both output and productivity, stagnant or falling real wages, worsening trade-offs between inflation and unemployment, and a regression toward greater distributive inequality. Ever-increasing government budget deficits have failed to provide sustained economic stimulus, while a generally falling dollar (except for the period 1980 to early 1985) has failed to prevent continued large foreign trade deficits.

In the early 1990s, the U.S. economy has become stuck in the most prolonged contraction since the 1930s. The much deeper recession of 1981–82 had ended abruptly as the economy surged in 1983–84 and entered (to many people's surprise) the longest uninterrupted expansion since the 1960s boom.[2] An enormous fiscal stimulus from Ronald Reagan's tax cuts and defense spending, assisted by falling energy prices and (at certain crucial times) expansionary monetary policy,[3] produced the rapid recovery of 1983–84 and continued to bolster growth in the mid-1980s. But toward the end of the cycle, in the late 1980s, growth slowed substantially before a recession officially began in mid-1990. Only a falling dollar and an improving trade balance kept the economy going in the late 1980s, but this stimulus too eventually faltered. And while output bottomed out in the first quarter of 1991, the subsequent recovery was so sluggish that the previous peak level of real gross domestic product (GDP) from the second quarter of 1990 was not reached again until the third quarter of 1992, over two years later. One year after the cycle

2 The 1960s expansion lasted thirty-five quarters ($8\frac{3}{4}$ years), from a trough in 1961-I to a peak in 1969-IV. The 1980s expansion lasted thirty quarters ($7\frac{1}{2}$ years), from a trough in 1982-IV to a peak in 1990-II.

3 Of course, monetary policy was generally tight through most of the early 1980s, as Fed Chairman Paul Volcker sought to wring inflation out of the economy. But in late 1982 and early 1983 the Fed temporarily eased rates, in order to help end the recession and spark a recovery. Then again, in 1985 and 1986, when growth was faltering, the Fed stepped in again with monetary expansion, helping to bring down both interest rates and the overvalued dollar.

trough, the GDP growth rate for 1992 was only 2.6 percent, compared with 3.9 percent in 1983 after the previous recession ended. And the 6.2 percent growth rate of 1984 seemed highly unlikely to be duplicated in 1993.

Indeed, new U.S. President Bill Clinton was greeted with the news of an anemic 0.8 percent annual growth rate for the first quarter of 1993, followed by a mere 1.8 percent for the second quarter. By then the sluggish expansion that had begun in mid-1991 was known as the "jobless recovery," as business firms did not hire back laid off workers while they downsized and restructured – and moved offshore. While government spending was being cut to reduce the budget deficit, private investment remained flat, and net exports were worsening again (due partly to recessions or slow growth in Europe and Japan). With the Republicans in Congress having blocked even a token $16 billion fiscal stimulus, the prospects were for continued sluggish growth throughout the mid-1990s.

At the end of 1993, a five-year, $500 billion deficit reduction package (reaching an annual maximum of $140 billion in the final year) has been the main economic achievement of the new administration, and it is one guaranteed to slow growth and keep unemployment higher for several years to come. Even though this measure will leave the federal government with a considerable deficit (especially if tax revenues fall short of projections due to slow growth or tax evasion), it is the first down payment on an austerity plan for the American economy. While no one in Washington wants to pronounce the "S" word (sacrifice), that is exactly what this plan promises. The question which no one in Washington wants to ask is, why is the sacrifice needed, and what will it accomplish?

1. THE SAVING SHORTFALL VIEW

In the 1980s, it became common among economists to blame a major portion (if not all) of the nation's economic ills on what was broadly defined as a crisis of "overconsumption" or a "shortfall of savings."[4] This analysis was soon picked up by editorialists and pundits who decried a

4 For further discussion of this argument see Robert A. Blecker, *Are Americans on a Consumption Binge? The Evidence Reconsidered* (Washington, DC: Economic Policy Institute, 1990); and Robert A. Blecker, "Low Saving Rates and the 'Twin Deficits': Confusing the Symptoms and Causes of Economic Decline," in *Economic Problems of the 1990s,* ed. Paul Davidson and Jan A. Kregel (Aldershot, UK: Edward Elgar, 1991).

massive "consumption binge" that was lowering the nation's saving rate and reducing investment in the country's future. The low saving rate had two main components: the dramatic decline in the official personal saving rate in the national income and product accounts, and the enormous increase in the federal government budget deficit. Both individual Americans and their government were said to be "living beyond their means," thus depleting the funds available to finance investment domestically. As a result, it was alleged, the nation had to run a trade deficit – not because of declining industrial competitiveness, as many people believed, but simply because excessive domestic spending relative to income compelled the country to borrow from abroad, which created a deficit on the current account in the balance of payments. And in the long run, it was claimed, the shortage of savings would inevitably "crowd out" investment, thus endangering the growth of the nation's productive capacity.

In the mid-1980s, this argument became popularized into the notion that the trade deficit was a "twin" of the budget deficit. Most serious economists recognized the "twin deficit" notion to be too simplistic, but it was maintained by some as a useful fiction to keep the public focused on the evils of the budget deficit rather than other causes of the trade imbalance.[5] Whether or not the two deficits were actually twins, siblings, or "distant cousins,"[6] both the trade deficit and the shortfall in private

5 For example, Martin Feldstein recently wrote:

> The link between the U.S. budget deficit and trade deficit in the 1980s was so clear that the two were popularly labeled the twin deficits. In the public's mind, the two deficits appeared as Siamese twins that could not be separated. Only by reducing the budget deficit would the trade deficit be made to shrink.
>
> There is of course some truth to this oversimplified picture, *indeed more truth and a much more benign policy implication than to the alternative view that our exploding trade deficit in the 1980s was due to the trade policies of Japan and our other trading partners.*

"The Budget and Trade Deficits Aren't Really Twins," *Challenge* (March–April 1992): 60 (italics added). Of course, Feldstein did much as chairman of the Council of Economic Advisors under President Reagan in the early 1980s to promote "twin deficits" thinking in the public mind, through his stern admonitions about the dangers of the rising budget deficit at that time.

6 This expression is due to Walter Enders and Bong-Soo Lee, "Current Account and Budget Deficits: Twins or Distant Cousins?" *Review of Economics and Statistics* 72 (August 1990): 373–81. Some economists have confused matters more by asserting that *any* connection between the budget and trade deficits, however small, makes them "twins." A good example is found in Jeffrey A. Rosensweig and Ellis W. Tallman, "Fiscal Policy and Trade Adjustment: Are the Deficits Really Twins?" Working Paper No. 91-2, Federal Reserve Bank of

investment spending in the late 1980s and early 1990s were widely attributed to the overall low national saving rate, resulting from both individual and public improvidence.

This view has led in turn to a desperate search for measures to raise the national saving rate.[7] These range from Republican proposals to lower taxes on capital gains to Democratic advocacy of greater tax incentives for Individual Retirement Accounts (IRAs). All such proposals to raise private savings through tax incentives suffer from the problem that they might exacerbate the budget deficit, thus failing to raise total national saving (in which the government deficit counts as dissaving). To avoid this problem, one policy analyst has even advocated legally forcing people to save through "mandatory savings accounts."[8] But most of all – especially among those who are skeptical of any government efforts to stimulate private saving – this view has led to the conclusion that the most important place to start is by reducing the budget deficit, and perhaps even moving to a budget surplus in order to offset reduced private saving.[9]

The standard saving shortfall view was well expressed in a policy report entitled *Overconsumption:*

> The greatest single problem of the U.S. economy in the late 1980s is its extremely low level of national saving. The current low national saving rate . . . lies at the root of both our unprecedented trade deficits and our inadequate level of domestic investment, which in turn is a major cause of low U.S. productivity growth.[10]

Atlanta, March 1991, who state that their results "provide evidence supporting the twin deficit notion that government deficits impact trade balances" (Abstract, n. pag.). But according to their highest estimates, the government budget deficit explains no more than 30 percent of the trade deficit. By this accounting, two cousins who share 25 percent of the same genetic make-up are virtually "twins."

7 See, e.g., Charls E. Walker, Mark A. Bloomfield, and Margo Thorning, *The U.S. Savings Challenge: Policy Options for Productivity and Growth* (Boulder, CO: Westview Press for the American Council on Capital Formation, Center for Policy Research, 1990).

8 See Robert E. Litan, "Force-Feeding Our Piggy Banks: Cutting the Deficit by Making Americans Save More of Their Incomes," *Washington Post,* May 30, 1993.

9 This is the view expressed by Barry Bosworth, "There's No Simple Explanation for the Collapse in Saving," *Challenge* 32 (July–August 1989): 27–32; and Lawrence Summers and Chris Carroll, "Why Is U.S. National Saving So Low?" *Brookings Papers on Economic Activity, 2:1987,* pp. 607–42.

10 George N. Hatsopoulos, Paul R. Krugman, and James M. Poterba, *Overcon-*

Within this perspective, there are subtle differences depending on the relative importance attributed to the government deficit and private over-spending in depressing national savings. In the ominously titled book *Day of Reckoning*, Benjamin Friedman aims his wrath at the fiscal policy of the Reagan administration:

> The decision to mortgage America's economic future has not been a matter of individual choice but of legislated public policy. Popular talk of the 'me generation' to the contrary, most individual Americans are . . . saving nearly as much, as their parents and grandparents did. What is different . . . [are the] tax and spending policies that the U.S. government has pursued throughout Ronald Reagan's presidency.[11]

At the other extreme, Lawrence J. Kotlikoff argues that the decrease in the national saving rate in the 1980s is most attributable to falling private saving, when the latter is properly measured; in his view, officially reported government deficits are not reliable indicators of the true impact of fiscal policies on overall national saving.[12] The *Overconsumption* study takes an intermediate position, however, putting roughly equal blame on public and private profligacy. Lawrence Summers and Chris Carroll concur with this consensus position:

> . . . rising deficits can account for only about half of the decline in the national saving rate between the two periods [1960–81 and 1982–86]. The remainder is attributable to a roughly equal decline in the private saving rate. Much of that decline is in turn traceable to a fall in the personal saving rate.[13]

Of course, there have been strong dissents against this saving shortfall view, in all of its variants. From the Right, "new classical" economists such as Robert Barro have disputed whether a saving shortfall exists and especially whether deficit financing of government deficits is truly a net

sumption: The Challenge to U.S. Economic Policy (New York and Washington: American Business Conference and Thermo Electron Corporation, 1989), p. 6.

11 Benjamin M. Friedman, *Day of Reckoning: The Consequences of American Economic Policy Under Reagan and After* (New York: Random House, 1988), pp. 5–6.

12 Lawrence J. Kotlikoff, "The Crisis in U.S. Saving and Proposals to Address the Crisis," *National Tax Journal* 18 (September 1990): 233–46. Kotlikoff admits, however, that "there is no 'smoking gun' explanation for the critically low level of U.S. saving" (p. 237).

13 Summers and Carroll, "U.S. National Saving," p. 607.

drain on national saving. In Barro's "Ricardian equivalence" view, far-sighted individuals offset increased government deficits by additional private saving in anticipation of higher future taxes, and if the higher saving rates are not found in the official savings statistics then this is due to mismeasurement.[14]

From the Left, Keynesian economists such as Robert Eisner have also argued that official saving rates are mismeasured, but mostly because they omit large parts of what a society sets aside to provide for the future such as expenditures on consumer durables, public education, and public infrastructure. More importantly, Keynesians believe that government deficits need not crowd out private investment but can actually stimulate it by boosting demand and thus contributing to growth. In fact, Eisner has found that his measure of the "real" federal deficit (adjusted for inflation effects and correcting for the treatment of public capital expenditures) has a positive effect on business investment.[15]

In spite of these criticisms, the saving shortfall view has clearly won the day, both within the mainstream of the economics profession and in the public mind. This is perhaps most obvious from the fact that the first Democratic president in twelve years made reducing the budget deficit his number one economic priority, whether by choice or as a result of political pressure, in spite of 1992 campaign pledges to "grow the economy" and "invest in America."

The saving shortfall view appears to rest on a logically solid foundation, especially the macroeconomic accounting relationship or "identity" which links the trade balance, total national saving (private and public), and domestic investment.

Trade balance = National saving − Domestic investment, where "national saving" is the sum of private saving and the government budget

14 See Robert Barro, "The Ricardian Approach to Budget Deficits," *Journal of Economic Perspectives* 3 (Spring 1989): 37–54. Barro points out that official saving rates do not include as saving the appreciation of existing stocks of assets. Yet asset appreciation provides for future consumption just as well as asset accumulation out of current income.

15 See Robert Eisner, "Budget Deficits: Rhetoric and Reality," *Journal of Economics Perspectives* 3 (Fall 1989): 73–93; Robert Eisner, "The Real Rate of U.S. National Saving," *Review of Income and Wealth,* series 37 (March 1991); and Robert Eisner, "Sense and Nonsense About Budget Deficits," *Harvard Business Review* (May–June 1993): 99–111.

surplus (which is negative if the government has a deficit).[16] From this identity, it appears that if the nation is "living beyond its means" and saving too little, the low level of savings must result in either a trade deficit (negative trade balance), or a low amount of domestic investment, or a combination of the two. This logical foundation gives the saving shortfall view a certain *a priori* plausibility.

Nevertheless, it is evident that the direction of causality in this equation need not run from saving to the other variables.[17] If the trade balance is depressed by an overvalued exchange rate or by declining industrial competitiveness, this could cause a reduction in national saving by depressing domestic employment and national income. This would work partly through reduced private saving of individuals and businesses with lower incomes, and partly through reduced tax revenue of the public sector. Alternatively, there could be a common factor depressing both saving and investment. This occurs in a recession, for example, when private saving, public saving, and domestic investment all fall together (although investment usually falls more than saving in a recession, so that the trade balance improves). Saving and investment can also move together when the retained earnings of corporations (which are counted as part of private saving) are an important source of finance for investment, and firms adjust the level of their retained earnings to the level of investment spending they plan to undertake.[18]

In reality, it is likely that all these causal mechanisms as well as others are operating, with some mechanisms being stronger at some times and others at other times. What is clearly *not* true is that the saving rate is *necessarily* the independent factor that drives changes in the trade balance or the investment rate. Sometimes this is true, and undoubtedly the rising U.S. government deficit in the early 1980s contributed to some extent to the worsening trade deficit. But that was a special case, and even

16 Note that this must be the *consolidated* budget surplus of the federal, state, and local governments. In the 1980s, state and local government budget surpluses partly offset the federal budget deficit, as shown in Table 8.2 below.

17 See also the discussion of this point in Blecker, "Low Saving Rates and the 'Twin Deficits' "; and Robert A. Blecker, *Beyond the Twin Deficits: A Trade Strategy for the 1990s* (Armonk, NY: M. E. Sharpe, Inc., for the Economic Policy Institute, 1992).

18 See Alfred S. Eichner, *The Macrodynamics of Advanced Market Economies* (Armonk, NY: M. E. Sharpe, Inc., 1991).

then most estimates show that no more than half (and possibly much less) of the rise in the trade deficit in the 1980s can be explained by the U.S. budget deficit.[19] In the late 1980s and early 1990s, the trade and budget balances generally moved in opposite directions, clearly showing that other factors were at work. Figure 8.1 shows that the overall trade balance (measured by net exports of goods and services in the GDP accounts) generally followed the budget deficit downward from 1980–87, with a lag of about two years, but then the former improved substantially while the latter worsened notably from 1989–92. On the whole, the 1980–87 period is unusual in terms of the strong correlation exhibited between the trade and budget balances, but even then the correlation is far from perfect.

In fact, some of the research produced by advocates of the saving shortfall view in the economics profession actually reveals anomalies which at least partly undermine the validity of that view. A good example is the very carefully done study of *Saving and Investment in a Global Economy* by Barry Bosworth. The author concludes that

> the conventional model of international macroeconomics works surprisingly well in explaining economic developments over the 1980s. A perspective that emphasizes divergences between domestic rates of investment and saving as the primary driving force behind changes in the current account can account for a large portion of the imbalances that developed during the 1980s.[20]

Nevertheless, at least one of Bosworth's major findings seems inconsistent with the conventional emphasis on the saving rate as the underlying cause of the nation's economic ills. Not only for the U.S., but also for twelve other industrialized nations, Bosworth found that "lower rates of income growth are primarily responsible for reduced rates of private saving."[21] In other words, the low saving rate, supposedly the *cause* of low investment and slow growth, is actually an *effect* of slow growth. Thus, the conventional wisdom is revealed to rest on circular reasoning: in order to grow faster, we must raise the saving rate, but in order to raise the saving rate, we would have to grow faster.

Interestingly, Bosworth also finds that the main cause of lower invest-

19 See the sources cited in Blecker, *Beyond the Twin Deficits,* pp. 49–51.

20 Barry Bosworth, *Saving and Investment in a Global Economy* (Washington, DC: Brookings Institution, 1993), p. 27.

21 Ibid., p. 78.

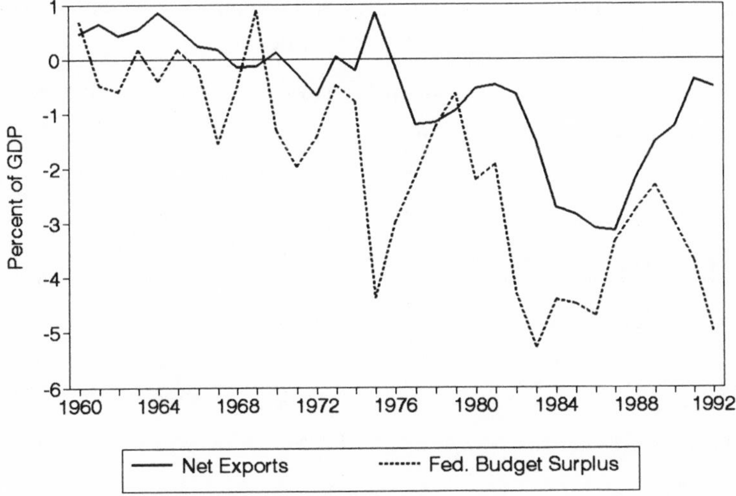

Figure 8.1. Trade and budget balances.

ment rates in the U.S. and elsewhere recently is also slower output growth. The effect of interest rates on investment was found to be small and, in the case of the U.S., was statistically insignificant. "The main result that emerges . . . is that private rates of saving and investment are linked over the long term, moving up and down together in response to variations in the growth of the overall economy."[22] This result clearly undermines the view that an autonomous drop in the nation's private saving rate has been a major *independent cause* of the growth slowdown, or that the low national saving rate is constraining investment spending by raising interest rates.

Nevertheless, the private saving rate did fall off sharply in the mid-1980s, and the budget deficit certainly grew substantially. The next section examines exactly how, when, and why these changes occurred, and how they were linked to broader changes in the U.S. economy.

2. THE GROWTH SLOWDOWN AND THE EVIDENCE ON SAVINGS

By almost all indicators, U.S. economic performance worsened in the 1970s and 1980s compared with the previous two decades. Table 8.1 gives some standard indicators. The time periods have been chosen to

22 Ibid., p. 92.

Table 8.1. U.S. economic growth rates and related indicators – selected periods, 1947–90 (in percent)

	1947-59	1960-69	1970-79	1980-90
Real gross domestic product	3.7	4.5	2.9	2.9
Real gross national product per capita	2.0	3.2	2.0	1.9
Real personal disposable income per capita	2.0	3.4	2.1	1.8
Labor productivity[a,b]	2.5[c]	2.6	1.4	1.1
Real hourly compensation[b]	3.2[c]	2.6	1.2	0.4
Real weekly earnings[d]	2.5[c]	1.6	-0.4	-0.4
Inflation rate[e]	3.4	2.7	7.0	5.1
Unemployment rate[f]	4.5	4.8	6.2	7.1

Sources: U.S. Department of Commerce, Bureau of Economic Analysis, National Income and Product Accounts; U.S. Department of Labor, Bureau of Labor Statistics, data reported in U.S. Council of Economic Advisors, *Economic Report of the President* (Washington, DC: Government Printing Office, various years); U.S. Congress, Joint Economic Committee, *Economic Indicators* (various issues); and author's calculations.

Notes: All variables are measured as average annual percentage growth rates except the inflation and unemployment rates, which are averages of annual rates. Growth rates were calculated by log-linear least squares regressions. Real variables were measured in constant 1987 dollars except as noted.

[a]Output per hour of all persons.

[b]For nonfarm business sector, based on 1982 = 100 index, except as noted.

[c]Old series, based on 1977 = 100 index.

[d]Total private nonagricultural, in constant 1982 dollars, except as noted.

[e]Measured by the annual rate of change in the implicit price deflator for gross domestic product.

[f]Average rate for all civilian workers.

begin with years of depressed output and to end at cycle peaks, although every period except 1960–69 covers more than one official business cycle.[23] Real GDP growth slowed down in the 1970s and 1980s compared

23 Due to the use of annual data, and the desire to roughly cover decades,

with the 1950s and 1960s. Real gross national product (GNP) and personal disposable income per capita also slowed down in the 1970s and 1980s compared with the 1960s, although they did not grow very rapidly in the 1950s due to rapid population growth (the 1947–59 period was the height of the postwar "baby boom"). Productivity growth also slowed down notably in the 1970s and 1980s compared with both previous periods. Both inflation and unemployment were worse in the 1970s and 1980s than in 1947–69, although inflation subsided somewhat in the 1980s while unemployment worsened compared with the 1970s.

Turning to wages, real hourly compensation of all nonfarm business employees grew at a negligible 0.4 percent per year in the 1980s, after slowing down from 3.2 percent annual growth in 1947–59 to 2.6 percent in 1960–69 and 1.2 percent in 1970–79. Another measure of labor income, the real weekly earnings of nonagricultural private sector employees, actually fell at a −0.4 percent annual rate in both the 1970s and 1980s, after growing positively throughout the 1950s and 1960s. The worse performance of this latter measure reflects the omission of non-wage benefits from the earnings variable, as well as falling average weekly hours of private sector employees since the 1960s. Overall, more detailed analysis of labor compensation statistics shows that production and non-supervisory workers have done worse than managers and supervisors; that workers with less education have done worse than those with more education; and that there has been a shift of employment toward lower-compensation jobs mainly in the service sector.[24] All these factors indicate a trend toward greater inequality both within the American work-

however, the time periods in Table 8.1 do not exactly correspond to official business cycles. The 1947–59 period begins during the recovery from the postwar recession and includes three recessions (1949, 1953–54, and 1957–58). The 1960–69 period contains essentially one prolonged expansion (there was a mild recession in the second half of 1960). The 1970–79 period starts in a recession year, includes the subsequent recession of 1974–75, and ends at a cycle peak. The 1980–90 period starts in a recession year, includes the deeper recession of 1982, and ends at a cycle peak. Growth rates for all four periods have been calculated using least squares time trends of the natural logarithms of the variables, which lessens any biases due to the precise selection of starting and ending years.

24 For further details on the adverse trends in U.S. labor income and working conditions see Lawrence Mishel and Jared Bernstein, *The State of Working America, 1992–93* (Washington, DC: Economic Policy Institute, 1993).

Table 8.2. U.S. saving and investment rates and trade balances – selected periods, 1960–92 (in percent of GDP, except as noted)

	1960-69	1970-79	1980-89	1985-92
Gross national saving	16.6	16.9	15.4	13.5
Gross private saving	16.7	17.9	17.9	16.4
Corporate	8.4	8.3	8.7	8.5
Noncorporate[a]	8.3	9.6	9.2	7.9
Total government saving (budget surplus)	-0.1	-1.0	-2.5	-2.9
Federal	-0.2	-1.7	-3.6	-3.7
State and local	0.1	0.7	1.1	0.8
Fixed investment	14.7	16.2	16.6	15.1
Net exports of goods and services	0.4	-0.4	-1.9	-1.9
Current account balance[b]	0.6	0.2	-1.7	-2.0
Memoranda				
Personal saving rate[c]	6.7	7.8	6.5	4.9
Net national saving rate[d]	8.9	7.9	4.3	2.7
Consumption of fixed capital (depreciation rate)	8.5	9.8	11.5	11.1

Source: U.S. Department of Commerce, Bureau of Economic Analysis, National Income and Product Accounts (NIPAs), and author's calculations.

Notes: Budget surpluses are measured on a NIPA basis, and deficits are shown as negative surpluses.

[a]Includes personal saving plus depreciation allowances for households and unincorporated businesses.

[b]Measured by the NIPA concept of "net foreign investment."

[c]Percent of personal disposable income.

[d]Percent of net domestic product.

force, and between wage employees and other members of society (especially large property owners and highly educated professionals).

One point that emerges clearly from Table 8.1 is that the growth slowdown and worsened macroeconomic performance date back to the 1970s. Nevertheless, by most measures the "saving shortfall" did not begin until the early or mid-1980s. Table 8.2 presents data relating to saving and investment rates and the trade balance. Average saving and investment rates are given for the three decades 1960–69, 1970–79, and 1980–89, plus the period 1985–92. Although this last time period is not strictly comparable to the others,[25] it is included because it covers the years during which most measures of saving rates show their greatest declines. Even for the 1980s, as may be seen, the data in this table reveal a mixed picture which is very sensitive to the particular measures and time periods used.

The broadest measure of national saving is the gross national saving rate, which dipped from an average of 16.9 percent in the 1970s to 15.4 percent in the 1980s as a whole, and fell more sharply to 13.4 percent in the 1985–92 period. Gross domestic saving consists of two parts, gross private saving and public saving (the government budget surplus). As may be seen, the entire drop in the gross domestic saving rate in the 1980–89 period is attributable to a rise in the overall government deficit (public sector dissaving), which fell by 1.5 percent of GDP between 1970–79 and 1980–89. The rising government deficit is more than accounted for by the increasing federal budget deficit, as state and local governments ran increasing budget surpluses in the 1980s (mostly accounted for by pension fund contributions that would be counted in personal savings if they were paid by private companies). The government deficit also increased from the 1960s to the 1970s, but at that time the lower public sector savings were more than offset by *higher* private sector savings so that the gross national saving rate actually *increased* slightly in the 1970s – just when the growth slowdown began.

In 1985–92, there was also a decline of 1.5 percent of GDP in the gross private saving rate (compared with 1970–79 or 1980–89). Even then, the gross private saving rate remained over 16 percent in 1985–92, very close to its level in the 1960–69 "Golden Age" period. Within the private sector, gross corporate saving remained steady at over 8 percent of GDP throughout the periods covered in Table 8.2. Noncorporate gross saving dipped to an average rate of 7.9 percent of GDP in 1985–92, well below the 1970–79 level of 9.6 percent, but not far below the 1960–69 level of 8.3 percent.

25 The years 1985 to 1992 go from midexpansion during one business cycle to early recovery in another cycle. I decided to use this longer period rather than 1990–92 alone because the latter is dominated by a recession and is too short to be compared with entire decades.

However, the more narrow measure of the official personal saving rate fell from an average of over 6 percent (of personal disposable income) in the 1960s, 1970s, and early 1980s, to barely 4.9 percent in 1985–92. Also, another measure called the net national saving rate declined even more alarmingly, from nearly 9 percent of net domestic product in the 1960s to under 3 percent in the 1985–92 period. In fact, this last measure dipped to a meager 0.6 percent in 1992, leading to claims that the country had virtually zero savings for that year.[26] Why do these alternative measures of saving rates, which have been the basis for most of the saving shortfall hysteria, show much greater decreases?

The answer lies largely in the esoteric area of depreciation allowances, or what the national income accounts call "consumption of fixed capital." The national income accounts include estimates of the economic depreciation of the nation's capital stock, which are subtracted from gross savings to get net savings. The official personal saving rate is a net measure, from which depreciation of household capital stocks (mostly residential housing) has already been subtracted.[27] And the net national saving rate excludes all depreciation allowances, for corporate and noncorporate businesses as well as for households. What has driven the net national saving rate to such pitiful levels is, aside from the rising government budget deficit, mainly a notable increase in "consumption of fixed capital" as a share of GDP. It is largely the rising depreciation rate, along with the government deficit, and not a sudden decrease in private thriftiness that has made the net measures of the saving rate sink so low.

This raises the question of why the depreciation rate has risen and what, if anything, should be done about it.[28] Briefly, the depreciation rate has risen for two main reasons. First, thanks to the slowdown in the growth of current output and income documented in Table 8.1, the depre-

26 For example, Litan, "Force-Feeding Our Piggy Banks," writes that "it is especially distressing that the U.S. national saving rate (*after depreciation of existing public and private capital*) has dropped precipitously: from 7 percent of total output for much of the postwar period through 1980 to just 1 percent today" (italics added). What Litan fails to say is that rising depreciation (along with the government deficit, of course) accounts for most of this "distressing" decline in the *net* national saving rate, while gross private saving has fallen much less.

27 Personal saving is defined as personal disposable income minus personal consumption expenditures (and other outlays), and personal disposable income is a subset of the net national product from which depreciation allowances have already been removed.

28 For a more detailed discussion of this issue and additional references see Blecker, *Are Americans on a Consumption Binge?* pp. 43–46.

ciation on existing stocks of capital equipment and structures (which were created in the past, when growth was higher) looms ever larger in proportion to current GDP. And second, there has been a notable shift in the composition of investment away from structures (including residential housing) to producers' durable equipment, which has shorter economic lifetimes, and within the latter category toward more short-lived types of equipment such as computers. In other words, the rising depreciation rate that has depressed net savings measures is partly a symptom of the growth slowdown itself, and otherwise is mostly a reflection of changing technology.

Theoretically, a low net saving or investment rate means that a country is not adding much to its capital stock, beyond replacement of depreciating buildings and equipment. But this can be misleading. Especially in the case of producers' durable equipment, replacement investment almost invariably takes the form of new "vintages" of machinery embodying improved technology. For example, no one replaces an early 1980s IBM personal computer (PC) with an equivalent machine today. The new PCs being purchased today have capabilities that still required much more expensive mainframes ten years ago – yet cost less than an original IBM PC. While computers are an extreme case, they represent an increasing fraction of new equipment expenditures, and the same principle holds (albeit in less extreme fashion) for other types of equipment. For these reasons, the hysteria based on low *net* saving rates is simply misguided.

The bottom line in all of this is the extent to which there is investment in future productive capabilities. The data on investment reveal contradictory patterns. Throughout the 1980s, the U.S. devoted about the usual percentage of GDP to gross investment spending. The investment share of GDP averaged 16.6 percent in the 1980s, even higher than in the 1960s or 1970s. Even in the 1985–92 period, the investment share was still higher than in 1960–69. We may feel that some of this investment was misdirected (say, to shopping malls and office buildings instead of industrial plants and low-income housing), but there is no evidence that total investment spending was constrained by a shortage of capital funds through most of the 1980s. If anything, there was a surplus of corporate cash flow that was used for mergers and acquisitions, stock repurchases, and other nonproductive activities in the 1980s.[29] Investment did drop off

29 See Margaret M. Blair and Robert E. Litan, "Corporate Leverage and Leveraged Buyouts in the Eighties," in *Debt, Taxes, and Corporate Restructuring,* ed. John B. Shoven and Joel Waldfogel (Washington, DC: Brookings Institution, 1990).

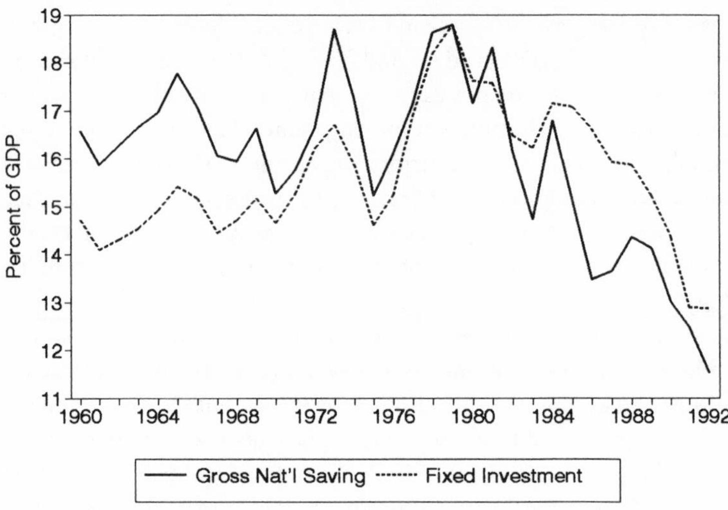

Figure 8.2. Gross national saving and investment rates.

sharply in the late 1980s and early 1990s. Figure 8.2 shows that the share of fixed investment in GDP plummeted after 1988 to its lowest level in recent history. But as Bosworth's study of *Saving and Investment in a Global Economy* suggests, this fall in the investment rate is perfectly understandable in light of the tremendous slowdown in output growth during that period. Indeed, real GDP growth averaged a meager 1 percent per year from 1989 to 1992, and this also largely accounts for the decline in the gross national saving rate seen in Figure 8.2 for the same years.

Both Table 8.2 and Figure 8.2 show that the national saving rate fell by more than the investment rate in the mid-1980s; the difference is made up by the rising trade deficit shown in Figure 8.1. Both measures of the trade balance shown in Table 8.2 – net exports of goods and services and the current account balance — declined notably in the 1980s. After all, the data must satisfy the previously cited macroeconomic identity which says that the trade balance must equal the difference between national saving and domestic investment.[30] But it does not necessarily follow that the decline in the national saving rate was the *cause* (or the sole cause) of the

30 Domestic investment is the sum of fixed investment (shown in Table 8.2) and inventory accumulation (not shown). Inventory accumulation is omitted from Table 8.2 because it is small and cyclically volatile, and because it does not increase society's productive capabilities as fixed investment does.

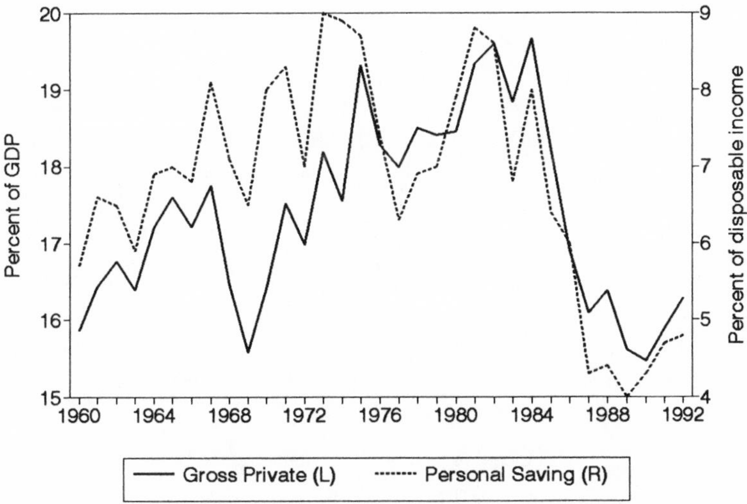

Figure 8.3. Private saving rates.

fall in the trade balance. Causality could also run at least partly the opposite way, as argued earlier.

The precise timing of the trends in private saving rates over the past decade does reveal a dramatic drop-off in the mid-1980s which cannot be attributed either to the budget deficit (which is not counted in private saving) or to rising depreciation (which is a gradual trend, and only affects net saving rates). As Figure 8.3 shows, both the gross private saving rate and the personal saving rate fell abruptly in 1984–87 (although the latter measure fell much more than the former compared with its own historical trend). Does this indicate that American families went on an unprecedented "consumption binge" in the mid-1980s, as was commonly alleged at the time?

A glance at Figure 8.4 reveals the fallacy in this view. What happened in 1985 to 1987 was that the growth of real per capita personal disposable income fell off abruptly, after rising rapidly in 1984. Per capita consumption growth also slowed down in 1985–87, but less quickly than disposable income growth, resulting in a higher ratio of consumption to income and, necessarily, a fall in the measured saving rate (since personal saving is defined as the difference between personal disposable income and consumption expenditures).[31] Consumers, it seems, were surprised

31 I am indebted to Milton Lower for originally suggesting this point to me.

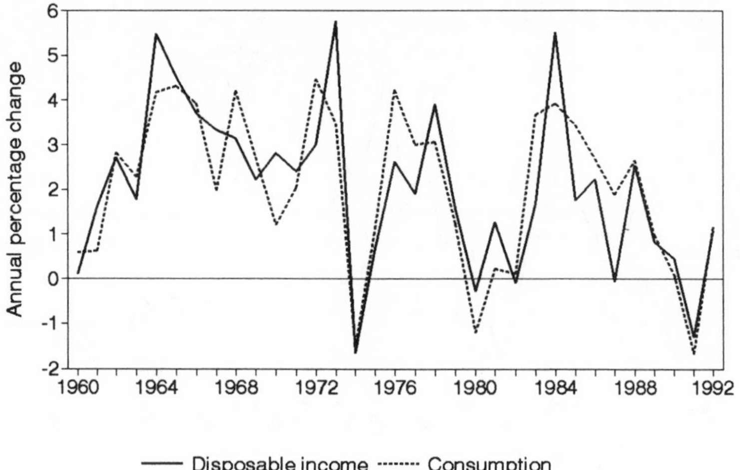

Figure 8.4. Growth rates of real per capita personal disposable income and consumption.

by the failure of disposable income to keep growing smoothly in the middle of the 1980s expansion. Consumers had good reason to be surprised, since it was unusual for disposable income growth to slow down so quickly in the middle of an economic expansion. Thus, consumption spending grew faster than income (albeit at a decreasing rate) for a few years, until consumers became convinced that slower income growth would not be reversed and were forced to adjust. The ease of obtaining consumer credit undoubtedly helped to make this possible and left consumers saddled with large debts at the end of the period, as some economists have suggested.[32] But the real question is not why the saving rate fell, but why income growth slowed down so abruptly after 1984.

3. REVERSE CAUSALITY AND THE TRADE DEFICIT

The slowdown in income growth in the mid-1980s is exactly where the "reverse causality" (of the trade deficit contributing to the low national saving rate) comes in. The years in the mid-1980s when private saving

32 See Summers and Carroll, "U.S. National Saving"; also Robert Pollin, *Deeper in Debt: The Changing Financial Conditions of U.S. Households* (Washington, DC: Economic Policy Institute, 1990).

rates collapsed were also the years of the most rapidly growing trade deficits.[33] Empirical evidence shows that the main *proximate* cause of the rising trade deficit at that time was the rising value of the U.S. dollar.[34] Slow growth in some of our major trading partners, especially in western Europe and Latin America, also contributed to stagnant exports. Indeed, exports actually *fell* slightly in real terms from 1980 to 1986, while imports soared from 1983 to 1986. The resulting trade deficit, which peaked at $160 billion in 1987 (as shown in Figure 8.1, above), in turn caused the loss of nearly 5 million jobs, while the surging imports kept a lid on industrial workers' wage increases.[35] There is thus a plausible mechanism by which the rise in the trade deficit could have contributed to slowing income growth at just around the time when the saving rate fell most dramatically.

Of course, the question remains why the dollar soared so high in the 1984–85 period, precipitating the subsequent peak in the trade deficit (which lagged the peak of the dollar by two years due to the time it takes for international trade flows to respond to changing exchange rates – the famous "J-curve"). The standard story is that the rising budget deficit of the federal government pushed up interest rates and thus drew in large amounts of foreign capital, aided by recent liberalizations of capital flows in Japan and elsewhere, along with the generally more favorable investment climate in the U.S. in the early 1980s. As foreigners bought dollars

33 The following discussion of the trade deficit draws in part on the author's previous work in "Low Saving Rates and the 'Twin Deficits'" and *Beyond the Twin Deficits.*

34 See William L. Helkie and Peter Hooper, "An Empirical Analysis of the External Deficit," in *External Deficits and the Dollar: The Pit and the Pendulum,* ed. Ralph C. Bryant et al. (Washington: Brookings Institution, 1988).

35 According to Faye Duchin and Glenn-Marie Lange, "Trading Away Jobs: The Effects of the US Merchandise Trade Deficit on Employment" (Working Paper No. 102, Economic Policy Institute, Washington, DC, October 1988), the 1987 U.S. trade deficit accounted for a loss of 5.1 million jobs. This was based on the original trade deficit figure for 1987, which was $171.2 billion. Since then, the 1987 trade deficit has been revised down to $159.6 billion. Since $159.6 is 93 percent of $171.2, their job loss estimate should be multiplied by a factor of 0.93, resulting in a loss of 4.8 million jobs (still close to 5 million). For evidence on the negative effects of imports on wages, see Ana L. Revenga, "Exporting Jobs? The Impact of Import Competition on Employment and Wages in U.S. Manufacturing," *Quarterly Journal of Economics* 107 (February 1992): 255–84.

to pay for their investments in U.S. assets (everything from government bonds to bank deposits to real estate), they drove up the value of the dollar.[36]

While there is undoubtedly some truth in this story, even economists sympathetic to this argument have been unable to show that more than a part of the dollar's rise can be attributed to the budget deficit.[37] One reason is that this story omits a crucial factor: the tight monetary policies of the Federal Reserve under Paul Volcker. While strict monetary targets were abandoned in 1982, monetary stringency returned with a vengeance in late 1983 and 1984, when the Fed refused to monetize the rising government deficit, and thus caused interest rates to go back up after having fallen the previous year. A second reason is that, by the end of 1984 and early 1985, the dollar went on a final surge which cannot be explained by any objective factors such as interest rates, and which has been attributed to a "speculative bubble."[38] Thus, the overvaluation of the dollar in the mid-1980s was not simply a result of the budget deficit, and hence cannot be written off as just another manifestation of the "saving shortfall." And in the late 1980s and early 1990s, the dollar fell back to about its 1980 value in spite of continued large budget deficits.

Moreover, the trade deficit grew worse than any macroeconomic factors alone could explain in the 1980s because of an underlying declining trend in U.S. industrial competitiveness. This decline has been identified by numerous economists in various ways, but most would agree on one thing: the U.S. needs a continuously *depreciating* dollar in order to keep its merchandise trade balance from deteriorating, for otherwise U.S. imports will tend to grow faster than U.S. exports.[39] Others would put the

36 This story can be found in Bosworth, *Saving and Investment in a Global Economy,* as well as in Rachel McCulloch and J. David Richardson, "U.S. Trade and the Dollar: Evaluating Current Policy Options," in *Current U.S. Trade Policy: Analysis, Agenda, and Administration,* ed. Robert E. Baldwin and J. David Richardson (Cambridge, MA: National Bureau for Economic Research, 1986); and Rudiger Dornbusch, *Dollars, Debts, and Deficits* (Cambridge, MA: MIT Press, 1986).

37 See especially Helkie and Hooper, "An Empirical Analysis of the External Deficit," as well as Bosworth, *Saving and Investment in a Global Economy.*

38 See Paul R. Krugman, *Exchange-Rate Instability* (Cambridge, MA: MIT Press, 1989).

39 Many studies have found that the U.S. income elasticity of import demand is on the order of about 2.5, while income elasticity of export demand is well below 2. These studies include Robert A. Blecker, "Structural Roots of U.S.

point differently: for any given real value of the dollar, the U.S. is constrained to grow more slowly than its trading partners in order to avoid rising trade deficits.[40] However this long-term trend is conceptualized, it made the trade deficits of the 1980s worse than they would otherwise have been. The cumulative effect of declining competitiveness on the trade deficit between 1980 and 1989 has been estimated at $86 billion.[41] As a result, the trade balance remained over $100 billion per year at the end of the decade (before the recession of 1990–91 lowered import demand), even after the dollar had returned to about its 1980 value.

Thus, the facts are not consistent with the frequently heard story that Americans went on a "spending spree" in the mid-1980s which lowered the saving rate and thus caused the trade deficit to rise. Rather, the facts are more consistent with the view that the country suffered a growing trade imbalance due to a combination of factors, and that the soaring trade deficit contributed to a rapid slowdown in income growth in the years 1985–87. With average real wages flat or falling (depending on the precise measure used), it is apparent that most households felt an "income squeeze" which reduced their ability to save out of current income at that time. The low saving rate was a symptom, not the underlying cause, of the slow growth plaguing the country.

While this income squeeze story makes sense for the great majority of families which depend on wages, there is another side to the falling saving

Trade Problems: Income Elasticities, Secular Trends, and Hysteresis," *Journal of Post Keynesian Economics* 14 (Spring 1992): 321–46; William R. Cline, *United States External Adjustment and the World Economy* (Washington: Institute for International Economics, 1989); and Robert Z. Lawrence, "U.S. Current Account Adjustment: An Appraisal," *Brookings Papers on Economic Activity, 2:1990*, pp. 343–89. Helkie and Hooper, "An Empirical Analysis of External Deficit," found these income elasticities to be closer, but included another variable (relative U.S.–foreign capital stocks) which picked up the unfavorable trends in U.S. trade.

40 This idea was developed by A. P. Thirlwall, "The Balance of Payments Constraint as an Explanation of International Growth Rate Differences," *Banca Nazionale del Lavoro Quarterly Review*, No. 128 (March 1979): 45–53. Blecker, "Structural Roots of U.S. Trade Problems," p. 340, estimates that U.S. growth is constrained to be roughly 60 percent of foreign growth.

41 See Blecker, *Beyond the Twin Deficits*, p. 68. A similar estimate is found in Lawrence, "U.S. Current Account Adjustment," p. 368, who calculates the structural decline in the trade balance at $75 billion between 1980 and 1990. Both estimates exclude agricultural exports and petroleum imports.

rate story which pertains more to upper-income households that receive substantial amounts of income from asset ownership.[42] Traditionally, such households could be expected to save much larger fractions of their current income on average than lower-income, wage-earning households. But in the mid-1980s, the incentives for affluent families to save were reduced for several reasons. First, booming asset markets in stocks and (except in certain regions) real estate led to an enormous increase in household net worth, in spite of greater debt loads. Since the purpose of saving is to increase the value of assets, and assets were rising in value anyway, there was less incentive to save out of current income. Or, put another way, families with assets that appreciated in value could make extra expenditures on consumption goods based on the capital gains that they were receiving (whether realized or not), but since those capital gains were not counted in national income the corresponding expenditures appeared to lower the saving rate.[43] Second, rich people's expenditures received a special boost from the corporate takeover activity, some of which involved stock repurchases that put extra cash in the hands of former equity owners. There is evidence that a large fraction of this extra cash, perhaps more than 50 percent, was spent rather than reinvested.[44] Thus, the reasons for the falling saving rate were different at the top of the income distribution than at the bottom.

4. THE BUDGET DEFICIT AND TAX POLICY

While the fall in the private saving rate can be understood more as a symptom of the economic growth slowdown, the federal budget deficit appears to be another matter. Reagan's infamous tax cuts and increased military spending in the early 1980s produced a major shift in fiscal policy which resulted in sustained increases in the federal budget deficit never before experienced in peacetime. Nevertheless, a closer look at U.S. fiscal policy in the 1980s casts doubt on the current hysteria about the

42 For further discussion of these issues and references see Blecker, *Are Americans on a Consumption Binge?* and "Low Saving Rates and the 'Twin Deficits.'"

43 See Josef Steindl, "Capital Gains, Pension Funds, and the Low Saving Ratio in the United States," *Banca Nazionale del Lavoro Quarterly Review* (June 1990): 165–77.

44 See the statistical appendixes in Hatsopoulos, Krugman, and Poterba, *Overconsumption*, and Blecker, *Are Americans on a Consumption Binge?*

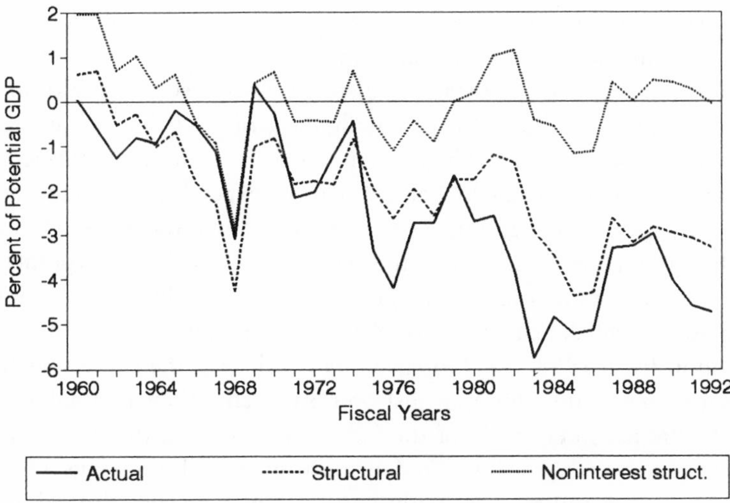

Figure 8.5. Alternative federal budget balances.

budget deficit and the supposed need to prioritize deficit reduction over all other economic policy objectives.

In the first place, although the dollar value of the budget deficit is now on the order of $300 billion annually, as a percentage of potential GDP (defined as what GDP would be with a "standardized unemployment rate"[45]) the deficit was actually *smaller* in fiscal 1992 than in fiscal 1983–86 (see the solid line in Figure 8.5). Second, a better measure of the burden of the government's borrowing is the net debt to the public as a percentage of GDP. This percentage had stabilized at just over 40 percent in the late 1980s, before the recession and subsequent slow recovery

45 The Congressional Budget Office defines the standardized unemployment rate as a "nonaccelerating inflation unemployment rate" (NAIRU), which has varied between 5.0 and 6.0 percent over the last thirty-five years, and is estimated at 5.5 percent for 1992. See U.S. Congressional Budget Office, *Economic and Budget Outlook* (Washington, DC: Government Printing Office, January 1993, and Errata Sheet dated February 1993). Obviously, a more generous definition of full employment (say, as a 4 percent unemployment rate) would yield a larger estimate of potential GDP and higher estimates of the "structural budget surplus" (discussed below). But we can make our argument even using the more conservative standardized unemployment rate or NAIRU.

raised it again. This percentage is not unusually high either by historical or international standards.[46] Put in this perspective, current deficits are not as frightening as they may appear.

Furthermore, it is important to distinguish the fiscal *deficit* from the underlying fiscal *policies*. To begin with, the actual deficit is influenced by the state of the economy, as high unemployment results in diminished tax revenues (and somewhat higher entitlement expenditures) which automatically increase the gap between revenue and outlays. Thus, as shown by the dashed line in Figure 8.5, the "structural" deficit (the hypothetical deficit at the "standardized unemployment rate") has been notably lower than the actual deficit for most of the past decade, except for a brief period in fiscal 1988–89. Moreover, by fiscal 1992 the *entire* structural deficit (about $200 billion, or just over 3 percent of potential GDP) was due to the net interest bill of the federal government, that is, what the government owes to the bondholders for its previous borrowings. In other words, the government is actually raising enough revenue through taxes that it could afford to pay for all its current programs, including entitlements, if the country had a very conservative measure of full employment (5.5 percent unemployment). The noninterest structural deficit (the dotted line in Figure 8.5) is virtually zero. And if the country had something closer to true full employment – say, a 4 percent unemployment rate – it would have a whopping surplus of revenue over all noninterest outlays.

The growing net interest burden – the bulging gap between the dashed and dotted lines in Figure 8.5 – was the result of a net national debt (owed to the public) that more than trebled from under $1 trillion to about $3 trillion during the twelve years of Republican rule from 1981 to 1992. This extraordinary net interest burden represents a gigantic drain on the national treasury, soaking up $200 billion of tax revenue that could otherwise go to more useful purposes such as education or infrastructure – or which could be used for stimulative tax cuts in times of depressed demand. In addition, the large net interest bill of the federal government constitutes an enormous regressive transfer program to the wealthy. That is, since the tax burden is more evenly distributed than the ownership of government bonds, the average taxpayer is effectively paying money to the wealthier individuals who have lent money to the government to cover its past deficits.[47]

46 See Robert Heilbroner and Peter L. Bernstein, *The Debt and the Deficit* (New York: Norton, 1989).

47 See the evidence in Thomas R. Michl, "Debts, Deficits, and the Distribution of Income," *Journal of Post Keynesian Economics* 13 (Spring 1991): 351–65.

Table 8.3. Federal income and payroll tax rates – selected periods, 1950–89 (in percent)

	1950-66	1967-82	1983-89
Personal tax rates:[a]			
top bracket	84.5[b]	69.6	42.1
median family[c]	19.6	18.9	15.4
Social security rate[d]	5.1	11.2	14.3
Corporate top bracket	50.8	48.2	41.7

Sources: Tax rates are from tables in Appendix A of Joseph A. Pechman, *Federal Tax Policy*, 5th edition (Washington, DC: Brookings, 1987). Median family income is from U.S. Department of Commerce, Bureau of the Census, *Current Population Reports*, Series P-60, various issues. Ratio of taxable income to personal income is from U.S. Department of the Treasury, Internal Revenue Service, *Statistics of Income Bulletin*, vol. 10, no. 1 (Summer 1990).

[a]Personal rates are for married couples filing jointly and include all applicable surcharges, but not alternative minimum taxes or earned income credits.

[b]For 1950-63, the maximum effective rate was used in place of the nominal top bracket rate, which was even higher for those years.

[c]Median family taxable income was estimated by multiplying median family income by the average ratio of taxable income to personal income.

[d]Combined employer and employee payroll tax rates for old age, survivors, disability, and hospital insurance.

Moreover, this transfer to the rich comes on top of the fact that the fiscal policy changes that led to the rising budget deficits in the 1980s were themselves profoundly skewed in favor of the wealthy. The generally regressive distributional impact of the tax policy changes of the 1980s is documented in Table 8.3. The top bracket marginal rate for the personal income tax was cut in half between 1950–66 and 1983–89, while the rate on median family taxable income was reduced only slightly. Furthermore, labor income (up to a certain ceiling) is subject to payroll taxes, and the main payroll tax (the social security tax for old age, survivors, disability, and hospital insurance benefits) rose throughout the periods shown in Table 8.3.[48] At the same time, the top rate for corporate income

48 The payroll tax rates shown in Table 8.3 are the combined rates for employers and employees, since the employers' share of payroll taxes ("contributions for social insurance") are counted as an imputed part of employee compensation in personal disposable income in the national income accounts.

was cut from nearly 51 percent to under 42 percent. Clearly, the burden of taxation was shifted from capital owners to wage earners, and from the wealthy to the middle class.

The evidence on nominal income tax rates in Table 8.3 is buttressed by more rigorous studies of tax incidence. For example, Joseph Pechman found a steady reduction in effective taxation of capital income from 1966 to 1985, with no corresponding reduction in effective taxation of labor income, under a wide range of assumptions.[49] And Pechman concluded that the Tax Reform Act of 1986

> . . . restored only a small fraction of the progressivity lost in the preceding two decades. At the very top of the income distribution, the 1986 federal tax reform restored about half the reduction in effective tax rates between 1980 and 1985, but left them far below the 1966 levels: the top 1 percent paid only 26.8 percent in taxes in 1988 as compared with 39 percent in 1970.[50]

Another study[51] shows that it was only taxpayers in the upper 10 percent of the income distribution who received net cuts in their effective federal tax rates in the 1980s, and 90 percent of these tax breaks were received by the richest 1 percent (who had average annual incomes of over $500,000). Lower taxes on the richest 1 percent of taxpayers (compared with pre-1978 tax rates) accounted for a loss of $84 billion in tax revenue in 1990 alone, or more than a third of the total deficit for that year. And if we consider that the lost tax revenue in the preceding years contributed substantially to the rising national debt and growing net interest payments of the federal government, the actual deficit would have been reduced by considerably *more* than $84 billion in 1990 if higher tax rates on the rich had been maintained throughout the preceding decade.

Thus, the rich were "double dipping" in the 1980s, in the sense that they benefited not only from receiving the largest tax cuts, but also from lending the government money at exorbitant interest rates. Indeed, per-

49 In Joseph A. Pechman, *Who Paid the Taxes, 1966–85* (Washington, DC: Brookings Institution, 1985). Pechman's calculations include all federal, state, and local taxes, not just federal income and payroll taxes.

50 Joseph A. Pechman, "The Future of the Income Tax," *American Economic Review* 80 (March 1990): 4.

51 The following calculations are all from Robert S. McIntyre, "Inequality and the Federal Budget Deficit," in *Growth and Equity: Tax Policy Challenges for the 1990s*, ed. Bruce L. Fisher and Robert S. McIntyre (Washington, DC: Citizens for Tax Justice, 1990).

sonal interest income was the most rapidly growing part of personal disposable income throughout most of the 1980s. It was, in effect, a very profitable scam, to lend the government money at high interest rates rather than pay the same money to the government in taxes. Unfortunately for the country, this was a sure way of reducing the national saving rate as well as bankrupting the national treasury.

5. INCOME DISTRIBUTION, THE SAVING RATE, AND STAGNATION

These facts suggest that there is a "missing link" in all the discussions of low saving rates and the government budget deficit: the distributional angle. This can be conceptualized in terms of what economists call the "functional" or class distribution of income between owners of capital and sellers of labor. That is, the national income of a country like the United States can be divided into what might broadly be called "profits" and "wages."[52] Traditionally, it has been assumed by many economists that the propensity to save is notably greater out of profit income as compared with wage income. There are several reasons for this, including the fact that corporate retained earnings (which come entirely out of profits) are counted as savings, and the fact that personal capital income (dividends, interest, etc.) is received largely by wealthy households with relatively high personal saving rates. As a result, we expect that when the share of national income going to capital (the "profit share") rises, the private saving rate should increase. When we consider the national saving rate, including (as explained in section 2) the government budget surplus, as long as the tax system is reasonably progressive, we also expect a higher profit share to boost tax revenue and therefore to further raise the national saving rate.

Early postwar fears of economic stagnation were based in part on the fear that, if there was a secular rising tendency of the profit share (say, due to increasing monopoly power of corporations), the saving rate would rise, but this would depress aggregate demand via the Keynesian "paradox of thrift."[53] Such fears were not realized, however, as the profit share

52 The precise national income accounting definitions used to construct total profit and wage income are given in the appendix to this chapter.

53 This was the core of the argument in Josef Steindl, *Maturity and Stagnation in American Capitalism* (Oxford: Blackwell, 1952; reprint ed., New York: Monthly Review Press, 1976).

has not had a rising tendency and if anything has fallen since peaking in the mid-1960s. Moreover, private consumption and investment spending were able to increase rapidly throughout most of the postwar period through the expanded use of debt finance, and were frequently supplemented by government deficit spending and (until the 1980s) surpluses on the current account of the balance of payments (positive net exports of goods and services).

A situation in which there is a much higher combined saving-and-tax rate out of profit income, compared with wage income, is sometimes referred to as a case of "underconsumptionism" or "stagnationism."[54] This terminology reflects the fact that a redistribution of income toward profits in such a situation depresses aggregate demand, income, and employment. But such a situation also implies the possibility of what is sometimes called "wage-led growth." That is, if there is excess industrial capacity so that output is constrained by aggregate demand (as is normally the case in an industrialized country like the United States), then a redistribution of income to wages which *lowers* the national saving rate can nevertheless *stimulate* production, employment, and growth. This occurs because workers will spend a greater fraction of their income on goods and services than will owners of capital, and assumes that there are not offsetting reductions in investment demand or net exports.[55] In this case, there is the possibility of a "class compromise" in which capital owners accept a smaller share of the social pie in exchange for allowing the whole pie to grow bigger, with all benefitting.

If our analysis in the preceding sections is accurate, it implies that the changes in both private behavior and fiscal policy in the United States in the 1980s have made the U.S. economy less likely to experience wage-led growth. Reduced retention of corporate profits, lavish spending on luxury consumption by the wealthy, and regressive changes in the tax code in the

54 See, e.g., the work of Amitava K. Dutt, "Stagnation, Income Distribution, and Monopoly Power," *Cambridge Journal of Economics* 8 (March 1984): 25–40; and Lance Taylor, "A Stagnationist Model of Economic Growth," *Cambridge Journal of Economics* 9 (December 1985): 383–403.

55 The effects of such offsetting reductions are considered by Stephen A. Marglin and Amit Bhaduri, "Profit Squeeze and Keynesian Theory," in *The Golden Age of Capitalism,* ed. Stephen A. Marglin and Juliet B. Schor (Oxford: Oxford University Press, 1990); and Robert A. Blecker, "International Competition, Income Distribution and Economic Growth," *Cambridge Journal of Economics* 13 (September 1989): 395–412.

1980s all had the effect of reducing the degree to which a higher profit share of income results in higher national savings (private saving plus tax revenue). To test this hypothesis, I estimated how the relationship between the functional distribution of income (measured as the profit share of national income) and the gross national saving rate has changed since the early 1980s. The methodology for deriving those estimates is explained in the appendix to this chapter, but the results can easily be summarized here.

According to my estimates, prior to 1983, a 1 percentage point rise in the profit share of national income resulted in an 0.28 percentage point rise in the gross national saving rate (gross national saving as a percentage of GDP). After 1983, this effect was reduced by 0.11, implying that a 1 percentage point rise in the profit share would then cause only an 0.17 percentage point rise in the gross national saving rate. To assess the quantitative importance of this effect, we may compare the years 1979 and 1989, which are similar in terms of their business cycle characteristics (both were near-peak years of the business cycle, followed by recessions in the succeeding years). The gross national saving rate fell from 18.8 percent in 1979 to 14.1 percent in 1989. Of this 4.6 percent decrease in the saving rate,[56] slightly more than half (2.4 percentage points) can be explained by the reduced response of national saving to the profit share. Interestingly, most of the rest of the decrease in the national saving rate is not attributed to the budget deficit (since the higher budget deficit is partly offset by an induced increase in private saving), but rather to the falloff in the investment share noted earlier (which in turn can be explained mostly by slow growth).

While these precise estimates may be subject to some uncertainty, as all statistical estimates inevitably are, the point is that the reduced saving and taxation of capital income (and, more broadly, the income of the wealthy) in the 1980s had a measurable impact on the national saving rate. And this impact has two important policy implications. First, any discussion of who should sacrifice in order to reduce the budget deficit should be informed by the fact that the fiscal policies that created the large deficit (and reduced the national saving rate) largely benefitted the very wealthy in the first place. In this respect, "shared sacrifice" in the sense of everyone in society bearing some of the burden is actually *unfair,* in that it

56 The percentages do not add up exactly due to independent rounding. See the Appendix for more detail on the estimates.

penalizes some who were in no way responsible (and who in fact were actually paying higher taxes while suffering an income squeeze in the 1980s), while putting too little of the burden on those who got away with the greatest gains over the past decade.

Second, while the Reagan "supply-side" policies failed to create a sustained profit-led economic expansion,[57] they did substantially reduce the prospects for wage-led growth. This means that restoring more progressivity to the tax code, as Clinton's plan does to some extent, can actually help to revive the possibility of economic growth being consistent with a more equitable distribution of income. Even if raising any taxes (including those on the upper-income brackets) is contractionary in the short run, creating a greater differential between tax rates on the rich and the average family increases the demand-side boost which the economy gets when income is redistributed downward. Of course, this still requires policies to accomplish such a redistribution.

To sum up, the economic policies and structural changes of the 1980s created a perverse situation, in which those who normally provide most of the nation's savings (including the tax revenue which raises public saving as well as private saving) failed to do so. They failed to do so partly because of incentives to save less in the corporation, partly because of incentives for wealthy individuals to spend more on consumption, and especially because of less progressive income taxation. As a result, the national saving rate plummeted in the middle of the economic expansion of the mid-1980s, in spite of reasonably robust profits (the profit share of national income, before taxes, was actually slightly higher in 1989 than in 1979 – 20.6 versus 19.4 percent). This, combined with worsening international competitiveness and slowing growth, was responsible for the apparent "saving shortfall" – not a supposed decline in the thriftiness of average American families.

6. CONCLUSION

In the end, it appears that the low private saving rate is a symptom, not a cause, of the nation's economic problems. This assessment is critical because if policy is based on attacking the symptoms rather than the causes

57 The profit share did recuperate somewhat in the mid-1980s, at least relative to the 1970s if not to the 1960s. But this was not enough to prompt what Marglin and Bhaduri (in "Profit Squeeze and Keynesian Theory") call an "exhilarationist" response in the form of a profit-driven investment boom.

of slow growth, it may end up prolonging and worsening the disease rather than curing it. In the present case, the imposition of draconian tax increases on middle-class families (especially large regressive consumption taxes) would only worsen, not solve, the underlying problem of slow income growth. Indeed, such a policy would not even do much to raise the national saving rate, taking into account the fact that private saving would be further depressed if disposable income were further eroded by large tax increases. And even if the saving rate rose, the total amount of saving and investment would surely fall at least for several years.

Eventually, of course, faster growth will require more saving to finance the investment activity that promotes growth. But seeking to accomplish this by raising the saving rate *ex ante* is going about things exactly the wrong way. If we can restore a higher investment rate and stimulate growth – and that is no easy task – the higher income growth will allow businesses and families to save more. But if we try to induce or force people to save more (or pay more taxes) first, we will only depress demand, making it unlikely that businesses will want to carry out the rate of investment spending needed to foster sustained growth.[58] Moderate tax increases targeted mainly on the wealthy, as proposed by President Clinton, will only slow the recovery and perhaps help provoke another recession, while at least shifting more of the tax burden back to those who can best afford to pay – and who gained the most from Reagan's tax cuts in the 1980s. Titanic tax increases for all families, as proposed by "populist" billionaire H. Ross Perot, could push us into another Great Depression, and are blatantly inequitable in spite of their "shared sacrifice" appeal.

While there are no magic pills for reviving growth, some general guidelines can be sketched out. First, while restoring progressivity to the tax code is a good idea, excessive efforts to reduce the budget deficit are not. The "third deficit" (the public infrastructure shortfall) needs to be addressed, and increased spending in this area allows us to combine a modest short-term fiscal stimulus with long-term productivity enhancements.[59] Second, given the nation's competitive problems and the rising

58 For an analysis of this issue see Steven M. Fazzari, "Investment and U.S. Fiscal Policy in the 1990s," Briefing Paper, Economic Policy Institute, Washington, DC, June 1993.

59 On the importance of public investment see David Alan Aschauer, *Public Investment and Private Sector Growth: The Economic Benefits of Reducing America's "Third Deficit"* (Washington, DC: Economic Policy Institute 1990).

share of spending devoted to imports, it is imperative to design trade and industrial policies as part of a growth program. For starters, we need to pressure our trading partners (especially those with large trade surpluses, such as Japan and China) to open up their markets, stimulate their economies, and to maintain exchange rates consistent with balanced trade. But since such pressure is unlikely to succeed unless accompanied by a "credible threat," we may need to consider erecting trade barriers in some cases where cooperation is not forthcoming.[60]

Third and finally, it should be clear by now that the two-decade-old growth slowdown is something that cannot be cured by traditional macroeconomic policies alone. We are going to have to confront the sources of our slow productivity growth, declining competitiveness, and rising income inequality at the micro level, if we are going to restore an environment in which aggregate growth can be sustained and in which average workers and families can benefit from that growth.

APPENDIX

The relationship between the profit share of national income and the gross national saving rate was estimated by a multivariate statistical regression. The dependent variable is gross national saving rate (NATSAV), measured by the conventional national income accounting definition, and is displayed as the solid line in Figure 8.2. The profit share (PROFSHARE) is defined as total property income (rental income, corporate profits, and net interest) as a percentage of national income excluding proprietary income.[61] PROFSHARE was multiplied by a dummy for the years 1983–92 (D1983) to test for structural change in the effect of PROFSHARE on NATSAV.

Other independent variables were included to control for other determinants of NATSAV. To control for the effects of fiscal policy, the structural budget balance as a percentage of potential GDP was used.[62] This

60 For further discussion of these issues and the situations in which trade barriers may be warranted see Blecker, *Beyond the Twin Deficits,* pp. 116–23.

61 Proprietary income (i.e., the income of unincorporated businesses) is omitted because it may contain labor income of the business owners as well as returns to their property ownership. Proprietary income is small, however, and this exclusion makes little difference to the results.

62 The source for this variable is the Congressional Budget Office, *Economic and Budget Outlook,* January 1993, and Errata Sheet dated February 1993.

variable, labeled STRUCT_BUDGET, is shown as the dashed line in Figure 8.5. To control for business cycle effects, the share of fixed investment in GDP (INVEST) was used. This variable is the dashed line in Figure 8.2. Other business cycle proxies, such as the GDP gap (measured by the residuals from regressing the natural logarithm of real GDP on a linear time trend),[63] were tried and yielded similar results, but INVEST resulted in the best fit for the whole model.

The regression results were as follows:

$$\begin{aligned} \text{NATSAV} = \; & \underset{(-0.39)}{-0.785} + \underset{(1.57)}{0.181}\ \text{STRUCT\_BUDGET} + \underset{(9.93)}{0.773}\ \text{INVEST} \\ & + \underset{(3.88)}{0.284}\ \text{PROFSHARE} - \underset{(-7.39)}{0.115}\ \text{PROFSHARE} * \text{D1983} \end{aligned}$$

$$R^2 = 0.906, \quad \text{Adjusted } R^2 = 0.893, \quad \text{D.W.} = 1.713$$

Time subscripts have been omitted since there were no lags in the model, but it should be noted that STRUCT_BUDGET is measured for fiscal years which began on July 1 of the preceding year until 1976 and October 1 thereafter (the transitional quarter in 1976 was omitted).[64] Note that the coefficient on PROFSHARE itself measures the effect of this variable on NATSAV prior to 1983; the coefficient on the interactive dummy term represents the *change* in this effect starting in 1983, and the sum of the two coefficients (0.284 – 0.115 = 0.169) represents the total effect of PROFSHARE in 1983–92.

63 The current growth rate (annual percentage change in real GDP) performed less well. But Bosworth, *Saving and Investment in a Growing Economy*, shows that private saving is a fairly complex function of current and lagged growth rates.

64 I would have preferred calendar-year data on the structural budget deficit, but they were not available at the time of this writing. I also estimated the model using my own estimates of STRUCT_BUDGET (derived as the residuals from regressing calendar-year budget data from the national income accounts on the unemployment rate) and obtained similar results to those shown here.

Social and cultural perspectives

The quantitative concerns of economic analysis frequently distract our attention from the social and cultural impacts of macroeconomic change. As the American economy has suffered through two decades of slow and painful adjustment to altogether new historical, structural, and institutional conditions, the consequences for individuals and groups of individuals have been profound. Recognizing those impacts and pondering their significance must also be part of understanding and surmounting American economic decline.

Structural economic change has dramatically affected the distribution of wealth and income, and thereby the relative welfare of Americans. Refracted along the lines of race and gender, these welfare changes are particularly vivid. M. V. Lee Badgett and Rhonda M. Williams report striking new data concerning the social contours of structural economic change. In a society that for generations has grown used to unhindered economic growth and expansion, recent decline has been a shock. Utilizing the perspective of cultural anthropology, Katherine S. Newman deploys field research findings that speak, in human terms, of the troubled times in which we live.

9

The changing contours of discrimination: race, gender, and structural economic change

M. V. LEE BADGETT AND RHONDA M. WILLIAMS

1. INTRODUCTION

For many U.S. workers, the past twenty years have been an era marked by declining real wages and benefits, rising income inequality, a reduction in bargaining power relative to employers, and poorer working conditions. Through lived experience and media analysis, many workers know that corporate America's efforts to restore profitability and compete effectively have dramatically transformed the economic landscape. Businesses have relocated ("capital flight"), increased the use of contingent and "home" work, engaged in active union busting, and expanded the service sector in their quest to lower costs and restore profit levels.

This chapter focuses on the race and gender consequences of economic transformation for blacks and whites of both sexes. Specifically, we both document and seek to explain the divergent labor market outcomes for white women and African Americans during the 1970's and 1980's. Both our research and our critical reads of current scholarship affirm the importance of research and policies that use gendered race-based analysis (i.e., sort race-ethnic groups by gender) and racial gender-based discussions of restructuring and labor market outcomes (i.e., disaggregate sex groups by race, ethnicity, and nationality). Few analyses to date have examined systematically restructuring's impact on the race–gender distribution of earnings; fewer still have addressed the gender and race contours of unemployment.

We would like to thank Dave Marcotte for his committed research assistance and the Africa and Africa in the Americas Program at the University of Maryland for financial support.

We begin with an overview of the labor market status of blacks and white women prior to 1970. This assessment provides a context from which to assess the qualitative and quantitative dimensions of the race and gender restructuring that characterized U.S. labor markets during the past two decades. Section 3 then presents the theoretical perspectives on race–gender employment discrimination and labor supply that inform our empirical analysis, presented in section 4. The goal of our empirical analysis is to quantify the changing impact of being a black or a female on a given worker's location in the employment–unemployment hierarchy in three business cycle peak years, 1973, 1979, and 1987.

Several key findings define the race–gender contours of economic restructuring. First, it has enabled a subset of the white female workforce and imperiled economic viability for a significant proportion of the African American community. Our analysis of unemployment disrupts the commonly held notion that the 1970's were an era of unambiguous labor market improvement for black men and women. We find, as have others, evidence for widening racial income gaps in the 1980's that coincide with narrowing intra-racial gender income gaps. Our models indicate a shifting gender unemployment gap among African Americans: black women's unemployment probabilities decreased in the 1980's relative to black men. Finally, we note a sharp break in the relationship between marriage and earnings. In a reversal of historical trends, marriage increased white women's probability of having a high-wage job in the 1980's. For black women, marriage in the 1980's reduced the likelihood of high-wage employment, also a reversal of dynamics observed in the 1970's. This chapter concludes with an explanation of these changes that privileges changes in the contours and costs of discrimination.

2. RISING TIDES, DRIFTING BOATS: INCOMES AND GROWTH IN THE 1980'S

Post-war restructuring

Our perspective on the race and gender restructuring of labor markets rests upon the notion that we are witnessing an important reconfiguring of labor market hierarchies. In order to comprehend the particulars of this transformation, we must provide an overview of an earlier period of race and gender restructuring, from the end of World War II to 1970.

Between 1940 and 1970, blacks and whites of both sexes registered significant increases in their real earnings. Across educational levels, women and men of both races enjoyed this long upswing. While black women high school graduates saw their mean earnings more than triple between 1939 and 1969, white women's annual earnings did not quite double. The black–white earnings ratio for men with twelve years of schooling (again, measured in terms of average yearly earnings), for instance, climbed from 0.57 to 0.71.[1] Most of the changes in this earlier period stem from black workers' northward migration (and the simultaneous shift out of agriculture) and their rising levels of educational attainment.[2]

However, because earnings data mask occupational and employment hierarchies, they do not robustly capture all relevant labor market information. They do not, for example, indicate the prevalence of occupational segregation by race and gender. Although racial segregation for both men and women declined considerably in the 1960's, most women still worked in female-dominated occupations in 1970, and those jobs continued to be racially typed.[3] Approximately 70% of men or women would have had to change jobs in 1970 in order to achieve a gender-integrated occupational distribution. Because black women moved out of domestic work into clerical jobs, the greatest decline in occupational segregation occurred between black and white women during this period. To a much greater extent than black men, women of both races remained excluded from traditionally white male-dominated occupations.

Race- and gender-based occupational segregation meant that all women were more likely to be clerks, operatives, and service workers than professionals and managers. In 1970, white women were more likely than black women to work in clerical occupations; black women were more likely to be service workers or machine operatives.[4] Persistent intra-occupational wage gaps not reducible to gender gaps in experience suggested that employers set their wage offers based on the sex of the desired worker.[5]

1 Gerald D. Jaynes, "The Labor Market Status of Black Americans: 1939–1985," *Journal of Economic Perspectives* Vol. 4, No. 4, 1990: 9–24.
2 James P. Smith and Finis R. Welch, "Black Economic Progress After Myrdal," *Journal of Economic Literature* Vol. 27, No. 2, June 1989: 519–64.
3 Mary King, "Occupational Segregation by Race and Sex, 1940–88," *Monthly Labor Review* Vol. 115, No. 4, April 1992: 30–37.
4 Teresa Amott, *Caught in the Crisis: Women and the U.S. Economy Today,* New York: Monthly Review Press, 1993.
5 Barbara Bergmann, "Does the Market for Women's Labor Need Fixing?" *Journal of Economic Perspectives* Vol. 3, No. 1, 1989: 43–60.

Earnings data also mask racial differences in unemployment. Black unemployment did not surpass white unemployment before 1940.[6] Black unemployment rates began to consistently double white rates in 1954, and that pattern has persisted. Prior to 1970, black unemployment was more cyclically sensitive than white unemployment. In other words, blacks lost jobs earlier and more frequently than whites in recessions. In upswings, black employment increased faster than white employment, although these gains were not always equal to recession losses.

Toward the end of this period, the federal government outlawed employment discrimination by race and gender (Title VII of the 1964 Civil Rights Act) and, in 1965, instituted a policy of affirmative action to remove discriminatory employment practices among federal government contractors. Studies of average earnings and employment patterns covering this early period suggest that federal antidiscrimination policy somewhat improved the economic positions of women and black men.[7]

The 1970's and 1980's

Economic growth in the 1980's did not produce a rising tide that lifted all boats. On the contrary, the emergent consensus is that rising income inequality within groups was the norm during the past twenty years: income inequality increased among men and women and within racial groups.[8] In the 1980's, inequality also began to increase *between* groups: black men lost ground relative to white men from the late 1970's through 1980's. Both age-specific data and cohort data confirm a widening racial gap.[9] For example, the black–white median income ratio for year-round,

6 Steven Shulman, "Competition and Racial Discrimination: The Employment Effects of Reagan's Labor Market Policies," *Review of Radical Political Economics* Vol. 16, 1984: 111–28.

7 M. V. Lee Badgett and Heidi Hartmann, "Evidence of the Effectiveness of Equal Employment Opportunity Policies: A Review," Final Report for Joint Center for Political and Economic Studies, 1992.

8 Frank Levy and Richard J. Murnane, "U.S. Earnings Levels and Earning Inequality: A Review of Recent Trends and Proposed Explanations," *Journal of Economic Literature* Vol. 30, 1992: 1333–81; Norton W. Grubb and Robert H. Wilson, "Demographic and Labor Market Effects on Wage and Salary Inequality, 1968–1984," presented at 1986 APPAM Research Conference.

9 William Darity, Jr., "Race and Inequality in the Managerial Age," in *Social, Political, and Economic Issues in Black America,* Boston: William Monroe Trotter Institute, 1990, 29–82.

full-time working men dropped from 0.77 to 0.71 between 1978 and 1987. For young men age 25 to 29, the ratio plummeted from 0.90 to 0.75. The comparable ratio for the 20–24-year-old cohort in 1977 was 0.84. Ten years later, when that cohort was 30–34 years old, the black–white median income ratio had dropped to 0.69.

Occupational segregation increased between black and white men in the 1980's, and occupational status became more important in determining unemployment experiences. Between 1980 and 1988, the increase in occupational segregation was particularly pronounced among young men, those with less than an eighth grade education, and those with fewer than four years of college.[10] Throughout the period, much of the rising gap between black and white men's unemployment rates was explained by rising unemployment among black workers with blue-collar jobs. However, white-collar and college educated blacks were not exempt from this structural shift: unemployment for black workers in all educational and occupational groups grew relative to unemployment among similar white workers.[11]

As their unemployment experience would suggest, employment inequality soared among black men, who experienced significant declines in their share of total employment after 1970.[12] The declines were concentrated among men with twelve or fewer years of schooling, which Bound and Holzer attribute to declining demand for manufacturing workers.[13] In 1970, employment rates (employment population ratios) were identical for black high school and college graduates. By 1985, high school graduates had an employment rate 11 percentage points lower than their college counterparts, a result many analysts attribute to black men's disproportionate loss of better paying manufacturing jobs.

Although occupational segregation declined considerably in the 1970's, the gender wage gap remained largely unchanged until women's wages began to rise relative to men's in the 1980's.[14] Men's decline in earnings accounts for about 40% of the gender gap reduction, which is

10 King, "Occupational Segregation."

11 M. V. Lee Badgett, "Racial Differences in Unemployment Rates and Employment Opportunities," Ph.D. dissertation, U.C. Berkeley, 1990.

12 Jaynes, "Labor Market Status of Black Americans."

13 John Bound and Harry J. Holzer, "Industrial Shifts, Skills Levels, and the Labor Market for White and Black Males," National Bureau of Economic Research Working Paper No. 3715, 1990.

14 Amott, *Caught in the Crisis.*

partly explained by the consequences of industrial restructuring and the reduced demand for high school educated men.[15] Although corporate downsizing and capital flight reduced manufacturing's total share of employment, women increased their share of this shrinking pie. The job-generating service sector also hired women in increasing numbers, but in traditionally female-dominated jobs (service sector and administrative support).

However, women's labor market fortunes varied by race. As was the case among men, the widening of the earnings gap parallels slight increases in occupational segregation by race. Among women, occupational segregation increased most significantly for women with fewer than twelve years of education, and for those who had attended, but not graduated, from college.[16] While white women made the greatest inroads into traditionally white male-dominated occupations such as law and medicine,[17] black women increased their concentration in social work and teaching as white women vacated these positions. Hence the female black–white earnings gap (measured as median weekly earnings of full-time workers) increased in the 1980's, heralding a retreat from more than a decade of convergence toward equality.[18] The unemployment gap also widened between black and white women, with essentially the same pattern seen among men: unemployment increased for black women of all levels of education but was concentrated among the less-educated.

3. THE CHANGING CONTOURS OF DISCRIMINATION

Understanding these large shifts in the race and gender composition of the workforce and of the wage structure requires an analysis of the underlying interaction of social and economic forces. Racism and sexism may

15 Lawrence F. Katz and Kevin M. Murphy, "Changes in Relative Wages, 1963–1987: Supply and Demand Factors," *Quarterly Journal of Economics* Vol. 107, No. 1, 1992: 35–78.

16 King, "Occupational Segregation."

17 Amott, *Caught in the Crisis.*

18 Francine D. Blau and Andrea H. Beller, "Black–White Earnings over the 1970's and 1980's: Gender Differences in Trends," *Review of Economics and Statistics* Vol. 74, 1993: 276–86; John Bound and Richard B. Freeman, "What Went Wrong? The Erosion of Relative Earnings and Employment Among Young Black Men in the 1980's," *Quarterly Journal of Economics,* 1992: 203–32.

be directly related to economics through the competition for jobs.[19] Other aspects of racism and sexism reflect social or noneconomic attitudes, beliefs, and behaviors, but even these attitudes and behaviors may have direct economic effects through labor market discrimination. The adaptation of labor markets to forces of economic and social change means that the race and gender divisions of labor are dimensions of a complex dynamic process. Our framework highlights the race and gender dimensions of that process and builds on the assumption that labor market discrimination exists. Given the existence of discrimination, its extent and intensity both influence and are influenced by economic restructuring. Our framework proposes that employers compare the costs of ending discrimination with the costs of continuing discrimination. These costs are influenced by the policy environment, labor supply, labor costs, and the resistance of incumbent workers, each of which is affected by economic restructuring.

In a world without discrimination, workers would apply for jobs and be judged solely by their individual productivity characteristics. Changes in employers' labor needs are driven by changes in technology, the product market, and the relative cost of labor. For example, if restructuring increases the demand for high-skilled labor, employers should hire from each race–gender group in proportion to its share of workers with the necessary skills. If higher productivity workers get higher paying jobs, then income distribution differences between race–gender groups must simply reflect different average skill levels.

In a discriminatory world, a worker's race and gender become important determinants of which job – if any – he or she obtains with a given set of skills. Profit-maximizing employers' willingness to end discrimination depends on the interaction of two forces: the actual monetary costs of *continuing* discrimination and the monetary costs of *ending* discrimination. If the costs of continuing to discriminate are falling and the costs of ending discrimination are positive within the firm, discrimination will increase, resulting in differential shifts in labor demand in response to

19 William Darity, Jr., and Rhonda M. Williams, "Peddlers Forever? Culture, Competition, and Discrimination," *American Economic Review* Vol. 75, May 1985: 256–61; Steven Shulman, "Why Is the Black Unemployment Rate Always Twice as High as the White Unemployment Rate?" in *New Approaches to Economic and Social Analyses of Discrimination,* New York: Praeger, 1991: 5–38.

changes in product markets or in production technology. For example, a real estate firm in the Sunbelt with a largely white male workforce and no federal contracts or other direct antidiscrimination pressure might respond to an increase in demand for corporate office space by hiring a higher percentage of white male realtors than is in the company's applicant pool.

The costs to employers of continuing to discriminate include lost profits, increased hiring and search costs, and potential legal penalties if caught. Lost profits result from hiring higher priced white and/or male labor. As noted earlier, racial wage gaps fell during the 1970's, reducing lost profits from wage discrimination, but the gap began to widen again in the 1980's. The gender gap showed the opposite pattern (recall the earlier discussion of the impact of service sector growth), remaining steady before dropping somewhat in the 1980's.

Hiring and search costs will depend at least partly on the unemployment rate, with lower costs during recessions when a firm's applicant pool is larger and contains more of the favored employee group. Labor supply changes will also affect firms through search costs. As women's labor force participation rises (especially for white women), applicant pools will be increasingly female, making it more difficult for employers to hire qualified male applicants without passing over qualified female applicants.

The potential legal costs of discriminating depend on the strength of enforcement efforts and the likely penalties if caught. Leonard points out that both the probability of being caught discriminating and the potential monetary penalties fell in the 1980's after a relatively strong period of enforcement in the 1970's.[20]

Ending discrimination is also likely to be costly to employers. If employees see members of other groups as competitors for jobs (including future promotions), ending discrimination is likely to increase the resistance of majority workers, resulting in lower productivity and higher labor costs for employers, particularly if teamwork becomes more important in the production process.[21] Job competition intensifies for workers

20 Jonathan S. Leonard, "The Impact of Affirmative Action Regulation and Equal Employment Law on Black Employment," *Journal of Economic Perspectives* Vol. 4, 1990: 47–64.

21 This may explain the growing interest in "managing diversity" programs in companies that have diversified their workforces and have implemented

during recessions when job openings are relatively scarce[22] and may also intensify for good jobs when income inequality increases. The resistance of male workers to the increased hiring of female workers, which causes more competition, is also likely to depend on the effects of discrimination on family incomes (where families take the traditional heterosexual form). As restructuring increases the importance of women's financial contributions to the family income, male resistance to hiring women is likely to fall. Since most marriages are intra-racial, this effect is likely to improve the prospects of white women the most.

This framework allows us to predict how economic forces will affect an employer's propensity to discriminate and, therefore, the relative effects of economic change on different race and gender groups. One of the most important implications of this framework is that the costs of ending discrimination will obviously be nonexistent when no incumbent workforce exists, that is, in new plants or firms. Employers starting from scratch can hire from possibly lower-cost female or minority labor pools without the threat of retaliation by disgruntled male or white employees.[23] This suggests that white women and people of color will fare better economically when many new plants open, such as in fast-growing regions and growing or new industries. In earlier research, we found such a regional pattern in changes in the income distribution.[24] Employment growth in existing firms might not have the same effect since firms must balance the costs of diversifying their workforces. The effect of new technologies will depend on who uses them, that is, old or new firms, and how the organization of the workforce changes, for example, incorporating teamwork.

We summarize this model of the costs of discrimination in Table 9.1. With this framework, we can also look back over the past two decades to

team-oriented production. The cost of the programs would be a cost of ending discrimination.

22 Shulman, "Competition and Racial Discrimination."

23 This is a similar dynamic to that embodied in Becker's model of taste discrimination, where employers with a lower preference for discrimination increase their profits by taking advantage of available lower cost labor. (Gary S. Becker, *The Economics of Discrimination,* Chicago: University of Chicago Press, 2d edition, 1971.)

24 Rhonda M. Williams and M. V. Lee Badgett, "Redistribution and Restructuring by Race and Gender: A Regional and Industrial Analysis," unpublished, June 1993.

Table 9.1. *Determinants of the extent of discrimination*

	Race		Gender	
Factor	1970's	1980's	1970's	1980's
Cost of continuing discrimination				
Lost profits	+	−	−	+
Relative labor supply	−	+	−	−
Legal costs	−	+	−	+
Cost of ending discrimination				
Resistance from workers				
Job competition	+	+		
Family income effect			−	−
New firm creation	Varies by industry and region			

Note: A + means that the factor *increases* the extent of discrimination (i.e. either reduces the cost of continuing or increases the cost of ending discrimination), and a − means that the factor *decreases* the extent of discrimination.

explain the changes we observed earlier. The columns for the 1970's and 1980's predict the influence of that factor on the extent of discrimination, with the direction based on the empirical literature. In the 1970's, we would have expected most factors to reduce discrimination. The exception to that pattern comes from the falling racial wage gap, which would tend to reduce the cost of discrimination (and therefore increase the extent of discrimination) through lost profits. In the 1980's the rising wage gap for black workers and the falling wage gap for female workers reverse the influence of that force, predicting that employers will hire more black workers but fewer female workers. The other diverging factor between the *racial* forces and the *gender* forces that drives apart expected outcomes for white women and black women is the family income effect. White men's overrepresentation in well-paying jobs puts white women, who are more likely to marry white men, in the position of benefitting most from any increased acceptance of women.

Overall, then, in the 1970's we would expect to see some loosening of discriminatory practices that would allow white women and people of color increasing access to high-wage jobs. In the 1980's the effects are much less clear-cut, with the expectations differing when considering race versus sex discrimination. If labor supply and the family income effect are important relative to the other factors affecting discrimination, then white women's position may have improved relative to the position of black women and black men. In the empirical work discussed next, we measure the economic position of each race–gender group of workers and compare their progress over time.

4. EVIDENCE FROM THE 1970'S AND 1980'S

Our research asks how much race and gender influence a worker's likelihood of ending up in one of three economic status categories – serious unemployment, low-wage employment, and high-wage employment – and how that influence has changed over time, given the massive restructuring of the U.S. economy. To isolate the effects of race and gender, we must also take into account other factors that determine a worker's position, such as education, age (a measure of work experience), region, city residence, occupation, and industry. One method that allows us to measure the effect of different variables on the probability of being in a particular category when the categories have some natural order is the ordered probit procedure.[25] In this study the order arises from the downward progression of economic status from having a high-wage job to having a low-wage job to having no job (or, more precisely, having no job for a significant period of time). Details of our statistical method and data, which come from the Current Population Survey for 1973, 1979, and 1987, are described in the appendix to this chapter.

Table 9.2 shows how full-time (or usually full-time if unemployed) workers are distributed across the categories by gender (top half) and by race (bottom half). Unfortunately, small sample sizes for Hispanics, Asian Americans, and Native Americans force us to restrict our statistical comparison to blacks and whites. Not surprisingly, men and whites dominate the high-wage group. Women as a group have increased their share of high-wage jobs over the two decades. Black workers achieved modest improvement in access to high-wage jobs but greatly increased their share of serious unemployment.

Turning to our ordered probit model results, broadening the view of economic status to include unemployment shows that the supposed gains of black workers in the 1970's were limited even after controlling for

25 G. S. Maddala, *Limited-dependent and Qualitative Variables in Econometrics,* Cambridge: Cambridge University Press, 1983.

Table 9.2 *Percent distribution of the three economic status groups*

	1973		1979		1987	
Group	Women	Men	Women	Men	Women	Men
1	5.1	5.2	5.9	6.7	5.0	7.6
2	67.3	26.2	60.4	23.9	53.2	27.3
3	27.7	68.7	33.7	69.4	41.8	65.1
	Black	White	Black	White	Black	White
1	8.3	4.8	11.5	5.8	10.6	6.0
2	55.4	38.1	47.5	36.5	48.1	36.7
3	36.3	57.2	41.0	57.7	41.4	57.4

Note: Group 1 refers to those with eleven or more weeks of unemployment, Group 2 refers to those with weekly incomes below the workforce median, and Group 3 refers to those with weekly incomes above the workforce median.

other important determinants of economic position. Table 9.3 presents the partial derivatives from the coefficient on being black in the probit models split by gender and from the coefficient on being female in the probit models split by race. For black men the situation clearly worsened throughout the two decades of economic restructuring: the probability of high-wage employment fell, and the probability of low-wage employment gradually rose. The contribution of race to the probability of unemployment rose sharply for black men from 1973 to 1979, and remained at that high level in 1987.

Black women faced similar racial barriers relative to white women, and the pattern of the coefficients tells a similar story. Black women were increasingly likely to experience similar unemployment, although the contribution of race was smaller than for black men, and black women found it more and more difficult to find high-wage employment. These growing disadvantages were somewhat offset by a steadily rising ability to get low-wage jobs, suggesting that white women moved up the economic ladder, leaving the middle rung for black women.

The improvement in white women's position is clear from the second part of Table 9.3, where the effect of being female is measured for each race. The disadvantage of being a woman for obtaining a high-wage job

Table 9.3. *Partial derivatives on race and gender from probit models*

	1973			1979			1987		
Gender probit	Unemp.	Low wage	High wage	Unemp.	Low wage	High wage	Unemp.	Low wage	High wage
Women	.001	.006	−.007	.006	.017	−.023	.008	.023	−.030
Men	.006	.053	−.059	.015	.057	−.072	.015	.060	−.075
Race probit									
Black	.012	.167	−.179	.027	.134	−.160	.017	.095	−.112
White	.013	.241	−.254	.030	.229	−.259	.029	.162	−.191

Note: For gender probits, partial derivatives measure the effect of being black. For the race probits, partial derivatives measure the effect of being female.

fell by more than 20% from 1973 to 1987. White women were less likely to be in low-wage jobs and more likely to be in high-wage jobs. However, this move up the ladder came at the cost of increasingly serious unemployment. That finding is surprising considering that white women's and men's overall unemployment rates converged over this time period, moving in the *opposite* direction from what is found here: white women's rate fell and white men's rate rose.[26] The seemingly contradictory finding here suggests that either white women usually employed full time experienced a lower frequency of unemployment or those working part time experienced less unemployment.

In the probit model for black workers, we see further evidence that black women's position only improved relative to black men. As with white women, being female reduced the likelihood of black women having a high-wage job less in 1987 than in 1973. And the falling partial derivative for having a low-wage job suggests that black women moved up in economic status relative to black men. The relationship of gender to black unemployment is more complex, however, with black women's position worsening in the 1970's but improving in the 1980's.

Further splitting our sample into the four race–gender groups and

26 Badgett, "Racial Differences in Unemployment Rates."

running separate ordered probit models also reveals some interesting patterns over time. One widely reported phenomenon is also seen here: education became increasingly important for all four groups in helping reach the top category. For white men, an additional year of education improved their probability of getting a high-wage job by 1.7% in 1973 but 3.2% in 1987. The increase for white women was from 2.9% to 4.3%, and the value of a year of education increased for black women from 2.8% to 4.5%. The one exception is for black men, for whom another year of education gave less of a boost upward in 1987 than in 1979 (2.8% compared with 3.2%) but was still higher than in 1973 (2.3%).

Within the individual group statistical models, we also see evidence of the family income effect. In the 1970's, marriage reduced white women's probability of getting a high-wage job, by 0.5% in 1973 and by 1.3% in 1979. But in 1987, marriage *increased* a white woman's probability by 0.2% – not a large effect, but one in the opposite direction compared with the 1970's that suggests the family income effect may have helped remove some of the employment stigma of marriage and employers' presumptions that married women will soon leave the labor force. The family income effect would not just be seen for married white women, since unmarried white women might be seen by men as potential marriage partners, and the evidence for this effect was seen earlier in the improvements for white women in general. This family income effect is not visible for black women in the 1980's, however. To the contrary, marriage went from increasing a black woman's probability of high-wage employment (by 4.8% in 1973 and 3.1% in 1979) to reducing it in 1987 (by 0.2%).

5. THE INCREASING SIGNIFICANCE OF RACE?

Although by no means definitive, our results portend a transformation of race and gender hierarchies in U.S. labor markets. White men's relative dominance persists, however measured. Yet we find important directions of change in the labor market fortunes of black women, white women, and black men. The decline of manufacturing and the growth of the feminized service sector reduced employment opportunities for significant numbers of black men, throwing them into more intense competition with white workers. Restructuring has reduced the costs of employment discrimination against black men *and* increased the costs of ending discrimination.

Our analysis suggests that white women, much more than black workers of either sex, are on a path that leads more quickly to labor market convergence with white men. White women's probabilities for high-wage employment are increasing (relative to both white men and black women) in the post-industrial economy. Black women share black men's unemployment problems, but are increasing their share of high-wage jobs relative to black men.

We have conjectured that two forces have enhanced white women's labor market climb. The first is white women's status as potential or actual "female kin" to white men, which improves their acceptability as co-workers and therefore their economic status. From the perspective of an employer, the costs of ending discrimination against white women are declining. The second factor is white women's increasing share of the labor force, which increases an employer's costs of continuing discrimination.

Black people can duplicate labor market effects of neither white women's share of the population nor, in the foreseeable future, their attractiveness to most white men as marriage partners. When viewed in the context of the direct evidence of employment discrimination generated by matched pair studies,[27] our results suggest that competitive forces alone are insufficient to erode the increasing significance of race in shaping labor market outcomes. To us, this suggests the importance of a renewed federal commitment to ending racial employment discrimination. Without this commitment, the prognosis is one of a new era of resurgent racial inequality.

APPENDIX: DATA AND METHOD

Data for this study come from the March Annual Demographic File of the Current Population Survey for 1974, 1980, and 1988. (The form of the CPS used is from the Mare–Winship Uniform Files, which reconfigure the CPS data into a more tractable form for data manipulation.) The March surveys include information on the respondents' income and employment for the *previous* year, providing the annual data for 1973, 1979, and 1987 used in this chapter. The three years studied are three

27 Margery Austin Turner, Michael Fix, and Raymond J. Struyk, *Opportunities Denied, Opportunities Diminished: Racial Discrimination in Hiring*, Urban Institute Report 91-9, Washington D.C.: Urban Institute Press, 1991.

business cycle peaks. Respondents were included in the subsample if they were over sixteen years of age and worked at least one week in the year.

Industry of employment is defined by the industry of the longest job held in the previous year, that is, in the year studied. Changes in industry and occupation definitions combined with the issue of small cell sizes required the aggregation of categories for those two variables. Industry codes were aggregated into six categories, and occupation into seven categories.

The economic status dependent variable – serious unemployment, low-wage employment, high-wage employment – was constructed in two steps. First, the median weekly wage and salary income for the entire subsample was calculated (including the groups not included in this analysis because of their small sample sizes: Asian-Americans, Native Americans, and other individuals not coded as white or black). The weekly income variable was constructed by dividing total wage and salary income by weeks worked in the previous year. Only those workers with weekly incomes of at least $20 (in 1973 dollars) were retained in the sample. The calculation of the median included all workers, and that median constitutes the dividing line between "low-wage" and "high-wage" employment.

The second step involved determining the number of weeks of unemployment per individual. For those normally full-time workers experiencing some unemployment, in 1979 and 1987 the median was twelve weeks of unemployment, which we preferred as the dividing line to define "serious" unemployment. Unfortunately, the 1973 data only provided categories of weeks, one of which began at eleven weeks, leading us to choose eleven weeks as the dividing line to ensure consistency across years. Those individuals with eleven or more weeks were coded as unemployed, and those with less than eleven weeks of unemployment were allocated to the appropriate weekly income category.

Underlying the ordered probit model, the statistical method used in this chapter, is some unobserved continuous measure of economic status which is a function of the independent variables (e.g., age, education). What we do observe, however, is the worker's status category, which is a function of the unobserved process determining the distribution of all workers across the three categories. Maximum likelihood estimation gives estimates of the effect of the independent variables on the unobserved variable. Since many of our variables are dummy variables, we must exclude one dummy variable from each set. The excluded category in the models discussed here is living in the Midwest, with a farm or labor occupation, in the financial and health services industries.

The effect of changes in the independent variables on the probability of being in a particular category, that is, the partial derivatives, can be calculated from the ordered probit coefficients for particular values of the independent variables. (With a dependent variable using three categories, three sets of partial derivatives are calculated.) We calculate the partial derivatives at the means of the age and education variables and for a married white man employed in a clerical position in the professional services industry who lives in a midwestern central city. The partial derivative for being black or female cannot truly be thought of as what would happen if that prototypical person became black or female, but it does reveal the difference for an otherwise similar black person or for a woman.

10

Troubled times: the cultural dimensions of economic decline

KATHERINE S. NEWMAN

> I'll never have what my parents had. I can't even dream of that. I'm living a lifestyle that's way lower than it was when I was growing up and it's depressing. You know it's a rude awakening when you're out in the world on your own. . . . I took what was given to me and tried to use it the best way I could. Even if you are a hard worker and you never skipped a beat, you followed all the rules, did everything they told you you were supposed to do, it's still horrendous. *They lied to me.* You don't get where you were supposed to wind up. At the end of the road it isn't there. I worked all those years and then I didn't get to candy land. The prize wasn't there, damn it.
>
> – Lauren Caulder, age 40

There are many vantage points from which to approach the question of America's economic decline. Most of them, quite properly, involve the structural trends – demographic, industrial, and monetary – that constitute the intellectual terrain of economists and historians. But if we are to understand what the declining position of the United States means to ordinary people in the late twentieth century – workers, consumers, suburban folk, and urban dwellers – we have to consider how the macrotrends of job markets and housing markets, unemployment and underemployment have impacted upon individual lives.

For at the end of the day, it is the dashed hopes, and the conflicts between communities that accompany this post-industrial transformation that define the daily experience of economic decline. Anger and frustration have crystallized politically in the form of populist outbursts at elites, perceived as unfairly immune to economic pain, and at the poor, defined as parasitical elements intent on a free ride. The appeal of Ross

Perot, among other "outsider" politicians, is best understood as a response to the economic disarray of the past two decades in general and the declining fortunes of the middle class in particular. Trust in traditional politics, understood as the two-party system, has eroded considerably as the battered middle class loses faith in the capacity of government as usual to solve the structural problems of the American economy in the late twentieth century. Politicians appear to be as confused as practitioners of the dismal science; the result is a deepening crisis of confidence in the ability of the country's leaders – political and intellectual – to salvage the nation's prosperity and restore the "rightful" place of the middle class.

For anthropologists, the quest to understand the daily lived consequences of economic disarray must be grounded in ethnographic understanding. Statistics and documents can go only so far in representing the ordinary American's perspective on structural change; thereafter, there is no substitute for fieldwork, for intensive observation, structured and unstructured interviews, extended conversations, and close contact over a long period of time. Qualitative research methods of this kind provide the data for a grounded analysis of cultural responses to economic trends: the interpretive representation of experience at the level of individuals, families, and local communities.

This chapter draws upon two bodies of data of exactly this kind. The first, generated in the early years of the 1980s and discussed at greater length in *Falling From Grace* (Newman 1988), is based upon extensive fieldwork with both managerial/executive workers and blue-collar families left stranded by double-digit unemployment of the early Reagan years. The second, which draws upon fieldwork in a suburban community in northern New Jersey in 1989–91 (presented in detail in *Declining Fortunes* [Newman 1993]), focused on two generations in sixty families, particularly their experience of inter-generational downward mobility. Hundreds of interviews, not to mention countless casual conversations, fed into the data base for these two studies. Collectively, they represent a portrait of the personal, local experience of economic decline – unemployment, foreclosure, a crashing exposure to self doubt, and the growth of the calamitous assumption that America is no longer the country it once was.

The purpose of my analysis is to show how cultural constructions – of morality, of values, of worthiness, and of loyalty – have filtered and textured the experience of ordinary Americans on the receiving end of impersonal economic forces. I do so by examining two forms of downward mobility, two distinct kinds of dislocation which, in turn, parallel structural trends in the labor and housing markets noted by the economists and historians in this volume. *Intra-generational downward mobility* afflicts individuals who, in the course of their adult working lives, lose the jobs they have enjoyed for decades and discover, to their dismay, that they are unable to replicate them. This has become a national tragedy for legions of displaced white collar managers, particularly those dubbed "middle management" and dismissed as unneeded in the rush of American firms to become lean and mean. Having worked for decades to assure their stability and security, many of these people have lost both.

Inter-generational downward mobility is a different malady. When the post-war expansion period came to a halt, the fortunes of the baby boom generation eroded sharply. Compared with the experience of their parents in the 1950s and 1960s, the trajectory of the boomers has been a serious disappointment. This form of downward movement takes on a different cultural hue because it does not involve catastrophic loss, but rather the disappointment and frustration of millions of young Americans who will probably never get what they believe they deserve.

THE END OF PROSPERITY

In the expansive years between the end of the Great Depression and the middle of the 1970s, the experience of downward mobility was virtually invisible. Of course, frictional unemployment has always afflicted some Americans, and many fail to recover their previous standard of living. But beginning in the mid-1970s, downward mobility began to afflict groups of Americans who never thought they would have anything in common with the poor. Managerial and executive employees began to feel the brunt of recessions in ways they had not previously experienced. Solid blue-collar citizens began to see their jobs disappear in record numbers. For millions of middle-class and working-class families, this meant the loss of everything they had worked for – jobs, homes, stability, and a secure grip on the future. By the early 1980s, displaced workers found they were unable to find new jobs in a climate where neither educational credentials nor work experience seemed to offer much protection. Pink slips have rained down in the financial services industries as one major bank after another consolidates and sheds its staff.

In the 1990s, high-technology firms, from Apple to IBM to Raytheon, have let thousands go as they downsize in the hope that lower labor costs will put them back in competitive shape. Left behind, stranded in a no-man's-land of persistent joblessness are the thousands of high-skilled, white-collar workers, now joined on the unemployment lines by millions of working-class colleagues who have had longer and more bitter experience with economic insecurity.[1]

Refugees from the managerial world are undone by the descent into downward mobility. For unlike their blue-collar brethren, who have had to contend with layoffs and callbacks for most of their working life, white-collar managers were accustomed to thinking of themselves as above the fray, valued for their long years of experience, based in turn on their professional credentials. When the axe falls, shock and dismay are quickly followed by an enforced isolation that is almost as hard to endure as the financial duress that unemployment brings. Families that have been independent, cloistered behind suburban hedges, find themselves in need of help and understanding, only to discover that their very independence has become a major handicap. They have no links to trade upon, no meaningful networks that can stand the test of their newfound needy status. Instead, even in the midst of high unemployment across the nation, they discover how quickly they can become the subject of stigma, singled out as blameworthy.

David Patterson was a case in point. He was one of the forty former managers I interviewed in the course of my study of managerial downward mobility in 1981. A middle manager in a high-tech firm on Long Island, Patterson had moved his whole family from their long-time home in California to the East in the name of an internal promotion. He had been in the new job, a comfortable vice-presidency, for less than two years when the company went through a major contraction, shedding over fifty managers in one month. David worked his contacts, scoured the *Wall Street Journal* want ads, and called everyone he knew in the industry to inquire about a new position, initially confident that he would find a job without any trouble. He had been unemployed for nearly a year by the time we met in the smoky corridors of the "Forty Plus Club," a volunteer group for businessmen and -women who are out of work. David's family had "lost" the family home, moved into a small apartment in a suburb

1 See Lillian Rubin (1993) *Families on the Fault Line,* New York: HarperCollins, for more on the experience of working-class families in this era of economic instability.

outside of the Big Apple, and his wife had struggled to find a job as a receptionist. Their savings depleted and their teenage children in a total uproar, David and his wife were completely bewildered and beginning to tear into each other.

Most damaging for the Pattersons was the sense that no one around them believed their story. No one accepted the notion that there were no jobs to be had. Neighbors and "fair weather" friends had begun asking embarrassing questions that left David's wife, Julia, both traumatized and suspicious:

> Since becoming unemployed there's really nothing, especially for my wife – no place where a woman can talk about things. There are no real relationships. She's hurt. People say to her, "With all the companies on Long Island, your husband can't find a job? Is he really trying? Maybe he likes not working." This really hurts her and it hurts me. People don't understand that you can send out 150 letters to headhunters and get 10 replies. Maybe one or two will turn into something, but there are a hundred qualified people going after each job. The computer industry is contracting all over the place and as it [shrinks], my wife contracts emotionally.[2]

For David, and the others who spend their days at the Forty Plus Club, the dynamics of the American economy, the vagaries of their own particular industries, and the abstract fluctuation of the unemployment figures hold little meaning. These structural facts, these trends which "explain" so much of what has happened to the middle class, pale beside the introspective, self-blaming quality of their downward mobility. When friends become scarce and the phone never rings, the independence of the managerial man becomes his own prison, and his own character takes the center stage. David was forever asking himself what was wrong with *him*, why was *he* unable to find a new job? Even though millions of Americans have found themselves in the same dismal situation, all David can see are his own flaws, magnified a thousand times to expose what he takes to be the "real reasons" he has failed himself and his family. For the trends and statistics do not tell David why others have been more fortunate, even if only a few of them have been able to hang on. There must be something that separates the downwardly mobile from the persistently successful. For David that something can only be found within. He is a product of an

2 Quoted originally in Katherine Newman's (1988:5) *Falling From Grace: The Experience of Downward Mobility in the American Middle Class*, New York: Free Press.

individualistic culture that made him feel like a prince, when his life was a Depression-era boy's dream come true, and something of a criminal when it all fell apart. In either case, David – not the international economy – is the protagonist in this story, the one who, as master of his destiny, is responsible for his sorry fate.

Blue-collar workers are less likely to experience downward mobility this way. Those who live in the shadow of shuttered manufacturing plants often live in residential communities for whom the local plant has been the economic mainstay. When General Motors shuts down eleven plants across the country, idling thousands of assembly line workers with one stroke of the pen, the neighborhoods nearby each reel from the loss of their lifeline. Tertiary businesses – the suppliers of parts, the taverns and restaurants patronized by the workers – and the local governments that rely on the tax dollars of the now unemployed laborers are all cast into the abyss together. If there is a virtue in their loss, it is only that they may have friends to turn to who have been through the same catastrophe and an enemy or series of enemies[3] to blame for their misfortune.

Men and women from the factory world do not see themselves as masters of their own fate in the same way that their white-collar brethren do, recognizing as they do that forces beyond their control have a powerful impact on their well-being. Their personal fates are in the hands of the same large institutions that may have put them in jeopardy in the first place: unions, companies, politicians looking to do some favors. Scanning the newspaper for breakthroughs that will jump-start the plant, they often look in vain. With so many jobs permanently lost, deliverance is not forthcoming. When this reality sinks in and the unemployment compensation has run out, low-paid jobs in the service sector are all that seems to remain.

If they are protected from debilitating self-blame, however, they are also more inclined to feel helpless in their numbers. This much was evident in the course of a year-long study I did in 1983 on the impact of the closure of the Singer Sewing Machine factory in Elizabeth, New Jersey. The Singer Company was a major multi-national firm in the mid-nineteenth century, one of the most important manufacturing companies in the U.S. Its empire stretched around the globe, with plants in Russia (confiscated during the revolution of 1917), Scotland, and many other

3 Among the possibilities are foreign competitors, company management, and/or uncaring politicians, local and federal.

parts of the world. But the Elizabeth plant was the flagship, the proud home of thousands of craftsmen and assembly line workers. The town was synonymous with the firm, for Singer provided the bedrock of jobs and security for over 100 years. Indeed, throughout the 1930s, when thousands of Elizabeth families were on bread lines, the Singer plant kept its employees in work, opened soup kitchens for those less fortunate, and continued to play its life-long role as paternalistic underwriter of schools, softball clubs, hospitals, and city government in Elizabeth.

However, after World War II, the market for sewing machines began to contract. Ready-made clothing became widely available and less expensive, cutting into domestic demand. In the 1960s, the trend toward increased female labor force participation forced the sewing machine market into a deep downturn. Women no longer had time for sewing and they turned away from this mainstay appliance of the past. Singer, in turn, began to diversify away from its original product lines and to withdraw investment from the manufacturing plants. A long, slow bleed turned the Elizabeth factory from a model of industrial innovation into a dinosaur. A moratorium on hiring was followed by layoffs, with the death knell of the factory sounding at last in the early 1980s.

Elena Morales, a Cuban immigrant who settled in Elizabeth, New Jersey, in the early sixties, put nearly twenty years into the Singer Sewing Machine factory. Her job, together with her husband's wages, meant that she could send her kids to parochial school and look forward to a better future for them. She was, in many respects, typical of the plant's workforce in its last years of operation. Unfortunately, her experience of post-shutdown downward mobility was typical as well. Having worked her way up from an assembly line worker to a quality-control inspector, Elena discovered that her track record was of little value in finding a new job that was even close to the quality of the old one:

> I collected unemployment for a year . . . [I worked] part time [in a dry cleaning business]. Then I worked in a restaurant . . . until 1983. Finally I found [my present] part-time job in the airport cleaning the airplanes. I started as a cleaning lady.
>
> Losing my [Singer] job had a tremendous impact on me. I didn't have nothing. We still have bills and things. . . Factories are the worst in my mind now . . . Nothing is secure anymore . . . I think all the companies are going to close.[4]

4 Originally quoted in Newman, *Falling From Grace,* 181.

Elena's experience has been replicated by millions of others who found themselves thrown from the unionized, benefit-safe, world of stable blue-collar employment into the universe of unprotected, part-time, low-wage jobs that do not pay enough to keep a family. Having lost her seniority, Elena now works the night shift and hopes not only that she can hang on to this job but that her husband, also a blue-collar worker, will not be jettisoned as she was. There is no security left, certainly nothing to look forward to in the future that is half as reliable as the old Singer company once was.

For Elena, however, more than just the Singer firm is gone. A whole way of life, an entire social contract, has been destroyed. The loyalty that bound her family, and hundreds of immigrant families before her, to the firm has been replaced by a fragile, wary, and instrumental work relationship. She does not put her faith in the airline that employs her now; she does not believe any firm is likely to return the faith at all. Traditions that glued workers to management, even in the face of labor conflict, have disappeared across the manufacturing landscape. Craftsmanship, pride in the product – all of this appears to have gone by the boards as blue-collar workers discover that they are eminently replaceable: by computers, by non-union labor, by hungry people in far away lands willing to work for nickels.

Yet unlike David Patterson, Elena does not blame herself for the loss of the Singer job. Her anger is directed at a firm which she believes lost its soul and its character, and at the government which did nothing to protect blue-collar workers in the face of imports that beat domestic prices down. She holds herself responsible, as does David, for finding new work, but she does not subject herself to the withering internal critique that has debilitated him even as he continued to look for work.

These are two faces of downward mobility, the profiles of people who never expected to think of themselves as needy. They were the self-reliant ones who believed until recently that they could manage their own affairs, requiring help from no one. David Patterson discovered that he needed others badly, but that there was no one who was interested in his plight. Elena managed, but at the cost of her standard of living and her prospects for the future. She cannot look toward retirement, a pension, or health care, for none of this is provided by her new part-time job. Their experience is characteristic of the fate of millions of Americans who worked hard and thought they had it made, only to discover that they have lost virtually everything.

GENERATION GAPS

Downward mobility has other faces as well. Americans who came of age after the mid-1970s, including the lion's share of the baby boom generation, have discovered that even if they can keep unemployment at bay, they are not likely to see the standard of living with which they were raised. Women like Lauren Calder, whose words opened this chapter, are discovering that despite educational credentials and job records that surpass their parents, their standard of living leaves much to be desired. The generations that entered the labor market after the mid-1970s found themselves at a marked disadvantage in virtually every respect. Jobs, particularly good jobs, were more competitive, with hundreds more people chasing them than there were positions to fill. Housing markets boomed – fine for those already over the hump of home ownership – leaving those not yet in the market stranded by astronomical price increases and escalating interest rates.

According to the National Housing Task Force, a congressional panel formed in 1987 by Senator Alfonse D'Amato and Senator Alan Cranston, nearly two million *fewer* families own their own home today than there would have been if the rates of home ownership common just a decade ago had been sustained throughout the 1980s.[5] Yet even as these numbers went down, some people were doing fairly well in the housing market: Americans over the age of 60 and whites in general increased their share of the home ownership market. For one or two demographic groups to improve their lot while national averages decline can only mean one thing: somebody has to have done much worse in the housing sweepstakes. The somebodies were members of the baby boom generation who have been locked out of the American dream in increasing numbers.

Older Americans saw their rates of home ownership climb dramatically from the mid-1970s to the early 1990s. Particularly advantaged during this period were people in the 55–75 age group, the very group that benefited in the first place from the government policies of the postwar period that provided low-cost mortgages. This support made it possible for them to get into the housing market early and stay there. As William Apgar, associate director of Harvard University's Joint Center for Housing Studies, put it, "After World War II, we made home ownership

5 By 1991 the national home ownership rate recovered to 64.1%. But this upturn masks the profound generation gap discussed in the next section.

much more available to people at a younger age than before, with the Veterans Administration and Federal Home Authority and other programs. [The postwar generation] was able to start earlier and own their own homes longer, and that's where the equity build-up comes from . . ."[6]

Baby boomers had exactly the opposite experience. In every age group under 44, home ownership rates dropped dramatically between 1973 and 1990. Rates for boomers now in their midthirties suffered a drop of nearly 10% over that period, with younger people sustaining similar declines. Americans under the age of 35, which includes many of the nation's boomers, found themselves excluded from the home buying market. The younger members of the baby boom generation, the men and women who came of age in the Reagan era, were especially disadvantaged: in 1973 over 23% of the people in this age group owned their own homes; by 1990 that figure dropped to about 15%. Not surprisingly, these figures were reflected in a substantial jump in the average age of first-time home buyers. In the early 1980s, the median age of the first-time buyer was 27. By 1991 it had risen to 35 – an astonishing jump in less than a decade.[7]

These trends have had an impact that goes well beyond the roofs over the heads of the nation's boomers. They have taken an equal toll on their confidence, on their sense of belonging, and most especially on their capacity to care for the next generation – the children of the 1990s. This became clear in the course of a two-year study of a suburban enclave in northern New Jersey which I call "Pleasanton." This bedroom community, a mere 20 minutes from New York City, was a modest, middle-income, economically diverse community whose growth – such as it was – dates to the 1950s and 60s. The completion of the highway system that now links suburban New Jersey to the New York orbit made it possible for families to live in places like Pleasanton and ride the freeways to work. Low-cost housing and cheap mortgages put Pleasanton in reach of GIs and their brides, and they moved in droves to this quiet community, a stone's throw from the George Washington Bridge. Thirty years later –

6 Quoted in the *New York Times,* "Home Ownership – A Receding Dream," (20 October 1991), Sec. 10: 1, 10.

7 Joint Center tabulations of the 1973, 1976, and 1980 American Housing Survey, and the 1983, 1987, and 1990 Current Population Survey, compiled by the *San Francisco Chronicle,* "A Shift in Who Owns Homes" (29 November 1991), A1, A20.

and with no visible change in the housing stock – the dream began to fade for the boomers. Throughout the 1970s and 80s, housing prices in Pleasanton skyrocketed. At the same time, job opportunities flattened out, and even with two earners in a household, the bucolic suburbs of their childhood years became untouchable for the boomers. Pleasanton has become an affluent town populated by professionals and well-paid managers. The Lauren Caulders of the world, born and bred in Pleasanton, haven't a prayer of being able to move into the town now. It is out of reach.

Wendy Norman, a high school classmate of Lauren Caulder's, spends a lot of time thinking about the advantages her parents conferred upon her: comfort without extravagance, a life of cultural enrichment developed through ballet lessons, the occasional theater trip, and lazy summer days down at the pool. While Wendy was lucky to have all these things, her parents were fortunate too. The economic history of the 1950s made it possible for them to do far more for Wendy than their own parents had been able to do for them in the dreary days of the Great Depression. The Normans took pride and pleasure in watching Wendy absorb the cultural advantages they could provide. But Wendy is fairly certain she will not feel a similar glow of satisfaction that comes from knowing that she has "done right" by her own kids:

> I guess our grandparents and our parents, what kept them moving and motivated was that they were trying to do for their children. Improve their children's lot. I think they achieved that and for the most part were probably happy in it. That gave them the happiness, the self-fulfillment. I don't think we have that in our generation.

Wendy, and her baby boom counterparts across the nation, are worried that those critical advantages, those aspects of personal biography which sociologists call "cultural capital," may be lost to the children of the 1980s and 1990s. They may have to settle for much less: for mediocre schools, libraries that are closing down for lack of revenue, residence in less affluent communities with fewer amenities.

Today's middle-class parents are only too aware of how problematic such a scenario could be for their children. Kids who do not go to good high schools have a hard time finding their way into competitive colleges. They are disadvantaged in their efforts to get into professional schools or to land high paying jobs. In short, the connection between cultural advantage and social prestige has never been more definitive, particularly in the eyes of those baby boom parents who were, themselves, the beneficiaries of middle-class advantage. Nancy knows all too well that she would be doing even *worse* in the 1990s were it not for the educational credentials her parents bestowed upon her. She is bombarded daily with news headlines that proclaim education the key to the nation's prosperity, along with daily public hand wringing over the quality of America's schools. The message is abundantly clear: her child's future depends upon the educational and cultural resources she provides. If these are less than what it takes, Nancy's kid will reap the consequences.

If the baby boom generation is bewildered and disturbed by this sudden turn of events, their parents – the generation that entered adulthood in the affluent years following World War II – are even more confused. They see themselves as living proof of the vitality of the American dream. Children of the Great Depression who were raised in cramped working-class enclaves of the nation's cities, they came of age in a time of war, emerging into peace time along with the benefits of the GI Bill, the VA mortgage, cheap land, a booming housing market, and a seemingly endless expansion in every conceivable industry.[8] Young men whose fathers crossed the Atlantic in steerage (and were satisfied if they could land a steady job in a sweat shop), ended up in America's finest universities and fueled an unprecedented expansion of the country's middle class. They became engineers, doctors, lawyers, businessmen – the first professionals in their family lines. The sky was the limit. As these post-war parents tell the story, anyone who was willing to work hard could literally make their dreams come true.

Both generations – those who rode the wave of post-war affluence and those who have fallen into the trough of post-industrial decline – pose questions about their divergent paths, largely in the privacy of their homes and in casual conversation with friends. The declining fortunes of the baby boom cohort, while the subject of an occasional magazine piece or newspaper article, have yet to become the platform for a social movement, or the rallying cry of a new age politician.[9] Indeed, for many

8 Glen Elder's classic study of the long-term impact of the Depression on children shows that the cohort which endured its devastation as youngsters, emerging into the labor market during World War II, fared quite well in terms of overall life satisfaction as well as occupational experience, marital quality, and psychological health. *Children of the Great Depression: Social Change in Life Experience* (Chicago: University of Chicago Press, 1974).

9 Gary Hart, Democratic senator from Colorado, was among the first to try and capture a post-war generation through a vision of new values. Lee Atwater, the late mastermind of the Republican party, argued that the 1980s had given

Americans the personal strain of coping with disappointed expectations and dashed ambitions is so great that little energy is left over for analyzing their own experience as symptomatic of far-reaching, structural disorders in the U.S. economy.

In the long run these very issues will dominate the policy landscape in America as we move into the twenty-first century. For ultimately the question of who is entitled to the good life in America, and who must pay to help those excluded from the golden circle, must be resolved if we are to avoid the shredding of the social fabric. There is plenty of evidence to show, albeit in isolated ways thus far, that such a shredding process is already underway. If we are to avoid a future characterized by an "every man for himself" philosophy, a credo that cannot sustain any society for long, we must look long and hard at the impact of intergenerational downward mobility and ask what it means in cultural as well as practical terms.

WHAT HAPPENED TO THE AMERICAN DREAM?

Although Pleasanton residents are not economists, and do not lay claim to professional expertise in these matters, they have a fairly good grasp of the immediate culprits that have exiled the town's baby boomers from their native community. Four related phenomena come to their minds when they explain how their slice of the American dream has eroded away: escalating housing prices, occupational insecurity, blocked mobility on the job, and the cost of living squeeze that has penalized the boomer generation, even when they have more education and better jobs than their parents have.

That housing prices have escalated beyond all comprehension comes as no news to post-war parents. By sitting still and doing almost nothing, they have seen the value of their most important asset rise to levels that are, by their own standards, stratospheric. In the course of the 1980s, real estate became a language and a way of life. Dinner party gossip revolved around how much houses on the block were going for and who was making a killing on what piece of property. It seemed, and still seems to many in Pleasanton, as though there was nothing else to talk about,

birth to a new generation that could be captured by the conservatives. Bill Clinton and Albert Gore, taking a page from John Kennedy's book, show some signs of speaking to generational issues.

nothing as captivating as money being made in the form of four bedroom colonials.

The odd thing about this sudden wealth was that it made the process of accumulating capital effortless, almost magical. Compared to the effort involved in working for a living, real estate profits were incredibly easy to pile up. Dumb luck – being in the right place at the right time – and some modest resources were all that was needed to get into the game.

Simon Rittenberg was a salesman for nearly forty years for a factory that manufactures security devices for use in businesses and homes. He has the hearty, confident character of the ideal salesman even though he has been retired for some time. Like everyone else who grew up in a little apartment during the Depression, it had always been his dream to have a house of his own. Simon was always worried about how he would pay it off. It never occurred to him that he could pile up a little fortune just by hanging on to the house. But when he became a widower and the house was just too big for a lone man, he sold out and discovered how much "doing nothing" had done for his bank account:

> I don't think I had the intelligence to know that by moving, coming to this country, that I would do so well. All I knew was that my father had always rented. He never owned anything. He rented his store, and he rented his apartment. And now I was going to take this big leap into owning a home, which would be mine, my castle. I don't know if that was right or wrong, but I know I was lucky. Because after 35 years, my $17,000 became $285,000 when I sold [the house]. So was that brilliance on my part?
>
> Now I'm a big shot: I made some kind of great deal! The economics of it didn't have anything to do with me. It had to do with the world, what happened.

While Simon is happy enough to have this fat bank account, he takes greater pride in the achievements of his work life than he does the lucrative side effects of the housing mania of the 1980s. He does not feel responsible for his good fortune, though he is not unhappy to have it. It has become emblematic of a kind of real estate madness that seems to have descended on the world, or at least his small corner of it.

Were this madness only positive in its impact, Simon would not be troubled long by its benefits. Yet his son, Ron, has been driven out by the very same forces that provided him with such fantastic rewards. Ron Rittenberg is nearly 40 now and lives in Washington, D.C., where he works for a federal agency that provides information to criminal justice agencies around the country. He has a 3-year-old son and a wife who works full time. They live in suburban Maryland in a community that is nowhere near the level of affluence that Pleasanton represents. Ron just laughs when asked to compare the community he lives in now with the Pleasanton of his youth. The flip side of the father's good fortune is the son's flight to a less expensive community, far away from his kin.

Of course, the escalating cost of housing is not the only divide separating the post-war parents from their baby boom children. Jobs are harder to find and far more insecure in all respects. Pleasant's progeny were well-educated by any standard and they parlayed that advantage into job qualifications that often exceeded anything their parents had had to offer employers in years gone by. The sons of skilled blue-collar workers got college degrees and became accountants. The daughters of non-working, high school educated mothers, nearly all went on to higher education, often finding jobs as teachers or managers. Yet even with these credentials in hand, success did not come easily to the boomers. Where their parents found an expanding job market with an inexhaustible thirst for their talents, the baby boom generation has found a crowded, competitive market where they are often deemed expendable.

Security is not easy to come by these days; it is a concern that looms very large in the lives of those who were raised in the prosperous, stable 1950s and the roaring, expansive 1960s. Contractions, leveraged buyouts, bankruptcies, layoffs, and general despair over the state of American competitiveness – these are the watchwords of today's business pages. Nothing in the boomers' upbringing, schooling, or early experience in the labor market prepared them for what we must all confront now: the fact that the U.S. economy cannot provide the kind of job opportunities or personal security that the country took for granted in earlier generations.

Martin O'Rourke, now in his early forties, got a first-hand taste of this nasty medicine when he worked for an auto company in the early 1980s. Martin's father was a blue-collar man through and through, but Martin was a talented artist. Overruling family objections, he decided to go into commercial drawing. Ultimately he ended up starting his own small business where he continues to make a reasonable living today. But his early inclinations were not in an entrepreneurial direction. He thought he'd be a company man, until he witnessed what happens to loyal company men:

> The real reason I quit the company was that my office was next door to a man who had worked for the company since 1955. He was the oldest employee in the company, and he was 62 years old when I met him. On a Friday afternoon at 4:30 they fired him. He had been a very important man

> in the company and he lived and breathed his work. He was in charge of all the warehouses across the country – all the parts warehouses. They decided to consolidate the warehouses and figured he would be unnecessary. So they just fired him. I'll never forget that day. He was in his office and he was crying and I asked what happened. I thought maybe his wife died or something horrible happened and he just handed me this piece of paper that said he was no longer needed by the company.
>
> I went home and said to my wife, I've got to leave, quit. I can't go on with this job because I'm just as devoted to my work. I lived and breathed my job too and I was 100% a company guy and worked insane hours for them. For what? So I could wind up like him? Be just let off? At age 62, where's this man going to go? And my feeling was that I just had to be in control . . .

In the 1980s a new habit began to spread through corporate America, a tradition of declining loyalty of firm to worker and a consequent wariness among younger employees of depending upon any job for permanent security.[10] We are used to the fact that our manufacturing industries are on the skids and few of Pleasanton's progeny were headed in that direction. They were, and are now, white-collar bound. But this has hardly protected them, their parents, or their friends from the shakeouts and shutdowns that have plagued the service industries. New York City, where many Pleasanton boomers work, has lost over 100,000 jobs since 1987, many of them white-collar positions.[11] Martin O'Rourke watched the axe fall on an older, long-time employee, and it scared him enough to abandon the corporate world altogether. His fear was well justified since few age groups have been spared the pressure of mounting layoffs and white-collar dislocation. Many a 30- and 40-year-old has been handed a pink slip in the long aftermath of the stock market crash in 1987.[12]

10 For an ethnographic study of workers' views of American industry, see Katherine S. Newman, *Falling From Grace: The Experience of Downward Mobility in the American Middle Class* (New York: Free Press, 1988), Ch. 6; and Katherine S. Newman, "Turning Your Back on Tradition: Symbolic Analysis and Moral Critique in a Plant Shutdown," *Urban Anthropology,* 14:1–3 (1985): 109–150.

11 "Workers Must Choose as Jobs Move," *New York Times* (11 April 1991), B1.

12 Parents of the boomer generation find these trends equally frightening. The unpredictable swings in the local economy remind them all too easily of earlier economic disasters they lived through as children in the Depression. As Simon Rittenberg sees it, things are just going from bad to worse:

> I think there are going to be a lot of psychological breakdowns because of this economic uncertainty. I really do. I hope to hell it doesn't happen and I don't

Among those who *have* managed to escape the abyss of unemployment in the 1980s and early 1990s, other problems have contributed to an intergenerational decline. Upward mobility within the ranks of American firms is leveling out at an earlier age for baby boomers than was true for their fathers in the expansive post-war period. When business was booming in the U.S., management pyramids just kept on growing. A large cadre of newly minted B.A.s (courtesy of the GI Bill) flooded into the market place and advanced quickly up the ranks. Business growth remained strong as they reached their 40s and this was reflected in continuous career growth. For these post-war men, careers tended to level off in their 50s and began the slow descent to retirement as they entered their 60s. While some were caught and crushed by the years of high unemployment in the early 1980s, most managed to escape the crunch of the Reagan recession and are coasting still on reasonable pensions and high home equity.

Sons and daughters who began their careers in the 1970s and 1980s have encountered tremendous competition for the "good jobs" and flatter job pyramids that level off at distressingly early ages. Charles Aberstein, whose son Larry graduated from Pleasanton's main high school ten years ago, has noticed how much harder it is to make one's way in the job market now than it was when he started out:

> We're in a different kind of life environment today than we were thirty years ago. There's lots more competition. There's many more college graduates and fewer and fewer positions. Many of the good jobs have been exported to the Pacific. Major industries have fled the U.S. There are that many fewer executive level positions here and yet many candidates for them. It's a more competitive world than the one that I grew up in. [Larry's] aware of it. He'll find his way, but it won't be easy as it was for me.

Charles climbed the job ladder toward a vice-presidency in an insurance firm, but he knows that Larry will find the same kind of ascent less assured. Many baby boomers are discovering that the sheer size of their generation ensures that there are too many of them chasing too few

> think it will be as severe as what my parents went through [in the thirties], but I see it happening. You pick up the *New York Times* this morning, Wang Corporation is laying off 2,000 people. Oh boy, that's a lot of people. Mobil Oil, Esso, they're all laying off people. The economics of these takeovers that are taking place and then selling these companies in parts, only means one thing: the people lose jobs, the companies do not exist after they get through cutting them up.

options. Moving up from entry-level positions to middle management seemed easy enough; the next step has become increasingly difficult.

Under the best of circumstances only a few of the millions of baby boomers will see advancement into executive ranks. Many will see the zenith of their careers arrive in their 40s, leaving twenty or thirty more years of their work lives with unchanged horizons (if they are lucky enough to escape the pressures of downsizing or business collapse). Beyond the boredom leveling off entails, its financial consequences are significant as well: boomers will not see the continued increases in salaries that might eventually pull them up to an even point with their parents. Leveling off, coupled with increasingly frequent recessions, or inflationary pressures will translate into a long-term erosion in their standard of living, a standard which has fallen short of their expectations to begin with.

The combination of high housing costs, occupational insecurity, and slowing potential for advancement in the workplace has meant that the baby boom generation is subject to an intense squeeze. Stagnation is the lot of the boomers.[13] Yet the demands upon their resources, far from slowing, have accelerated. Now in the midst of their child-bearing years, they face mounting costs for everything from clothing to child care, education to transportation. The proportion of their income that must go toward these essentials seems, from their parents' perspective, far more than was required in "the good old days." As one older mother put it, her children are working hard not to get ahead of her but in order to prevent themselves slipping even farther backwards:

> Our income was so low when we first got married, but we got a brand new auto for $1,800. Our son David earns $20,000 teaching kids. For him a new car costs $16,000. It's just the proportion! When I went to Radcliffe, it cost $3,200 a year. Maybe my father was only earning $9,000. But for David, Harvard would cost $20,000 a year and that's a lot more than one-third of his father's income . . . Usually there's an improvement in each generation and what they're able to get. But I think with our kids they're going backwards. Much more austere kind of lifestyle.

13 After 1973, real wage growth and thus family income growth stagnated. As a result, individuals who came of age during this period face what Frank Levy calls an "inequality of prospects" relative to the generation that came before them. Frank S. Levy, *Dollars and Dreams: The Changing American Income Distribution* (New York: W. W. Norton, 1987); and Frank S. Levy and Richard C. Michel, *The Economic Future of American Families: Income and Wealth Trends* (Washington, D.C.: Urban Institute, 1991).

Disparities between generations along these basic economic lines inevitably lead to strain and a background jealousy. Boomers do not wish their parents ill or feel that their good fortune was undeserved. They just want to know why the run of luck did not hold long enough to include them, why they have to put up with the penny-pinching struggles that Lauren Caulder complains of so bitterly:

> You just sit there and look, and watch how everything that seemed reasonable to wish for has somehow flown – I really think in the last two or three years. Partly because there's so many of us pushing prices up . . . It's not as if it's a mystery why this should be happening. It's just a shame that you have to wake up and smell the coffee like that.

Lauren believes that an arbitrary force intervened to damage her time in the sun. She is having to pay the penalty for living in an era of economic disarray, for being part of a huge generation that has overwhelmed every market it touches – from the schools, to professions, and no doubt some day the retirement homes. But it is often hard for them to hold on to this structural explanation, this macropicture of demography and economics, interest rates and international competition. What they can see is the discordant biographies that put their own childhood experiences of normal middle-class existence out of reach now that they have reached their middle-aged years.

Many boomers have had the good fortune to exceed their parents in education and in occupational prestige. The problem is that these superior credentials no longer seem to "buy" a superior, or even equal, lifestyle. Mary Flory's experience provides a case in point. Her parents are working-class people who were fortunate enough to settle in Pleasanton when that was still possible for families of modest means. Mary and her husband have moved up in the world; he, in particular, is an educated white-collar man. Nonetheless, they have fallen way behind Mary's parents in terms of the lifestyle they can afford:

> My father was an elevator operator all his life. My husband is a teacher. I would have thought right away of course we could afford to live in Pleasanton. We have better jobs. But we couldn't. There is no way we could live there. I really couldn't believe that I couldn't live in the town that I grew up in. I don't know what it says.

American culture is based in large part on an underlying social Darwinism that sees survival of the fittest as a just rule. We believe that those who are well equipped to compete will reap material rewards and that, conversely, those who cannot "cut the mustard" will (and should) feel the sting of deprivation. For the past fifty years or more, the dominance of white-collar work in the U.S. prestige hierarchy has meant that we define the "fittest" as those who are educated, those who can lay claim to a professional identity.[14] On this view of the natural order of things, blue-collar employment should not be rewarded nearly as well as "mental" work. Jobs that require a strong back are honorable enough, but they do not deserve the kind of payoff that thought-jobs do.

In Mary Flory's case, the reverse rule seems to apply. Her perfectly respectable, but clearly unskilled father, could afford to buy into Pleasanton, but her educated, professional husband is locked out. The upside-down quality of this arrangement is entirely illegitimate from Mary's point of view, and there is considerable cultural support for her way of thinking. There is no justice in the notion that Mr. Flory was in the right place at the right time, while Mary and her husband had the bad taste to be born at the wrong historical moment. It is an arbitrary feature of post-war history. Yet arbitrariness barely begins to capture Mary's response. She is angry, frustrated, and above all bewildered by this reversal of what "ought to be."

For most of Pleasanton's boomers, the cost of living squeeze is here to stay. They do not see any way out of this mess and this conclusion, in and of itself, is a source of depression. Weathering hard times is one thing. Accepting that the inter-generational slide is a permanent fact of life is quite another. Yet, as Cathy Larson sees it, there is no reason for the realistic person to see the situation in a rosier light:

> This has gone on for so long, I don't know why it should be any different tomorrow. You know, you tell yourself constantly that you can get over the hump. But it's just an ongoing thing. It's a life of credit cards. It's a life of bills. It's a life of living beyond your means.

In Cathy's life, financial limitations create what she calls a "low-burning thing," a subtext of constraint, a feeling that she is not free. This, above all, is the meaning of the inter-generational slide: the freedom to consume

14 See Kathryn Dudley, *The End of the Line: Political Conflict and Cultural Antagonism in the Industrial Midwest* (Chicago: University of Chicago Press, 1993), for an interesting discussion of this Darwinist ideology in practice in Kenosha, Wisconsin, where auto workers are being told they deserve to lose their jobs and standard of living to the white-collar elites since they never really deserved to have these benefits in the first place.

is cut short, the ability to plan for the long run is limited, and the bitter sense of rules turned inside out makes people feel, to use Cathy's words, like "it was all a big lie."

THE END OF ENTITLEMENT

Financial pressures facing the baby boom generation have profoundly affected every aspect of their private and public lives. From the most intimate decisions about whether or when to have children, to the most pragmatic questions of career choices, virtually every serious decision they have had to make about their lives has been dictated by conflicting desires based on economic limitations. On the one hand, the boomers are loath to give up the critical hallmarks of middle-class life, and cling tenaciously to the idea that by working harder (more hours, more workers in a household) they can lay claim to their share of the American dream.

At the same time, they face pressures to conform to ideals of family organization and child rearing that were feasible in the 1950s and 1960s, but are no longer easily achieved. Despite the revolution of the women's movement, which has brought thousands of women (including mothers of young children) into the workplace, the image of nurturing, omnipresent mother has yet to fade away. Indeed, for the boomers themselves, she is a vivid memory, not just an abstraction. The post-war generation was largely raised by women who either retired from the factories and offices they had worked in during World War II or never worked in the paid labor market at all. The domestic front, they were told, was a woman's natural destiny.[15]

While the women's movement did succeed in dismantling the notion that women belong in the kitchen and the kitchen only, it did not succeed in shifting the burden of child rearing to a fifty–fifty proposition. As Arlie Hochschild has pointed out in her remarkable book, *The Second Shift,* women are still fighting that battle and mainly losing.[16] American society

15 In 1940, female labor force participation was at 27.9 percent. By 1944, it was up to 36.3 percent, dropping to 35.8 percent in 1945 and 30.8 percent in 1946. *Historical Statistics of the United States: Colonial Times to 1970* (Washington, D.C.: U.S. Department of Commerce, Bureau of the Census, 1975).

16 Arlie R. Hochschild, *The Second Shift: Working Parents and the Revolution at Home* (New York: Viking Press, 1989).

still looks upon women as the crucible of moral development in young children, charges them with the responsibility for making sure the kids "turn out right." Child-rearing women are told in so many ways that they cannot afford to "mess up." Where social movements encouraged women to broaden their horizons and take up their fair share of the burden of earning a living, personal history and cultural norms tell the same women that they had better be sure they have done a good job raising their children. Can this be done from the vantage point of the workplace? No one is sure it's possible; many are vocally skeptical.

The problem is, of course, that by the early 1980s it became clear that holding on to a middle-class lifestyle would be hard to do absent two income earners in a household. How could husbands support their families alone? How could wives live up to their obligations as moral mothers when their incomes were needed to keep the mortgage payments going? This core contradiction has found no easy resolution; for these cultural and political dilemmas, while usually understood as moral debates, are inseparably tied to the declining fortunes of the baby boom generation.

There are those – even in Pleasanton – who might say, "Why don't the post-war parents help out? If they benefited so much from the boom years, don't they have the resources to rescue their kids?" Even if Pleasanton parents were inclined toward rescue missions, inclined to ignore the cultural prescription that calls for every generation to stand on its own two feet, they lack the wherewithal to prop up their adult children's standard of living.[17] Having had their children at comparatively young ages, the post-war generation of parents find themselves relatively young, with many years of self-financed retirement left. Baby boomers in their 40s often find themselves with parents who are in their 60s, parents who can expect to live for twenty years or more on the resources they garnered during the boom years. In particular, the equity value of their homes – generally the largest single item of value in their personal portfolios – will serve as the main bank account they will draw upon in their retirement years. Where growing old once meant growing poor, social security, pub-

17 Marcia Millman, *Warm Hearts and Cold Cash: How Families Handle Money and What This Reveals About Them* (New York: Free Press, 1991), suggests that parents often bestow money on their children or grandchildren. She is talking about people who have a net worth in excess of $500,000 and income enough to support a lavish retirement. Most Pleasanton residents don't have resources like that. Indeed, most Americans don't have resources even close to that level.

lic and private pensions, and home equity now means that the golden generation that hit the post-war boom will also enjoy the most comfortable retirement ever made available to an American generation. They will, that is, if they can hold on to their resources and fund their sunset years themselves.

Medical care costs have skyrocketed in the past decade, as has the cost of maintaining a loved one in a nursing home. Pleasanton parents are all too aware of the expenses involved in the long haul. Moreover, they have little faith that they will be able to depend on anyone else, whether government or members of their own family, to provide for them as they age. Whatever pressure they may feel to help the next generation over the hump, especially over the hump of home ownership, collides with the knowledge that they must husband what they have for the long years ahead.

Were the long-term future the only concern, many Pleasanton parents would undoubtedly try to do something for their struggling boomers. But the present is causing enough problems all by itself, for the fiscal crisis that has beset many a suburban community has generated demands for property tax revenues that are proving ever more difficult for the post-war generation to meet. In Pleasanton itself, property taxes have increased nearly *sixfold* in the past twenty years. For many old timers, who moved to Pleasanton when it was a modest town (on the strength of modest incomes), taxes have proven to be the final straw.

Mary and Sam Kinder moved to Pleasanton in the 1950s, even though they could barely afford a down payment. Sam owned a local hardware store that was bought out by a chain. He now does construction work in the city, driving a tractor trailer on hauling jobs. Mary works for a perfume franchise that has concessions in big department stores and has done so since her youngest child was 10 years old. Married fresh out of high school, the Kinders raised four kids in Pleasanton and lived in one house for almost thirty-eight years. It has not been easy for them financially, but they scraped by and thought things would ease up now that the kids are largely on their own.

Tax increases have put an end to the dream of coasting into retirement. When Sam retires, they are selling out and moving south to join their oldest son who long ago concluded that he too could not afford to live in Pleasanton. Their neighbor Mrs. Floury found the tax problem an even bigger burden since she was a widow and truly unable to meet her legal obligations. Mary Floury speaks with considerable bitterness about the way her mother was chased out by the tax bite:

> The reason my mother moved to Florida was because the taxes had gone up again in Pleasanton. My father had died. She was still working at the local restaurant. This was in 1977. She was house poor. She was the only one living in a three-bedroom house and it was a struggle to keep afloat. She went to Borough Hall and said that she was really having trouble paying her taxes. What should she do? They told her to leave. She was so hurt. She had been living there since 1951. They don't have a heart. They just want her money. It really hurt her that they said leave.

Although many of the post-war migrants to Pleasanton have found themselves sitting on residential gold mines, the tax consequences of this increase have made it increasingly difficult for them to remain in the community they consider to be their own. Pressures to move out grow as they age and face the prospect of declining income.

A growing uneasiness with the social character of Pleasanton is also responsible for making the old timers feel that they are no longer entirely welcome. Pleasanton was, by all accounts, a very ordinary community in the 1950s and 1960s. It was (and still is) pretty and peaceful, but it was not socially exclusive. Mary Floury's father, the elevator operator, and Rhonda Carland's dad, the chemistry professor, lived together and accepted their differences since few in the community were "really rich." Pleasanton families thought of themselves as ordinary middle-class people (even though by national standards they were quite well off). People who wanted to "put on airs" did not move to Pleasanton; they settled in other, nearby communities that already had established reputations as havens of the wealthy, replete as they were with country clubs, chauffeurs, and genuine mansions.

Yet as the cost of housing grew, the new families who moved to Pleasanton in the 1980s were far more affluent as a group than many of the old timers. A social gap has opened up between the skilled blue-collar workers and middle-level management types who founded the post-war community, and the highly paid professionals who are the only people that can afford to buy into this desirable suburb these days. There are no manual workers, jewelry store clerks, or hardware store owners among today's migrants to Pleasanton. Newcomers are partners in big city law firms, executives in large corporations, and specialist physicians. Their tastes, their desires, and their more privatized lifestyle have subtly eroded the communal flavor of life in Pleasanton, setting the tone for a more genteel, upper-crust local culture. Long-time residents like the James family do not feel entirely comfortable with this shift. Keith James, who is in his late 20s now, looks back upon the change with the sense that something valuable has been lost in the shuffle:

> By the time I graduated from high school in 1980, the town was just barely affordable. But there were still all the same kind of families. I feel now that Pleasanton has totally turned around. It's become basically a very affluent neighborhood, you know, because it's near Manhattan. You see a lot of new . . . groups coming into town. And we're getting a lot of doctors. It's pushing people out. I can remember when someone's parents lived in town, maybe someone's grandparents lived in Pleasanton, and there was some sort of return to the town. But that's totally changing.

It is not unusual to hear those who know they cannot afford to live in the community now argue that it has changed so much they would not really want to locate there anymore. As one of Keith's classmates put the matter, "I wouldn't really want to live in Pleasanton now. They have a lot of rich people that have moved in that are kind of snobby." As the burden caused by the high cost of living mounts, the change in the social climate in town leaves old timers feeling that the community they may need to vacate is no longer quite the same place anyway. It belongs to a different class of richer Americans.

Mindful of the possibility that their worries will be discounted as so much bleating by spoiled, demanding, perfectly comfortable baby boomers to whom the nation owes nothing, they are quick to point out that in an absolute sense they have much to be grateful for. Neither the boomers nor their parents confuse their experience with that of the poor or believe that they deserve an outpouring of sympathy to soothe their disappointments. They understand that relative to the "truly disadvantaged,"[18] they live a charmed existence.

Nonetheless, they live simultaneously with a diffuse sense of dissatisfaction and an underlying desire to fix the blame on someone or some group of individuals who has derailed the journey they thought they had tickets for. They are especially perplexed by the arbitrary character of the trends that have had such a profound influence over their standard of

18 To use William Julius Wilson's phrase. *The Truly Disadvantaged: The Inner City, the Underclass, and Public Policy* (Chicago: University of Chicago Press, 1987).

living. It has escaped no one's attention that two generations living side by side have encountered drastically divergent life chances. As Martin O'Rourke puts it, "Times have changed. I don't expect to walk in my parents' footsteps. I won't have the same opportunities they had."

Americans believe themselves to be resourceful people. If there are obstacles in the way of prosperity, we will clear them away. If the rules of the game have changed, we will learn to play by the new ones. Unfortunately, it would appear that we cannot figure out what today's rules really are. We are drowning in a kind of national confusion, floundering in our attempts to find a way out, all the while wondering why the old formula no longer pays off.

With every day that goes by, the unseen hands of the international economy seem to interfere more and more in our most intimate decisions: when to marry, when to have children, where we can live, how easily we can remain in our chosen communities, whether we will be able to enjoy our sunset years or will have to worry about every dime. And on all of these counts, the largest living generation of Americans are doing worse, enjoying less of the good life than those who came before them, most notably their own parents.

The baby boom generation experiences this decline as a boa constrictor wrapped around their eroding sense of freedom. Decisions that were once left to the vagaries of emotion are now calculated down to the last nickel; risks that could once be taken with educational pathways or careers are now out of the question, too dangerous by half. If being careful would cure the disease of downward mobility, baby boomers would at least have a strategy for overcoming the obstacles the economy has placed in their way. But in truth, being careful, making all the right choices, is no guarantee that the future will work the way it is supposed to. Indeed, for many of the nation's youngest boomers – the Reagan generation – who put aside risks and dreams in favor of the pragmatic course, economic history has been unkind in the extreme. No amount of deferred gratification will buy them the gratification they want: sky-rocketing prices, stagnating wages, dissipating promotion prospects, and the relentless pressure of an economy that just does not seem to work any more – these are the forces and trends that are closing in like the vise grip of the boa.

But the boomers are hardly the only Americans in trouble. Indeed, there are few generations or regions that have managed to stay out of harm's way. Those who have experienced downward mobility in their own adult lives, who like David Patterson have had to watch their dreams flow down the drain, are often lost in the wilderness of downward mobility. Their numbers have grown as the economy has worsened, as unemployment remains persistently high, and as temporary jobs, or poorly paid jobs, come to replace what was once a well-endowed labor market. Politicians and educators alike speak about the importance of training, of skill, of education, issues that are like motherhood and apple pie. What can they say to people like David Patterson – well educated, hard working, and eager to get back into the game – who followed all the rules and now find themselves stranded, diplomas in hand?

THE SOCIAL CONTRACT UNDER STRESS

Most disturbing for the nation as a whole has been the erosion of a sense of national purpose and collective commitment in the face of these pressures. In many communities, and indeed in many families, the sense that one's back is up against the wall is contributing to a rampant form of individualism. School bond issues are turned back in record numbers as elderly residents refuse to pay for the educational needs of new generations. Suburban dwellers look with anger upon city dwellers who seem hungry for their tax dollars. Racial antagonism grows in urban centers and segregated suburbs, another unholy manifestation of the shrinking pie.

The United States is caught in the middle of a transition that few economists can explain and few politicians appear capable of addressing. For ordinary people, for those whose lives have been tossed about by structural trends not of their making, solutions to America's economic decline are eagerly awaited, but no longer confidently expected. Indeed, their very faith in the institutions of government has been seriously undermined.

Presidents Reagan and Bush assured the nation that their conservative policies would right the egregious wrongs of the Carter years and what they defined as the dismal performance of congressional Democrats. Old timers in Pleasanton gave credence to such a view until they realized, some twelve years down the Republican road, that their children were worse off than they were at the same age, with no end in sight to downward mobility. The rock-ribbed conservatives in the executive and managerial ranks who have now felt the sharp edge of corporate restructuring are similarly at a loss to explain why the policies of the past dozen years have left them stranded outside the labor market with little hope of a decent future. At the same time, having bought the Republican argument that liberal Democrats of the 1970s had ruined the nation's economy, these Americans were left with nowhere to turn. If neither liberals nor conservatives have "the answer," who is left to believe in? Outsiders, it would seem.

It remains to be seen what President Clinton and the fragile Democratic hold on Congress can produce. From the vantage point of Pleasanton, gridlock has become the normative expectation, constructive change the exceptional miracle. People in this community hope, feebly at times, that their concerns will be addressed, that security will return to their community and their families. But they no longer have great confidence that anyone can solve the economic dilemmas facing the United States.

The lived experience of these Americans, analyzed and interpreted via anthropological methods provides another perspective on the question of structural change. It recommends the qualitative orientation, the long-term fieldwork approach, for a subjective understanding of the meaning of the trends discussed at length by economists and historians. For if we are to comprehend the impact of change, especially change for the worse, we must take seriously the interpretive frames, the culturally grounded expectations, and the jarring ruptures that shape the understandings and responses of ordinary Americans to the experience of economic decline.

Conclusion

Economics has often been regarded as a science akin to meteorology – effective in explaining past events, but less useful in the prediction of the future. What the American economy of the twenty-first century will look like and how it will perform is decidedly unclear. Whether the future will be a prosperous one ultimately depends on our ability to overcome the contemporary economic decline that has been the theme of this book.

By way of conclusion, Michael A. Bernstein traces some of the historical roots of the evolution of contemporary economic knowledge that speak to our seeming inability to formulate novel and effective policy approaches for the solution of current problems.

11

American economics and the American economy in the American Century: doctrinal legacies and contemporary policy problems

MICHAEL A. BERNSTEIN

> At the present moment people are unusually expectant of a more fundamental diagnosis; more particularly ready to receive it; eager to try it out, if it should be even plausible. But apart from this contemporary mood, the ideas of economists and political philosophers, both when they are right and when they are wrong, are more powerful than is commonly understood. Indeed the world is ruled by little else. Practical men [and women], who believe themselves to be quite exempt from any intellectual influences, are usually the slaves of some defunct economist.
>
> – John Maynard Keynes, 1935[1]

Contemporary anxieties about the performance of the American economy have been paralleled by similar concerns about the ability of modern economic theory and policy to provide effective remedies for slow growth and inadequate domestic capital formation. It would be safe to say that the credibility and influence of economists, both within the academic community and in governmental service, have taken as much a battering in the past two decades as the domestic economic growth rate. There is a rather exquisite irony in this fact, for in many respects it was the faltering economic performance of the late 1970s, epitomized by the very high levels of the "misery index" (the sum of the rates of inflation and unemployment) during that decade, that laid the foundations for a major transformation in American economic policy during the 1980s, with the

1 John Maynard Keynes, *The General Theory of Employment, Interest, and Money* (New York: Harcourt, Brace and World, 1964), 383.

advent of so-called supply-side economics. But that policy revision too has fallen into disrepute. As several of the essays in this volume have demonstrated, not only has supply-side theory failed to live up to its promises, it has in many instances made matters worse.

Our comprehension of the late-twentieth-century history of the American economy, not to mention any successful formulation of new policy strategies today, depends upon our reckoning with the history of policy development and implementation itself. Economics has, after all, emerged as one of the dominant social sciences in late-twentieth-century America, and this has been illustrated by the displacement of almost all other social scientists by economists in major positions of political and bureaucratic authority. This development is often viewed as symptomatic of a contemporary impatience with what are regarded as the wasteful and inefficient practices of reformers. In a time of economic retrenchment, it is argued that the state has necessarily turned to the systematic, hard-headed, and thrifty realism of economists.

But economic thought itself and the policy initiatives that emerge from its application have not and do not exist in a vacuum waiting to be applied to national needs as circumstances warrant. On the contrary, the evolution of American economic doctrine has been and is intimately linked with the history of American government and with the social history of the economics profession. As the past eighty years have witnessed the rise of the United States to unprecedented levels of military and political power, and of economic power at least until the early 1970s, so too have they seen an increasing interaction and visibility of economists in the federal government. But there has been a high price paid for this ascendancy of a particular social science in the councils of government. On the one side, alternative approaches to economic analysis and understanding have been increasingly ignored or marginalized in favor of a mainstream point of view. On the other, as now poignantly apparent, the ability of American economics to adjust and respond to changing material challenges and needs has been dramatically compromised.

A substantial part of this book has been concerned with the documentation and analysis of the faltering and inadequate steps taken to facilitate economic transition in a new era of growth and development. It is just as important and pressing to assess the reasons for the apparent inflexibility of economic theory and policy analysis in grappling with such new macroeconomic conditions. They are to be found in the same historical contexts of world war and cold war that so powerfully shaped the aggregate performance of the American economy for the past fifty years. If the end of the Cold War era has ripped away the peculiar structures upon which American prosperity had been built since 1945, then it has also robbed mainstream economic theory of both its conceptual raison d'être and the material contexts within which its analytical apparatus made the most sense.

The opportunities afforded to and the claims made upon economists by the federal government since the 1930s unrelentingly shaped the research agenda and practical applications of American economics. Those opportunities and claims – focused on achieving specific policy objectives – were uniquely linked with the successful prosecution of major war efforts as well as with peacetime military planning, procurement, and mobilization. Hot and cold wars certainly stimulated American economic growth and development since midcentury. They also focused economic research and policy making in historically specific and uniquely defined ways – orientations that nevertheless have proved less useful in solving contemporary policy problems.

More than all this, what the statist-inspired development of such new fields in economics as operations research, allocative programming, and game theory served to do was to legitimize a transformation in the object of economics research that had been in the making since the turn of the century. Ever since the "marginalist revolution" in economic theory (during which the nineteenth-century focus on the labor theory of economic value was replaced with a subjective calculus of individual preferences), American economists had been very much part of a redefinition of the science. No longer the study of "the nature and causes of the wealth of nations" (as Adam Smith and other classical theorists had claimed), nor "a critical analysis of capitalist production" (as Karl Marx had suggested), the discipline became, in this century, the formal study of what Lionel Robbins had so deftly called in his 1932 *Essay on the Nature and Significance of Economic Science* "the adaptation of scarce means to given ends."[2] While the work of marginalist theorists had gained increasing respectability since the 1870s, earlier (and quite famous) works in this tradition had had a distinctly polemical, usually anti-Marxist quality. That tone was sharply distinguished from and ultimately displaced by the

2 See Lionel Robbins, *An Essay on the Nature and Significance of Economic Science* (London: St. Martin's Press, 1969).

ostensibly objective, apolitical, and elegant formulations of mid- and later-twentieth-century mathematical economic theorists.[3]

The "new economics" of the post–World War II era and the interventionist fiscal and monetary policies pursued by the American government since 1945 did not simply issue from the published text of Keynes' *General Theory,* nor did they emerge *de novo* from college and university seminar rooms, faculty offices, and typewriters. They depended upon military mobilization and war in particular, upon imperial power and global authority in general. This "new economics" could not subsist without national power. On the one side, American hegemony in the American Century was crucially linked with the expansion of the scope and size of government activity, and with a significant commitment by the government to deploying the means (diplomatic, political, military, and economic) of that power. On the other side, fiscal activism and the economic doctrines associated with it made no sense, at least within the social context of laissez faire capital accumulation and social Darwinist conceptions of inequality, except within the framework of an American dominion in world affairs. Put simply, American power in an American century required an American economics.

It was of course during World War II that the groundwork was laid for the participation of the American economics profession in the Cold War itself. Future Nobel Economics Laureate Paul Samuelson commented in 1945 "that the last war was the chemist's war . . . this one [was] the physicist's. It might equally be said that this [was] the economist's war."[4] The usefulness of the economics discipline to the American war effort was demonstrated in two broad areas of endeavor – mobilization and resource allocation, and strategic decision making. Economists quickly took up positions in government agencies established to meet the various needs and challenges thrown up by American entry into World War II – as epitomized by the creation of such entities as the Board of Economic Warfare, the Combined Production and Resources Board, the Defense

3 See, e.g., Eugen von Böhm-Bawerk, *Karl Marx and the Close of His System* (P. M. Sweezy, ed.) (London: Merlin Press, 1975); and John B. Clark, *The Distribution of Wealth: A Theory of Wages, Income and Profits* (New York: Kelley, 1967).

4 From Paul Samuelson, "A Warning to the Washington Expert," *New Republic* 111:11 (September 11, 1945), 298, as quoted in Barry M. Katz, *Foreign Intelligence: Research and Analysis in the Office of Strategic Services, 1942–1945* (Cambridge: Harvard University Press, 1989), 103.

Plant Corporation, the Foreign Economic Administration, and the Office for Coordination of National Defense Purchases.[5]

To be sure, the entire wartime experience of American economists played a major role in the postwar evolution of the discipline. In large measure a direct outcome of the wartime experience, the development of input–output analysis, new statistical estimation techniques, national income account conventions, and international financial and commodity flow tabulations demonstrated beyond doubt that the 1940s were an extremely innovative decade in the history of American economic thought. That most of these intellectual developments took place within the context of a crusade against fascism and totalitarianism powerfully suggests that World War II "imparted to a community of humanist and social scientific scholars a concrete sense of the embeddedness of their ideas – and themselves – in history." "They brought [this attitude] back with them to their universities" and, it should be added, they sought to convey it to their respective disciplinary colleagues.[6]

Not surprisingly, the American armed services and allied government agencies were particularly eager to develop allocative techniques for wartime production, transportation, and distribution that would minimize costs and waste and that would have as their corollary the maximization of objectives such as output, frequency, or endurance. Research on such programming problems had a tremendous impact on the future course of research in mathematical economics in particular and economic theory in general.[7]

Tjalling C. Koopmans, a Dutch physicist who came to the United States in 1940, played a significant role in relevant research in applied mathematics that in the short run stimulated a wide variety of investiga-

5 See, e.g., Bureau of the Budget, War Records Section; *The United States at War: Development and Administration of the War Program by the Federal Government* (Washington, D.C.: United States Government Printing Office, n.d.).

6 Katz, *Foreign Intelligence,* 198.

7 See E. Roy Weintraub, *General Equilibrium Analysis: Studies in Appraisal* (New York: Cambridge University Press, 1985), 90; and Tjalling C. Koopmans (ed.), *Activity Analysis of Production and Allocation: Proceedings of a Conference* (New York: John Wiley and Sons, 1951). An impression of how dramatic an impact wartime developments had on the future evolution of economic theory in the United States may also be won from Robert Dorfman, Paul A. Samuelson, and Robert M. Solow, *Linear Programming and Economic Analysis* (London: McGraw-Hill, 1958).

tions on programming and allocation problems. Serving on the Combined Shipping Adjustment Board, a joint American–British effort to marshall most effectively the merchant fleets of the allied nations, Koopmans developed a static programming model of transportation routes, schedules, and tonnage for the world-wide war effort. His work became a linchpin in the articulation of a wide array of applications that were the foundation of the future evolution of economic theory in the 1950s and 1960s. By 1949, Koopmans' research and that of many investigators in mathematics and economics had reached sufficient maturity under the stimulus of the recent war years to allow for a special conference to be held at the Cowles Commission for Research in Economics in Chicago. The conference generated information and publications that were dramatic in their impact and significance.[8]

The Cowles conference grew essentially out of Koopmans' conviction that there was a connection between much of the allocation and operations research studies done during World War II and economic theory more generally. As one eminent participant in the meeting remembered, Koopmans was "like a man on fire," and the collaboration that the conference sustained brought "instant respectability to the field" of programming and operations research in the eyes of many economic theorists. By "mechanizing" the problem of the maximization of some objective subject to constraints of various sorts, the work of the conference participants served to unify, at least in the formal constructs of mathemat-

8 The major (and arguably the most famous) publication to come out of the Chicago meetings was the anthology edited by Koopmans titled *Activity Analysis of Production and Allocation*. In his impressive introduction to the volume, Koopmans quite interestingly wrote on p. 4: "There is, of course, no exclusive connection between defense or war and the systematic study of allocation and programming problems. It is believed that the studies assembled in this volume are of equal relevance to problems of industrial management and efficiency in production scheduling. They also throw new light on old problems of abstract economic theory. If the apparent prominence of military application at this stage is more than a historical accident, the reasons are sociological rather than logical. It does seem that governmental agencies, for whatever reason, have so far provided a better environment and more sympathetic support for the systematic study, abstract and applied, of principles and methods of allocation of resources than private industry. There has also been more mobility of scientific personnel between government and universities, to the advantage of both."

ics, a wide array of problems in economics having to do with such things as the maximization of profits and the minimization of costs.[9]

It was on matters of resource allocation and decision making, therefore, where economists made perhaps their most significant contributions, and with which they (collectively as a profession) had their most significant experience during the war. Even before the Japanese naval offensive at Pearl Harbor, conversion to defense production had created virtually intractable problems of resource scarcity and waste for government officials. How to choose efficiently the timing and distribution of various productive activities necessary for the war effort became a major concern. With American entry into the war, allocation problems became only more intense. In a particularly vivid description of the confusion, waste, and unintended consequences of rising military production, the War Records Section of the Bureau of the Budget noted:

> Merchant ships took steel from the Navy. . . . The Navy took aluminum from aircraft. Rubber took valves from escort vessels, from petroleum, and from the Navy. . . . Many a plant was changed over to war production when its normal product was more needed than its new product. Locomotive plants went into tank production, when locomotives were more necessary – but the Tank Division did not know this. Truck plants began to produce airplanes, a change that caused shortages of trucks later on. In some cases, plants were converted at great cost of steel and copper, when a fraction of the previous metals involved would have brought a greater return at some other place in the economy. The scramble for a production we could not attain, brought us waste instead.[10]

It was but a short and logical step from a preoccupation with the analytics of resource allocation to the study of strategic decision making. Situating allocative choice problems within the context of conflict and uncertainty made obvious sense for wartime planning. Thus emerged "game theory," by which the intellectual evolution of American econom-

9 Interview with Professor Emeritus George B. Dantzig (Department of Operations Research, Stanford University), by the author (3 May, 1989). Dantzig was a central figure in the development of programming techniques – work he had undertaken in the late forties for the United States Air Force. His now classic essay "Maximization of a Linear Function of Variables Subject to Linear Inequalities" was a central piece in the Koopmans conference volume. See Tjalling Koopmans, *Activity Analysis of Production and Allocation,* 339–47.

10 From *The United States at War,* 113–14.

ics and the concerns of a burgeoning national security state truly melded. On a strictly mathematical level, the development of both linear programming techniques to solve allocation problems and game theory itself was premised upon similar advances in the mathematical understanding of particular equation systems known as linear inequalities. Yet game theory had a powerful appeal for strategic and tactical analysis because of its focus on counteraction and opposition in decision-making. It was for this reason that the theory of games, while greatly stimulated by the World War II experience, did not achieve its full status until the coming of the Cold War.

The 1940s work of John von Neumann and Oskar Morgenstern signaled the entrance of game theory as a major part of economic analysis.[11] Their demonstration that it was possible to derive definite results from mathematical simulations of complicated scenarios of conflict and uncertainty was revolutionary. They showed that under certain conditions and assumptions, game participants could implement strategies that would secure at least certain minimum gains (or their parallel, at most certain minimum losses). While it was immediately clear that their findings would be useful in conventional microeconomic theory – especially with regard to estimating pricing outcomes in oligopolistic markets – over time it also became obvious that they would be applicable to strategic choice problems and national defense planning.

Game-theoretic approximations and simulations of two-person conflicts seemed appropriate scenarios in which to investigate the implications of the nuclear duopoly, between the United States and the Soviet Union, of the early Cold War era.[12] The dramatic intellectual impact of

11 See John von Neumann and Oskar Morgenstern, *Theory of Games and Economic Behavior* (Princeton: Princeton University Press, 1947); and R. Duncan Luce and Howard Raiffa, *Games and Decisions* (New York: Wiley, 1958).

12 Dorfman, Samuelson, and Solow give an excellent summary of the essential ideas of game theory in their *Linear Programming and Economic Analysis*, p. 2: "The theory of games rests on the notion that there is a close analogy between parlor games of skill, on the one hand, and conflict situations in economic, political, and military life, on the other. In any of these situations there are a number of participants with incompatible objectives, and the extent to which each participant attains his [or her] objective depends upon what all the participants do. The problem faced by each participant is to lay his [or her] plans so as to take account of the actions of . . . opponents, each of whom, of course, is laying . . . plans so as to take account of the first

the work of von Neumann and Morgenstern among academic economists was thus, not coincidentally, paralleled by the willingness of the federal government to support the continued evolution of this line of inquiry. Research funding, distributed by the Department of Defense and affiliated agencies – most notably the Office of Naval Research – was rapidly made available to those economic theorists, in particular mathematical economists, whose work in game theory and allocative programming seemed to have potential value for the missions of the national defense and security establishment – all this at a time when the mission of the American defense agencies was expanding in novel and global ways.

The U.S. Navy and Air Force proved most eager to lend support to the work of game theorists and mathematical economists. The Navy, in particular, supported much of the work in general equilibrium theory – in large part done by Kenneth Arrow and Gerard Debreu (both future Nobel Laureates) – that, during the 1950s and early 1960s, propelled the field into great visibility and prominence. During the 1950s, what had been the Air Force's Project RAND (an acronym for research and development), and what later became the non-profit RAND Corporation known today, underwrote much of the work on allocative programming that had been stimulated by the 1940s work of people like Tjalling Koopmans.

Indeed, under RAND auspices, continued research in game theory and allocative programming flourished throughout the 1960s and 1970s. The corporation funded what it called "Defense Policy Seminars" at U.C.L.A., the University of Chicago, Columbia, Dartmouth, Johns Hopkins, M.I.T., Ohio State, Princeton, and the University of Wisconsin. In 1965, RAND created a graduate fellowship program to support relevant training in economics and international relations. In that year, eight such fellowships were distributed among Berkeley, Chicago, Columbia, Harvard, Princeton, Stanford, and Yale. Not infrequently, talented graduate students and young postdoctoral investigators received major support from RAND (and, through RAND, from the federal government) for their work in economics that touched upon matters of strategic decision making.[13] One such individual for whom this was true, whose career as a

participant's actions. Thus each participant must surmise what each of [the] opponents will expect [them] to do and how these opponents will react to these expectations."

13 See Bruce L. R. Smith, *The Rand Corporation: Case Study of a Nonprofit Advisory Corporation* (Cambridge: Harvard University Press, 1969), 16, 111–12. Smith also notes that, as a RAND consultant, Thomas Schelling

national security analyst would take many twists and turns, was Daniel Ellsberg, one of the primary actors in the 1971 "Pentagon Papers" scandal surrounding the Vietnam War. His research at Harvard University and at RAND dealt primarily with strategic choice under risk and uncertainty, and in this regard his work was representative of the new trends in economic theory that dovetailed so closely with the concerns of the American government during the Cold War.[14]

The authority and legitimacy of the new work in economic theory that had been, in large measure, an outgrowth of the war years, carried over to the postwar era and the years of the Cold War. In a wide array of activities related to the defense establishment and the new global power of the United States, economic analysis came to play a significant role. From defense cost minimization, to budgeting techniques and strategies, to transportation and logistical-support scheduling, to shadow-price estimation of the burdens of military-industrial procurement, the research of the World War II years paid off. Even in the private corporate economy, not to mention in the civilian activities of government, what came to be known as the operationally useful methods of economists came of age. For example, RAND economists developed a Planning, Programming, Budgeting System (known as the P.P.B.S.) for national defense policy formulation as well as for general government spending procedures; Stephen Enke worked on algorithms to assist in Air Force logistics; several investigators formulated a cost–benefit calculus regarding nuclear war; joint-product output and interdependent activity analysis in oil refining came within the purview of the new economics of allocative decision making; and in 1963 a brief effort was made to apply operations research programs to the functioning of the British National Health Service. With demonstrations like these, the prestige of those engaged in such research, along with

wrote another classic text in game theory and economic analysis, *The Strategy of Conflict* (Cambridge: Harvard University Press, 1960). Also see Schelling's "Bargaining, Communication, and Limited War," *Journal of Conflict Resolution* 1 (March, 1957), 19–36.

14 See, for example, the work Ellsberg did at RAND in "The Crude Analysis of Strategic Choices," *American Economic Review* 51:2 (May, 1961), 472–78, in which the U.S.–Soviet postwar confrontation is described by a 2×2 gaming matrix giving each superpower two choices – "wait" or "strike." Also see his "Risk, Ambiguity, and the Savage Axioms," *Quarterly Journal of Economics* 75 (1961), 643–69 – an essay that reports on some of his work as a Harvard University graduate student in economics.

the academic, governmental, and private foundation support for their research activity, were powerfully enhanced.[15]

As the United States deployed a growing world-wide influence and power throughout the postwar era, it is also true that the American economics profession expressed an increasing self-confidence during the 1950s. This poise represented the seasoning of a powerful new field that, in at least the formal sense of collegiate and university organization within the United States, was in most cases less than a half-century old.[16] New subfields of the economics discipline, such as growth and development

15 See, e.g., David Novick, *Efficiency and Economy in Government Through New Budgeting and Accounting Procedures* (RAND Corporation, Report R-254, February 1, 1954); Tibor Scitovsky, Edward S. Shaw, and Lorie Tarshis, *Mobilizing Resources for War* (New York: McGraw-Hill, 1951); S. Enke, "An Economist Looks at Air Force Logistics," *Review of Economics and Statistics* 40 (August, 1958), 230–39; C. J. Hitch, "Economics and Military Operations Research," *Review of Economics and Statistics* 40 (August, 1958), 199–209; L. J. Sterling, "Decision Making in Weapons Development," *Harvard Business Review* 38 (January–February, 1958), 127–36; H. Mendershausen, "Economic Problems in Air Force Logistics," *American Economic Review* 48 (September, 1958), 632–48; Charles J. Hitch and Roland N. McKean, *The Economics of Defense in the Nuclear Age* (Cambridge: Harvard University Press, 1961); A. Charnes, W. W. Cooper, and B. Mellon; "Blending Aviation Gasolines: A Study in Programming Interdependent Activities in an Integrated Oil Company," *Econometrica* 20 (April, 1952), 135–59; H. C. Levinson, "Experiences in Commercial Operations Research," *Journal of the Operations Research Society of America* 2 (August, 1953), 220–39; and M. S. Feldstein, "Economic Analysis, Operational Research, and the National Health Service," *Oxford Economic Papers* (New Series) 15:1 (March, 1963), 19–31.

16 It is, of course, important to remember that if the Cold War years privileged certain kinds of academic research, they also witnessed the enervation of other intellectual traditions by both the passive means of deprivation of support (by universities and foundations, as well as the government), and the active efforts of academic and state and federal officials to deny employment and advancement to those deemed to be, at the least, outside the mainstream, at the worst, disloyal and treasonous. The most recent contribution in this regard is Ellen W. Schrecker's *No Ivory Tower: McCarthyism and the Universities* (New York: Oxford University Press, 1986). Also see, of specific interest, J. E. King, *Economic Exiles* (New York: St. Martin's Press, 1988); and Lawrence Lifschultz, "Could Karl Marx Teach Economics in the United States?" originally published in *Ramparts* magazine, reprinted in J. Trumpbour (ed.), *How Harvard Rules: Reason in the Service of Empire* (Boston: South End Press, 1989), 279–86.

theory, garnered attention and resources (not to mention audiences) owing to the interests of the federal government in fostering decentralized market growth in developing nations; a design imagined as a means both to further U.S. foreign policy interests and to forestall Chinese and Soviet initiatives around the world.[17] Policy makers also hoped to secure greater access for American entrepreneurs to the economies of once colonial and now newly independent states. American economics assumed greater visibility on a global scale, in this regard, in addition to its growing reputation and status at home. And the creation of a Council of Economic Advisers (C.E.A.) within the executive branch of the federal government during the Truman presidency created high expectations as to the value and weight of economics within the political realm.

Created by the Employment Act of 1946, the C.E.A. is composed of three senior members, professional economists appointed by the president upon the consent of the Senate. Assisted by a research staff also composed of professionals, the council members have the major responsibility of preparing an annual *Economic Report of the President* for submission to the Congress. They are also expected to lend assistance and counsel in the formulation of economic policy. Conceived of by most economists as a demonstration of the inherent usefulness and importance of the discipline, the council stands as the only executive branch unit (other than, perhaps, the Office of the Surgeon General) that, by the terms of its enabling legislation, represents a *specific* professional entity in the White House.[18]

17 On the matter of development economics and growth theory, there is perhaps no better example of the resonances between that field and the Cold War concerns of the American government than Walt W. Rostow, *The Stages of Economic Growth: A Non-Communist Manifesto* (New York: Cambridge University Press, 1971).

18 There is a vast literature on the history of the creation of the council, and of its operations over time. See, e.g., Herbert Stein, *The Fiscal Revolution in America* (Chicago: University of Chicago Press, 1969), ch. 9; Stephen K. Bailey, *Congress Makes a Law* (New York: Columbia University Press, 1950); and Edwin G. Nourse, *Economics in the Public Service: Administrative Aspects of the Employment Act* (New York: Harcourt, Brace, 1953). Also see R. M. Collins, "The Emergence of Economic Growthmanship in the United States: Federal Policy and Economic Knowledge in the Truman Years," in Mary O. Furner and Barry Supple (eds.), *The State and Economic Knowledge: The American and British Experiences* (New York: Cambridge University Press, 1990), 138–70.

The globalist perspective of the Truman administration, as epitomized in the so-called "Truman Doctrine" calling for containment of the military, political, and diplomatic influence of the Soviet Union and mainland China, posed vast challenges to the macroeconomic management of American postwar affairs. It was within this context that the first Council of Economic Advisers, composed of Edwin Nourse as chair (an agricultural economist who for many years had been resident at the Brookings Institution), Leon Keyserling (an attorney from Washington, D.C., and New York with extensive New Deal experience in economic matters), and John Clark (a Ph.D. economist and attorney serving as Dean of the College of Business Administration at the University of Nebraska), took office.

Global containment, and its first great test in the Korean peninsula in the early 1950s, confronted the Truman administration with the need to finance a vast expansion in American military capabilities. Under the aegis of the "new economics," this extraordinary fiscal requirement, one that in fact ultimately exceeded those of World War II, was met. Yet this achievement was realized at the cost of creating enormous tensions and strains within the economic advising community over the role of economists in government and the purpose of economic learning. There quickly emerged a power struggle between those in the profession, like Nourse, who believed in keeping to modest dimensions the spending commitments of the federal government, and those, led often by Keyserling, who linked projects of military and political intervention world-wide with increased fiscal spending targets at home. These latter "inflationists," as Nourse called them, found in a diplomatic and military strategy, epitomized by the Truman Doctrine, the blueprint for a more aggressive pump-priming strategy for the federal budget in general.[19]

Interestingly enough, Nourse construed this contest as not so much about levels and rates of growth in government spending, although he did argue that federal spending should always fall in the upswing of the business cycle (contrary to Keyserling and his allies), as about the professional role and legitimacy of economists in governmental service. He conceived of the council, as he wrote to a colleague in the University of Michigan economics department in the summer of 1946, as a scientific

19 The narrative constructed here is based upon evidence in the Papers of Edwin G. Nourse housed at the Harry S. Truman Library in Independence, Missouri (hereafter Nourse Papers).

entity, that would ideally serve beyond each presidential term. He compared the council, in this sense, to the Supreme Court – appointed by presidential authority, but wielding influence above and beyond the vagaries of electoral politics. Nourse went so far as to refuse invitations to testify before the Joint Economic Committee of the Congress, on the grounds that such public appearances would detract from the objective and non-partisan status of the council. "[The] prime function [of the Council of Economic Advisers]," he wrote President Truman in the summer of 1946, "is to bring the best available methods of social science to the service of the Chief Executive. . . . There is no occasion for the Council to become involved in any way in the advocacy of particular measures or in the rival beliefs and struggles of the different economic and political interest groups." Nourse's colleagues, Keyserling and Clark, did not agree with him, and often went up to Capitol Hill to testify.[20]

This early history of the council suggests that the fiscal demands and opportunities associated with the birth of the national security state were both a boon and a burden for the economics profession as a whole. On the one side, fiscal activism became identified with the global as well as the domestic initiatives of the federal government. Guns *and* butter were very much the order of the day.[21] On the other side, however, were sown the seeds not only of dissension among economists (for that is normal enough) but also for the politicization of economics policy practice that, while perhaps inherent in the very creation of a C.E.A., nevertheless so worried mainstream economists like Nourse himself.

By the spring of 1948, conservative Republicans in Congress, predictably led by the formidable Senator Robert Taft of Ohio, sought to reduce dramatically the funding for the C.E.A.. Taft excoriated the council as a holdover from New Deal anti-depression policies. Given that military

20 See Nourse to Truman, July 29, 1946, Nourse Papers, Box 3 (File: "Daily Diary 1946-2 E.G.N. letter accepting chairmanship of Council of Economic Advisers July 29, 1946 Nourse Papers"); and Nourse to William Haber (Department of Economics, University of Michigan), August 23, 1946, Nourse Papers, Box 1 (File: "CEA Staff File Appointments, 1946–47 Nourse").

21 See, for a particularly persuasive case that increased military production was possible along with enhanced consumer product output during World War II, Harold Vatter, "The Material Status of the U.S. Civilian Consumer in World War II: The Question of Guns or Butter," in G. T. Mills and H. Rockoff, eds., *The Sinews of War: Essays on the Economic History of World War II* (Ames, Iowa: Iowa State University Press, 1993), 219–42.

spending would now guarantee full employment, he argued provocatively, what was the need for a C.E.A. or the 1946 Employment Act anyway? A year later, Nourse would complain to Truman that the "dangers to the domestic economy from financing [military-industrial] expenditures out of continuing deficits and with a growing national debt are no less real than [those] military and diplomatic dangers as now confront us."[22]

The Council of Economic Advisers, as an institution if not as individual members, weathered the uncertainty of the Truman years. Nourse felt compelled, in the fall of 1949, to resign; Leon Keyserling succeeded him as chair. Under President Eisenhower, and most vividly under President Kennedy, the C.E.A. achieved a relatively unchallenged respect and standing. At the same time, it became, like much else of American economics, an object of acute interest to foreign governments and scholars. Some governments, for example, rather quickly imitated the American institutional form of the council. West Germany formed in 1970 a Council of Experts to advise the Chancellor on economic matters; the Canadian government added to its ministries an Economic Council. Council member Roy Blough (of the University of Chicago) undertook a revision of fiscal procedures in 1950 at the request of the Turkish government. Much of his work was underwritten by the Economic Cooperation Administration (the institutional representation of the Marshall Plan) of the Truman White House. Blough also met frequently, as did Raymond Saulnier (chair of the C.E.A. under Eisenhower and later a professor at Barnard College), with representatives of Japan's Economic Planning Agency. Arthur Okun, a prominent C.E.A. member under Kennedy and Johnson (for whom he also served as council chair), directly advised the Canadian government on the establishment of its Economic Council. Arthur Burns, chair of the council under Eisenhower and later chair of the Federal Reserve System Board of Governors under Nixon, hosted a steady stream of economics policy makers from India, Japan, Poland, Singapore, the Soviet Union, and Yugoslavia during his tenure both in the Executive Office Building and at the Fed. Clearly, American economics had, in a wide variety of ways, made itself an essential part of both American governance and the evolution of the discipline and policy practice worldwide.[23]

22 Nourse to Truman, August 15, 1949, Nourse Papers, Box 6 (File: "Daily Diary 1949–92").

23 Hirotaka Kato (Japan Economic Research Institute) to Burns, September 3, 1965; Fumio Aoba (Secretary-General, Japan Economic Research Institute)

In addition, throughout the latter part of this century, the sway of American ideas in the social and policy sciences, quite notably in mainstream economics, has steadily increased. As instruments of international authority, and as tools with which the legitimacy of particular forms of

to Burns, July 2, 1965; Aoba to Burns, July 8, 1965; Burns to Aoba, May 10, 1965; Aoba to Burns, April 10, 1965; Aoba to Burns, February 28, 1965, all in Box 126 (File: "Exchange of Economists – Japan Economic Research Institute – Kato [1965]"), Arthur F. Burns Papers, 1928–69 (hereafter Burns Papers), Dwight D. Eisenhower Library, Abilene, Kansas. Also see Memo, Douglas H. Eldridge (Secretary, National Bureau of Economic Research) to Burns et al., February 9, 1967, regarding visit by a team of economists from the Industrial Bank of Japan, Ltd.; Takeo Kurai (Chief, Research Department of International Management Association of Japan) to Solomon Fabricant, September 1, 1964; K. N. Wahal (Commercial Consul of India in New York) to William J. Carson (Executive Director, National Bureau of Economic Research), August 24, 1964; Yoh Poh Seng (Department of Economics, University of Singapore) to Burns, May 10, 1964; Memo, Carson to Burns et al., December 20, 1963, regarding visit of M. S. Dragilev of Moscow State University; Memo, Louise Smith (National Bureau of Economic Research staff member) to Carson, June 26, 1963, regarding visit of Nicoli Cobeljic, Assistant Director of Yugoslavia Economic Planning; Memo, Fabricant to National Bureau of Economic Research staff, March 29, 1963, regarding visit of Kazushi Ohkawa of Hitosubashi University; and Memo, Fabricant to Burns et al., April 25, 1963, regarding visit of Z. Bidinski, Economic Counselor at the Polish Embassy, Washington, D.C.; Box 126 (File: "Foreign Visitors to the National Bureau [1958–1967] (1)"), Burns Papers. Also see Arthur J. R. Smith (Chair, Economic Council of Canada) to Okun, September 15, 1970; Okun to Smith, November 2, 1970; Smith to Okun, December 16, 1970; and Okun to Smith, December 10, 1970, all in Box 30A (B series) (File: "Economic Council of Canada Seminar Nov. 20, 1970"), Papers of Arthur Okun, Lyndon Baines Johnson Library, University of Texas at Austin. See "Diary of Roy Blough, Council of Economic Advisers, June 29–December 31, 1950," entry for Wednesday, August 30, 1950, in Box 13 in the Papers of Roy Blough, Truman Library. Also see Saulnier to Okita, March 12, 1958, in Box 25 (File: "Chron[ological File]; January, February and March 1958"), "Records of the Office of the Council of Economic Advisers, 1953–61," in the Eisenhower Papers – C.E.A. Files, Eisenhower Library. Finally see Nahit Alpar (Financial Counselor of the Turkish Embassy, Washington, D.C.) to Blough, March 29, 1950; Henry W. Wiens (Program Review Officer, Economic Cooperation Administration – Special Mission to Turkey) to Blough, April 11, 1950, both in Box 15 (File: "Improving Fiscal System of Turkish Republic"), Papers of Roy Blough, Truman Library; and the "General File ECA Mission to Turkey – 1950" and "General File – Tax Mission to Turkey 1949" also in Box 15.

power may be established, such "creations of the intellect," as Joseph Schumpeter once referred to them, should indeed garner as much attention from scholars of world systems as trade flows and direct investment patterns. Not only how ideas are shared, but why they are promulgated and accepted across (as well as within) national boundaries should afford a more profound understanding of geopolitical regimes and, in the case of United States history, of how deeply international supremacy as a "way of life" (as William Appleman Williams called it in 1980) has made its way into the interstices of American society.[24]

It was precisely the impact of the peculiar political-economic history of the immediate post–World War II era, and indeed of its attendant "way of life," that have had such a deleterious effect upon the ability of the federal government to respond to contemporary economic decline. As the United States moves from a position of global economic hegemony to one of economic interdependence, even of economic retardation, new theoretical approaches are necessary in order to understand and explain the dramatic changes that have occurred in the economy since 1945. Such analytical departures are especially urgent since received wisdom and mainstream theory have not allowed us to formulate effective or unambiguous responses to current economic problems. That wisdom and theory did not, of course, emerge in a vacuum. Indeed, the very world authority that fostered and encouraged its development and practice has now apparently been lost. As a consequence, we are now (like the interwar generation of whom Keynes wrote in 1935) "unusually expectant of a more fundamental diagnosis [of the myriad economic troubles with which we are faced]; more particularly ready to receive it; eager to try it out, if it should be even plausible." And yet the signs of such a reformulation of economic inquiry are as rare in the economics profession itself as in the wider polity. Weaned, as we all have been, on the special material and social conditions of the Cold War and American global hegemony, professional economists, political leaders, and the public at large find themselves largely incapable of articulating new agendas for the further refine-

24 See William Appleman Williams, *Empire as a Way of Life: An Essay on the Causes and Character of America's Present Predicament Along with a Few Thoughts About an Alternative* (New York: Oxford University Press, 1982); and Joseph A. Schumpeter, *Capitalism, Socialism and Democracy* (New York: Harper & Row, 1962), 3.

ment of economic doctrine and analysis. It is not surprising, in this context, to note that one of Keynes' most famous students could argue in 1975 that mainstream economics had more applicability in a planned or wartime economy than in a decentralized market setting. That characterization has great merit given that history shows that armed conflict brings a necessary centralization of control within societies along with a powerful "simplification of objectives" by which leaders and the public can quickly and efficiently make decisions. As a corollary to this well-documented social and political impact of war there emerges an attenuation of political conflict and economic contestation as societies make efforts to position themselves adequately with respect to a common enemy.[25] Modern American economics, viewed in this light, emerges as the product of an effort to understand and interact with an altogether unique and contingent set of circumstances – conditions that have little if anything to do with a peacetime economy structured to foster the accumulation of private wealth in decentralized market settings.

Thus, a particular kind of economics, which helped explain (and which was exemplified by) a growing, wartime economy, and was oriented towards problems of resource allocation, matured in the United States during the 1940s and 1950s.[26] The development of this kind of economics was a direct result of an unprecedented government involvement in the economy during World War II and the ensuing Cold War. An orthodoxy thereby emerged among professional economists in government, business, and academia. It became institutionalized, and it drove

25 See Joan Robinson's essay on "Consumer Sovereignty in a Planned Economy," in her *Collected Economic Papers,* vol. 3 (Oxford: Basil Blackwell, 1975), 70–81. On war as a "simplification of objectives," see Lionel Robbins, *The Economic Problem in Peace and War: Some Reflections on Objectives and Mechanism* (London: Macmillan, 1947), as well as Forest H. Capie and Geoffrey E. Wood, "The Anatomy of a Wartime Inflation: Britain, 1939–1945," in *The Sinews of War,* 21–42, esp. 21.

26 I do not mean to suggest that this doctrinal development took place solely within the United States. In fact, it emerged throughout the industrialized world and even gained legitimacy in the developing nations. I would argue that the forces molding such theoretical evolution were similar to those in this country: wartime and Cold War mobilization, the impact of an emergent American hegemony not simply in political and military terms but also in intellectual and academic contexts, and the effort to confront and overthrow the appeal and stature of Marxist and other critical approaches in the social sciences more generally.

rival forms of economic explanation to the margins of serious discussion. During the 1960s and 1970s this economics became increasingly stale, lifeless, and inappropriate for the economic problems facing the nation. While the seeds of this inexpediency were presumably present in the 1940s and 1950s, the weaknesses of the dominant economic theories were not apparent during periods of nation-wide mobilization and sustained growth. The problem today is that the very ascendancy of this mainstream economics prevents analysts, whether in government, the corporate arena, or the academic world, from recognizing its contemporary ineffectiveness.

Perhaps the best example of the theoretical inflexibilities that plague contemporary economic analysis, especially given the concerns of this volume, is to be found in the modern theory of economic growth.[27] In its mathematical sophistication and quantitative focus, that theory was very much a product of the peculiar contexts within which economic analysis evolved during the 1940s and early 1950s. It has enjoyed a remarkable hegemony in the professional discourse of mainstream economists, and it has received substantial recognition in, among other accolades, the award of the 1987 Nobel Memorial Prize in Economics to one of its leading architects, Robert M. Solow of the Massachusetts Institute of Technology.

The modern theory of economic growth conceives of economic production as essentially a technological relationship. It attempts to situate a conceptual understanding of the growth process within the context of economic models that focus on rational choice and individual decision making. A "production function" is posited that expresses output as the result of a technically specified interaction between inputs of labor, machinery, tools, and natural resources like land. Growth is understood as the result of production that exceeds the annual requirements for maintenance of the labor force, replacement of consumed resources and worn-out machinery and tools, and amortization of the capital stock. Thus, a proportion of annual output is saved every year – assuming that technology and labor productivity are sufficient to generate a surplus. Savings are

27 The following exposition is based on Robert M. Solow, "Contribution to the Theory of Economic Growth," *Quarterly Journal of Economics* 70 (February, 1956), 65–94, as well as his *Growth Theory: An Exposition* (Oxford: Oxford University Press, 1970). Also see Trevor W. Swan, "Economic Growth and Capital Accumulation," *Economic Record* 32:63 (November, 1956), 334–61.

then converted into additions to the stock of productive capacity by means of the investment activities of firms and individuals.

Given the availability of capital for production, generated via the savings prevailing at any given moment in time, the growth process is also modulated through changes in the supply of labor. Mainstream economists generally assume that the supply of labor is the result of an exogenously given rate of population growth and changes in the labor-force participation rate of that population. Alterations in the natural rate of reproduction, in a given society, will affect labor supply both extensively through changes in the aggregate size of population and intensively through changes in the proportion of that population actively seeking employment. These latter movements in the available labor supply will depend on such parameters as the age composition of the population (a very young or a very old population will normally have a lower labor-force participation rate), socially specified attitudes toward the participation of certain segments of the population (such as women and racial and ethnic minorities) in various forms of remunerated work, and cultural and social expectations as to the normal age at which individuals would enter the labor force after appropriate schooling and exit through retirement.

Focused as it is on the relationship between individual choice and aggregate economic performance, mainstream growth theory investigates the means by which expansion is achieved with the full employment of available human and non-human inputs. Put simply, the increase in the capital stock occasioned by the savings–investment relationship must coincide with the increase in the supply of labor for growth stability and full employment to be secured. In this model of the growth process, such adjustment occurs through changes in the technique of production.

Variation in the choice of production technique is a core principle in modern economic growth theory. With production understood to be managed by entrepreneurs, modern economic theory grasps the decision making of producers in terms of particular objectives such as the minimization of costs or the maximization of output. Indeed, it was one of the most influential findings of those investigators who had developed allocative programming and rational choice models during the 1940s and 1950s that particular objectives, such as cost minimization, always had counterparts (known as "duals") such as output maximization. Doing one thing would ensure achievement of the other – minimizing costs would maximize output, maximizing output would minimize costs.[28] Armed with this insight, modern growth theorists were able to formulate a rigorous and elegant model of economic expansion. Central to this conception was the notion of resource scarcity – a principle rigorously systematized in the work of the World War II and Cold War researchers who had had to grapple with the daunting material constraints of waging actual or potential war on a global scale.

The technique employed in production is conceived, in modern economic theory, to be the result of the rational choices made by producers who have assessed the marginal productivities of the inputs to the production process. That technique may change by producers either increasing the ratio of capital employed to labor (moving into a "capital intensive" production technique) or decreasing that ratio (moving into a "labor intensive" production technique). For stable growth with full employment of all available inputs, the growth in the stock of productive capacity must keep pace with the naturally and socially specified rate of growth in the labor force.

A stable process of growth, according to this theory, is the result of the competitive and rational behavior of producers. If the capital stock grows disproportionately faster than the labor supply, diminishing returns to the employment of capital would obtain. The relatively larger return accruing to the employment of labor provided with an excess of capital would signal to producers that a more labor-intensive production process would be more rational. Conversely, if the growth of the labor force disproportionately exceeds the net increase in the capital stock, the marginal return indices would prompt producers to increase the capital intensity of their enterprises. Stability is achieved, according to this model of economic structure and behavior, where any changes in technique would decrease output.

This mainstream model of the growth process is premised upon an

28 The notion of the "dual" in economic theory is powerfully explained by Robert Dorfman, Paul Samuelson, and Robert Solow in *Linear Programming and Economic Analysis,* 39–63, esp. 41, where these authors point out that "the dual of a maximizing problem is a minimizing problem, and vice versa." Also see the extremely influential work by Paul Samuelson in the *Foundations of Economic Analysis* (New York: Atheneum, 1976), specifically recognized in 1970 when Samuelson received the Nobel Memorial Prize.

assumption that producers face a spectrum of available techniques from which to choose the most rational and productive process. Changes in techniques are here assumed to be achieved costlessly, although transformation costs could be, and have been, introduced into the model without altering its basic findings. The model can also be further complicated by the introduction of either fixed techniques of production or truncated spectrums of available techniques, thereby making the model more realistic but again not altering its primary import.[29]

Adjustment to the full employment of productive resources can also be less formally explained, within the modern theory of economic growth, as owing to the effects of changes in the interest rate upon savings and thereby upon the rate of increase in the capital stock. Should the capital stock become too large relative to the available labor supply, the prevailing interest rate will fall. Savings would thus decrease as individuals saw less to be gained in large savings accounts. Ultimately the capital stock would decrease as investment fell due to the attenuation in the supply of savings economy-wide. On the other hand, if capital were relatively limited in supply, the rate of interest would rise, savings would increase, and the capital stock would ultimately expand. By making savings a function of the interest rate, the modern theory of economic growth ties the rate of savings to the size of the capital stock. Most importantly, the variability of production technique that this model posits allows for adjustments to full employment of inputs to be caused by systemic effects such as the relative availabilities of production inputs and of savings.

Clearly the modern theory of economic growth, given its focus on individual maximizing behavior and rational choice concepts, understands expansion in primarily quantitative terms, by means of a notion of a "natural" rate of growth in the labor force and associated rates of increase in the available capital stock. Qualitative change, within this theoretical context, is most often relegated to the status of an exogenous factor.[30] There is perhaps no more vivid representation of this rather

29 One of the best known efforts to "complicate" the mainstream model of economic growth is R. M. Solow, J. Tobin, C. C. von Weizsacker, and M. Yaari, "Neoclassical Growth with Fixed Proportions," *Review of Economic Studies* 33 (1966), 79–116. Also see C. E. Ferguson, *The Neoclassical Theory of Production and Distribution* (New York: Cambridge University Press, 1975), 280–93.

30 For one of the best overviews of modern growth theory, see F. H . Hahn and R. C. O. Matthews, "The Theory of Economic Growth: A Survey," *Economic Journal* 74 (December, 1964), 779–902.

wooden characteristic of modern growth theory than its treatment of labor. The supply of labor, whether indexed in numbers of persons or quantities of labor time, is measured simply as a scalar. But in reality the amounts of labor available for employment at any given point in time are specified by particular skills, training, experience, and behavior tied to past experience, patterns of hiring, and educational practice. As economic growth proceeds, it is not infrequently the case that the stock of labor skills and training on hand does not conform with newly emergent loci of investment and expansion. Yet modern economic theory regards such qualitative considerations as these as necessarily secondary to the core precepts of received wisdom.

Put another way, mainstream economic growth theory limits its effectiveness in two ways: (1) by often ignoring structural and qualitative changes within economic variables and aggregates and (2) by implicitly assuming that fluctuations in rates of expansion are the result of cyclical forces that are inherently the same irrespective of the point in the history of a given economy at which they occur.[31] Such an approach, born of the doctrinal legacies of the mid-century evolution in orthodox economics discussed here, denies the existence of long-term growth patterns that are the outgrowth of institutional and historical forces that underlie cyclical processes themselves.

In addition to the theoretical weaknesses that the unwillingness to address long-term phenomena embeds in modern economic analysis, there are as well obvious, and at times painful, policy consequences. Investment both to build and to restore infrastructure, now understood to be an essential part of the wealth of nations, was ignored in the United States during the 1960s and 1970s in no small part because mainstream economists focused their research and their public pronouncements on short-run, easily quantifiable data. During the sustained "stagflation" of the 1970s, American economists preoccupied themselves with assess-

31 For example, see the explanation of Nobel Laureate James Tobin in his *Essays in Economics* (London: North-Holland, 1971), vol. 1, p. vii: "Macroeconomics concerns the determinants of entire economies. . . . The theoretical concepts and statistical measures involved are generally economy-wide aggregates or averages such as national income, total employment, or a national cost-of-living index. The objective is to explain ups and downs of these magnitudes and their interrelations. The basic assumption is that this can be done without much attention to the constituents of the aggregates, that is, to the behavior and fortunes of particular households, business firms, industries, or regions."

ments of the impact of rising oil prices, poor crop yields, and high-wage labor-union contracts while at the same time ignoring what we now know were obvious signs of a secular shift in the nation's position in the global marketplace. Thus relegated to making various policy suggestions based on short-run perceptions of the inverse trade-off between the rates of inflation and of unemployment, mainstream professional economists had little or nothing to say about such matters as industrial policy, the establishment of hemispheric and worldwide trading networks, or investment both to retrain the labor force and to retool the capital stock.

As this book has tried to explain, a systematic analysis of macroeconomic performance over time requires that attention be given to the fact that the performance of an economy is dependent upon both short-run factors and long-run development mechanisms. As an economy evolves, major structural and institutional characteristics of the system are transformed: demand patterns, amounts of income available for discretionary expenditure, technological knowledge, raw material stocks, market size – all change, along with fundamental alterations in communication, in transportation, and in the economic role of government. The basis of most of these changes in economic structures and institutions is the continuing elaboration of the nature and scope of enterprise. The stage of long-run development an economy has reached will influence responses to short-run shocks and fluctuations and the forms that recovery will assume. Indeed, it has been the burden of the research reported in this book that the relative absence of forces contributing toward a robust upturn in the American economy of recent decades has been in great degree due to secular mechanisms of development rather than to the impact of short-run shocks.

To move beyond the narrow view of orthodox economic analysis, and thereby fashion more promising conceptual and applied solutions to contemporary economic decline, it is necessary (as several essays in this volume have either explicitly or implicitly shown) to develop analytical propositions that are rooted in historical experience. The modern economy may on one level be characterized as a system of production that fashions useful or desired objects by the sale of which it accumulates wealth. Thus, the cost conditions affecting supply as well as the determinants of needs and desires affecting demand play a central role in delimiting growth performance. It is the secular changes in these factors of which a long-term perspective on economic growth and development is made.

In its earliest historical manifestation, modern economic growth proceeds on the basis of a strictly limited set of commodities. Immaturity in technological knowledge, raw material constraints due to technical bottlenecks and difficulties in transportation, and a scarcity of sufficiently disciplined and skilled workers severely circumscribe the set of goods that can actually be produced. At the same time, the market for commodities is small for two reasons. First, the modest extent of production as a whole, coupled with the fairly primitive techniques in use, dictates a low level of demand for producers' goods. Second, the generally low level of income of the population, along with the existence of much productive activity that is either traditional or household based, generates a very small demand for marketed consumer goods.

Expansion, then, is dependent on the rate of growth of the industrial labor force.[32] On the one hand, levels of output and of profits are directly proportional to levels of employment. On the other, the greater the size of the wage-earning population, the more extensive the market. An increase in the labor force, however, depends on certain mechanisms. First, household (which is to say, subsistence) labor must be displaced by the purchase of commodities. Second, artisans and petty-commodity producers must be driven out of the market. The former will depend on the extent to which the prices of products also made in the home can be lowered. The latter will involve the achievement of greater productive efficiency by the merging in space (in a "manufactory") of processes once carried out in isolation, and by the increasing division of tasks.

Yet the inherent limit to growth in this period remains the low level of wages. Given the labor-intensive character of production, the preservation of the profitability of enterprise depends on keeping labor costs down. This contradiction in the character of accumulation may be temporarily relieved by increasing the rate of capacity utilization, thereby increasing the amount of labor expended at a given wage, and by lowering per-unit labor costs by means of the elimination of skill requirements and by the introduction of secondary laborers, who historically have often tended to be women and children, into the work force. These strategies, however, tend to interfere with the production of labor to the extent that they jeopardize the cohesiveness of families and the health and education

32 See W. A. Lewis, "Economic Development with Unlimited Supplies of Labour," *Manchester School of Economic and Social Studies* 22 (May, 1954), 139–191; and John C. H. Fei and Gustav Ranis, *Development of the Labor Surplus Economy: Theory and Policy* (Homewood, Ill.: Irwin, 1964), ch. 2.

of children. They have often, in fact, prompted widespread reform campaigns, as notably demonstrated in nineteenth-century Britain and early-twentieth-century America, to regulate the employment of children and the length of the work day. They also may poison, by virtue of the labor–management hostility they engender, the political environment in which the wage bargain is made. As a result, the drive to increase labor productivity is frustrated. But this need not be a permanent state of affairs – and historically it was not. The potential for growth eventually becomes linked with process innovation and the impact of labor-saving technical change.

Growth in an economy in the earliest stages of industrialization is therefore based on goods that are rudimentary and labor intensive in their production and enjoy flexible responses to price changes by both supply and demand. Historically, such commodities have been simple consumer items – nonluxury clothing, foods, and household implements, although certain luxury goods may also be produced (as the historical evidence shows) to meet the demands emanating from elite classes such as landowners. The early production of textiles in the nineteenth-century United States, for example, took advantage of certain key characteristics of the product such as a natural resource base (i.e., cotton and wool) easily cultivated and prepared for use, as well as cheaply transported; a relative simplicity in production technique; and an ability to encourage the substitution of manufactured clothing for household production of clothing, given what economists call a high price elasticity of demand, thereby releasing labor inputs from homes to a growing labor market.[33]

Over time, the initial focus on consumer goods generates linkages with other sectors and broadens to include an ever-increasing range of consumption items. Linkages arise for two reasons: (1) market development calls forth transportation improvements that in turn stimulate development in producer-goods sectors; (2) the opportunities for growth center on reduction of costs in the production process, which in turn requires the development of new, non-human inputs. But given some minimum level of wages, for both political and biological reasons, the lowering of costs

33 The notion of "elasticity" in economics refers to the relative response of one variable to a given change in another. In the case of price elasticity of demand, the concept refers to the percentage change in the quantity of a good demanded given a particular change in the good's price. Many empirical studies have demonstrated, across time and regions, that with respect to basic clothing the price elasticity of demand is fairly high.

necessarily becomes linked with process innovation – that is, labor-saving technical progress. (If the costs of raw material inputs are fundamentally dependent on improvements in transportation and the technique of extraction, process innovation will lower these costs as well.) The increasing mechanization of production creates new sectors whose outputs are the machinery and tools to be used by the consumer-product industries.

The potential for continued growth thus ultimately shifts, in principle, from the extensive increase in markets owing to the growth of the labor force to the intensive development of profitability by means of lowering the costs of production. For the individual firm, expansion, at one time primarily dependent on the extent to which output could displace petty and household producers, is now constrained by the market share of other enterprises. Growth thus becomes tied to the elimination of competitors by price cutting. Hence, process innovation becomes even more important as a mechanism of expansion.[34]

As process innovation proceeds, the growth of other industrial sectors is stimulated. A related factor in the rise of producer goods and "heavy" industries is the increasing extent and improving quality of transportation, communication, and other elements of the infrastructure. The incentives to reduce costs, originally arising in the leading consumer-product sectors, also emerge in the producer-goods industries themselves. Production of machinery itself becomes more and more mechanized, and the creation of machinery by machinery becomes widespread. As a result, this epoch of development is characterized by high rates of investment in producer durables and other heavy industries.

The development of producer goods and heavy industries has fundamental implications for subsequent long-term patterns of growth. Techniques in use in these industries require large investments of capital in plant and equipment. In addition, production and management tasks require higher degrees of skill and expertise. Because of larger capital requirements, economies of scale, and the need for a well-trained, highly motivated, and disciplined workforce, the rise of these industries most often coincides with the concentration of capital in a smaller number of firms over time. This structural trend also takes hold in the consumer-goods sectors for similar reasons.

Increasing capital concentration alters the growth performance and

34 See Paolo Sylos-Labini, *Oligopoly and Technical Progress,* trans. E. Henderson (Cambridge: Harvard University Press, 1969), 33–77, 161–73.

stability of the economy. Consider that a firm's potential market, say in a given year, is a function of the number of potential customers that year and the frequency with which the given product is consumed per individual per year. The number of potential consumers is linked with the rate of growth of population and with the level of disposable income that population commands. Frequency of purchase is linked with the durability and characteristics of the commodity itself. A durable good may be purchased once every several years; a non-durable good, like food, is purchased virtually every day. To the extent that the expansion of markets by price reductions is limited, durable-goods firms will face severely limited growth opportunities. Their sales prospects become tied ever more closely with general income standards, the rate of increase of the buying population, and the overall rate of economic growth. In addition, as the proportion of the nation's industry that is conducted in oligopolistic markets increases, the destabilizing impact of cyclical fluctuations increases. A large decline in the aggregate rate of growth, in an economy now predominantly concentrated, has the potential to initiate a continuous decline in utilization, output, and employment. The prospects for a reversal of this process, as a consequence of the long-term alteration in the economy's structure, become increasingly dim. Unless the macroeconomy grows in a steady-state fashion with full employment of all inputs, a business cycle can indeed precipitate a long period of cumulative decline. Given the many factors militating against the achievement of balanced expansion, such as population changes, alterations in the geographic size of markets, differential rates of growth among national economies within a global trading system, natural events, and the uncoordinated actions of firms themselves, the likelihood of the system's avoidance of fluctuations in growth rates is small.

In a major sense, the foregoing is the foundation of an argument concerning economic stagnation – a claim that was seriously debated in the American economics profession during the Great Depression of the 1930s.[35] Typically the continuation of such an argument would view further growth as dependent on intervention by the government. It was this conviction, of course, that was the foundation of Keynes' argument that fiscal spending and monetary stimulus could move an economy out

35 See my "Explaining America's Greatest Depression: A Reconsideration of an Older Literature," *Rivista di storia economica* 2 (second series) (1985), 155–74.

of the doldrums more effectively than reliance on the presumed efficacies of competitive markets. Even so, Keynes shared with his more orthodox colleagues an impatience for and lack of interest in historical arguments about the pitfalls of long-term growth in capitalist economies. For many of Keynes' generation, the long period was not worth discussing in great detail.[36]

Historical experience reminds us, however, that revivals of activity in a "mature" economy can be linked with the creation of new markets through product innovation and with the increasing intensity of sales efforts, advertising, and the provisioning of consumer credit. Product innovation can also provide an avenue for further expansion by virtue of the competitive pressures it unleases to slow or reverse the trend of increasing concentration and relatively stagnant investment activity set in motion in the past. The precise venue of the innovative activity undertaken is difficult to specify abstractly, but contingencies having to do with technology, income levels, and world-wide patterns of competition will clearly be decisive.[37]

It is precisely questions about the means of sustained recovery and economic revitalization that now confront both the economics profession in particular and the American public, and their elected political representatives, in general. But there are few if any traditions or instincts in the

36 On Keynes' reluctance to discuss the long run, see Joan Robinson, *The Accumulation of Capital* (London: Macmillan, 1971), v, as well as her "The Model of an Expanding Economy," originally published in the *Economic Journal* (1952), republished in her *Collected Economic Papers,* vol. 2 (Oxford: Blackwell, 1975), 74–87, esp. 81. Also see Walt W. Rostow, *Theorists of Economic Growth from David Hume to the Present: With a Perspective on the Next Century* (New York: Oxford University Press, 1990), 190.

37 There will also be influences on the location of innovative activity that are tied to conditions in international trade having to do with costs differentials prevailing between national economies. In other words, historical factors will affect not only the sectoral location but also the geographic location of innovative activity. See, for one of the most influential articles on this matter, R. Vernon, "International Investment and International Trade in the Product Cycle," *Quarterly Journal of Economics* 80 (May, 1966), 190–207. This issue has become especially vivid in recent debates concerning the further economic integration of the European Community and the establishment of a North American Free Trade Agreement between Canada, Mexico, and the United States.

mainstream economics profession to confront squarely the long-term problems that the American economy faces at century's end. With its focus on individual decision-making, its preference for quantitative measurement that ignores qualitative reflection, and its insistence that market-driven solutions are in principle a superior means for the achievement of public policy objectives, modern economic analysis attains a professional respectability and discursive rigor while at the same time forfeiting the opportunity to have a decisive, practical, and effective impact in public affairs.[38]

In the final analysis, those issues about which modern American economics is virtually silent – economic nationalism, global economic interdependence, technological innovation and the sources of growth, corporate organization and managerial practice, financial institutions and the political economy of monetary policy, economic and social power as it is utilized by and as it affects various segments of society, and the economic role of government as it evolves over time – constitute the terrain upon which the ultimate resolution of America's contemporary economic difficulties will necessarily be found. The essays in this volume have attempted to offer some suggestions as to how that ground might initially be mapped.

Ironically, even in the midst of its present economic difficulties and worries, orthodox American ideology and its associated policies involving economic and social matters have today become almost prescriptive in a large part of the world. Devolution in the former Soviet Union and the economic privations currently encountered throughout Eastern Europe and much of Latin America have facilitated the penetration of individualistic concepts and values into societies that have been, for many decades, steadfastly hostile to such intellectual and cultural transplantation.

38 In his efforts to confront what he called the "classical theory" of his day, John Maynard Keynes spoke eloquently of the concerns he had regarding the role of economic theory in policy debates. In the Preface to his *General Theory*, p. v, he wrote: "The matters at issue are of an importance which cannot be exaggerated. But, if my explanations are right, it is my fellow economists, not the general public, whom I must first convince. At this stage of the argument the general public, though welcome at the debate, are only eavesdroppers at an attempt by an economist to bring to an issue the deep divergences of opinion among fellow economists which have for the time being almost destroyed the practical influence of economic theory, and will, until they are resolved, continue to do so."

In ways quite reminiscent of the activities of the immediate post–World War II years, American economists and businesspeople are once again positioned to bring their authority to bear abroad. A "U.S. Business School" has been founded in Prague, for example, to speed the transition to decentralized market decision making. In 1992, students and professors at the University of North Carolina-Chapel Hill sent over a thousand mainstream economics and business textbooks to ten institutions of higher learning in Hungary, Poland, and the former states of Czechoslovakia and Yugoslavia. At Yale University, with the assistance of the Charter 77 Foundation of Budapest and New York, a "Civic Education Project" began in 1991 that will send graduate instructors and professors in economics to assist in curricular development in social science departments at Central and Eastern European universities and institutes. And most recently, the business schools at Harvard, M.I.T., Northwestern, the University of Pennsylvania, and Stanford made plans to bring to their campuses 120 management and economics professors from Russia and Eastern Europe for what they have labeled a "retraining program" in their fields. These are but a few suggestive examples of the continuing and growing influence of American social scientific thought around the world. That this trend has been accompanied, in various circles, by a rejoicing in America's international influence, and that it is invoked as an explicit rationalization for American policy, power, and international position goes without saying.[39]

To be sure, the mechanisms by which this state of affairs has emerged have much to do with objective patterns of compulsion and coercion. International Monetary Fund (I.M.F.) assistance to Russia has now been premised, for example, upon the acceptance of what has been called "technical assistance" from the fund to, in the words of a recent I.M.F.

39 See, e.g., E. Kelly, "Business School in Prague Trains Future Capitalists," *Los Angeles Times* (January 12, 1992), D3; the "Student Affairs" announcements column in the *Chronicle of Higher Education* 36:46 (August 1, 1990), A25; J. W. Schmotter, "Business Schools After the Cold War," *Chronicle of Higher Education* 38:29 (March 25, 1992), A44; and the "Program Announcement and Application of the Civic Education Project, 1992–93" (in author's possession). Economic transition in the Commonwealth of Independent States and in Eastern Europe is also receiving increased attention from academic circles. For instance, see the *Journal of Economic Perspectives* 5:4 (Fall, 1991) – a publication of the American Economic Association. The entire number is devoted to articles derived from a "Symposium on Economic Transition in the Soviet Union and Eastern Europe."

report, "advise [that nation] on moving from a state-owned, government-run economy toward one based on the market forces of supply and demand and private enterprise." Market pricing principles have also been invoked, quite revealingly, to support a World Bank memorandum of two years ago (written by a current deputy secretary of the U.S. Treasury – Lawrence Summers) suggesting that toxic waste dumping be focused in low-wage countries – as potential losses of income due to environmental injury would be relatively lower. Yet they have been effective nonetheless. It remains that they be understood and described within a historical setting, not by the invocation of the assumptions of internalist intellectual histories or reified claims about the "end of history" or the start of a "New World Order."[40]

Whether a so-called Americanized approach to understanding economic life, and formulating an associated policy agenda on the basis of that reasoning, persists as a dominant motif in the wider world remains to be seen. Indeed, it would be unsound to suggest that there has not been resistance to such predominance. For some parts of Asia and Latin America, altogether different notions of economic coordination and justice are part of a continuing debate. In North Africa and the Middle East, there are in some cases active and strenuous (and, at times, quite violent) efforts to sustain differences with the "West." What will ultimately happen in the former communist nations of Europe, not to mention in the former Soviet Union itself, is also, at this point, manifestly unclear.

This is to say that the supremacy of particular points of view is not, of course, simply a matter of scholarly debate or pedagogy. A real environment of wealth distribution, corporate control, diplomatic pressure, and military force also plays a crucial role in distinguishing between, and differentially empowering, dominant and oppositional ideologies. It is imperative, therefore, that we turn our attention to the role of both

40 See M. Parks, "Soviets Gain IMF Status: Expert Advice Promised," *Los Angeles Times* (October 6, 1991), A1, A12; and D. Henwood, "Toxic Banking," *Nation* (March 2, 1992), 257. Also see, e.g., Mark Blaug, *Economic Theory in Retrospect* (New York: Cambridge University Press, 1978) – one of the best known of the "internalist" histories of modern economic thought that, at the same time, remains quite open-minded and intellectually generous. Speculations regarding the advent of an altogether new historical epoch and global "order" have found a rather large and diverse (as well as an often misinformed) readership as with Francis Fukuyama's *The End of History and the Last Man* (New York: Free Press, 1991).

political-economic processes and of ideas in structuring the history within and between nations. Surely we all very much remain, to paraphrase Keynes, enthralled by economists – living, canonized, vilified, and extinct. Liberating ourselves from this predicament, by critically rethinking its origins and consequences, is undoubtedly an essential part, as well, of understanding and overcoming the American economic decline of the late twentieth century.

Contributors

David Adler was educated at Columbia University and Oxford University. He received his M.A. in Economics from Columbia in 1987. He has written several books on American popular culture and currently works in television-broadcasting finance.

M. V. Lee Badgett is a labor economist and an Assistant Professor in the School of Public Affairs at the University of Maryland, College Park. Her research considers the role of race, gender, and sexual orientation in labor markets, and it assesses the need for anti-discrimination policies.

Michael A. Bernstein is Associate Professor and Chair of the Department of History and Associated Faculty Member in the Department of Economics at the University of California, San Diego. He is the author of *The Great Depression: Delayed Recovery and Economic Change in America, 1929–1939* (New York: Cambridge University Press, 1989), and of numerous articles on the economic and political history of twentieth-century America.

Robert A. Blecker is Associate Professor of Economics at American University and Research Associate of the Economic Policy Institute in Washington, D.C. He is the author of two institute studies – *Are Americans on a Consumption Binge?: The Evidence Reconsidered* and *Beyond the Twin Deficits: A Trade Strategy for the 1990s*. He has also published extensively on international competition, foreign trade, and American economic growth and income distribution.

Samuel Bowles, co-author of *Democracy and Capitalism* (New York: Basic Books, 1987), is Professor of Economics at the University of Massachusetts, Amherst, and a Staff Economist at the Center for Popular Economics.

Paulo Du Pin Calmon is Assistant Professor of Public Affairs and Economics at the University of Brasilia. He holds an M.A. in Economics from Vanderbilt University and a Ph.D. in Latin American Studies from the University of Texas, Austin.

James K. Galbraith is Professor at the Lyndon B. Johnson School of Public Affairs and in the Department of Government at the University of Texas, Austin. His most recent book, *Macroeconomics* (Boston: Houghton-Mifflin, 1993), was co-authored with Professor William Darity of the University of North Carolina, Chapel Hill.

David M. Gordon, co-author of *Segmented Work, Divided Workers* (New York: Cambridge University Press, 1982), is Professor of Economics at the New School for Social Research in New York City.

Jeffrey A. Hart is Professor of Political Science at Indiana University, Bloomington, where he teaches international politics and international political economy. He was a professional staff member of the President's Commission for a National Agenda for the Eighties, and has worked at the Office of Technology Assessment of the United States Congress. His publications include *The New International Economic Order* (New York: St. Martin's, 1983), *Rival Capitalists* (Ithaca: Cornell University Press, 1992), and numerous scholarly articles in such leading political science journals as *World Politics, International Organization,* and the *Journal of Conflict Resolution.*

Robert L. Heilbroner is the Norman Thomas Professor Emeritus of Economics at the New School for Social Research. The author of numerous articles and books on economic thought, economic history, and economic policy, his most recent publication is *21st Century Capitalism* (New York: Norton, 1993).

Jane Knodell is Associate Professor of Economics at the University of Vermont. The author of several articles on monetary theory and monetary history, she is currently serving as an elected member of the City Council of Burlington, Vermont.

William Lazonick is the author of numerous books and articles on the economic and business history of Western Europe and the United States. His publications include *Competitive Advantage on the Shop Floor* (Cambridge, Mass.: Harvard University Press, 1990) and *Business Organization and the Myth of the Market Economy* (New York: Cambridge University Press, 1991). He is currently Professor of Economics at the University of Massachusetts, Lowell.

Katherine S. Newman is Professor of Anthropology at Columbia University, and the author of two volumes on the subject of downward mobility, *Falling From Grace* (New York: Free Press, 1988) and *Declining Fortunes* (New York: Basic Books, 1993). Her current research is on the meaning of work among inner-city minority adolescents – a project supported by the Russell Sage Foundation, the Ford Foundation, the Spencer Foundation, and the Rockefeller Foundation.

Thomas E. Weisskopf, co-author of *The Capitalist System* (New York: Prentice-Hall, 1986), is Professor of Economics at the University of Michigan, Ann Arbor.

Rhonda M. Williams is an Assistant Professor of Afro-American Studies at the University of Maryland, College Park. Her most recent publications include "Accumulation as Evisceration: Urban Rebellion and the New Growth Dynamic," in Robert Gooding-Williams (ed.), *Reading Rodney King, Reading Urban Uprising* (forthcoming); "Racial Inequality and Racial Conflict: Recent Developments in

Radical Theory," in William Darity (ed.), *Labor Economics: Problems in Analyzing Labor Markets* (Norwell, Mass.: Kluwer Academic, 1992); and "Race, Deconstruction, and the Emergent Agenda of Feminist Economic Theory," in Marianne Feber and Julie Nelson (eds.), *Beyond Economic Man: Feminist Theory and Economics* (forthcoming). She has served as an economic advisor to the Institute for Women's Policy Research and to the Joint Center for Political and Economic Studies, both in Washington, D.C.

Index